MAKING COPYRIGHT WORK
FOR THE ASIAN PACIFIC

JUXTAPOSING HARMONISATION WITH FLEXIBILITY

MAKING COPYRIGHT WORK FOR THE ASIAN PACIFIC

JUXTAPOSING HARMONISATION WITH FLEXIBILITY

EDITED BY SUSAN CORBETT
AND JESSICA C LAI

Australian
National
University

PRESS

ANU PRESS

Published by ANU Press
The Australian National University
Acton ACT 2601, Australia
Email: anupress@anu.edu.au

Available to download for free at press.anu.edu.au

ISBN (print): 9781760462383
ISBN (online): 9781760462390

WorldCat (print): 1057230592
WorldCat (online): 1057230434

DOI: 10.22459/MCWAP.10.2018

Cover design and layout by ANU Press

Contents

Abbreviations

ACTA	Anti-Counterfeiting Trade Agreement
ALRC	Australian Law Reform Commission
APCA	Asian Pacific Copyright Association
APEC	Asia-Pacific Economic Cooperation Forum
ARIPO	African Regional Intellectual Property Organization
ASEAN	Association of Southeast Asian Nations
ASEAN+3	ASEAN, China, Japan and South Korea
ASEAN+6	ASEAN+3, Australia, India and New Zealand
AUSFTA	Australia – United States Free Trade Agreement
CBD	Convention on Biological Diversity
CER	Australia – New Zealand Closer Economic Relations Trade Agreement
CLRC	Copyright Law Reform Committee
CMA	Canadian Copyright Modernization Act
CPTPP	Comprehensive and Progressive Agreement for Trans-Pacific Partnership
DMCA	Digital Millennium Copyright Act
EU	European Union
FTA	free trade agreement
FTAAP	Free Trade Area of the Asia-Pacific
GDP	gross domestic product
GDPR	General Data Protection Regulation
HDCA	New Zealand Harmful Digital Communications Act 2015

ICESCR	International Covenant on Economic, Social and Cultural Rights
IP	intellectual property
IPRs	intellectual property rights
ISP	internet service provider
JSCOT	Joint Standing Committee on Treaties
KORUS	Korea – United States FTA
LIANZA	Libraries and Information Association of New Zealand
MBIE	Ministry of Business, Innovation and Employment
MED	Ministry of Economic Development
MPAA	Motion Picture Association of America
MTA	multilateral trade agreement
NSW	New South Wales
NTD	notice and takedown
OGCIO	Office of the Government Chief Information Officer
OGD	open government data
OGP	Open Government Partnership
OKI	Open Knowledge International
OSP	online service provider
P2P	peer-to-peer
P4	Trans-Pacific Strategic Economic Partnership Agreement (Pacific 4)
PIPA	Personal Information Protection Act
PSI	public sector information
RCEP	Regional Comprehensive Economic Partnership
RIS	Regulatory Impact Statement
SEM	Single Economic Market
TCE	traditional cultural expressions
TK	traditional knowledge
TPM	technological protection measure
TPP	Trans-Pacific Partnership Agreement
TRIPS	Trade-Related Intellectual Property Rights

UNCRC	United Nations Convention on the Rights of the Child
UNDRIP	United Nations Declaration on the Rights of Indigenous Peoples
UNEP	United Nations Environment Programme
UNESCO	United Nations Educational, Scientific and Cultural Organization
US	United States
USTR	United States Trade Representative
UTS	University of Technology Sydney
WCT	WIPO Copyright Treaty
WIPO	World Intellectual Property Organization
WIPO IGC	WIPO Intergovernmental Committee on Intellectual Property and Genetic Resources, Traditional Knowledge and Folklore (the IGC)
WPPT	WIPO Performances and Phonograms Treaty
WTO	World Trade Organization

Introduction

Susan Corbett and Jessica C Lai[1]

The copyright laws of most countries of the Asian Pacific region[2] rarely constitute the subject of international academic commentary, which tends to focus mainly upon the judicial rulings and laws deriving from the European Union (EU) and the United States (US). This is due to many factors, including that much of the Asian Pacific region does not have the history implicit in western copyright law and the subject is therefore relatively new for the region. Moreover, many Asian Pacific nations simply have not had (and many continue not to have) the financial or intellectual resource capacity to deal with the finer details of copyright law. For example, it is well documented that many nations in the region signed up to international intellectual property obligations in the Agreement on Trade-Related Intellectual Property Rights (TRIPS) in exchange for other trade benefits, sometimes not fully appreciating the implications of such obligations or perhaps believing they had no real choice in the matter. This is related to the fact that the Asian Pacific region is mainly populated by countries that are overall users and importers of copyright works, whereas the EU and US – the main drivers of stronger intellectual property norms – are characterised (at least in copyright terms) by significant numbers of owners and exporters of copyright works. Indeed, absent the pressure imposed by their more powerful trading partners, there would arguably be no real incentive for the poorer countries of the region to introduce strong copyright laws into their domestic regimes.

---

1   Copyright © 2018 Susan Corbett and Jessica C Lai.
2   The Asian Pacific region is defined in the Statutes of the Asian Pacific Copyright Association as 'the Region embracing the countries and territories located in or bordering on the Pacific Ocean west of the International Date Line'.

This book aims to address a gap in the copyright discourse by providing a contemporary overview of developing areas of copyright law in the Asian Pacific region, particularly as they pertain to the potential for some degree of regional harmonisation. The time is ripe, with several Asian Pacific jurisdictions, such as China, Hong Kong and Singapore, now reflecting a mature level of scholarship in the field and challenging the regional dominance of frontrunners Australia and New Zealand. In recent years, nations of the Asian Pacific region have been highly active in the realm of free trade agreements (FTAs), and the heated manner in which the copyright provisions have been debated emphasises the importance and complexity of the relationship between copyright, development, trade and society.

This book is made up of selected papers from the second annual conference of the Asian Pacific Copyright Association (APCA). APCA was established on 15 November 2011 and includes countries and territories located in or bordering on the Pacific Ocean west of the International Date Line. The purpose of this demarcation was to offer the included countries a forum to discuss issues concerning copyright and related rights, specifically with respect to the region and its particular concerns. Furthermore, APCA aims to ensure that the needs and concerns of the people of the Asian Pacific region are taken into consideration by the international community in all discussions and international negotiations concerning such rights.

In view of this, Adrian Sterling, the founder of APCA, drafted a Code in 2015 to spark discussion about the possibility of harmonising protection of copyright and related rights in the Asian Pacific region. In the introduction to the Code, Sterling stated:

> *Undoubtedly*, regional harmonisation in this field is of value to right owners and the public …[3]

> … the application of the Code would greatly strengthen the recognition of copyright and related rights in the Asian Pacific Region to the benefit of rights owners, users of protected material and the general public.[4]

---

3   Adrian Sterling 'Asian Pacific Copyright Code' in this volume at 1 (emphasis added).
4   At 1.

Underlying these statements are the presumptions that copyright and neighbouring rights are implicitly beneficial and that harmonisation across the region would ultimately be advantageous, from the perspective of right owners, users and the general public.

Furthermore, Sterling noted the importance of providing a counter to FTAs, specifically referring to the Trans-Pacific Partnership Agreement (TPP), which 'reflect many aspects of United States law which, it is submitted, are not necessarily those which apply or should apply in the countries and territories of the Asian Pacific Region'.[5] Of course, while the TPP has caused much controversy, especially with respect to the US and the intellectual property chapter of the Agreement, the notion that the Asian Pacific nations might profit from allying with one another stands potentially true in the face of other forces, such as the EU.

Each of Sterling's propositions is distinct, complicated and debatable. 'Pirate parties', the 'open movement' and academic literature on the aptness of copyright in the modern global and digital world,[6] would suggest that we cannot presume that copyright and neighbouring rights are implicitly beneficial, whether for right owners, users or the general public. Similarly, the discourse regarding the putative harmonising effects of the multilateral Agreement on TRIPS and FTAs that include TRIPS-plus provisions (requiring stronger protections than embodied in TRIPS), especially in developing countries,[7] would indicate that harmonisation comes with downsides. Policymakers, interest groups and civil society in the Asian Pacific are increasingly challenging the intellectual property chapters in FTAs with the EU and US. The TPP is a case in point, having spurred protests across the Asian Pacific region. As an illustration, a key issue was the increase of the copyright term to 70 years. Another was increased protection for technological protection measures. Thus, harmonisation via a Code across the region must differ from coerced 'harmonisation' via multilateral trade agreements (MTAs) and FTAs.

---

5   At 1.

6   See e.g. Rebecca Giblin and Kimberlee Weatherall (eds) *What if We Could Reimagine Copyright?* (ANU Press, Canberra, 2017) (doi.org/10.22459/WIWCRC.01.2017); and Jessica Litman 'Fetishizing Copies' in Ruth L Okediji (ed) *Copyright in an Age of Limitations and Exceptions* (Cambridge University Press, Cambridge, 2017).

7   Gustavo Ghidini, Rudolph JR Peritz and Marco Ricolfi (eds) *TRIPS and Developing Countries: Towards a New IP World Order?* (Edward Elgar, Cheltenham, 2014); and Joseph Strauss 'The Impact of the New World Order on Economic Development: The Role of Intellectual Property Rights System' (2006) 6 J Marshall Rev Intell Prop L 1.

One could view the extent to which the intellectual property chapter of the TPP was debated as highlighting the increasing importance of intellectual property as a tool of trade and development in the Asian Pacific region. Moreover, the controversy exemplifies the burgeoning importance of the Asian Pacific region and the potential strength it may have as a regional unit. This leads to two observations. First, that there is a lot of potential for the nations of the Asian Pacific region to work together, find common ground and shift international bargaining power. Second, in so doing, the region could tailor any regional agreements to suit local needs. These are the ways that a Regional Code could differentiate itself from existing MTAs and FTAs as a more inclusively negotiated agreement.

At the same time, it is questionable whether defensive harmonisation is possible or desirable. Harmonisation requires a certain level of shared legal culture, policy aims and – related to this – economic and technological position.[8] As noted by Melanie Johnson, Robin Wright and Susan Corbett in this volume, harmonisation has proved challenging even between Australia and New Zealand, which have a common language, shared history and culture, and comparatively similar laws. Furthermore, harmonisation inevitably entails the surrender of some sovereignty. This then raises the question of why the Asian Pacific region would want to do this in the realm of copyright and related rights. Put another way, what would the region gain in return? In FTAs, the answer is ostensibly that nations can 'cash in' their 'intellectual property chips' in exchange for something that is considered to be to their benefit, such as access in the agricultural sector. Free of such an exchange, the benefits of harmonising copyright and related rights are less obvious. Moreover, harmonisation of copyright and related rights would raise the concern of whether this would benefit the region as a whole, as envisaged by the Code, or just a few nations within the region.

It is trite to write that the social, economic and cultural situation varies in every jurisdiction and that extant flexibility in international obligations is key to addressing such variance. A Code will, thus, only be desirable

---

8   See e.g. Susy Frankel and Megan Richardson 'Trans-Tasman Intellectual Property Coordination' in Susy Frankel (ed) *Learning from the Past, Adapting to the Future: Regulatory Reform in New Zealand* (LexisNexis, Wellington, 2011) 527; Susy Frankel and others 'The Challenges of Trans-Tasman Intellectual Property Coordination' in Susy Frankel and Deborah Ryder (eds) *Recalibrating Behaviour: Smarter Regulation in a Global World* (LexisNexis, Wellington, 2013) 101; and Susy Frankel and others 'The Web of Trade Agreements and Alliances and Impacts on Regulatory Autonomy' in Susy Frankel and Deborah Ryder (eds) *Recalibrating Behaviour: Smarter Regulation in a Global World* (LexisNexis, Wellington, 2013) 17.

if it deals with common aims and concerns, but allows much flexibility in regard to the specific domestic situations pertaining to each of its signatories. Moreover, one must recognise that much harmonisation has already taken place through the TRIPS Agreement and the myriad of existing FTAs. That is, a Code for the Asian Pacific region has to cover common goals and areas that the region can realistically harmonise, and has to accept that certain spaces have more or less been filled by existing international obligations.

As it is, the proposed Code does not take us beyond existing norms and obligations found in international instruments and FTAs. In other words, it does not include anything specifically relevant for or important to the region. Given the preponderance of FTAs (such as the lingering TPP and the impending Regional Comprehensive Economic Partnership (RCEP)), which include a significant number of Asian Pacific countries, a Code needs to bring something different. The authors of this volume deal with several such possibilities, such as the relationship between copyright and privacy (discussed by Doris Estelle Long) and copyright and data licensing (examined by Jyh-An Lee). Perhaps most striking is the strong proposition that having indigenous peoples and traditional communities is a core commonality among Asian Pacific jurisdictions. Three chapters in this volume specifically focus on how a regional Code could address these interests of indigenous peoples and traditional communities (Lida Ayoubi, Natalie Stoianoff and Evana Wright, and Jonathan Barrett).

The remainder of this Introduction provides an outline of the structure of the book and a brief taste of the various topics addressed by its authors.

Part 1 of the book provides analysis and commentary on norm-making in the Asian Pacific region. **Peter Yu** discusses the potential regional FTAs (namely RCEP and the TPP), and the copyright provisions contained within these Agreements. **Lida Ayoubi** then addresses the potential for a Code to bring the region together, in particular through recognising that the Asian Pacific nations share common goals with respect to their indigenous peoples and traditional communities. The third chapter in Part 1, by **Natalie Stoianoff and Evana Wright**, discusses the move to introduce fair use into Australian copyright law and suggests how the potential risks fair use presents for indigenous cultural expressions more generally might be addressed in the Code.

Closely connected to this, Part 2 examines the idea of taking norms from other jurisdictions and fields of law. **Doris Estelle Long** highlights the opportunity to address the copyright and privacy interface in the Code, while **Susan Corbett** investigates partial norm-taking (with respect to anti-circumvention provisions) and explains how, without the rulemaking feature of US copyright law, strengthened anti-circumvention measures will likely be to the detriment of Asian Pacific jurisdictions.

Because many Asian Pacific jurisdictions are developing countries and net importers of copyright works, the ability to use and access copyright works is of crucial importance to the Asian Pacific region. In other words, getting the balance correct between owners and users is imperative. Accordingly, Part 3 of the book explores this theme, including the fact that the correct balance is specific to the particular situation in different parts of the region, underscoring the importance of harmonisation providing certain flexibilities. **Melanie Johnson, Robin Wright and Susan Corbett** discuss the potential of 'fair use' in New Zealand and Australia, particularly highlighting the disjunction between increasing levels of protection, often at the behest of the US, but not similarly adopting the broad and flexible fair use doctrine. **Jyh-An Lee** then addresses the licensing of government data and the concept of 'openness'.

Of similar importance, and related to the aforementioned balance, are the copyright implications of the availability of locally created art and culture, including traditional indigenous cultural expressions, to the citizens of the Asian Pacific region. The final part of the book, therefore, discusses the complexity of including exceptions from the perspective of indigenous peoples and the need for performers' rights for incentivising and supporting cultural creation. **Jonathan Barrett** scrutinises the permitted use 'freedom of panorama' vis-à-vis indigenous works, while **Jessica C Lai** analyses the historical background to performers' rights provisions in copyright law, and questions whether the extensive rights required by the World Intellectual Property Organization (WIPO) Performances and Phonograms Treaty are in reality of no practical use to many performers, particularly those in the Asian Pacific region.

An insightful and thought-provoking conclusion to the book is provided by **Shubha Ghosh**, whose carefully structured critique and commentary on each chapter adds an important dimension to this work.

The Asian Pacific Copyright Code

Copyright is basically a legal discipline that deals with the rights of authors of literary, dramatic, musical and artistic works, and is considered in association with the related rights of performers. Protection may also be extended by these rights to the associated rights of broadcasters, cable distributors etc., and internet transmissions.

Three fundamental systems of copyright are distinguishable: the copyright system, applicable in common-law countries, i.e. the United Kingdom, the US and countries with similar systems; the author's right system, applicable in France and other civil-law countries; and the independent system, giving protection by other categories of rights (as in China).

The three categories of rights are distinguishable in the countries of the Asian Pacific region.

These distinct systems inevitably lead to discrepancies in the application of protection in these countries.

The aim of the Asian Pacific Copyright Code is to provide a record of the generally accepted principles in this area, so that right owners in one country of the region are accordingly assured of protection in all other countries of the region. As author of the Code, I am conscious of the great service to international understanding provided by the copyright system, which provides the possibility that authors and others protected by the laws in the region can claim and receive protection in other countries of the region.

---

1   Copyright © 2018 JAL Sterling.

I believe that copyright, in providing a forum that brings together people of different countries and traditions, makes an important contribution to international understanding between the nations of the world.

I am grateful to the Asian Pacific Copyright Association (APCA) for the studies it has initiated on the Code, and the conference APCA arranged in connection with this in Hong Kong in 2016 – also to Associate Professor Susan Corbett for all the work she has put in to this area over many years.

Asian Pacific Copyright Code: Proposal for discussion

Adrian Sterling[2]

Introduction

While national and international copyright laws are well developed, the only specifically developed regional copyright law is that applying in the 28 States of the European Union, where Directives and other Union instruments provide harmonised protection of the copyright of authors and of related rights, including those of performers, film and phonogram producers, broadcasters (by wireless or wire) covering the majority of critical issues in this field (the only major area not being harmonised throughout the European Union being that concerning moral rights, which apply in all Union States, but with different provisions).

Undoubtedly, regional harmonisation in this field is of value to right owners and the public, providing as it does that neighbouring countries can develop their relations and mutual protection in this field.

In October 2015, the Trans-Pacific Partnership members (Australia, Brunei Darussalem, Canada, Chile, Japan, Malaysia, Mexico, New Zealand, Peru, Singapore, United States and Vietnam) announced the conclusion of the Trans-Pacific Partnership Agreement on trade, including provisions on intellectual property. The provisions of the Agreement reflect many aspects of United States law which, it is submitted, are not necessarily

---

2   Barrister, New South Wales (1949) and of the Bar of England and Wales (1953); Professorial Fellow, Queen Mary Intellectual Property Research Institute, University of London.

those which apply or should apply in the countries and territories of the Asian Pacific Region (i.e. countries and territories located in or bordering on the Pacific Ocean west of the International Date Line).

The Draft Asian Pacific Copyright Code here proposed reflects the objectives which, it is submitted, should be adopted in the countries and territories of the Asian Pacific Region.

The Draft Code proposes definitions, and provisions concerning beneficiaries, rights, limitations and exceptions, term of protection, infringement and remedies. The ultimate aim could be the setting up of an administration system to provide a central point of contact between participating countries and an Asian Pacific Copyright Arbitration Tribunal for settling disputes between rights owners in the Asian Pacific Region.

It is submitted that the application of the Code would greatly strengthen the recognition of copyright and related rights in the Asian Pacific Region to the benefit of rights owners, users of protected material and the general public.

Two general aims of the Code principles are firstly, to incorporate the principles recognised in the relevant international copyright and related rights instruments, and secondly, to incorporate on particular points higher standards of protection than in these instruments.

Procedure

The following Draft Asian Pacific Copyright Code is submitted for discussion by APCA. The draft is only an outline and is intended to bring to attention issues which need discussion and decision in this area. Additional issues may also need discussion.

Copyright is always developing and at a later stage updated versions of the Code may need consideration.

When APCA has formulated the final version of the Draft, the Code could be opened for signature by members of APCA and by other organisations and individuals interested in copyright and related rights (for example, authors, performers, broadcasters, internet service providers and administration societies).

When a sufficient number of signatories are obtained, the Code could be submitted to the Governments of countries and territories throughout the Asian Pacific Region, with the aim of adoption of the Code by them. It may be anticipated that consideration of the establishment of the Asian Pacific Copyright Arbitration Tribunal could be given by Governments adopting the Code.

The author of the Draft Code is Adrian Sterling, who proposes to license his copyright in the Code to the Asian Pacific Copyright Association.

[20 November 2015]

Draft Asian Pacific Copyright Code
Part I: General

Preliminary

A. Definitions
B. Beneficiaries
C. Rights
D. Limitations and exceptions
E. Term of protection
F. Infringement
G. Formalities, remedies and procedure
H. Administrative provisions

Part II: Asian Pacific Copyright Arbitration Tribunal

[text to be established]

Annex: International Copyright and Related Rights instruments – Membership (Asian Pacific Region)

Preliminary

The Asian Pacific Copyright Code sets out the principles which the signatories hereto recognise as representing the standards of protection of copyright and related rights which apply or should apply in the countries and territories of the Asian Pacific Region being those countries and territories located in or bordering on the Pacific Ocean west of the International Date Line.

A. Definitions

Authors: creators of original works including all categories mentioned in Article 2 of the Berne Convention, computer programs and databases.

Broadcasting organisations: Organisations engaged in transmission by wire or wireless, other than internet service providers.

Communication to the public: the act of bringing material protected by copyright or related rights to the perception of members of the public by means of performance in the presence of such members or by transmission of any kind including broadcast and on-demand.

Copyright: rights of authors in their works, including economic and moral rights.

Film producer: producer of moving image recordings.

Internet service provider: entity communicating to the public by on-demand transmission.

On-demand transmission: communication to the public by wire or wireless means by making available works, material protected by related rights and other material in such a way that members of the public may access such works and material from a place and at a time individually chosen by them.

Phonogram producer: producer of sound recordings.

Related rights: rights of performers, film and phonogram producers, broadcasting organisations and internet service providers in their respective performances, productions and transmissions.

Relevant international instruments: Berne Convention for the Protection of Literary and Artistic Works 1971, ('Berne'), Universal Copyright Convention 1971 ('UCC'), Convention for the Protection of Performers, Phonogram Producers and Broadcasting Organisations 1961 ('Rome'), Convention for the Protection of Producers of Phonograms against Unauthorised Duplication of their Phonograms 1971 ('Phonograms'), Convention relating to the Distribution of Programme-carrying Signals transmitted by Satellite 1974 ('Sat'), Agreement on Trade-Related Aspects of Intellectual Property Rights 1994 ('TRIPS'), WIPO Copyright Treaty 1996 ('WCT'), WIPO Performances and Phonograms Treaty 1996 ('WPPT'), and, when entered into force, WIPO Audiovisual Performances Treaty 2012 ('WAVPT') and WIPO Visually Impaired Persons Treaty 2013 ('WVIPT').

B. Beneficiaries

1. Beneficiaries under the Code are authors, performers, film and phonogram producers, broadcasters and internet service providers, such beneficiaries being either beneficiaries under the relevant international instruments or nationals of or resident in or incorporated in countries or territories of the Asian Pacific Region.

2. Countries and territories acknowledging this Code may apply reciprocity provisions in accordance with their regional or international obligations.

C. Rights

1. Authors have the rights in respect of their works to claim authorship, to prevent degradation and to prevent unauthorised copying or communication to the public, as well as the other rights granted to them by the relevant international instruments.[3]

2. Performers have the rights to authorise copying or communication to the public of their performances, as well as the other rights granted to them by the relevant international instruments.[4]

3. Film and phonogram producers have the rights to authorise copying and communication to the public of their respective film and sound recordings, as well as the other rights granted to them by the relevant international instruments.[5]

4. Broadcasting organisations and internet service providers have the rights to authorise copying or communication to the public of their respective transmissions, as well as the other rights granted to them by the relevant international instruments.[6]

---

3   Compare Berne Arts 5, 6bis, 8, 9, 11–12, 14, 14bis; TRIPS Arts 10, 11; WCT Arts 5–8.
4   Compare Rome Arts 7, 12; WPPT Arts 5–10, 15; WAVPT Arts 5–11.
5   Compare Rome Arts 10, 12; WPPT Arts 11–15.
6   Compare Rome Art. 13.

D. Limitations and exceptions

1. Limitations and exceptions under this Code are confined to those which are permitted by the relevant international instruments in certain special cases and which do not conflict with a normal exploitation of the work and do not unreasonably prejudice the legitimate interests of the rights owners.[7] In accordance with Article 12 of the Rome Convention 1961, remuneration rights instead of rights of authorisation may be granted to performers and phonogram producers in regard to the communication to the public of published phonograms.

2. Signatories to the Code agree to seek amendments to the Code which will provide a specific list of permissible limitations and exceptions under the Code.

E. Term of protection

1. The term of protection of author's rights is the life of the author plus 70 years after his/her death. The term of 70 years shall apply in respect of all categories of works mentioned in Article 7 of the Berne Convention instead of the respective durations of protection there specified.

2. The term of protection for performers' rights is 50 years from the year of the giving of the performance, or if the performance is published during that period, 50 years from the year of first publication of the performance.

3. The term of protection for film and phonogram producers' rights is respectively 50 years from the year of making of the film or sound recording concerned or if the recording is published during that period, 50 years from the year of first publication of the recording.

4. The term of protection for broadcasting organisations' and internet service providers' rights is respectively 50 years from the year of first transmission of the transmission concerned.

F. Infringement

Infringement of copyright and related rights is committed by doing any act in any territorial or extraterritorial area including Space without the necessary authorisation of the owner of the rights in the protected material involved in such act.

---

7   TRIPS Art. 13.

G. Formalities, remedies and procedure

1. The provisions of UCC Article III and Phonograms Article 5 apply regarding satisfaction of formalities.

2. Criminal and civil remedies are to be imposed for infringement of rights under this Code, as decided by the respective legislatures, together with notice and takedown measures in respect of unauthorised transmissions of protected material.

3. (a) A person who is within the jurisdiction of the courts of a particular country may in addition to proceedings for infringement in that country be prosecuted or sued in that country for infringement of copyright or related rights in any other country and the law of that other country will apply in this respect.[8]

    (b) Any person irrespective of country of residence, nationality or incorporation may in a particular country be prosecuted or sued for infringement of copyright or related rights in that country.

H. Administrative

1. The Asian Pacific Copyright Code is administered by the Asian Pacific Copyright Association.

2. The Association promotes the maintenance and development of the Code through meetings between signatories to the Code and persons and organisations and others interested in copyright and related rights in the Asian Pacific Region.

Part III: Asian Pacific Copyright Arbitration Tribunal

The Asian Pacific Copyright Arbitration Tribunal on establishment provides the means for settlement of disputes as to the recognition and application of copyright and related rights in the Asian Pacific Region.

© Asian Pacific Copyright Association 2015

Signatories
[to be applied]

---

8   Compare UK case *Lucasfilm Ltd and ors v Ainsworth and anor* [2011] UK SC 39 (27 July 2011, UK Supreme Court).

Annex: International Copyright and Related Rights instruments – Membership (Asian Pacific Region)

20 November 2015

Annex:

International Copyright and Related Rights instruments – Membership

(Asian Pacific Region)

COUNTRY	BERNE	UCC	ROME	PHONOGRAMS	TRIPS	WCT	WPPT	SAT
Australia	1928(P78)	1969(P78)	1992	1974	1995	2007	2007	1990
Brunei Darussalam	2006(P)				1995			
Cambodia		1953(G)			2004			
China	1992(P)	1992(GP)		1993	2001	2007	2007	
Fiji	1971(B)	1971(G)	1972	1973	1996			
Indonesia	1997(P)				1995	2002	2005	
Japan	1899(P75)	1956(P77)	1989	1978	1995	2002	2002	2000
Kiribati								
Korea, Dem People's Rep. of	2003(P)							
Korea, Rep. of	1996(P)	1987(GP)	2009	1987	1995	2009	2009	2012
Malaysia	1990(P)				1995	2012	2012	
Marshall Islands								
Micronesia, Fed. State of	2003(P)							
Nauru								
New Zealand	1928(R47)	1964(G)		1976	1995			
Palau								
Papua New Guinea					1996			
Philippines	1951(P97)		1984		1995	2002	2002	
Russian Federation	1995(P)	1973(P95)	2003	1995	2012	2009	2009	1989

COUNTRY	BERNE	UCC	ROME	PHONOGRAMS	TRIPS	WCT	WPPT	SAT
Samoa	2006(P)				2012			
Singapore	1998(P)				1995	2005	2005	2005
Solomon Islands					1996			
Taiwan					2002			
Thailand	1931(P95)				1995			
Timor-Lesté								
Tonga	2001(P)				2007			
Tuvalu								
Vanuatu	2012(P)				2012			
Vietnam	2004(P)		2007	2005	2007			2006

20 November 2015

NOTE: The instruments to which reference is made in the above listing are:

- Berne Convention: Convention for the Protection of Literary and Artistic Works 1886, 1971 ('Berne') (R = Rome Act 1928, B = Brussels Act 1948, P = Paris Act 1971);
- Universal Copyright Convention 1952, 1971 ('UCC') (G = Geneva Act 1952, P = Paris Act 1971);
- Rome Convention: International Convention for the Protection of Performers, Producers of Phonograms and Broadcasting Organizations 1961('Rome');
- Phonograms Convention: Convention for the Protection of Producers of Phonograms against Unauthorised Duplication of their Phonograms 1971 ('Phonograms');
- Agreement on Trade-Related Aspects of Intellectual Property Rights 1994 ('TRIPS');
- WIPO Copyright Treaty 1996 ('WCT');
- WIPO Performances and Phonograms Treaty 1996 ('WPPT');
- Satellites Convention: Convention relating to the Distribution of Programme-carrying Signals Transmitted by Satellite 1974 ('SAT').

Part 1: Norm-making

.

1

TPP, RCEP and the Future of Copyright Norm-setting in the Asian Pacific

Peter K Yu[1]

1 Introduction

The past decade has seen two mega-regional intellectual property norm-setting exercises focusing on countries in the Asian Pacific region. The first was part of the effort to establish the Trans-Pacific Partnership[2] (TPP), a mega-regional pact that was intended to cover '40% of global GDP [gross domestic product] and some 30% of worldwide trade in both goods and services'.[3] The negotiations surrounding this partnership ran from 15 March 2010 until the signing of the final agreement on 4 February 2016. In January 2017, shortly after the inauguration of the Trump Administration, the United States withdrew from the TPP,

1   Copyright © 2018 Peter K Yu. Professor of Law, Professor of Communication and Director, Center for Law and Intellectual Property, Texas A&M University. An earlier version of this chapter was delivered as the keynote opening address at the 2016 Meeting of the Asian Pacific Copyright Association at the Faculty of Law of the University of Hong Kong. The author is grateful to the participants for valuable comments and suggestions. The chapter draws on research from the author's earlier articles in the *SMU Science and Technology Law Review* and the *Vanderbilt Journal of Transnational Law*.
2   Trans-Pacific Partnership Agreement (signed 4 February 2016) [TPP Agreement].
3   David A Gantz 'The TPP and RCEP: Mega-Trade Agreements for the Pacific Rim' (2016) 33 Ariz J Int'l & Comp L 57 at 59.

thereby placing the regional pact on life support.[4] A year later, however, the 11 remaining TPP partners established the Comprehensive and Progressive Agreement for Trans-Pacific Partnership (CPTPP), which they eventually signed in March 2018. If this modified pact enters into force, it will cover Australia, Brunei Darussalam, Canada, Chile, Japan, Malaysia, Mexico, New Zealand, Peru, Singapore and Vietnam.

The second norm-setting exercise is part of the ongoing negotiations surrounding the Regional Comprehensive Economic Partnership (RCEP). Launched in November 2012, these negotiations built on past trade and non-trade discussions between the Association of Southeast Asian Nations (ASEAN)[5] and its six major Asian Pacific neighbours (Australia, China, India, Japan, New Zealand and South Korea). Although policymakers, commentators and the media have seldom analysed the RCEP until a few years ago, its 16 negotiating parties 'account for almost half of the world's population, almost 30 per cent of global GDP and over a quarter of world exports'.[6] Once established, this partnership will cover not only China and India but also two high-income Asian economies (Japan and South Korea) and six other TPP/CPTPP partners (Australia, Brunei Darussalam, Malaysia, New Zealand, Singapore and Vietnam).

Taken together, these two mega-regional norm-setting exercises will have unlimited potential to shape future copyright norms in the Asian Pacific region. For countries that have joined either the CPTPP or the RCEP, legal obligations concerning new protection and enforcement standards will have to be incorporated into domestic law once the applicable agreement enters into force. These standards can be quite burdensome, as they often exceed what is currently required by the Agreement on Trade-Related Aspects of Intellectual Property Rights (TRIPS Agreement) of the World Trade Organization (WTO).[7] Countries that have joined both the CPTPP and the RCEP will also have to be ready to resolve conflicts between these two agreements, should they arise.

---

4   Peter K Yu 'Thinking about the Trans-Pacific Partnership (and a Mega-regional Agreement on Life Support)' (2017) 20 SMU Sci & Tech L Rev 97.
5   The 10 current members are Brunei Darussalam, Cambodia, Indonesia, Laos, Malaysia, Myanmar, the Philippines, Singapore, Thailand and Vietnam. They negotiate as a bloc in the RCEP negotiations.
6   'Regional Comprehensive Economic Partnership' Department of Foreign Affairs and Trade (Australia) dfat.gov.au.
7   Agreement on Trade-Related Aspects of Intellectual Property Rights 1869 UNTS 299 (adopted 15 April 1994, entered into force 1 January 1995) [TRIPS Agreement].

Even those countries that remain outside of the CPTPP or the RCEP may end up accepting norms enshrined in either agreement, or both, despite their lack of legal obligation to do so. While some of these countries may introduce new laws or amendments in an effort to harmonise their laws with those of their Asian Pacific neighbours, others, especially the less powerful ones, may face considerable external pressure to accept higher standards stipulated in the new mega-regional agreements.

Moreover, if an Asian Pacific Copyright Code is to be developed – a recurring theme of this volume – such development will have to take into account the new copyright norms in the CPTPP and the RCEP, regardless of whether the Code incorporates any of these norms in the end. Any effort to develop such a regional code will also have to anticipate the potential inconsistencies, tensions and conflicts between the CPTPP and the RCEP in the intellectual property area.

In view of these complications and the potentially considerable change in the intellectual property norm-setting landscape in the Asian Pacific region, this chapter closely examines the roles of the (now inoperative) TPP, the CPTPP and the RCEP in shaping future regional copyright norms. It begins by discussing the historical origins of the TPP and the RCEP. It then highlights the similarities and differences between the copyright and intellectual property enforcement provisions in the TPP Agreement and a leaked draft of the RCEP intellectual property chapter. This chapter continues to explore the ramifications for the United States' withdrawal from the TPP and the eventual adoption of the CPTPP.[8] It concludes by outlining the future of copyright norm-setting in the Asian Pacific region.

---

8   Donald J Trump 'Withdrawal of the United States from the Trans-Pacific Partnership Negotiations and Agreement' (2017) 82 Fed Reg 8497 [Presidential Memorandum].

2 Historical Origins

2.1 TPP

The origin of the TPP Agreement can be traced back to the early 2000s. The predecessor of this agreement was a quadrilateral agreement known as the Trans-Pacific Strategic Economic Partnership Agreement, more commonly referred to as the 'P4' or 'Pacific 4'. As Meredith Lewis recounted:[9]

> [The negotiations were initially] launched by Chile, New Zealand and Singapore at the APEC [Asia-Pacific Economic Cooperation Forum] leaders' summit in 2002. These original negotiations contemplated an agreement amongst the three participating countries, to be known as the Pacific Three Closer Economic Partnership … . However, Brunei attended a number of rounds as an observer, and ultimately joined the Agreement as a 'founding member'. The Agreement was signed by New Zealand, Chile and Singapore on July 18, 2005 and by Brunei on August 2, 2005, following the conclusion of negotiations in June 2005.

In March 2010, negotiations for an expanded agreement began between Australia, Peru, Vietnam, the United States and the P4 members. Malaysia, Mexico, Canada and Japan joined the negotiations afterwards.

From its inception, the TPP was negotiated as a highly ambitious and comprehensive trade agreement. As the then United States Trade Representative (USTR), Ronald Kirk, declared at the first round of the TPP negotiations in Melbourne, Australia:[10]

> Trans-Pacific Partnership negotiations offer a unique opportunity to shape a high-standard, broad-based regional pact. In line with the President's goal of supporting two million additional American jobs through exports, a robust TPP agreement would expand our exports to one of the world's fastest-growing regions. Our team's aim is to achieve the biggest economic benefits for the American people, and these negotiators will be working to set a new standard for 21st century trade pacts.

---

9   Meredith Kolsky Lewis 'Expanding the P-4 Trade Agreement into a Broader Trans-Pacific Partnership: Implications, Risks and Opportunities' (2009) 4 Asian J WTO & Int'l Health L & Pol'y 401 at 403–404.

10   Office of the United States Trade Representative 'USTR Begins TPP Talks in Australia' (press release, 15 March 2010).

After nearly six years of negotiations, an agreement was finally reached in Atlanta in October 2015.[11] This agreement contains 30 chapters, covering a wide range of issues, such as market access, textiles and apparel, sanitary and phytosanitary measures, investment, financial services, telecommunications, electronic commerce, government procurement, competition, intellectual property, labour, the environment and regulatory standards. The agreement also includes various annexes and side letters regarding tariff commitments, product-specific rules, country-based arrangements and non-conforming measures.

Chapter 18 is devoted entirely to intellectual property matters.[12] It covers a wide variety of areas, including cooperation,[13] trademarks,[14] country names,[15] geographical indications,[16] patents and undisclosed test or other data,[17] industrial designs,[18] copyright and related rights,[19] enforcement[20] and internet service providers.[21]

2.2 RCEP

The RCEP negotiations did not start until more than two years after the beginning of the TPP negotiations. Launched in November 2012, the RCEP negotiations were established not solely as a reactive response or a defensive measure. Instead, they built on prior efforts in various fora to facilitate economic integration and cooperation in the Asian Pacific region. These fora include ASEAN+3 (ASEAN, China, Japan and South Korea), ASEAN+6 (ASEAN+3, Australia, India and New Zealand) and APEC.

---

11   Office of the Press Secretary 'Statement by the President on the Trans-Pacific Partnership' (press release, 5 October 2015) [TPP Press Release].
12   TPP Agreement, above n 2, at ch 18.
13   Section B.
14   Section C.
15   Section D.
16   Section E.
17   Section F.
18   Section G.
19   Section H.
20   Section I.
21   Section J.

In October 2001, the East Asian Vision Group, which was charged with 'develop[ing] a road map to guide future regional cooperation',[22] recommended to ASEAN+3 leaders the establishment of the East Asia Free Trade Area.[23] Although China strongly supported this proposal, Japan and other Asian countries had serious reservations about China's potential dominance in this pact.[24]

Five years later, Japan advanced an alternative proposal concerning the Comprehensive Economic Partnership in East Asia.[25] Covering not only ASEAN+3 members but also the three remaining ASEAN+6 members (Australia, India and New Zealand), this partnership would dilute China's influence in the regional pact while adding to the mix a major source of natural resources – namely, Australia.[26]

Around that time, APEC members also actively explored regional integration and cooperation efforts. In November 2006, APEC began studying the concept of a Free Trade Area of the Asia-Pacific (FTAAP).[27] Three years later, APEC leaders pledged to create an agreement to realise this conceptual vision. Since then, APEC leaders have endorsed various declarations laying down the incremental steps needed to realise the FTAAP, including the *Pathways to FTAAP* and the *Beijing Roadmap for APEC's Contribution to the Realization of the FTAAP*.[28]

In November 2011, ASEAN, with the support of both China and Japan, proposed to merge the initiatives concerning the East Asia Free Trade Area and the Comprehensive Economic Partnership in East Asia to form the

---

22   Mark Beeson *Institutions of the Asia-Pacific: ASEAN, APEC and Beyond* (Routledge, London, 2009) at 78.

23   Shujiro Urata 'Japan's FTA Strategy and a Free Trade Area of the Asia-Pacific' in Charles E Morrison and Eduardo Pedrosa (eds) *An APEC Trade Agenda? The Political Economy of a Free Trade Area of the Asia-Pacific* (ISEAS Publishing, Singapore, 2007) 99 at 106.

24   Beeson, above n 22, at 88; Shintaro Hamanaka 'Trans-Pacific Partnership versus Regional Comprehensive Economic Partnership: Control of Membership and Agenda Setting' (Asian Development Bank, Working Paper Series on Regional Economic Integration No. 146, December 2014) at 10; Meredith Kolsky Lewis 'Achieving a Free Trade Area of the Asia-Pacific: Does the TPP Present the Most Attractive Path?' in CL Lim, Deborah Kay Elms and Patrick Low (eds) *The Trans-Pacific Partnership: A Quest for a Twenty-First Century Trade Agreement* (Cambridge University Press, Cambridge, 2012) 223 at 227 (doi.org/10.1017/CBO9781139236775.022).

25   Lewis, above n 24, at 228; Urata, above n 23, at 106–107.

26   Mark Beeson *Regionalism and Globalization in East Asia: Politics, Security and Economic Development* (Palgrave Macmillan, Basingstoke, 2007) at 224; Urata, above n 23, at 111.

27   Lewis, above n 24, at 223.

28   Asia-Pacific Economic Corporation Forum *Pathways to FTAAP* (14 November 2010); Asia-Pacific Economic Cooperation Forum *The Beijing Roadmap for APEC's Contribution to the Realization of the FTAAP* (11 November 2014).

RCEP.[29] At the 19th ASEAN Summit in Bali, Indonesia, ASEAN leaders adopted the *Framework for Regional Comprehensive Economic Partnership*.[30] Formal negotiations were finally launched in November 2012 at the 21st ASEAN Summit in Phnom Penh, Cambodia. As ASEAN+6 leaders declared at that time, the RCEP negotiations were established to:[31]

> [a]chieve a modern, comprehensive, high-quality and mutually beneficial economic partnership agreement establishing an open trade and investment environment in the region to facilitate the expansion of regional trade and investment and contribute to global economic growth and development; [and]

> [b]oost economic growth and equitable economic development, advance economic cooperation and broaden and deepen integration in the region through the RCEP, which will build upon our existing economic linkages.

Although the ASEAN+6 leaders' joint declaration did not specifically mention the TPP, there is no denying that the development of this United States–led partnership greatly accelerated the RCEP negotiations.[32] The latter negotiations were particularly urgent when two major ASEAN+6 economies, China and India, were intentionally excluded from the TPP.[33] Also excluded were other key ASEAN+6 members, such as Indonesia, the Philippines, South Korea and Thailand. While some of these countries had been invited to the TPP negotiations but declined to participate,[34] others were simply ignored.

Undoubtedly, there were both economic and non-economic reasons for not inviting these countries to the TPP negotiations. Yet the outcome was the same: while the excluded countries could still join the partnership once it had been established, they would not be able to shape the standards involved and could only accept the final terms as agreed upon by the

---

29   Hamanaka, above n 24, at 11; Ganeshan Wignaraja 'The Regional Comprehensive Economic Partnership: An Initial Assessment' in Tang Guoqiang and Peter A Petri (eds) *New Directions in Asia-Pacific Economic Integration* (East-West Center, Honolulu, 2014) 93 at 94.

30   ASEAN *Framework for Regional Comprehensive Economic Partnership* (12 June 2012).

31   ASEAN Plus Six *Joint Declaration on the Launch of Negotiations for the Regional Comprehensive Economic Partnership* (20 November 2012).

32   Du Ming 'Explaining China's Tripartite Strategy toward the Trans-Pacific Partnership Agreement' (2015) 18 J Int'l Econ L 407 at 424; Hamanaka, above n 24, at 13; Michael Wesley 'Who Calls the Tune? Asia Has to Dance to Duelling Trade Agendas' (19 October 2014) The Conversation theconversation.com.

33   Peter K Yu 'TPP and Trans-Pacific Perplexities' (2014) 37 Fordham Int'l LJ 1129 at 1132–1163.

34   Yoo Choonsik 'South Korea Moves Closer to Joining TPP Trade Talks' *Reuters* (online ed, 29 November 2013); Alan Raybould 'Thailand Says to Join Trans-Pacific Partnership Trade Talks' *Reuters* (online ed, 18 November 2012).

original negotiating parties. Such an outcome was highly unattractive, if not unacceptable, to large Asian economies such as China and India. It is therefore unsurprising that these countries have turned their time, attention and energy towards the RCEP to develop regional standards based on their own preferences and experiences.[35]

At the time of writing, ASEAN+6 members have already entered into over 20 rounds of negotiations. Once the RCEP Agreement is completed, the final text is anticipated to cover a wide range of areas, including 'trade in goods, trade in services, investment, economic and technical cooperation, intellectual property, competition [and] dispute settlement'.[36] Beyond these areas, working or sub-working groups have also been established to address rules of origin; customs procedures and trade facilitation; legal and institutional issues; sanitary and phytosanitary measures; standards, technical regulations and conformity assessment procedures; electronic commerce; financial services; and telecommunications.[37]

Given this large number of working and sub-working groups, it remains to be seen whether their establishment will result in the creation of standalone chapters in each specific area. Regardless of how the final agreement is structured, however, that agreement is likely to be as ambitious as the TPP Agreement, which contains 30 different chapters in the final text. In light of this expansive and comprehensive coverage, questions have already been raised about the potential rivalry, compatibility and complementarity between these two mega-regional agreements.

3 TPP and RCEP Norms

Although no draft text has thus far been officially released to the public, Knowledge Ecology International made available online a leaked 15 October 2015 draft of the RCEP intellectual property chapter (draft RCEP chapter).[38] To better understand the copyright norms that are being developed in the Asian Pacific region, it will be instructive to compare this leaked draft with the TPP intellectual property chapter (TPP chapter).[39]

---

35   Hamanaka, above n 24, at 12–15.
36   ASEAN Plus Six *Guiding Principles and Objectives for Negotiating the Regional Comprehensive Economic Partnership* (30 August 2012) at preamble [*Guiding Principles*].
37   'Regional Comprehensive Economic Partnership: News' Department of Foreign Affairs and Trade dfat.gov.au.
38   '2015 Oct 15 version: RCEP IP Chapter' (19 April 2016) Knowledge Ecology International keionline.org [Draft RCEP Chapter].
39   TPP Agreement, above n 2, at ch 18.

Despite the recent signing of the CPTPP, this comparison continues to focus on the TPP for three reasons. First, the comparison between the TPP chapter and the draft RCEP chapter highlights the significant differences between the two mega-regional norm-setting exercises. These differences not only reflect the varied positions taken by leading players in the Asian Pacific region, but they also underscore the limited divergence between the TPP and RCEP intellectual property norms. Since these two sets of norms have not diverged significantly, it is likely that the CPTPP and RCEP norms will diverge even less. Second, the present comparison paves the way for the discussion of the CPTPP in the next section. That discussion will enable readers to take stock of the select TPP intellectual property provisions that the CPTPP has suspended. It will also allow them to compare the TPP and CPTPP intellectual property norms. Third, this section will become useful should the United States choose to revive the TPP or incorporate its intellectual property norms into future bilateral, regional or plurilateral trade agreements.

Because the scope and coverage of this volume do not allow for a detailed exploration of the large number of intellectual property provisions in the draft RCEP chapter, this section focuses on only the draft sections on copyright and related rights[40] and enforcement of intellectual property rights.[41] It is nonetheless worth remembering that other sections or other draft chapters, such as those on investment and electronic commerce, could deeply affect or be relevant to intellectual property protection and enforcement. For example, the TPP investment chapter, which seeks to establish an investor–state dispute settlement mechanism, became highly controversial after Eli Lilly and Philip Morris used similar mechanisms in bilateral or regional trade agreements to address their intellectual property disputes.[42]

---

40   Section 2.
41   Section 9.
42   *Eli Lilly and Company v Government of Canada (Final Award)* ICSID UNCT/14/2 16 March 2017; *Philip Morris Brands Sàrl v Oriental Republic of Uruguay (Award)* ICSID ARB/10/7 8 July 2016; *Philip Morris Asia Ltd v Commonwealth of Australia (Award on Jurisdiction and Admissibility)* UNCITRAL PCA 2012-12 17 December 2015. For these disputes and the use of the investor–state dispute settlement mechanism, see Cynthia M Ho 'Sovereignty under Siege: Corporate Challenges to Domestic Intellectual Property Decisions' (2015) 30 Berkeley Tech LJ 213; Ruth L Okediji 'Is Intellectual Property "Investment"? *Eli Lilly v Canada* and the International Intellectual Property System' (2014) 35 U Pa J Int'l L 1121; Peter K Yu 'Crossfertilizing ISDS with TRIPS' (2017) 49 Loy U Chi LJ 321; and Peter K Yu 'The Investment-Related Aspects of Intellectual Property Rights' (2017) 66 Am U L Rev 829.

3.1 Copyright and Related Rights

In the area of copyright and related rights, the draft RCEP chapter includes the usual language[43] found in free trade agreements (FTAs) requiring the accession to the two internet-related treaties of the World Intellectual Property Organization (WIPO) – the WIPO Copyright Treaty and the WIPO Performances and Phonograms Treaty.[44] Going beyond the terms of the TPP Agreement, the draft chapter[45] also requires accession to the Beijing Treaty on Audiovisual Performances,[46] the International Convention for the Protection of Performers, Producers of Phonograms and Broadcasting Organizations (Rome Convention)[47] and the Marrakesh Treaty to Facilitate Access to Published Works for Persons Who Are Blind, Visually Impaired or Otherwise Print Disabled.[48]

In addition, the draft RCEP chapter includes the usual provisions on technological protection measures and electronic rights management information,[49] which are both significantly shorter and more flexible than their counterparts in the TPP Agreement.[50] Targeting online streaming and other new means of digital communication, the draft RCEP chapter also includes provisions addressing the unauthorised communication, or the making available, of a copyright work to the public.[51] The push for such provisions is understandable considering the increasing volume of copyright infringement litigation concerning works disseminated through streaming or other digital technologies.[52]

---

43   Draft RCEP Chapter, above n 38, art 1.7.6(g)–(h).
44   WIPO Copyright Treaty 2186 UNTS 121 (adopted 20 December 1996, entered into force 6 March 2002) [WCT]; WIPO Performances and Phonograms Treaty 2186 UNTS 203 (adopted 20 December 1996, entered into force 20 May 2002).
45   Draft RCEP Chapter, above n 38, art 1.7.6(h)–(*ibis*).
46   Beijing Treaty on Audiovisual Performances (adopted 24 June 2012).
47   International Convention for the Protection of Performers, Producers of Phonograms and Broadcasting Organizations 496 UNTS 43 (adopted 26 October 1961, entered into force 18 May 1964).
48   Marrakesh Treaty to Facilitate Access to Published Works for Persons Who Are Blind, Visually Impaired or Otherwise Print Disabled (adopted 27 June 2013, entered into force 30 September 2016).
49   Draft RCEP Chapter, above n 38, arts 2.3, 2.3*bis* and 2.3*ter*.
50   See Susan Corbett 'Free Trade Agreements with the United States, Rulemaking and TPMs: Why Asian Pacific Nations Should Resist Increased Regulation of TPMs in Their Domestic Copyright Laws' in this volume.
51   Draft RCEP Chapter, above n 38, art 2.1.1–2.1.2.
52   Among the leading cases in this area are *American Broadcasting Companies v Aereo Inc* 134 SCt 2498 (2014) before the United States Supreme Court; *ITV Broadcasting Ltd v TVCatchup Ltd (Main Proceedings)* [2017] ECLI 144 C-275/15 before the Court of Justice of the European Union; and *Maneki TV* Saiko Saibansho (18 January 2011) 65 Minshū 121 before the Japanese Supreme Court.

Among the negotiating parties, there was some effort – notably by Australia – to push for stronger language on copyright limitations and exceptions beyond the mere recitation of the three-step test in the TRIPS Agreement and the WIPO Copyright Treaty.[53] Article 2.5.3 of the leaked draft states:

> Each party shall endeavour to provide an appropriate balance in its copyright and related rights system by providing limitations and exceptions ... for legitimate purposes including education, research, criticism, comment, news reporting, libraries and archives and facilitating access for persons with disability.

The purposes listed in this provision are very similar to those found in the preamble of the United States fair use provision.[54]

Like the TPP chapter, the draft RCEP chapter includes a provision prohibiting government use of infringing computer software.[55] Unlike the TPP chapter, however, the draft RCEP chapter does not extend the copyright term beyond the life of the author plus 50 years – the minimum required by the Berne Convention for the Protection of Literary and Artistic Works.[56] The draft RCEP chapter also does not include detailed TPP-like provisions on internet service providers, secondary liability for copyright infringement, and the notice and takedown mechanism (although those provisions could easily have been negotiated as part of the yet-to-be-disclosed electronic commerce chapter, if that chapter indeed exists).

To the disappointment of consumer advocates and civil society organisations, South Korea proposed language that would require countries to 'take effective measures to curtail repetitive infringement of copyright and related rights on the Internet or other digital network'.[57] In addition, Japan called for the disclosure of information concerning the accounts of allegedly infringing internet subscribers.[58] It further advanced a footnote supporting 'a regime providing for limitations on the liability of, or on the remedies available against, online service providers while preserving the legitimate interests of [the] right holder'.[59]

---

53   TRIPS Agreement, above n 7, art 13; WCT, above n 44, art 10(1).
54   17 USC § 107.
55   Draft RCEP Chapter, above n 38, art 4.2.
56   Berne Convention for the Protection of Literary and Artistic Works 1161 UNTS 31 (adopted 9 September 1886, entered into force 5 December 1887, revised at Paris 24 July 1971) art 7(1).
57   Draft RCEP Chapter, above n 38, art 9*quinquies*.3.
58   Article 9*quinquies*.4.
59   Article 9*quinquies*.2, n 43.

Even more alarming to many developing countries, the draft RCEP chapter offers stronger and more expansive protection to broadcasters than the TPP chapter, covering such issues as the unauthorised retransmission of television signals over the internet.[60] As Jeremy Malcolm commented:[61]

> Based on the current text proposals, [the] RCEP may actually impose more stringent protections for broadcasters than the TPP does. The TPP allows authors, performers and producers to control the broadcast of their work, but it does not bestow any independent powers over those works upon broadcasters. [The] RCEP, in contrast, could create such new powers; potentially providing broadcasters with a 50 year monopoly over the retransmission of broadcast signals, including retransmission of those signals over the Internet.

3.2 Intellectual Property Enforcement

With respect to intellectual property enforcement, the draft RCEP chapter includes the usual provisions concerning civil, criminal and administrative procedures and remedies, as well as provisional and border measures. Although a considerable portion of the draft language in the enforcement section merely reaffirms the existing rights and obligations under the TRIPS Agreement, the proposed language increases the obligations concerning the seizure and destruction of allegedly infringing goods, including the grant of authority to take ex officio action[62] and to seize or destroy the materials or implements used to create infringing goods.[63] The draft chapter also seeks to empower judicial authorities to determine damages for intellectual property infringement based on lost profits, the market price or the suggested retail price.[64]

Like the TPP chapter, the draft RCEP chapter calls for criminal procedures and penalties for unauthorised camcording in cinemas.[65] Unlike the TPP, however, the draft RCEP chapter does not have extensive provisions on criminal procedures and penalties. These provisions do not apply to

---

60   Article 2.6.
61   Jeremy Malcolm 'RCEP: The Other Closed-Door Agreement to Compromise Users' Rights' (20 April 2016) Electronic Frontier Foundation www.eff.org.
62   Draft RCEP Chapter, above n 38, art 9*ter*.5.
63   Articles 9*bis*.5, 9*bis*.6, 9*bis*.10 and 9*quater*.6.
64   Article 9*bis*.2(i).
65   Article 9*quinquies*.5.

either trade secret infringement or the circumvention of technological protection measures. The draft provisions on border measures are also less detailed and less invasive.[66]

At the time when the leaked draft was being negotiated, the RCEP negotiating parties strongly disagreed on the appropriate standards concerning criminal liability for aiding and abetting,[67] the award of attorneys' fees[68] and obligations relating to intellectual property enforcement in the digital environment.[69] Facing strong opposition from its negotiating partners, South Korea remained the lone party calling for the provision of pre-established damages.[70]

In sum, the draft RCEP chapter, like any other treaty in the middle of the negotiation process, includes a wide array of bracketed texts. While some draft provisions are stronger than, or similar to, what is found in the TPP Agreement, other language is much weaker. The draft text also includes language that cannot be found in the TPP Agreement or other TRIPS-plus FTAs. Given that 'nothing is agreed until everything is agreed'[71] – a favourite aphorism of treaty negotiators and other government officials – it remains to be seen what the final RCEP intellectual property chapter will look like.

4 United States' TPP Withdrawal and the Adoption of the CPTPP

The previous section has shown that both the TPP chapter and the draft RCEP chapter have called for higher protection and enforcement standards that go beyond what is required by the TRIPS Agreement. While differences still exist between the two chapters, it will not be far-fetched to assume that the copyright norms in the Asian Pacific region will be greatly strengthened once either agreement, if not both, enters

---

66   Article 9*ter*.
67   Article 9*quater*.4.
68   Article 9*bis*.4.
69   Article 9*quinquies*.
70   Article 9*bis*.3.
71   Henrique C Moraes 'Dealing with Forum Shopping: Some Lessons from the Negotiation on SECURE at the World Customs Organization' in Li Xuan and Carlos Correa (eds) *Intellectual Property Enforcement: International Perspectives* (Edward Elgar Publishing, Cheltenham, 2009) 159 at 176.

into force. Nevertheless, this seemingly predictable norm-setting picture has been complicated by the United States' withdrawal from the TPP in January 2017.[72]

Although the Obama Administration described this mega-regional agreement as a 'cardinal priority and a cornerstone of [its] Pivot to Asia',[73] its successor made an about turn within a year of signing the TPP Agreement. On the first day of his first full week in office, President Trump signed a memorandum directing the USTR to 'withdraw the United States as a signatory to the [TPP and] ... from the TPP negotiations'.[74] As the document stated, 'it is the intention of [the new] Administration to deal directly with individual countries on a one-on-one (or bilateral) basis in negotiating future trade deals'. Not only did the Trump Administration abandon the TPP Agreement after six years of exhaustive negotiations, but it also shifted the policy emphasis away from regional and plurilateral trade agreements.[75]

Given the United States' new policy position, one cannot help but wonder what the future will hold for the TPP Agreement and its high TRIPS-plus intellectual property norms. Will this mega-regional agreement meet the same fate as the widely criticised Anti-Counterfeiting Trade Agreement (ACTA),[76] which was signed by most negotiating parties but failed to attain the requisite number of ratifications?[77] Will the Trump Administration eventually change its course? Or will other TPP partners manage to salvage the agreement even without the United States' participation?

Shortly after the announcement of the United States' withdrawal, Australia, Japan, Singapore and New Zealand explored ways to resuscitate the TPP Agreement.[78] At a May 2017 APEC meeting in Hanoi, Vietnam, these countries, along with other remaining TPP partners, reaffirmed their commitment to establishing the regional partnership and agreed to explore the development of a process to move the pact forward even

---

72 Presidential Memorandum, above n 8.
73 Kurt M Campbell *The Pivot: The Future of American Statecraft in Asia* (Twelve, New York, 2016) at 268.
74 Presidential Memorandum, above n 8.
75 Peter K Yu 'Trump's Trade Policy Is More Predictable and Less Isolationist than Critics Think' (3 February 2017) MarketWatch www.marketwatch.com.
76 Anti-Counterfeiting Trade Agreement 50 ILM 243 (adopted 15 April 2011) [ACTA].
77 Despite its adoption in April 2011, the ACTA has thus far been ratified by only one country – Japan, the country of depositary.
78 Bhavan Jaipragas 'Can the Trans-Pacific Partnership Be Salvaged? Forget Trump – Malaysia, Australia, New Zealand Think So' *South China Morning Post* (online ed, 24 January 2017).

without the United States' participation.[79] These proactive remedial efforts made good sense considering that Japan and New Zealand had already ratified the agreement.

A few months later, the 11 remaining TPP partners 'agreed on the core elements' of the CPTPP, opting to retain the majority of the original pact while suspending those provisions that had been pushed by United States negotiators but were of no interest, or of very limited interest, to the remaining partners.[80] On 23 January 2018, exactly a year after President Trump signed his controversial presidential memorandum, the CPTPP negotiations concluded in Tokyo, Japan. The agreement was subsequently signed in Santiago, Chile, on 8 March.

Although art 1 of the CPTPP incorporates by reference all 30 chapters of the TPP Agreement,[81] including the intellectual property chapter, art 2 suspends the following provisions:[82]

- art 18.63 (Term of Protection for Copyright and Related Rights);
- art 18.68 (Technological Protection Measures);
- art 18.69 (Rights Management Information);
- art 18.79 (Protection of Encrypted Program-Carrying Satellite and Cable Signals); and
- art 18.82 (Legal Remedies and Safe Harbours).

For comparative purposes, the above list includes only those provisions that relate to copyright and related rights and enforcement of intellectual property rights. It is worth noting that the CPTPP has also suspended many provisions in the areas of patents and undisclosed information.

The suspension of all of these provisions has greatly impacted on the future of intellectual property norm-setting in the Asian Pacific region. Not only has such suspension minimised the differences between the TPP/CPTPP and RCEP intellectual property norms, it has also caused the draft RCEP chapter to offer stronger protection than the CPTPP. Notwithstanding these complications, a proper comparison between the TPP/CPTPP and

---

79 'Pacific Ministers Commit to Move Ahead with Pact without US' *US News & World Report* (online ed, 21 May 2017).
80 'Trans-Pacific Partnership Ministerial Statement' (press release, 11 November 2017) at para 3.
81 Comprehensive and Progressive Agreement for Trans-Pacific Partnership (signed 8 March 2018) art 1 [CPTPP].
82 Annex, art 7(g)–(k).

RCEP intellectual property norms will have to take into consideration not only the recent suspension of select TPP provisions, but also the time that has elapsed since the leaked RCEP draft chapter.

The draft RCEP chapter was leaked more than two years ago. Most certainly, the negotiations of that chapter have already advanced beyond what the October 2015 draft has revealed. Moreover, the TPP/CPTPP and the RCEP were established as two rivalrous, though potentially complementary, norm-setting exercises. It will therefore be no surprise if the RCEP has been negotiated in the shadow of the TPP negotiations and the post-TPP developments. Now that the CPTPP offers much weaker protection than the TPP, many RCEP negotiating partners will understandably demand lower standards that correspond to the CPTPP.

Nevertheless, while the CPTPP has played an important and fast-growing role in intellectual property norm-setting in the Asian Pacific region, we should not ignore the lingering impact of the TPP. As I noted in an earlier article, regardless of whether the TPP is dead or alive, it may exert four types of influence that will deeply affect the future of intellectual property norm-setting in the Asian Pacific region.[83]

To begin with, the various chapters in the TPP Agreement, including its intellectual property chapter, may continue to provide the much-needed templates for drafting future bilateral, regional and plurilateral trade agreements. Thus far, the United States has relied heavily on templates to maximise effectiveness and efficiency in trade negotiations.[84] As policies change and new issues arise, these templates will be updated. Indeed, many terms in the earlier FTAs developed by the United States have already found their way to later agreements. In the intellectual property arena, for instance, ACTA and the TPP Agreement have all incorporated terms from these agreements, most notably the Korea – United States Free Trade Agreement.[85]

---

83   Yu, above n 4, at 101–110.
84   Peter Drahos 'BITs and BIPs: Bilateralism in Intellectual Property' (2001) 4 J World Intell Prop 791 at 794; Susy Frankel 'Challenging TRIPS-Plus Agreements: The Potential Utility of Non-Violation Disputes' (2009) 12 J Int'l Econ L 1023 at 1025; Peter K Yu 'Sinic Trade Agreements' (2011) 44 UC Davis L Rev 953 at 1011–1013.
85   Peter K Yu 'Trade Agreement Cats and the Digital Technology Mouse' in Bryan Mercurio and Ni Kuei-Jung (eds) *Science and Technology in International Economic Law: Balancing Competing Interests* (Routledge, London, 2014) 185 at 196.

Even more disturbing, South Korea injected the terms of its FTA with the United States into the RCEP negotiations, despite the fact that the United States is not a party to those negotiations.[86] As Jeremy Malcolm lamented:[87]

> Far from setting up a positive alternative to the TPP, South Korea is channeling the USTR at its worst here – what on earth are they thinking? The answer may be that, having been pushed into accepting unfavorably strict copyright, patent, and trademark rules in the process of negotiating its 2012 free trade agreement with the United States, Korea considers that it would be at a disadvantage if other countries were not subject to the same restrictions.

The second type of influence relates to the potential development of new international intellectual property norms that will incorporate the TPP Agreement by reference. A widely cited example of such development is the TRIPS Agreement's incorporation of the Washington Treaty on Intellectual Property in Respect of Integrated Circuits. Although the latter treaty has never entered into force, art 35 of the TRIPS Agreement explicitly incorporates its obligations as follows:[88]

> Members agree to provide protection to the layout-designs (topographies) of integrated circuits … in accordance with Articles 2 through 7 (other than paragraph 3 of Article 6), Article 12 and paragraph 3 of Article 16 of the Treaty on Intellectual Property in Respect of Integrated Circuits … .

The third type of influence concerns the potential use of the terms of the TPP Agreement to determine whether a country has adequately protected intellectual property rights. Of great notoriety regarding this type of determination is the USTR's Special 301 process.[89] As the United States Trade Act stipulates, the USTR can take Special 301 actions against

---

86   Peter K Yu 'The RCEP and Trans-Pacific Intellectual Property Norms' (2017) 50 Vand J Transnat'l L 673 at 700–701.

87   Jeremy Malcolm 'Meet RCEP, a Trade Agreement in Asia That's Even Worse than TPP or ACTA' (4 June 2015) Electronic Frontier Foundation www.eff.org.

88   TRIPS Agreement, above n 7, art 35.

89   19 USC §§ 2411–2420. On this process, see Jagdish Bhagwati and Hugh T Patrick (eds) *Aggressive Unilateralism: America's 301 Trade Policy and the World Trading System* (University of Michigan Press, Ann Arbor, 1990); Joe Karaganis and Sean Flynn 'Networked Governance and the USTR' in Joe Karaganis (ed) *Media Piracy in Emerging Goods* (Social Science Research Council, New York, 2011) 75 at 75–98; Paul C B Liu 'U.S. Industry's Influence on Intellectual Property Negotiations and Special 301 Actions' (1994) 13 UCLA Pac Basin LJ 87.

countries that have failed to provide 'adequate and effective protection of intellectual property rights *notwithstanding the fact that [they] may be in compliance with the specific obligations of the [TRIPS] Agreement*'.[90]

For instance, the USTR has repeatedly put Canada on the Special 301 Watch List, citing the country's failure to ratify the WIPO Internet Treaties, among other reasons.[91] Likewise, before China acceded to those treaties, the USTR stated in the 2005 *National Trade Estimate Report on Foreign Trade Barriers* that 'the United States consider[ed] the WIPO treaties to reflect many key international norms for providing copyright protection over the Internet'.[92] The report further stated that 'China's accession to the WIPO treaties [was] an increasingly important priority for the United States'.[93]

The final type of influence pertains to the potential misguidance provided by technical assistance experts. Given the politically driven circumstances surrounding the United States' withdrawal from the TPP, these experts may continue to treat the intellectual property provisions in the TPP Agreement as the world's best practices – or, worse, the gold standard for intellectual property protection and enforcement.[94] Oftentimes, these so-called 'best practices' are introduced without regard to a particular country's local needs, interests, conditions or priorities. For developing countries, overemphasis on the high TPP intellectual property standards as international benchmarks may ultimately undermine the countries' individual abilities to take advantage of the traditional limitations, safeguards and flexibilities provided in the TRIPS Agreement or other WIPO-administered international intellectual property agreements.[95]

In sum, although the TPP Agreement will not have any legal effect like the CPTPP, nor will it have as big an impact as it would have had upon taking effect, it may continue to exert considerable influence on intellectual property norm-setting in the Asian Pacific region. Thus, as important as it is to appreciate the growing role of the CPTPP and the ramifications

---

90   19 USC § 2411(d)(3)(B)(i)(II) (emphasis added).
91   Office of the US Trade Representative *2010 Special 301 Report* (Washington, 2010) at 25.
92   Office of the US Trade Representative *2005 National Trade Estimate Report on Foreign Trade Barriers* (Washington, 2005) at 96.
93   Ibid.
94   Kimberlee Weatherall 'Intellectual Property in the TPP: Not "the New TRIPS"' (2016) 17 Melb J Int'l L 257 at 276.
95   Peter K Yu 'The International Enclosure Movement' (2007) 82 Ind LJ 827 at 869–870.

for the suspended TPP intellectual property provisions, policymakers and commentators in the region should not overlook the lingering influence of the TPP.

5 Future of Copyright Norm-Setting

Although the ratification of the TPP sparked considerable debate, the United States' subsequent withdrawal from the regional pact has generated a new line of inquiry concerning the future of intellectual property norm-setting in the Asian Pacific region. Will the United States finally lose ground to China in its effort to shape future regional intellectual property norms?[96] Will the developments surrounding the TPP and the CPTPP accelerate or retard the RCEP negotiations? Will the RCEP negotiating parties eventually reject the inclusion of an intellectual property chapter in their regional pact in light of the complications surrounding the TPP and the CPTPP?

To address this line of inquiry, this section focuses on three specific questions. First, will the United States' withdrawal from the TPP and the recent adoption of the CPTPP lead to the omission of an intellectual property chapter in the RCEP Agreement? Second, if such a chapter indeed exists, will it contain high protection and enforcement standards? Third, will the ultimate standards adopted in the RCEP Agreement conflict with those stipulated in the CPTPP or other FTAs developed by the United States, including a revived or modified TPP Agreement?

5.1 An Intellectual Property Chapter?

The first question concerning whether the RCEP Agreement will contain an intellectual property chapter is easy to answer. Although it is still possible for the RCEP negotiating parties to reject the inclusion of such a chapter, especially in light of the wide variation in intellectual property protection

---

96   Giovanni Di Lieto 'If the TPP Dies, Australia Has Other Game Changing Trade Options' (4 September 2016) The Conversation theconversation.com; Nicholas Ross Smith 'China Will Be the Winner if US Backs Out of the TPP' (1 August 2016) The Conversation theconversation.com.

and enforcement across the Asian Pacific region,[97] past negotiations and ongoing developments have indicated a strong likelihood for this chapter to exist.

There are at least three strands of evidence to support such an existence. First, when ASEAN+6 members adopted the *Guiding Principles and Objectives for Negotiating the Regional Comprehensive Economic Partnership* in August 2012, they agreed to include an intellectual property text in the RCEP Agreement.[98] After the establishment of the Working Group on Intellectual Property at the third round of the RCEP negotiations in January 2014, that group has also worked actively to develop the draft text of the intellectual property chapter.[99] Absent any catastrophic developments in the RCEP negotiations, the time and effort invested in this working group is just too substantial for the chapter to be abandoned at this late stage.

Second, given the importance of intellectual property industries to countries such as Australia, Japan, New Zealand and South Korea, it is very unlikely that these countries will be content with a regional trade and investment agreement that does not contain an intellectual property chapter. If these countries threaten to pull out of the RCEP negotiations, the key question for the remaining ASEAN+6 members will no longer be about whether the agreement should omit an intellectual property chapter, but whether such omission is so important to them that they would rather lose the entire regional pact or the participation of key neighbours in this pact than include the chapter.

Third, apart from the developed country members of ASEAN+6, China, India and other emerging countries in the region – or what I have called 'middle intellectual property powers'[100] – have begun to appreciate the strategic benefits of stronger intellectual property protection and enforcement. Although these countries have yet to embrace the very high protection and enforcement standards found in the European Union, Japan or the United States, they now welcome standards that are higher

---

97   Peter K Yu 'Clusters and Links in Asian Intellectual Property Law and Policy' in Christoph Antons (ed) *Routledge Handbook of Asian Law* (Routledge, Milton Park, 2017) 147 at 148; Peter K Yu 'Intellectual Property and Asian Values' (2012) 16 Marq Intell Prop L Rev 329 at 339–370.

98   *Guiding Principles*, above n 36, s V.

99   'Regional Comprehensive Economic Partnership: News', above n 37.

100   Peter K Yu 'The Middle Intellectual Property Powers' in Randall Peerenboom and Tom Ginsburg (eds) *Law and Development in Middle-Income Countries: Avoiding the Middle-Income Trap* (Cambridge University Press, New York, 2014) 84 at 84.

than those currently available in the Asian Pacific region. These countries are therefore unlikely to block the inclusion of an intellectual property chapter in the RCEP Agreement.

5.2 High Intellectual Property Standards?

The second question concerning whether the RCEP intellectual property chapter will contain high protection and enforcement standards is much harder to answer. To begin with, it is difficult to predict the actual content of any unfinished and fast-evolving chapter. That the RCEP Agreement will provide for special and differential treatment[101] – a key distinction from the TPP or the CPTPP – has made such prediction particularly difficult. After all, the more special accommodation the agreement will provide to developing countries, the more eager their developed counterparts are to demand high overall standards.

At first glance, lower protection and enforcement standards will provide greater benefits to countries in the Asian Pacific region. Because many of these countries are still developing countries, they will be better off declining the adoption of high intellectual property standards, which tend to ignore their local needs, national interests, technological capabilities, institutional capacities and public health conditions.[102] At the time of writing, there remain significant regional variations in economic condition, imitative or innovative capacity, research and development productivity and availability of human capital. An innovative model that works well in the developed world is therefore unlikely to work well in the developing world.[103] Not only may the unquestioned adoption of high intellectual property standards from abroad fail to result in greater innovative efforts,

---

101 Shujiro Urata 'A Stages Approach to Regional Economic Integration in Asia Pacific: The RCEP, TPP, and FTAAP' in Tang Guoqiang and Peter A Petri (eds) *New Directions in Asia-Pacific Economic Integration* (East-West Center, Honolulu, 2014) 119 at 127.

102 Yu, above n 95, at 866–870.

103 Claudio R Frischtak 'Harmonization versus Differentiation in Intellectual Property Rights Regime' in Mitchel B Wallerstein, Mary Ellen Mogee and Roberta A Schoen *Global Dimensions of Intellectual Property Rights in Science and Technology* (National Academy Press, Washington, 1993) 89 at 93–97; David Silverstein 'Intellectual Property Rights, Trading Patterns and Practices, Wealth Distribution, Development and Standards of Living: A North-South Perspective on Patent Law Harmonization' in George R Stewart, Myra J Tawfik and Maureen Irish (eds) *International Trade and Intellectual Property: The Search for a Balanced System* (Westview Press, Boulder, 1994) 155 at 156; Yu, above n 95, at 889.

industrial progress and technology transfers, such adoption may drain away the resources needed for dealing with the socioeconomic and public health problems created by the new legislation.

Even worse, the introduction of legal reforms based on foreign intellectual property systems may exacerbate the dire economic plight of many developing countries, as these new laws would enable foreign rights holders in developed and emerging countries to crush local industries through lawsuits or litigation threats.[104] Even if these new laws could be beneficial in the long run, many of these countries might not have the wealth, infrastructure and technological base to take advantage of the opportunities created by the system in the short run.[105] For countries with urgent public policy needs or a dying population due to inaccessibility to essential medicines, the realisation of the hope for a brighter long-term future seems far away, if not unrealistic. If protection were strengthened beyond the point of an appropriate balance, the present population would undoubtedly suffer greatly.

As if these challenges were not difficult enough, greater harmonisation of intellectual property standards, while potentially beneficial, can take away valuable opportunities for experimentation with new regulatory and economic policies.[106] The lack of diversified standards can also reduce competition among jurisdictions while preventing each jurisdiction from deciding for itself what rules and systems it wants to adopt, thereby rendering the lawmaking process less accountable to the local populations.[107] In the digital age, when laws are hastily introduced and often without convincing empirical evidence, greater experimentation and competition are badly needed.[108]

Notwithstanding the many potential problems and challenges brought about by transplanting intellectual property standards from abroad, the technological rise of China, India and other emerging countries in the Asian Pacific region in the past decade has called for a pause to rethink appropriate intellectual property norm-setting strategies. During the

---

104 Ellen 't Hoen 'TRIPS, Pharmaceutical Patents, and Access to Essential Medicines: A Long Way from Seattle to Doha' (2002) 3 Chi J Int'l L 27 at 30–31.
105 Keith E Maskus *Intellectual Property Rights in the Global Economy* (Institute for International Economics, Washington, 2000) at 237.
106 John F Duffy 'Harmony and Diversity in Global Patent Law' (2002) 17 Berkeley Tech LJ 685 at 707–708.
107 At 706–707.
108 Peter K Yu 'Anticircumvention and Anti-Anticircumvention' (2006) 84 Denv U L Rev 13 at 40–58.

TRIPS negotiations, developing countries were repeatedly told that the TRIPS Agreement, along with other commitments in the WTO, would provide the painful medicine needed to boost economic development.[109] Although it is easy to dismiss the sales pitch of TRIPS advocates and supporters, it is much harder to evaluate whether China, India and the now-emerging countries in the Asian Pacific region have in fact benefited from the many economic reforms pushed on them by the WTO Agreement.

Consider China, for example. Many policymakers and commentators have now taken the view that China would not have been as economically developed and as technologically proficient as it is today had it not embraced the reforms required by WTO accession.[110] Moreover, as China moved from the stage of transplanting foreign laws to the stage of developing indigenous standards,[111] it has skilfully deployed 'selective adaptation' strategies[112] to ensure the incorporation of only beneficial features from the outside without also transplanting the harmful and unsuitable elements.[113]

In sum, even though one could continue to debate how much China, India and other emerging countries have benefited from TRIPS-induced intellectual property reforms, it is much harder to deny the contributions the TRIPS Agreement has provided to the economic development and technological proficiency in these countries. Thus, as much as policymakers and commentators are eager to criticise the deleterious effects of TRIPS-plus bilateral, regional and plurilateral agreements, such as the TPP, the CPTPP and the RCEP, they cannot lose sight of the agreements' potential positive benefits.

---

109 Daniel J Gervais 'The TRIPS Agreement and the Doha Round: History and Impact on Economic Development' in Peter K Yu (ed) *Intellectual Property and Information Wealth: Issues and Practices in the Digital Age* (Praeger Publishers, Westport, 2007) vol 4, 23 at 43.

110 Campbell, above n 73, at 195; Peter K Yu 'The Rise and Decline of the Intellectual Property Powers' (2012) 34 Campbell L Rev 525 at 550–551; Gordon G Chang 'TPP vs. RCEP: America and China Battle for Control of Pacific Trade' *National Interest* (online ed, 6 October 2015).

111 Guo He 'Patents' in Rohan Kariyawasam (ed) *Chinese Intellectual Property and Technology Laws* (Edward Elgar Publishing, Cheltenham, 2011) 25 at 28; Peter K Yu 'Building the Ladder: Three Decades of Development of the Chinese Patent System' (2013) 5 WIPO J 1 at 3–13.

112 Pitman B Potter 'China and the International Legal System: Challenges of Participation' in Donald C Clarke (ed) *China's Legal System: New Developments, New Challenges* (Cambridge University Press, Cambridge, 2008) 145 at 147–148; Wu Handong 'One Hundred Years of Progress: The Development of the Intellectual Property System in China' (2009) 1 WIPO J 117 at 118–119.

113 Peter K Yu 'The Transplant and Transformation of Intellectual Property Laws in China' in Nari Lee, Niklas Bruun and Li Mingde (eds) *Governance of Intellectual Property Rights in China and Europe* (Edward Elgar Publishing, Cheltenham, 2016) 20 at 26.

5.3 A Battle between the TPP, the CPTPP and the RCEP?

The last question concerning the conflicts between the TPP and the RCEP sometimes arises in view of the different leaderships involved. The adoption of the CPTPP has further complicated this question. While the TPP and the CPTPP evidence the leadership of the United States and Japan, respectively, many policymakers and commentators consider the RCEP a China-led mega-regional agreement. In light of such different leadership, it is logical to ask whether the TPP, the CPTPP and the RCEP would create conflicting obligations – or precipitate what I have described as the 'battle of the FTAs'.[114]

These conflicting obligations will be problematic for not only developing countries in the Asian Pacific region but also their developed counterparts. Juggling different standards within the same region will be costly, inefficient and highly challenging. Even more importantly, the conflicts between the TPP/CPTPP and the RCEP will make Asia 'a vital battleground in setting the rules of the global economic order'.[115] As President Barack Obama declared after the conclusion of the TPP negotiations in Atlanta in October 2015:[116]

> When more than 95 percent of our potential customers live outside our borders, we can't let countries like China write the rules of the global economy. We should write those rules, opening new markets to American products while setting high standards for protecting workers and preserving our environment.

Interestingly, this proverbial battle between the TPP and the RCEP did not materialise before the United States withdrew from the TPP. Although the standards in the draft RCEP chapter still differ from their counterparts in the TPP Agreement, they were closer to each other than many anticipated. With the adoption of the CPTPP and the suspension of a number of TPP intellectual property provisions, the TPP/CPTPP and RCEP standards have become even closer. Thus, one could make a strong case that the two mega-regional norm-setting exercises, whether

---

114 Yu, above n 84, at 1018–1027.
115 Campbell, above n 73, at 267.
116 TPP Press Release, above n 11.

before or after the adoption of the CPTPP, reflect a growing convergence of regional intellectual property standards, similar to that induced by the TRIPS Agreement.[117]

There are at least five reasons why the TPP/CPTPP and RCEP negotiations have not led to significant conflicting obligations. First, seven of the 16 RCEP negotiating parties – or, to be more precise, three and a half of the seven parties (Australia, Japan, New Zealand and close to half of ASEAN) – are TPP/CPTPP partners. As a result, they will have strong incentives to ensure that they can join the RCEP without violating the commitments made under the TPP Agreement or the CPTPP.[118] If conflicts do arise, they are unlikely to be blatant, but will instead be more subtle and highly specific.

Second, as noted earlier, China, India and other emerging countries within ASEAN+6 have begun to realise the growing benefits of increased intellectual property protection and enforcement. As a result, they no longer mount as much resistance as they did to those high intellectual property standards that have already been widely adopted in the developed world. In fact, some leaders of these countries may welcome new RCEP standards, as these standards will provide the much-needed external push to accelerate domestic intellectual property reforms.[119]

Third, although China has wielded considerable influence in the RCEP negotiations, it has thus far kept a rather low profile. This negotiation posture is consistent with the approach China has taken in other international trade and intellectual property negotiations.[120] In regard to the draft RCEP chapter, for instance, China did not even advance a proposal. As revealed by Knowledge Ecology International, the draft proposals came from other negotiating parties – namely, ASEAN, India,

---

117 Yu 'Clusters and Links', above n 97, at 150–151.
118 Meredith Kolsky Lewis 'The TPP and the RCEP (ASEAN+6) as Potential Paths toward Deeper Asian Economic Integration' (2013) 8 Asian J WTO & Int'l Health L and Pol'y 359 at 369–370.
119 Peter K Yu 'Intellectual Property, Economic Development, and the China Puzzle' in Daniel J Gervais (ed) *Intellectual Property, Trade and Development: Strategies to Optimize Economic Development in a TRIPS Plus Era* (1st ed, Oxford University Press, Oxford, 2007) 173 at 192.
120 Henry S Gao 'China's Participation in the WTO: A Lawyer's Perspective' (2007) 11 Singapore Yearbook of International L 41 at 69; Peter K Yu 'The Middle Kingdom and the Intellectual Property World' (2011) 13 Or Rev of Int'l L 209 at 229–237.

Japan and South Korea.[121] The only area in which China has taken a more assertive position concerns the disclosure in patent applications of the source of origin of genetic resources used in the inventions,[122] a requirement that already exists in art 26 of the Chinese Patent Law.[123]

Fourth, if the RCEP is to successfully compete with the TPP/CPTPP as a viable alternative for setting trade norms in the Asian Pacific region, it will need to provide effective standards in the intellectual property area. Otherwise, it will lose the support of those economies that are driven heavily by intellectual property and technology industries. Although the United States' withdrawal from the TPP has greatly reduced the competition the RCEP faces, the adoption of the CPTPP has revived such competition while retaining the possibility for the United States to resuscitate the TPP. In view of such competition, the RCEP will need to provide standards that are high enough to entice existing and future TPP/CPTPP partners to embrace the partnership as a dominant forum for setting regional intellectual property norms. Without such participation, a new regional pact could easily emerge to displace the RCEP even if the CPTPP is not eventually ratified.

Finally, ASEAN+6 leaders anticipate the coexistence of the TPP/CPTPP and the RCEP, as revealed in the key documents relating to the development of the FTAAP.[124] Adopted in November 2010, the *Pathways to FTAAP* registered the ASEAN+6 leaders' belief that 'an FTAAP should be pursued ... by developing and building on ongoing regional undertakings, such as ASEAN+3, ASEAN+6, and the Trans-Pacific Partnership, among others'.[125] The *Beijing Roadmap for APEC's Contribution to the Realization of the FTAAP*, which was released four years later, further stated that '[t]he FTAAP should aim to minimize any negative effects resulting from the proliferation of regional and bilateral [trade agreements]'.[126]

---

121 '2014 Oct 3 Version: Korea Proposal for RECP IP Chapter (Regional Comprehensive Economic Partnership)' (3 June 2015) Knowledge Ecology International www.keionline.org; '2014 Oct 3 Version: Regional Comprehensive Economic Partnership, Japan IPR Proposals, RCEP' (9 February 2015) Knowledge Ecology International www.keionline.org; '2014 Oct 10: ASEAN Proposals for RECP IP Chapter, Also India' (8 June 2015) Knowledge Ecology International www.keionline.org; Yu, above n 86, at 683–684.

122 Draft RCEP Chapter, above n 38, art 7.1.

123 Patent Law of the People's Republic of China (promulgated 12 March 1984, amended 27 December 2008, effective 1 October 2009) art 26.

124 Urata, above n 101, at 128–129.

125 Asia-Pacific Economic Corporation Forum *Pathways to FTAAP* (14 November 2010).

126 Asia-Pacific Economic Cooperation Forum *The Beijing Roadmap for APEC's Contribution to the Realization of the FTAAP* (11 November 2014).

Indeed, many policymakers and commentators believe the two mega-regional agreements will eventually merge.[127] As Kurt Campbell observed, '[f]or many in Asia, both the TPP and the RCEP are way stations on the path to the ultimate destination'.[128] The anticipated merger is easy to understand considering that no ASEAN member – or, for that matter, Australia, New Zealand or any other RCEP negotiating party – wants to pick between Beijing and Washington in developing their trade relations, despite their ongoing concern about China's growing economic and military strength.[129] Many ASEAN+6 members and their industries also cannot afford to have two expansive yet conflicting sets of regional trade and trade-related standards.[130] At some point, they will have to decide whether they want to focus on one or the other.

6 Conclusion

Regardless of the intellectual property standards ultimately included in the RCEP Agreement, that agreement, if established, will have serious ramifications for future intellectual property norm-setting in the Asian Pacific region. These ramifications will be similar to those concerning the establishment of the TPP or the CPTPP. To some extent, the mega-regional norm-setting exercises surrounding both the TPP/CPTPP and the RCEP reflect the ongoing policy dilemma confronting intellectual property policymakers in the region. If the protection and enforcement standards are set too low, the participating countries will have squandered a rare and valuable opportunity to promote regional harmonisation. If the standards are set too high, however, they will also have hurt themselves

---

127 Matthew P Goodman 'US Economic Strategy in the Asia-Pacific Region: Promoting Growth, Rules, and Presence' in Tang Guoqiang and Peter A Petri (eds) *New Directions in Asia-Pacific Economic Integration* (East-West Center, Honolulu, 2014) 169 at 174–175; Lewis, above n 24, at 235; Robert Scollay 'The TPP and RCEP: Prospects for Convergence' in Tang Guoqiang and Peter A Petri (eds) *New Directions in Asia-Pacific Economic Integration* (East-West Center, Honolulu, 2014) 235 at 235.
128 Campbell, above n 73, at 193.
129 Ann Capling and John Ravenhill 'The TPP: Multilateralizing Regionalism or the Securitization of Trade Policy' in CL Lim, Deborah Kay Elms and Patrick Low (eds) *The Trans-Pacific Partnership: A Quest for a Twenty-First Century Trade Agreement* (Cambridge University Press, Cambridge, 2012) 279 at 293 (doi.org/10.1017/CBO9781139236775.025); Ellen L Frost 'China's Commercial Diplomacy in Asia: Promise or Threat?' in William W Keller and Thomas G Rawski (eds) *China's Rise and the Balance of Influence in Asia* (University of Pittsburgh Press, Pittsburgh, 2007) 95 at 105; David Shambaugh 'Introduction: The Rise of China and Asia's New Dynamics' in David Shambaugh (ed) *Power Shift: China and Asia's New Dynamics* (University of California Press, Berkeley, 2006) 1 at 17; Yu, above n 33, at 1151.
130 Lewis, above n 24, at 235; Lewis, above n 118, at 369–370; Yu, above n 33, at 1177.

by impeding future development, eroding global competitiveness and jeopardising access to essential medicines, educational materials and information technology.

To complicate matters even further, the TPP chapter, the chapter as modified by the CPTPP and the draft RCEP chapter all feature protection and enforcement standards that have already been widely accepted by the developed country members of the Asian Pacific region. Overemphasis on these standards can be problematic, as such emphasis could undermine the region's ability to undertake the reform needed to target problems that are commonly found in developing countries. Indeed, except for those concerning the protection of genetic resources, traditional knowledge and traditional cultural expressions, none of the intellectual property provisions found in the TPP Agreement, the CPTPP or the draft RCEP chapter seem to target those specific problems.

As I have noted in previous works, developing countries in the Asian Pacific region continue to face a wide array of policy challenges, including a significant discrepancy between law on the books and enforcement on the ground; a woeful lack of access to essential medicines, educational materials, computer software, information technology, scientific and technical knowledge, and patented seeds and foodstuffs; and the growing need for alternative innovation models and other measures to address the highly uneven economic and technological developments within these countries.[131] If the intellectual property chapters in the TPP Agreement, the CPTPP or the RCEP Agreement will not address these challenges, one has to wonder what other measures will have to be taken to eventually improve the intellectual property systems in the developing country members of the Asian Pacific region.

---

131 Yu 'Intellectual Property and Asian Values', above n 97, at 379–397.

2

Copyright Harmonisation in the Asian Pacific Region: Weaving the Peoples Together?

Lida Ayoubi[1]

1 Introduction

In 2015, Professor Adrian Sterling proposed an 'Asian Pacific Copyright Code' that would harmonise the copyright laws of Asian Pacific countries that adopt the code.[2] The Code was proposed within the framework of the Asian Pacific Copyright Association (APCA) established in 2011 with members throughout the region.[3] This chapter argues that the proposed draft Code, as it stands, does not adequately take the interests of indigenous peoples and the impact of regional copyright harmonisation on those interests into account.

Regional, as well as international, copyright harmonisation has proven to be a complex issue. The Agreement on Trade-Related Aspects of Intellectual Property Rights (TRIPS) 1994 was arguably the most

1   Copyright © 2018 Lida Ayoubi. Lecturer in Law, Auckland University of Technology (AUT). The author would like to thank the AUT Faculty of Business, Economics and Law for provision of funding that facilitated the author's research. The author also wishes to acknowledge the research assistance of Mariyam Sheeneez and Sarah Lim and the valuable comments of the editors of this volume on the earlier drafts of this chapter.
2   See Adrian Sterling 'Asian Pacific Copyright Code' in this volume.
3   Asian Pacific Copyright Association www.apcacopyright.org [APCA].

significant step in harmonising intellectual property (IP) law, including copyright, on a global scale.[4] Much has been written about copyright harmonisation in Europe, and the extent of its success or failure remains subject to vigorous debate.[5]

While diverse and different from one another, many Asian Pacific countries have indigenous communities with rich cultural heritage and knowledge systems. However, as Kathy Bowrey explains, 'it has become conventional wisdom to assert that intellectual property provides inadequate protection to Indigenous peoples'.[6] The relationship between indigenous knowledge and culture and copyright has been a major component of the IP and human rights literature.[7] There are issues that arise at the intersection of IP and indigenous rights, both in terms of protection and exploitation (what should not be exploited and how to best use and protect the knowledge and cultural expressions that are available). The incompatibility of copyright and traditional cultural expressions (TCEs, or folklore as it was previously known) is mainly due to the fundamental differences between the values underpinning the western IP system and the worldviews of indigenous peoples.

In the face of an initiative to harmonise copyright law in the Asian Pacific region, this chapter explores the potential impact of harmonisation on the rights of the region's indigenous peoples to their TCEs. In doing so, the chapter focuses on what needs to be considered when developing a harmonised copyright *de lege ferenda* in the region.[8]

---

4   Agreement on Trade-Related Aspects of Intellectual Property Rights 1869 UNTS 299 (adopted 15 April 1994, entered into force 1 January 1995) [TRIPS].
5   See Agnès Lucas-Schloetter 'Is There a Concept of European Copyright Law? History, Evolution, Policies and Politics and the Acquis Communautaire' in Irini Stamatoudi and Paul Torremans (eds) *EU Copyright Law: A Commentary* (Edward Elgar, Cheltenham, 2014); P Bernt Hugenholtz, 'Harmonisation or Unification of European Union Copyright Law' (2012) 38(1) Monash University Law Review 4; Christina Angelopoulos 'The Myth of European Term Harmonisation: 27 Public Domains for the 27 Member States' (2012) 43(50) IIC 567; Maria Lillà Montagnani and Maurizio Borghi 'Promises and Pitfalls of the European Copyright Law Harmonisation Process' in David Ward (ed) *The European Union and the Culture Industries: Regulation and the Public Interest* (Ashgate, Farnham (UK), 2017).
6   Kathy Bowrey 'Indigenous Culture, Knowledge and Intellectual Property: The Need for a New Category of Rights' in Kathy Bowrey, Michael Handler and Dianne Nicole (eds) *Emerging Challenges in Intellectual Property* (Oxford University Press, Oxford, 2011) 46 at 46.
7   See generally on intellectual property harmonisation in Asia Pacific Christoph Antons, Michael Blakeney and Christopher Heath (eds) *Intellectual Property Harmonisation within ASEAN and APEC* (Kluwer Law International, The Hague, 2004).
8   'Of the law [that is] to be proposed'.

The chapter is divided into three main sections. Following this introduction is a brief overview of the treatment of TCEs or indigenous culture more generally during the course of copyright law harmonisation internationally. Part 3 outlines the relationship between copyright harmonisation and the protection of TCEs and the significance of that relationship. Finally, Part 4 identifies some possibilities for addressing the challenges regarding protection of TCEs from misappropriation that arise because of regional copyright harmonisation.

2 Copyright Harmonisation and Protection of TCEs: An Overview

Some of the factors that make copyright incompatible with TCEs are its focus on the individual author, the type of subject matter that attracts protection, the fixation requirement, the scope of moral and material rights of the author and copyright owner and copyright flexibilities, including the term of protection and limitations and exceptions to copyright. Many scholars have written extensively on indigenous peoples' claims to legal rights in their cultural expressions and their relationship to IP.[9] Therefore, this chapter will not repeat those claims. The chapter instead focuses on the treatment of TCEs in the context of copyright law harmonisation regionally and globally.

The lack of consideration for the value of indigenous TCEs and their treatment by copyright law is not surprising considering that a change in the international community's attitude towards indigenous rights in

---

9   See Matthew Rimmer (ed) *Indigenous Intellectual Property: A Handbook of Contemporary Research* (Edward Elgar, Cheltenham, 2015) at Part Two and chs 11 and 21; Peter Drahos and Susy Frankel (eds) *Indigenous People's Innovation: Intellectual Property Pathways to Development* (ANU E Press, Canberra, 2012) at chs 1, 5 and 7; Christoph Antons 'Intellectual Property Rights in Indigenous Cultural Heritage: Basic Concepts and Continuing Controversies' in Christoph Graber, Karolina Kuprecht and Jessica Lai (eds) *International Trade in Indigenous Cultural Heritage* (Edward Elgar, Cheltenham, 2012) 144; Christoph Antons 'At the Crossroads: The Relationship Between Heritage and Intellectual Property in Traditional Knowledge Protection in Southeast Asia' (2013) 29 Law Context A Socio-Legal J 74; Christoph Antons (ed) *Traditional Knowledge, Traditional Cultural Expressions and Intellectual Property Law in the Asia-Pacific Region* (Wolters Kluwer, Alphen aan den Rijn, 2009) at chs 5, 7, 11, 12 and 15.

general did not happen until the 1960s and 1970s,[10] and the United Nations Declaration on the Rights of Indigenous Peoples (UNDRIP) was adopted only 10 years ago.[11]

Bowrey argues that:[12]

> since the late twentieth century the major obstacle to better protection of Indigenous intellectual property has not been a lack of legal interest, or disagreement about the need for reform, but the considerable uncertainty about *how* to achieve this objective.

This lack of certainty has resulted in 'forum shopping' for the recognition of rights of indigenous people to their culture and knowledge and has led to international law on indigenous IP rights (IPRs) being 'fragmented and fractured'.[13] Meaningful regulation of indigenous traditional knowledge (TK) and TCEs has largely happened either outside of the main international IP fora,[14] or outside the traditional framework of IP law.[15] This is partly because TK and TCEs do not form part of the traditional western IP laws.

Early attempts to provide protection for the then termed works of 'folklore' within the framework of copyright led to the adoption of art 15(4) of the Berne Convention for the Protection of Literary and Artistic Works 1886 (Berne Convention) as part of its 1967 Stockholm revisions.[16] The article leaves it to Member States to designate a competent authority

---

10   See Convention (No. 107) Concerning the Protection and Integration of Indigenous and other Tribal and Semi-Tribal Populations in Independent Countries 328 UNTS 247 (opened for signature 26 June 1957, entered into force 2 June 1959); Convention for the Safeguarding of the Intangible Cultural Heritage 2368 UNTS 3 (adopted on 17 October 2003, entered into force 20 April 2006); Convention on the Protection and Promotion of the Diversity of Cultural Expression 2440 UNTS 311 (adopted on 20 October 2005, entered into force 18 March 2007).

11   United Nations Declaration on the Rights of Indigenous Peoples GA Res 61/295 A/Res/61/295 (2007) [UNDRIP].

12   Bowrey, above n 6, at 66.

13   Matthew Rimmer 'Introduction: Mapping Indigenous Intellectual Property' in Matthew Rimmer (ed), *Indigenous Intellectual Property: A Handbook of Contemporary Research* (Edward Elgar, Cheltenham, 2015) at 32.

14   See Convention on Biological Diversity 1760 UNTS 79 (opened for signature 5 June 1992, entered into force 29 December 1993) [CBD]; Nagoya Protocol on Access to Genetic Resources and the Fair and Equitable Sharing of Benefits Arising from their Utilization (adopted 29 October 2010, entered into force 12 October 2014).

15   The latest example of this is the negotiations at the World Intellectual Property Organization (WIPO) see WIPO Draft Articles for Protection of Traditional Cultural Expressions WIPO/GRTKF/IC/28/6 (2014).

16   Berne Convention for the Protection of Literary and Artistic Works 1161 UNTS 31 (opened for signature 9 September 1886, entered into force 5 December 1887), art 15(4) [Berne Convention].

that represents unknown authors of 'unpublished works' where 'there is every ground to presume' that the author is a national of the country.[17] By leaving the regulation of folklore to Member States, the article does not provide the same level of protection for, or clarity regarding, what we today know as TCEs as other copyright subject matters. So far, only India has announced the designation of such authority to the Berne Union Director General, as required by art 15(4)(b).[18] However, other countries such as the United Kingdom[19] and Canada[20] have implemented laws that assign a designated authority to deal with works with an untraceable author.

The two decades following the adoption of art 15(4) of the Berne Convention saw further national and international initiatives that aimed for the provision of better protection for TCEs. In 1976, with the assistance of the United Nations Educational, Scientific and Cultural Organization (UNESCO) and the World Intellectual Property Organization (WIPO), Tunis adopted the Tunis Model Law on Copyright for Developing Countries, which focused on folklore.[21] Nearly a decade later in 1985, a joint expert committee of UNESCO and WIPO stated that 'legal protection of folklore by copyright laws and treaties does not appear to have been particularly effective or expedient'. The joint Working Group then developed the Model Provisions for National Laws on the Protection of Expressions of Folklore Against Illicit Exploitation and other Prejudicial Actions.[22]

---

17   Article 15(4).

18   Article 15(4)(b) provides that 'countries of the Union which makes such designation under the terms of this provision shall notify the Director General by means of a written declaration giving full information concerning the authority thus designated. The Director General shall at once communicate this declaration to all other countries of the Union'. On 1 February 1984, India declared that it has designated 'the Registrar of the Copyrights of India as a competent authority in terms of Article 15, paragraph 4(a) of the Convention'. WTO Council for TRIPS 'Notification Provisions of Intellectual Property Conventions Incorporated by Referencing into the TRIPS Agreement but not Explicitly Referred to in It' IP/C/W/15 (20 November 1995) at 7.

19   The Copyright (Recording of Folksongs for Archives) (Designated Bodies) Order 1989 (UK) designates the bodies who maintain the archives of sound recordings of performances of folksongs as prescribed by s 61 of the Copyright, Designs and Patents Act 1988 (UK) where the words of the folksong are 'unpublished and of unknown authorship at the time the recording is made'.

20   Section 77(1) of the Canadian Copyright Act RSC1985 c C-42 allows the Copyright Board (established as per s 66(1)) to grant licences for use of published works where the copyright owner cannot be located. See for an analysis of the implications of s 77(1) Jeremy de Beer and Mario Bouchard *Canada's 'Orphan Works' Regime: Unlocatable Copyright Owners and the Copyright Board* (Copyright Board of Canada, December 2009).

21   WIPO *Tunis Model Law on Copyright for Developing Countries* (UNESCO, 1976). This model law remains soft law.

22   UNESCO/WIPO *Model Provisions for National Laws on the Protection of Expressions of Folklore Against Illicit Exploitation and other Forms of Prejudicial Actions* (Paris and Geneva, 1985) at [10].

When trade-related aspects of IP were being 'cooked up' in 1994 as part of the TRIPS negotiations, trade in TCEs was not properly considered, if at all. Approximately a year before the adoption of the TRIPS Agreement, the Bellagio Declaration highlighted that:[23]

> Intellectual property laws have profound effects on issues as disparate as scientific and artistic progress, biodiversity, access to information, and the cultures of indigenous and tribal peoples. Yet all too often those laws are constructed without taking such effects into account, constructed around a paradigm that is selectively blind to the scientific and artistic contributions of many of the world's cultures and constructed in fora where those who will be most directly affected have no representation.

Subsequent IP treaties follow the same wording and approach of the Berne Convention.[24] The TRIPS Agreements and the WIPO Copyright Treaty 1996 (WCT) require their Contracting Parties to comply with arts 1 to 21 of the Berne Convention.[25] The Beijing Treaty on Audiovisual Performances 2012 (not yet in force)[26] and the WIPO Performances and Phonograms Treaty 1996 (WPPT) both extend their afforded protections to performers of expressions of folklore.[27]

In addition to international attempts, there have been national initiatives that deal with the recognition, protection and management of indigenous TCEs and potentially enforcement of the rights associated with those TCEs by indigenous communities or custodians of the cultural expressions. Throughout the Asian Pacific region, a number of countries have adopted different initiatives to protect the rights of indigenous communities in their TCEs.[28]

---

23   'The Bellagio Declaration' in James Boyle *Shamans, Software, and Spleens: The Construction of the Information Society* (Harvard University Press, Cambridge, 1996) 193.

24   Berne Convention, above n 16.

25   TRIPS, above n 4, art 9(1) (excluding art 6*bis*); WIPO Copyright Treaty 2186 UNTS 121 (opened for signature 20 December 1996, entered into force 6 March 2002), art 1(4) [WCT]; Berne Convention, above n 16, arts 1–21.

26   Beijing Treaty on Audiovisual Works (adopted 24 June 2012, not yet in force) [Beijing Treaty]. In the Asia Pacific, Indonesia has signed while China, Japan, and the Russian Federation have ratified the Beijing Treaty.

27   WIPO Performances and Phonograms Treaty 2186 UNTS 203 (adopted 20 December 1996, entered into force 20 May 2002) [WPPT]. In addition to international treaties, regional instruments such as the Swakopmund Protocol within the Framework of the African Regional Intellectual Property Organization (ARIPO) also recognise the expressions of folklore as a matter for protection. Swakopmund Protocol on the Protection of Traditional Knowledge and Expressions of Folklore (adopted by the Diplomatic Conference of ARIPO at Swakopmund (Namibia) August 9, 2010) art 1.

28   For a list of national legislation see WIPO Traditional Knowledge, Traditional Cultural Expressions & Genetic Resources Laws, available at www.wipo.int.

Aware of the exclusion or lack of effective protection for TCEs in international copyright instruments, in 2008, the WIPO Intergovernmental Committee on Intellectual Property and Genetic Resources, Traditional Knowledge and Folklore (IGC) commissioned a gap analysis on The Protection of Traditional Cultural Expressions.[29] The focus of the gap analysis was on describing the existing international possibilities for the protection of TCEs, identifying the gaps that existed for protection internationally and, finally, outlining the options available for addressing those gaps.

Since 2011, the IGC has been working on a new international instrument for the protection of TCEs.[30] At the time of writing this chapter, the IGC planned to continue its text-based negotiations on TCEs in its upcoming sessions as part of its 2018/2019 Mandate. Many Asian Pacific countries have been closely involved with the negotiations at the IGC. For instance, Indonesia currently coordinates the 'group of Like-Minded Countries' consisting of countries from the Asian Pacific, as well as the Latin American and Caribbean groups. Australia and New Zealand have been particularly engaged in securing financial support for enabling the participation of indigenous and local communities at the negotiations.[31]

3 Why Copyright Harmonisation Matters

3.1 Countries' Obligations under Human Rights Law

One cannot resist drawing parallels between the protection of TCEs and copyright and the interface of human rights and IP law.[32] Similar reasons can be identified for the current state of the interface in both areas. Generally, human rights and IP law (and its connection to trade) have developed separately. Furthermore, there is still a lack of clarity regarding

---

29   WIPO *The Protection of Traditional Cultural Expressions: Draft Gap Analysis* WIPO/GRTKF/IC/13/4(b) (11 October 2008).

30   WIPO *The Protection of Traditional Cultural Expressions: Draft Articles* WIPO/GRTKF/IC/33 (March 2017) [WIPO Draft Articles].

31   WIPO IGC *Participation of Indigenous and Local Communities: Proposal for Subsidiary Contributions to the Voluntary Fund* WIPO/GRTKF/IC/2810 (19 May 2014); See also WIPO 'Australian Donation Means New Life for Fund that Involves Indigenous Peoples in International Negotiations' (press release, 1 March 2017).

32   See for an overview Laurence Helfer and Graeme Austin *Human Rights and Intellectual Property: Mapping the Global Interface* (Cambridge University Press, Cambridge, 2011).

the definition and scope of human rights and TCEs. Consequently, the international community has not sufficiently explored or recognised the human rights implications of trade in TCEs.

Concepts such as public interest and flexibility have been an integral part of international IP treaties. However, it was not until 2013, when WIPO adopted the Marrakesh Treaty to Facilitate Access to Published Works for Persons Who Are Blind, Visually Impaired or Otherwise Print Disabled, that human rights and their importance were expressly mentioned in an IP instrument.[33]

UNDRIP is generally viewed as the most prominent authority on the rights of indigenous people, complementing and emphasising the human rights previously recognised in key international human rights agreements.[34] With the exception of a few countries in the region, most Asian Pacific countries initially voted in favour of the Declaration.[35]

The legal status of UNDRIP is the subject of debate. Since it was drafted in the form of a declaration, as opposed to a convention or treaty, UNDRIP arguably has a non-binding status. However, some commentators argue that because of the universal acceptance of the Declaration and the subsequent endorsement of the opposing countries, including Australia and New Zealand, the Declaration has become part of customary international law.[36]

---

33   Marrakesh Treaty to Facilitate Access to Published Works for Persons Who Are Blind, Visually Impaired or Otherwise Print Disabled (opened for signature 27 June 2013, entered into force 30 September 2016) [Marrakesh Treaty].

34   UNDRIP, above n 11.

35   Australia and New Zealand initially voted against UNDRIP. Cambodia, China, India, Indonesia, Japan, Malaysia, Maldives, Micronesia, Nepal, Philippines, Singapore, Sri Lanka, Thailand, Timor-Leste and Vietnam voted in favour of the Declaration. Bangladesh, Russian Federation and Samoa abstained from voting. UNDRIP Voting Record, United Nations Bibliographic Information System unbisnet.un.org.

36   See Mauro Barelli 'The United Nations Declaration on the Rights of Indigenous Peoples: a human rights framework for intellectual property rights' in Matthew Rimmer (ed) *Indigenous Intellectual Property: A Handbook of Contemporary Research* (Edward Elgar, Cheltenham, 2015) at 47; S James Anaya and Siegfried Wiessner 'The UN Declaration on the Rights of Indigenous Peoples: Towards Re-Empowerment' in S James Anaya (ed) *International Human Rights and Indigenous Peoples* (Wolters Kluwer, Austin, 2009) at 99–102; Stephan Allen 'The UN Declaration on the Rights of Indigenous Peoples: Towards a Global Legal Order on Indigenous Rights?' in Andrew Halpin and Volker Roeben (eds) *Theorising the Global Legal Order* (Hart Publishing, Oxford, 2009) 187; and Emmanuel Voyiakis 'Voting in General Assembly as Evidence of Customary International Law?' in Stephen Allen and Alexandra Xanthaki (eds) *Reflections on the UN Declaration on the Rights of Indigenous Peoples* (Hart Publishing, Oxford, 2011) 209.

Of relevance to the discussion of this chapter is art 11(2) of UNDRIP, which states:[37]

> States shall provide redress through effective mechanisms, which may include restitution, developed in conjunction with indigenous peoples, with respect to their cultural, intellectual, religious and spiritual property taken without their free, prior and informed consent or in violation of their laws, traditions and customs.

Furthermore, arts 12 and 13 recognise rights of indigenous people towards their 'spiritual and religious traditions, customs and ceremonies' and their 'histories, languages, oral traditions, philosophies, writing systems and literatures'.[38] On the issue of participation of indigenous communities, art 18 of UNDRIP provides that:[39]

> Indigenous peoples have the right to participate in decision-making in matters which would affect their rights, through representatives chosen by themselves in accordance with their own procedures, as well as to maintain and develop their own indigenous decision-making institutions.

Finally, art 31 of UNDRIP stipulates that:[40]

> Indigenous peoples have the right to maintain, control, protect and develop their cultural heritage, traditional knowledge and traditional cultural expressions, as well as the manifestations of their sciences, technologies and cultures, including ... oral traditions, literatures, designs, sports and traditional games and visual and performing arts. They also have the right to maintain, control, protect and develop their intellectual property over such cultural heritage, traditional knowledge, and traditional cultural expressions.[41]

Viewing rights of indigenous people to their TCEs through the lens of human rights necessitates two sets of actions by governments. First, by protecting TCEs from misappropriation, countries ensure that human

---

37   UNDRIP, above n 11, art 11(2).
38   Articles 12 and 13.
39   Article 18.
40   Article 31.
41   See for an analysis of the scope and meaning of an indigenous right to intellectual property in the context of New Zealand Valmaine Toki 'An Indigenous Rights to Intellectual Property' (2015) Intellectual Property Quarterly 370; and Jessica C Lai 'What is an "Indigenous Right to Intellectual Property"?' (2017) 1 Intellectual Property Quarterly 78.

rights associated with TCEs are respected, protected and fulfilled.[42] Second, similar to other human rights, rights of indigenous communities should be balanced against the human rights of others. This includes balancing both IPRs of indigenous peoples (as creators) as well as non–IP related human rights of indigenous peoples (as custodians of TCEs) against others' human rights (such as the right to freedom of expression or culture). Therefore, countries would engage in a balancing act that defines the scope of permissible uses of TCEs by artists, creators or the general public.[43] For instance, the Waitangi Tribunal in New Zealand has provided extensive guidelines on how a balance should be struck between the protection of Māori interests in their TCEs and the interests of others.[44]

This may appear the same as the balancing of different rights under art 15 of the International Covenant on Economic, Social and Cultural Rights (ICESCR) regarding the interests of authors and those of the public.[45] However, the unique relationship between indigenous peoples and their cultural expressions requires a different balancing strategy. Harmonising copyright law across the Asian Pacific region, with diverse indigenous communities, without taking local customs and social values into account as part of a balancing act, undermines the human rights obligations of the countries in the region.

---

42   See, for example, *Universal Declaration of Human Rights* GA Res 217/A (1948), art 27 [UNDHR] recognising everyone's right to participation in the cultural life of the community and protection of the material interests resulting from any scientific, literary or artistic works they create; International Covenant on Civil and Political Rights 999 UNTS 171 (opened for signature 16 December 1966, entered into force 23 March 1976), art 27 [ICCP]; International Covenant on Economic, Social and Cultural Rights 999 UNTC 3 (opened for signature 16 December 1966, entered into force 3 January 1976), art 15 [ICESCR]; Convention on the Elimination of All Forms of Discrimination against Women 1249 UNTS 13 (opened for signature 18 December 1979, entered into force 3 September 1981), art 13(c) [CEDAW]; Convention on the Rights of the Child 1577 UNTS 3 (opened for signature 20 November 1989, entered into force 2 September 1990), art 31 [CRC]; UNDRIP, above n 11, arts 8 (recognising the rights for indigenous peoples not to be subjected to 'destruction of their culture') 11, 31 (recognising the right to maintain, control, protect and develop indigenous culture and traditional cultural expressions) and 13 (specifically recognising the indigenous peoples right to 'maintain, control, protect and develop their intellectual property over such cultural heritage … and traditional cultural expressions').

43   See for a discussion of balancing of indigenous-derived art and freedom of expression in New Zealand Jessica C Lai 'Bicultural Art: Offensive to the Māori or Acceptable Freedom of Expression? Wai 262, the CCPR and NZBORA' (2013) 19(2) AJHR 47.

44   Waitangi Tribunal *Ko Aotearoa Tēnei: A Report into Claims Concerning New Zealand Law and Policy Affecting Māori Culture and Identity* (Wai 262, 2011) especially at ch 1 [Wai 262 Report].

45   ICESCR, above n 42, art 15.

3.2 Reinforcing the Existing Incompatibilities

Further global or regional harmonisation allows copyright to assert itself in indigenous communities where cultural expressions and the knowledge that accompanies them are not traditionally viewed as commodities that can be financially exploited. Protection and exploitation of TCEs and TCE-derived works through copyright law is therefore bound to create tensions.

Indigenous communities have similarities but also differences, and those differences in creation, exploitation and conservation of indigenous works are closely tied to indigenous artists and their communities' identities and ways of life.

Harmonisation should be evaluated and addressed on its own merits and in the cultural context of the countries of the region. Simply following existing copyright law or merely adopting new legislation or policy is not appropriate because it not only reinforces a system that is ineffective in protecting TCEs from misappropriation but it also imposes the same ineffective system on indigenous communities with diverse and varying cultural heritage and worldviews. The provisions of the draft Asian Pacific Copyright Code do not acknowledge this and currently reflect the international copyright law and its shortcomings in protection of indigenous TCEs that have been repeated and reinforced through ongoing harmonisation.[46]

Expressions of diverse knowledge structures of indigenous communities should not be subjected to the same copyright rules and principles as non-indigenous works. A certain country's indigenous communities differ not only from those in other countries but also from one another. For instance, indigenous communities may have differing views as to what can be freely used, used upon seeking permission and what cannot be used and should not form part of the public domain.[47]

---

46   Sterling, above n 2.
47   See Jessica C Lai *Indigenous Cultural Heritage and Intellectual Property Rights: Learning from the New Zealand Experience?* (Springer, Cham, 2014) at 69.

The application and enforcement of IPRs is not going to be simple and straightforward where there are local institutions, traditional ideas and social values in place that resist or complicate such application.[48] Transplanting laws is problematic to begin with, let alone when that law would treat very different subject matters in the same way.[49]

Doris Long argues that 'indigenization' of IPR protection is an example of the rejection of the harmonisation of western IPRs.[50] While this 'indigenization' offers some solutions for protection of TCEs, it does not solve the problem of conflict of laws or adoption of initiatives for protection of TCEs.

Furthermore, one of the fundamental differences between indigenous worldviews and the IP system is the holistic view of indigenous communities regarding culture and knowledge and their indivisibility. Peter Drahos describes the holistic indigenous worldviews as 'a set of doctrines, precepts or directions left by ancestors for finding the correct path in the world'.[51] TCEs are linked to other concepts such as TK that form part of the now recognised 'cultural heritage' of indigenous peoples.[52] As Michael Blakeney argues, international debates often start with acknowledging the holistic nature of TK and TCEs but the negotiators' 'industrial property and copyright influenced habits of mind' cause them to try to fit indigenous concepts into 'familiar categories with tight definitions'.[53] Harmonising an area of law that affects TCEs will undoubtedly affect other aspects of indigenous cultural heritage and should be carefully considered.[54]

---

48   Elain Gin 'International Copyright Law: Beyond WIPO and TRIPS Debate' (2004) 86 JPTOS 771.

49   See for on overview of the impact of transplanting IP laws in the Asian Pacific Pham Duy Nghia 'Transplanted Law – An Ideological Cultural Analysis of Industrial Property Law in Vietnam' in Christoph Antons, Michael Blakeney and Christopher Heath (eds) *Intellectual Property Harmonisation within ASEAN and APEC* (Kluwer Law International, The Hague, 2004) at 125.

50   Doris Long '"Democratizing" Globalization: Practicing the Policies of Cultural Inclusion' (2002) 10 Cardozo J International and Comp L 217.

51   Peter Drahos *Intellectual Property, Indigenous Peoples and their Knowledge* (Cambridge University Press, Cambridge, 2014) at 18–19.

52   Christoph Antons 'Intellectual property rights in indigenous cultural heritage: Basic concepts and continuing controversies' in Christoph Graber, Karolina Kuprecht and Jessica Lai (eds) *International Trade in Indigenous Cultural Heritage* (Edward Elgar, Cheltenham, 2012) at 154.

53   Michael Blakeney 'The negotiations in WIPO for international conventions on traditional knowledge and traditional cultural expressions' in Jessica C Lai and Antoinette Maget Dominicé *Intellectual Property and Access to Im/material Goods* (Edward Elgar, Cheltenham, 2016) at 254.

54   See Debora Halbert *The State of Copyright: The Complex Relationships of Cultural Creation in a Globalized World* (Routledge, London, 2014) at 14, which states 'indigenous communities see traditional cultural expressions and knowledge as part of the larger struggle for autonomy, sovereignty, and self-governance'.

Further harmonisation of copyright law in the absence of a well-established and binding international legal framework for the protection of TCEs could create more problems, unless the impact of copyright on TCEs is accounted for in the harmonisation framework.

3.3 Potential Conflict of Copyright and Sui Generis Systems

Copyright harmonisation would be particularly problematic in the absence of mechanisms, such as sui generis systems, for the protection of TCEs. In that scenario, the same copyright rules and regulations would apply to TCEs and their custodians, which have diverse customs in different countries.

However, even in the presence of protection mechanisms that would limit the application of copyright law, there would still be an issue of conflict between local laws on protection of TCEs and the country's obligations under international or regional copyright laws that apply to instances of TCEs or works derived from them. As Susy Frankel argues, conflict between IP and other systems of protecting traditional knowledge and culture 'will inevitably arise'.[55] For instance, what happens when a country member to the main international copyright treaties does not join initiatives protecting TCEs and does not pass protective domestic legislation either?

The WIPO Draft Articles for Protection of Traditional Cultural Expressions (WIPO Draft Articles),[56] if and when adopted, will form an international sui generis system for the protection of cultural heritage from misappropriation. However, the legal nature of the final outcome of the negotiations at WIPO is still unclear and, similar to other international agreements, its effectiveness will rely on its adoption by countries. Even when adopted, it will be up to its contracting parties to create appropriate domestic policy and legislation to implement the principles of such a sui generis system. Therefore, it is crucial to ensure that copyright law does not conflict with the operation of existing or future sui generis systems that protect national interests.

---

55   Susy Frankel 'A New Zealand perspective on the protection of mātauranga Māori' in Christoph Graber, Karolina Kuprecht and Jessica C Lai (eds) *International Trade in Indigenous Cultural Heritage* (Edward Elgar, Cheltenham, 2012) at 441.
56   WIPO Draft Articles, above n 30.

4 Copyright Harmonisation and TCEs: Looking Ahead

Amending the existing IP framework is a rather cumbersome, if not impossible, task. However, future harmonisation attempts can provide an opportunity to address some of the existing difficulties instead of reinforcing them.

Long argues that 'international IP harmonisation threatens to exacerbate further the division between North and South by continuing to marginalise the participation of developing and non-industrialised countries'.[57] Therefore, a regional copyright code would be an opportunity to bridge this gap by giving developing countries, particularly those with indigenous communities, a seat at the table.

International regulation of indigenous interests in TCEs has proven difficult. Regional harmonisation of copyright on the other hand, provided it is limited to setting minimum standards, can provide an opportunity for overcoming the disagreements that are slowing down the international process. Fewer actors and more common ground, due to geographical similarities, give countries the chance to innovate and adopt norms based on local effective practices. While leaving sufficient policy manoeuvre space for countries to incorporate their national needs, a regional harmonising instrument can incorporate successful national practices instead of imposing an absolute top-down approach.

Generally, harmonisation can offer certainty for creators and users of TCEs, and authors of derivative works with indigenous origin. Harmonising copyright can also particularly help address the issue of protection of cross-border TCEs that span over multiple jurisdictions.[58] It can address the disputes in Asia over multiple claims over IPRs in cross-border TCEs through a dispute resolution mechanism.[59]

---

57   Long, above n 50, at 224.

58   See for some examples of such TCEs in relation to copyright (discussed in the context of geographical indications in the article) Mohammad Towhidul Islam and Ahsan Habib 'Introducing Geographical Indications in Bangladesh' (2013) 24(1) Dhaka University Law Journal 51 at 62–66. One example is the production of Nakshi Kantha (a type of embroidered quilt) in Bangladesh and India where the patterns are claimed by both countries to belong to their indigenous peoples.

59   See for an overview of cross-border disputes concerning TCEs Christoph Antons 'At the Crossroads: The Relationship Between Heritage and Intellectual Property in Traditional Knowledge Protection in Southeast Asia', above n 9, at 92–94.

4.1 Recognition and Acknowledgement of Human Rights

Any initiative that further harmonises copyright globally or regionally needs to be in line with the obligations of states under the existing international treaties on the protection of copyright. Even if considered incompatible with the protection of TCEs, amending the existing international copyright instruments is rather politically, even if not legally, unrealistic or impracticable. However, the interpretation of existing laws or adoption of new IP law and policy, whether in IP or trade platforms, can be subjected to broad international law principles and rules, including human rights law. Therefore, harmonising copyright without due consideration of its impact on TCEs and indigenous rights, be it for instance through imposing limited terms of protection or individual authorship and ownership requirements, would violate human rights entrenched in international law.[60]

The function of recognising the human rights of indigenous people that are related to their TCEs, in regional or international instruments that harmonise copyright, is twofold. First, it highlights the social and cultural purpose and object of IP as partly identified in the Preamble to the TRIPS Agreement and its arts 7 and 8 regarding the balancing of rights and interests in the IP regime.[61] Second, it underlines the interconnectedness of copyright and states' obligations under international human rights law. The presence of human rights principles in harmonisation frameworks goes beyond semantics and is an acknowledgement of the potential effects of the latter on the former. It can also act as a reminder of the need for equilibrium between human rights and copyright when implementing the latter.[62]

Therefore, when incorporating the adopted norms into their domestic law, the signatories to a regional or international instrument should observe this balance and set of obligations. This is especially important

---

60   See above n 42.

61   TRIPS, above n 4, Preamble and arts 7 and 8.

62   See Human Rights Commission *Report of the High Commissioner on the Impact of the Agreement on Trade-Related Aspects of Intellectual Property Rights on Human Rights* E/CN.4/Sub.2/2001/13 (27 June 2001) at [61], which states that 'an important aspect of the human rights approach to IP protection is the express linkage of human rights in relevant legislation. Express reference to the promotion and protection of human rights in the TRIPS Agreement would clearly link States' obligations under international trade law and human rights law … . This would assist States to implement the "permitted exceptions" in the TRIPS Agreement in line with their obligations under ICESCR'.

in light of the provisions that leave states with room for flexibility in the way they implement international obligations. Reference to indigenous communities and their rights over TCEs in domestic legislation would acknowledge the position of indigenous people as creators and guardians of cultural expressions, equal in rights, if not similar, to other creators of copyright works.

An overarching and general principle that acknowledges the significance of TCEs that might fall under the definition of copyright subject matter in an instrument harmonising copyright in the region is a good start. Instruments that are too prescriptive in defining contentious concepts such as indigenous peoples, beneficiaries or cultural expressions may defeat the purpose of protecting indigenous interests by excluding certain groups from protection.

Such an instrument could also specifically allow or require member states to provide for measures in their copyright legislation that protect TCEs and are in line with international human rights law principles relevant to rights of indigenous peoples. However, provisions that are too broad and give too much discretion to national states run the risk of not being implemented consistently with the intent of the drafters.

Furthermore, human rights are enforceable through many existing mechanisms. Evaluation of the impact of copyright policy, including harmonisation, on rights of indigenous communities to their TCEs in different countries could be achieved through monitoring mechanisms designed for IP law or human rights law instruments.

In reporting on their compliance with IP agreements, states could be required to include the steps they have taken to guarantee the protection of TCEs from the negative impact of copyright law.[63] Such steps might consist of their innovations within the framework of copyright law, sui generis systems (and their relation to copyright) or both. This could include both attempts at enabling indigenous communities to enjoy copyright protection over their TCEs when desired, as well as stopping the misappropriation of TCEs through copyright protection by third parties such as non-indigenous authors. Protection from misappropriation could also include measures that would stop authors from using indigenous

---

63   Human Rights Commission, above n 62, at [61] encouraging states to 'monitor the implementation of the TRIPS Agreement to ensure that its minimum standards are achieving … [the] balance between the interests of the general public and those of the authors'.

TCEs for the creation of new works when it is not culturally appropriate. Furthermore, countries could report on specifically designed exceptions they have adopted that lay out the permissible uses of TCEs. Such exceptions separate TCEs from other copyright works and would ensure that they are not subject to the standard built-in flexibilities of copyright law as stipulated under the Berne and TRIPS three-step tests.[64]

For instance, the impact of copyright harmonisation on TCEs could be evaluated under the umbrella of public interest as recognised in the TRIPS Agreement.[65] Under its existing transparency requirements, the World Trade Organization (WTO) requires its Member States to report about their specific measures, policies or laws, and the WTO itself regularly reviews the Members' trade policies.[66] States' performances in terms of safeguarding the public interest could be added to the current revision mechanism. This, however, would first require political will and a paradigm shift regarding rights of indigenous people to their cultural heritage.

Alternatively, human rights reporting mechanisms could be used for the same purpose. Countries that are members of the ICESCR have an obligation to report on the actions they have taken and on their progress with realising of the rights recognised in the Covenant.[67] The Committee on Economic, Social and Cultural Rights has in the past provided guidelines regarding the reporting process.[68] Therefore, the Committee could require the ICESCR Member States to specifically report on the impact of their copyright law and policy on misappropriation of TCEs.

---

64   The Berne and TRIPS three-step tests set out the requirements for inclusion of copyright flexibilities in national legislation. Berne Convention, above n 16, art 9(2), and TRIPS, above n 4, art 13.

65   TRIPS, above n 4, arts 7 and 8.

66   Some examples of such reports and reviews are the Reviews of Legislation on Enforcement of Intellectual Property Rights, Checklist of Issues on Enforcement of Intellectual Property, and the Annual Reports submitted to and published by the Council for Trade-Related Aspects of Intellectual Property Rights as well as countries' Trade Policy Reviews produced by the Trade Policy Review Body, available at docs.wto.org.

67   ICESCR, above n 42, art 16(1).

68   TRIPS, above n 4; see ICESCR, above n 42, art 16(2), which assigned the United Nations Economic and Social Council (ECOSOC) the task of monitoring the implementation of the Covenant. See *Review of the composition, organization and administrative arrangements of the Sessional Working Group of Governmental Experts on the Implementation of the International Covenant on Economic, Social and Cultural Rights* ECOSOC Res 1985/17 (1985), which established the Committee on Economic, Social and Cultural Rights to monitor states' reports and provide country-specific and general comments.

Countries that have ratified the United Nations Convention on the Rights of the Child (UNCRC) have to report to the Committee on the Rights of the Child two years after ratification of the Convention and every five years thereafter.[69] The Committee has provided guidelines for state reports and can request further information regarding the implementation of the UNCRC.[70] Articles 30 and 31 of the UNCRC recognise the right of children (particularly indigenous children) to enjoyment of and participation in his or her cultural life.[71] Alternatively, countries' laws and policies on the interface of TCEs and copyright could be evaluated in the UN Special Rapporteur's country reports on the rights of indigenous peoples.[72]

4.2 A Pluralistic View of Harmonisation

Many contentious issues still exist regarding protection of TCEs from misappropriation and their relationship with copyright law. The WIPO IGC has been addressing and debating these issues in the framework of the WIPO Draft Articles.[73] It is not expected that international copyright treaties or national legislation will or can fully address these questions or provide answers for them. However, such instruments can highlight that standard copyright rules should not apply to matters such as authorship, ownership, scope, term and exceptions in relation to TCEs. Countries can be required to refer to other international frameworks, such as the WIPO Draft Articles,[74] or to pass national legislation that ensure their copyright laws comply with their human rights obligations towards indigenous rights.

---

69   CRC, above n 42, arts 44(1) and (2).
70   Article 44(4). See also *General Guidelines Regarding the Form and Content of Initial Reports to be Submitted by States Parties under Article 44, paragraph 1 (a), of the Convention* CRC/C/5 (30 October 1991) [CRC, General Guidelines]; and *Treaty-specific guidelines regarding the form and content of periodic reports to be submitted by States parties under article 44, paragraph 1 (b), of the Convention on the Rights of the Child* CRC/C/58/Rev.3 (3 March 2015) [CRC, Treaty-specific guidelines].
71   CRC, above n 42, arts 30 and 31.
72   Special Rapporteur on the rights of indigenous people 'Country reports' OHCHR United Nations Human Rights Office of the High Commissioner www.ohchr.org.
73   WIPO Draft Articles, above n 30.
74   WIPO Draft Articles, above n 30.

As Hannu Wager and Jayashree Watal argued, 'if we consider the IP system as a tool of public policy, human rights considerations may be helpful in defining the objectives of the policy'.[75] Boundaries of what attracts copyright protection and what does not are not unchangeable. As Frankel noted, what IP protects is a 'cultural construct'.[76] Countries have been creating new forms of rights or subject matters on an ongoing basis. International copyright instruments harmonise the minimum standards of protection. Therefore, countries may provide for greater protection and may extend the minimum required protection to new categories of works.

In adopting a tiered approach to protection of TCEs from misappropriation, countries need to identify those aspects of indigenous culture for which IP is a suitable means of protection. When harmonising copyright and recognising the rights of indigenous communities to the TCEs, any such initiative should allow states enough flexibility to protect TCEs according to their national needs.

Antony Taubman suggests that three policies can inform the interface of IP and indigenous peoples' rights: a 'more effective use of existing mechanisms to protect communities' interests'; 'adapting the existing principles of intellectual property law and extending their effect to respect more effectively community interests'; and 'creating altogether new, stand-alone forms of protection for traditional knowledge and traditional cultural expressions'.[77] In the realm of copyright, countries have used one or a combination of these measures to protect indigenous rights within their national context. For instance, the South African Intellectual Property Law Amendment Act 2013 extends copyright protection to:[78]

> a literary, artistic or musical work with an indigenous or traditional origin, including indigenous cultural expressions or knowledge which was created by persons who are or were members, currently or historically, of an indigenous community and which literary, artistic or musical work is regarded as part of the heritage of such indigenous community.

---

75   Hannu Wager and Jayashree Watal 'Human rights and intellectual property law' in Christophe Geiger (ed) *Research Handbook on Human Rights and Intellectual Property* (Edward Elgar Publishing, Cheltenham, 2015) at 159; see also on how copyright can be used to protect indigenous interests Silke von Lewinski (ed) *Indigenous heritage and intellectual property: Genetic resources, traditional knowledge and folklore* (2nd ed, Kluwer Law International, London, 2008) at 350–413; and Daphne Zografos *Intellectual Property and Traditional Cultural Expressions* (Edward Elgar, Cheltenham, 2010) at ch 2.

76   Susy Frankel 'From Barbie to Renoir: Intellectual property and culture' (2010) 41 VUWLR 1 at 9.

77   Antony Taubman *A Practical Guide to Working with TRIPS* (Oxford University Press, Oxford, 2011) at 185–189.

78   Intellectual Property Laws Amendment Act 2013 (South Africa), s 1(1).

The Act also recognises communal ownership of traditional expressions by considering the author of an indigenous work 'the indigenous community from which the work originated'.[79]

The WIPO Draft Articles adopt the language of the Berne Convention and TRIPS Agreement three-step tests,[80] when it comes to limitations and exceptions to rights over TCEs, with an additional requirement for treatment of expressions not to be derogatory or offensive.[81] This is an attempt at extending the existing protection of IPRs to TCEs. However, it remains unclear whether this approach can sufficiently respond to the problems caused by applying the existing standards of copyright flexibility to TCEs.

Moral rights present another possible means for extending the protection of IP to TCEs. Article 6bis of the Berne Convention protects the moral rights of the author.[82] The TRIPS Agreement, however, does not explicitly provide for the protection of moral rights.[83]

A few factors deem the existing moral rights ineffective for protection of indigenous TCEs. First, moral rights are personal to the author and authorised persons or institutions after his or her death.[84] However, many indigenous communities do not recognise an individual as the author of a TCE or TCE-derived work. Second, similar to economic rights, moral rights are generally protected for a limited time.[85] This feature can also clash with the cultural significance of existing or future TCEs that requires perpetual protection. Finally, the scope of rights established under the

---

79   Section 1(1).
80   Berne Convention, above n 16, art 9(2), and TRIPS, above n 4, art 13. See above n 64.
81   WIPO Draft Articles, above n 30, art 5.
82   Berne Convention, above n 16, art 6bis.
83   TRIPS Agreement, above n 4, art 9, which states 'Members shall comply with Articles 1 through 21 of the Berne Convention (1971) and the Appendix thereto. However, Members shall not have rights or obligations under this Agreement in respect of the rights conferred under Article 6bis of that Convention or of the rights derived therefrom'; See also Sam Ricketson and Jane Ginsburg *International Copyright and Neighbouring Rights: The Berne Convention and Beyond* (2nd ed, Oxford University Press, Oxford, 2006) vol 1 at 615–619 for a detailed discussion of the moral rights in the TRIPS and its connection with the Berne Convention, arguing that members of TRIPS still have an obligation towards some moral rights that fall outside the scope of art 6bis, such as the right to disclosure or divulgation. The WCT requires its Contracting Parties to comply with arts 1 to 21 of the Berne Convention including art 6bis that confers the moral rights. WCT, above n 25, art 1(4).
84   Berne Convention, above n 16, art 6bis(1).
85   Article 6bis(2) of the Berne Convention prescribes that moral rights should 'be maintained, at least until the expiry of the economic rights'. Some civil-law jurisdictions, however, have perpetual moral rights, e.g. France's Code de la propriété intellectuelle, art. Article L121-1.

Berne Convention and further interpreted by case law may not align with the interests of indigenous communities in their TCEs.[86] Article 6bis(1) of the Berne Convention recognises the author's right to:[87]

> claim authorship of the work and to object to any distortion, mutilation or other modification of, or other derogatory action in relation to, the said work, which would be prejudicial to his or her honour or reputation.

This approach fails to reflect that, with respect to certain works of indigenous origin, the mere use of the work without distortion, mutilation or other modification may still be prejudicial to the interest of the indigenous community.[88] Therefore, when further harmonising copyright, countries could include innovative provisions on protection of moral rights of indigenous communities as collective guardians of TCEs.[89]

An approach for further copyright harmonisation, through either international and regional instruments or bilateral and multilateral trade agreements, should take advantage of the combination of policy responses that Taubman proposes.[90]

However, when creating sui generis protection systems, countries should ensure the compatibility of sui generis protection of TCEs and copyrights within the framework of copyright law.[91] As Frankel and Christoph Graber have argued, procedural mechanisms that protect the relationship of indigenous peoples with their culture and knowledge can facilitate the interface of sui generis protection and copyright law.[92]

---

86   Berne Convention, above n 16.

87   Berne Convention, above n 16, art 6bis(1).

88   See, for example, *Yumbulul v Reserve Bank of Australia* [1991] FCA 332; (1991) 21 IPR 481 where the image of an indigenous artwork was reproduced on a bank note. The indigenous community to which the artist belonged deemed the use inappropriate. However, the Court found the reproduction legitimate under the terms of a licensing agreement between the indigenous artist and an intermediary agency. See also Zografos, above n 75, at 48–49.

89   In Australia, the legislature did not pass the proposed Copyright Amendment (Indigenous Communal Moral Rights) Bill 2003. For an analysis of the Bill, see Jane Anderson 'Indigenous Communal Moral Rights: The Utility of an Ineffective Law' (2004) 5(30) ILB 15.

90   Taubman, above n 77, at 185–189.

91   An example is ensuring the compatibility of copyright with sui generis protection of TCEs through geographical indications (GI). A potential benefit of GI protection of TCEs is the perpetual nature of the right. A major problem with GI protection of TCEs is determining the GI holder and the boundary of geographical area.

92   Susy Frankel 'A New Zealand perspective on the protection of mātauranga Māori' in Christoph Graber, Karolina Kuprecht and Jessica C Lai (eds) *International Trade in Indigenous Cultural Heritage* (Edward Elgar, Cheltenham, 2012) at 454; Christoph Graber 'Institutionalization of Creativity in Traditional Societies and in International Trade Law' in Shubha Ghosh and Robin Malloy (eds) *Creativity Law and Entrepreneurship* (Edward Elgar, Cheltenham, 2011) 234 at 251–252.

Instruments harmonising copyright law can accommodate overarching principles regarding such procedural mechanisms without interfering with already existing international copyright norms. Countries can retain the freedom to choose the policy approach for the adoption of such mechanisms most suitable to their domestic context.[93]

Frankel explains that in New Zealand, the introduction of the Advisory Committees by the Trade Marks Act 2002 and Patents Act 2013[94] was intended to bridge the gap between the IP system and sui generis methods of protecting traditional knowledge and culture.[95] The Committees advise the Patents and Trade Mark Commissioners regarding any conflict between the interests of Māori and granting of a patent or registration of a trade mark.[96] These measures were designed to ensure that Māori knowledge and culture is not misappropriated under the framework of patents and trade marks legislation.

However, it is not possible to replicate the exact same checks and balances within the copyright law framework. The automatic protection[97] of copyright law means that any TCE-derived work that fits the copyright

---

93 See Christoph Graber, Karolina Kuprecht and Jessica C Lai 'The trade and development of indigenous cultural heritage: Completing the picture and a possible way forward' in Christoph Graber, Karolina Kuprecht and Jessica C Lai (eds) *International Trade in Indigenous Cultural Heritage* (Edward Elgar, Cheltenham, 2012) at 468–469, which highlights the importance of ensuring that procedural measures facilitate the interface of sui generis systems of protection of indigenous cultural heritage and IP laws.

94 Trade Marks Act 2002; Patents Act 2013; The Trade Marks Māori Advisory Committee was formed as a result of consultations with Māori in the mid-1990s and on the grounds that previous trade marks laws did not protect the interests of Māori sufficiently. Upon the passage of the Geographical Indications (Wine and Spirits) Registration Act 2006, the Committee provides advice regarding the proposed use or registration of a geographical indication likely to be offensive to Māori. The Patents Māori Advisory Committee was part of the broader changes introduced by the Patents Act 2013.

95 Susy Frankel 'A New Zealand perspective on the protection of mātauranga Māori' in Christoph Graber, Karolina Kuprecht and Jessica C Lai (eds) *International Trade in Indigenous Cultural Heritage* (Edward Elgar, Cheltenham, 2012).

96 Patents Act 2013, s 226; Trade Marks Act 2002, s 178.

97 The majority of countries have stepped away from subjecting copyright protection to formalities such as registration, notice and deposit after the adoption of the Berne Convention, above n 16. Fixation requirements are, however, a common feature of many national copyright legislations.

subsistence requirements is considered a copyright work.[98] The creation of TCE-derived works by non-indigenous authors and without the consultation of the indigenous community from which the TCE originates raises two sets of overlapping problems. First is the issue of compensation, which, in some instances, may be compared to the violation of the material interests of the author in the absence of licensing schemes. The second is where the creation of derivative works is contrary to the cultural values of the indigenous community.[99]

This second problem may also arise when copyright flexibilities (namely, the three-step test)[100] are applied to copyright works created by indigenous artists based on their heritage. Susan Corbett has dealt with this issue in the context of permissible uses of copyright works by libraries and archives in New Zealand.[101] In the way of exclusion, countries could indicate that the harmonised provisions on fair use or limitations and exceptions to copyright do not apply to subject matters that are TCEs or derivative works of indigenous origin.[102] The copyright legislation should make it clear that the use of TCEs for creation of derivative works will be governed by sui generis systems in place and copyright infringement rules including substantiality and originality should not apply. Adjusting the national copyright flexibilities in light of works of indigenous origin (created

---

98   However, as per art 17 of the Berne Convention, above n 16 (and art 9(1) of the TRIPS Agreement, above n 4) countries can control or prohibit the 'circulation, presentation, or exhibition of any work or production' without violating their obligations under these instrument. While this does not stop unauthorised, offensive or culturally inappropriate TCE-derived works from attracting copyright protection, countries can use their discretion to limit the exclusive rights of authors of such works. See for a further discussion of art 17 of the Berne Convention, Lai, above n 47, at 277–278. There is also an ongoing debate on whether certain types of works such as pornography or works generally seen as contrary to public order or morality are copyright protected. See, for example, Ann Bartow 'Copyright Law and Pornography' (2012) 91(1) Oregon Law Review 1, and Yasuto Shirae 'Copyright Protection on Pornography in Japan' (2014) 3(2) NTUT Journal of Intellectual Property Law and Management 213.

99   The balance of the cultural values of the indigenous community and the rights of the public is of significance and discussed within the context of New Zealand in Lai, above n 43.

100   Berne Convention, above n 16, art 9(2), and TRIPS, above n 4, art 13.

101   Corbett has recommended that s 55(3) of the New Zealand Copyright Act 1993 be amended to require libraries and archives to 'consult with Maori before digitising and providing online public accessibility to cultural heritage originating from Maori. An assessment of the balance between the public interest in culture versus the owners' rights in their property should also be required'. Susan Corbett *Archiving our culture in a digital environment: Copyright law and digitisation practices in cultural heritage institutions* (New Zealand Law Foundation, 2011) at 41.

102   On how permitted uses and fair use can impact negatively on indigenous concerns and TCEs, see Natalie P Stoianoff and Evana Wright, and Jonathan Barrett, in this volume.

by both indigenous and non-indigenous authors) would represent one means of protecting TCEs from misappropriation caused by the way the copyright law is set up internationally.

In the absence of consideration for indigenous rights in copyright legislation, claims against misappropriation of TCEs will be either secondary to copyright protection by resorting to sui generis methods (e.g. cultural heritage legislation) or hard to defend when such methods do not exist.

Countries should explore their options regarding the interface of sui generis measures and copyright law. One way of addressing this issue is establishing a body that provides guidelines on treatment of TCEs as copyright works or creation of new works using TCEs.[103] Alternatively, countries could introduce a registration requirement for copyright subsistence generally or limited to derivative works created using TCEs.

Acknowledgement that nothing in the copyright agreement stops the member states from adopting policy and law that are necessary for management of TCEs within their territory and meeting their obligations under other international human rights law is another option.[104]

Copyright treaties can allow indigenous peoples themselves to decide what TCEs can be subject to copyright protection or flexibilities. However, this in itself does not address the situations where there are no recognised custodians of certain TCEs or alternatively where multiple communities lay a claim to an expression.

An instrument harmonising copyright should also require states to adopt suitable national remedies for when misappropriation of TCEs occurs.

---

103 For example, in New Zealand, creation of such a body in the form of a commission was among the Waitangi Tribunal's recommendations for better protection of Māori knowledge and culture. The Waitangi Tribunal hears claims from the Māori regarding their rights under the Treaty of Waitangi. See Wai 262 Report, above n 44, at 92.

104 For instance, New Zealand often includes a clause in its free trade agreements to retain the ability to meet its obligations towards its indigenous population under the Treaty of Waitangi. See Susy Frankel and Megan Richardson 'Limits of Free Trade Agreements: The New Zealand/ Australia Experience' in Christoph Antons and Reto M Hilty (eds) *Intellectual Property and Free Trade Agreements in the Asia-Pacific Region* (Springer, Heidelberg, 2015) at 315–333; Susy Frankel 'Attempts to protect indigenous culture through free trade agreements' in Christoph Graber, Karolina Kuprecht and Jessica C Lai (eds) *International Trade in Indigenous Cultural Heritage* (Edward Elgar, Cheltenham, 2012) at 118–143.

To benefit from the proposed policy responses, conducting studies or consultations before further harmonisation is essential. To avoid reinforcing the existing problems, harmonising copyright law regionally or globally should be done only after thorough analyses of the existing national customs, values, laws and concepts.

Meaningful and independent representation from indigenous communities in the copyright harmonisation process should also be ensured. Indigenous representation is by no means easy to achieve.[105] The involvement of indigenous communities in negotiating a potential instrument on the protection of TCEs in WIPO, as a primarily IP-focused forum (rather than indigenous rights forum), has further brought this issue to the fore. However, the alternative, meaning representation that is dependent on states acting as messengers, might lead to cherry-picking of interests that states deem important or relevant.[106]

Therefore, to comply with their international human rights obligations,[107] countries need to consult their indigenous communities and have regard for their rights in relation to TCEs when joining regional or international agreements and regulating copyright law domestically. Such obligation is also specifically reflected in some national legal frameworks.

---

105 See Christoph Graber, Karolina Kuprecht and Jessica Lai 'The trade and development of indigenous cultural heritage: Completing the picture and a possible way forward' in Christoph Graber, Karolina Kuprecht and Jessica C Lai (eds) *International Trade in Indigenous Cultural Heritage* (Edward Elgar, Cheltenham, 2012) at 469–471.

106 Steps taken by the WIPO in the negotiation process of the WIPO Draft Articles, above n 30, to ensure participation of indigenous peoples can be used as guidelines for similar processes. These steps include the WIPO Voluntary Fund (effective in enabling underprivileged indigenous communities but dependent on states' voluntary contribution), experts selected by indigenous communities themselves, Indigenous Panels and a WIPO-funded secretariat for indigenous and local community participants. See, for example, UN Permanent Forum on Indigenous Issues 'Compilation of information received from agencies, funds and programmes of the United Nations System and other intergovernmental bodies on progress in the implementation of the recommendations of the Permanent Forum' E/C.19/2017/8 (13 February 2017) at [16] and 'Information Note from the Secretariat of the World Intellectual Property Organization to the Fourteenth Session of UN Permanent Forum on Indigenous Issues' (20 April – 1 May 2015). These can be seen as WIPO's ongoing attempts to respect the UNDRIP, above n 11, as the UN Permanent Forum on Indigenous Issues has called on WIPO to improve its implementation of the UNDRIP. See, for example, UN Permanent Forum on Indigenous Issues *Report of the Eleventh Session (7–18 May 2012)* E/2012/43-E/C.19/2012/13, at [47] stating that 'the Permanent Forum demands that WIPO recognize and respect the applicability and relevance of the Declaration as a significant international human rights instrument that must inform the Intergovernmental Committee process and the overall work of WIPO. The minimum standards reflected in the Declaration must either be exceeded or directly incorporated into any and all WIPO instruments that directly or indirectly impact the human rights of indigenous peoples'.

107 See UNDRIP, above n 11, art 18.

In New Zealand, for instance, the Waitangi Tribunal has stated that the Crown has to ensure the engagement of Māori in negotiation of international agreements that might affect their rights and interests in their culture and TK. The Tribunal states that normally 'Māori must have a say in identifying [their interests] and devising the protection'.[108] Additionally, the Tribunal went further by requiring the 'Māori voice' to be placed as the 'New Zealand voice' in international negotiations when Māori interests are overwhelming and other interests narrow or limited.[109]

5 Conclusion

Current copyright laws are mostly ineffective in protecting indigenous TCEs. This is due to the underlying mismatch between copyright law and the worldviews of indigenous peoples towards their cultural heritage and TK.

Further global or regional harmonisation of copyright reinforces the existing difficulties that arise at the intersection of copyright and TCEs. It does so by extending the reach of copyright law into communities where knowledge and cultural expressions are created and treated differently compared to regular copyright works. By adding to the IP obligations of countries, harmonisation also worsens the identified conflicts between copyright and sui generis mechanisms for the protection of TCEs.

The proposed Asian Pacific Copyright Code,[110] a regional copyright harmonisation initiative that inspired the writing of this chapter, does not currently address the impact of copyright on TCEs and indigenous interests in them. While regional harmonisation of copyright has benefits, such as establishing regional representation in global fora, giving a voice to developing countries and accommodating regional similarities, it should be approached with caution. This chapter has argued that further harmonisation of copyright law that does not take the mismatch between copyright and TCEs and its consequences into account can negatively impact the rights of indigenous peoples.

---

108 Wai 262 Report, above n 44, at 681.
109 At 685.
110 Sterling, above n 2.

In order to avoid the negative consequences of copyright harmonisation discussed in this chapter, and to comply with their obligations under human rights law, countries should consider the protection of TCEs when further harmonising copyright. This applies to all countries in general and to Asian Pacific countries interested in the proposed Copyright Code in particular.[111] The potential effects of harmonisation on TCEs should be examined in the local context of each country before going forth with such initiatives. A pluralistic approach to copyright harmonisation that gives countries the chance to choose policy measures that suit the interests of their indigenous communities best is preferred. Finally, indigenous communities should be directly involved in the process of harmonisation.

---

111 Sterling, above n 2.

3

Fair Use and Traditional Cultural Expressions

Natalie P Stoianoff and Evana Wright[1]

1 Introduction

> Yolngu art is part of the Yolngu system of knowledge both in itself and as a system of encoding meaning. The form of paintings is part of the ancestral knowledge that is transmitted from generation to generation, yet in addition, paintings encode meanings about the ancestral past and are one of the main ways in which people gain access to knowledge of the events of the ancestral past. More than that, paintings … are involved in the process of creating new meanings and understandings about the world, and in communicating these understandings to others.[2]

Indigenous knowledge may be broadly described as the system of knowledge developed and maintained by Indigenous and local communities and transmitted from generation to generation and includes:

---

1   Copyright © 2018 Natalie P Stoianoff and Evana Wright. Professor Natalie Stoianoff is the Director of the Intellectual Property Program at the Faculty of Law, University of Technology Sydney. She is the Chair of the Indigenous Knowledge Forum Committee and Lead Chief Investigator on the ARC Linkage Project Garuwanga: Forming a Competent Authority to Protect Indigenous Knowledge. Dr Evana Wright is a Lecturer in the Faculty of Law, University of Technology Sydney.
2   Howard Morphy *Ancestral Connections: Art and an Aboriginal System of Knowledge* (University of Chicago Press, 1991) at 75.

[L]iterary, artistic or scientific works; performances; inventions; scientific discoveries; designs; marks; names and symbols; undisclosed information; and all other tradition-based innovations and creations resulting from intellectual activity in the industrial, scientific, literary or artistic fields.[3]

Indigenous knowledge, including traditional cultural expressions, has been subject to misappropriation and exploitation by third-party interests resulting in spiritual, cultural and economic loss for Indigenous and local communities.[4]

To be clear, 'traditional' in the Indigenous knowledge context does not equate to old. Rather than denoting age, the term 'traditional' refers to the process by which the knowledge has been transmitted from generation to generation. The knowledge can be built upon, evolve and develop. Thus, new 'works' (in the copyright sense) can be created that constitute traditional cultural expressions.

The existing copyright system, however, does not provide adequate protection for Indigenous knowledge and cultural expressions that are collectively generated and held by an Indigenous or local community.[5] Even where protection does extend to traditional cultural expressions as a copyright work, the existing exceptions and limitations established under the copyright system do not take into account the special relationship between Indigenous communities and their cultural production.[6] Any exception or limitation to copyright must take into account this special relationship, as any use of traditional cultural expressions by a third party may be considered an affront to that community's culture and law.

3   World Intellectual Property Organization (WIPO) 'Intellectual Property Needs and Expectations of Traditional Knowledge Holders: WIPO Report on Fact-Finding Missions on Intellectual Property and Traditional Knowledge 1998–1999' (April 2001) at 25 [WIPO 'Intellectual Property Needs and Expectations of Traditional Knowledge Holders'].

4   Natalie P Stoianoff and others, 'Recognising and Protecting Aboriginal Knowledge Associated with Natural Resource Management – White Paper for the Office of Environment and Heritage' (UTS – Indigenous Knowledge Forum & North West Local Land Services, NSW, 2014) indigenousknowledgeforum.org at 1–3.

5   Natalie P Stoianoff and Alpana Roy 'Indigenous Knowledge and Culture in Australia – The Case for Sui Generis Legislation' (2015) 41(3) Mon LR 746.

6   WIPO Intergovernmental Committee on Intellectual Property and Genetic Resources (IGC) *Traditional Knowledge and Folklore, The Protection Of Traditional Cultural Expressions: Draft Gap Analysis* WIPO/GRTKF/IC/13/5(b) Rev, XIII (2008) at 13–17.

2 Traditional Cultural Expressions

In recent years, the western understanding of Indigenous knowledge has been divided into two categories: traditional knowledge and traditional cultural expressions.[7] Traditional knowledge involves knowledge, skills, know-how and innovations of Indigenous or local communities,[8] and this category of knowledge typically aligns with western patent law systems. By contrast, traditional cultural expressions include Indigenous or traditional artworks, music and songs, stories and performances that are typically generated collectively and cumulatively and passed on from generation to generation.[9] The works that fall within the category of traditional cultural expressions align with the works that may be protected under western copyright law, design law and even trade marks law.

As discussed further below, Indigenous communities do not view their knowledge in the categorical manner used in western intellectual property law. Reflecting a holistic worldview,[10] traditional cultural expressions are intimately connected to the spiritual, the land or Country and, often, express or communicate knowledge such as traditional medicinal knowledge or information of specific genetic resources.[11]

---

7   See, for example, efforts by WIPO to develop separate Draft Articles for the protection of the following categories of knowledge: traditional knowledge; traditional cultural expressions; and intellectual property and genetic resources. For the latest draft agreements see WIPO The Protection of Traditional Knowledge: Draft Articles (15 March 2017) www.wipo.int/meetings/en/doc_details. jsp?doc_id=368218; WIPO The Protection of Traditional Cultural Expressions: Draft Articles (16 June 2017) www.wipo.int/meetings/en/doc_details.jsp?doc_id=375036; WIPO *Consolidated Document Relating to Intellectual Property and Genetic Resources* (15 March 2017) www.wipo.int/ meetings/en/doc_details.jsp?doc_id=368344.
8   WIPO 'Traditional Knowledge' www.wipo.int.
9   WIPO 'Traditional Cultural Expressions' www.wipo.int.
10   On 'holism' in the international discourse, see Michael Blakeney 'The Negotiations in WIPO for International Conventions on Traditional Knowledge and Traditional Cultural Expressions' in Jessica C Lai and Antoinette Maget Dominicé (eds) *Intellectual Property and Access to Im/material Goods* (Edward Elgar, Cheltenham, UK, 2016) 227 at 247–254.
11   See, for example, the artwork on the cover page of the report 'Our Culture, Our Future' by Terri Janke and the description of the knowledge depicted in the artwork on the inner cover page. Terri Janke *Our Culture, Our Future: A Report on Australian Indigenous Cultural and Intellectual Property Rights* (Michael Frankel and Company, 1999) at Cover and Inner Cover.

Traditional knowledge and cultural expressions have been subject to a variety of forms of norm-setting including through several international instruments,[12] regional agreements[13] and national legal and policy instruments. One must remember that these western forms of regulation are additional to pre-existing customary legal systems of the holders/creators of the traditional knowledge and cultural expressions.

The protection of Indigenous knowledge from misappropriation and exploitation has been the subject of continued debate in the past three decades, with a number of attempts to develop legal frameworks at an international and regional level. The most relevant existing international instruments for the purpose of this paper are the Convention on Biological Diversity (CBD)[14] and Nagoya Protocol on Access to Genetic Resources and the Fair and Equitable Sharing of Benefits Arising from their Utilisation to the Convention on Biological Diversity (Nagoya Protocol)[15] as well as the United Nations Declaration on the Rights of Indigenous Peoples (UNDRIP).[16]

The CBD and Nagoya Protocol are focused on the protection of traditional knowledge associated with biological diversity and genetic resources. The CBD requires member countries to 'respect, preserve and maintain knowledge, innovations and practices of indigenous and local communities embodying traditional lifestyles relevant for the conservation and sustainable use of biological diversity' and to ensure that use of traditional knowledge is subject to the prior informed consent or approval and involvement of the relevant Indigenous or local community, and encourage equitable benefit sharing.[17] The Nagoya Protocol operationalises the access and benefit sharing provisions of the CBD and requires that member countries establish measures to ensure that

---

12   For example, Rio Convention on Biological Diversity, 1760 UNTS 79; 31 ILM 818 (opened for signature 5 June 1992, entered into force 29 December 1993) [CBD]; Nagoya Protocol on Access to Genetic Resources and the Fair and Equitable Sharing of Benefits Arising from their Utilization to the Convention on Biological Diversity UN Doc. UNEP/CBD/COP/DEC/X/1 (adopted 29 October 2010, entered into force 12 October 2014) [Nagoya Protocol]; and United Nations Declaration on the Rights of Indigenous Peoples, GA Res 61/295 LXI A/RES/61/295 (13 September 2007) [UNDRIP].

13   For example, Secretariat of the Pacific Community *Pacific Regional Framework for the Protection of Traditional Knowledge and Expressions of Culture* (2002).

14   CBD, above n 12.

15   Nagoya Protocol, above n 12.

16   UNDRIP, above n 12.

17   CBD, above n 12, art 8(j).

use of traditional knowledge associated with genetic resources is subject to prior informed consent or approval and involvement of the relevant Indigenous or local communities and upon mutually agreed terms.[18]

By contrast, UNDRIP is concerned with the protection of Indigenous knowledge more broadly and recognises the right of Indigenous peoples to:[19]

> [M]aintain, control, protect and develop their cultural heritage, traditional knowledge and traditional cultural expressions, as well as the manifestations of their sciences, technologies and cultures, including human and genetic resources, seeds, medicines, knowledge of the properties of fauna and flora, oral traditions, literatures, designs, sports and traditional games and visual and performing arts. They also have the right to maintain, control, protect and develop their intellectual property over such cultural heritage, traditional knowledge, and traditional cultural expressions.

While the terms of UNDRIP are non-binding, the provisions reflect the increasing recognition of the importance of Indigenous rights and the protection of Indigenous knowledge including traditional cultural expressions. This increasing recognition can also be seen in regional agreements for the protection of Indigenous knowledge, including the Pacific Regional Framework for the Protection of Traditional Knowledge and Expressions of Culture, along with national legal and policy instruments. The legal frameworks described above were developed under the western legal system and are in addition to the pre-existing customary legal systems of the holders or creators of the traditional knowledge and cultural expressions which regulate the use of Indigenous knowledge.

The World Intellectual Property Organization (WIPO) is also working to develop international instruments for the protection of Indigenous knowledge from an intellectual property perspective. As a result of collaboration between WIPO and the United Nations Environment Programme (UNEP), responsible for the introduction of the CBD, in 2000 the WIPO General Assembly established the Intergovernmental Committee on Intellectual Property and Genetic Resources, Traditional

---

18   Nagoya Protocol, above n 12, arts 7, 16. For a discussion on CBD art 8(j) and the Nagoya Protocol, see Jessica C Lai *Indigenous Cultural Heritage and Intellectual Property Rights* (Springer, Heidelberg, 2014) at 146–152.
19   UNDRIP, above n 12, art 31(1).

Knowledge and Folklore (IGC).[20] Working through the IGC, WIPO has prepared draft articles for the protection of traditional knowledge and traditional cultural expressions, and is negotiating an instrument on intellectual property rights and genetic resources, bringing together Indigenous knowledge and intellectual property within the framework of an access and benefit sharing regime.[21] This process has taken over 15 years and progress towards reaching a set of agreed terms continues to be slow. Despite the delays and the contentious areas remaining to be addressed, the WIPO IGC has identified a number of key provisions necessary for protecting traditional knowledge and traditional cultural expressions, including the scope and beneficiaries of protection, the governance framework for administering rights, and exceptions and limitations. According to the IGC Mandate for 2018/2019, the IGC will:[22]

> continue to expedite its work, with the objective of reaching an agreement on an international legal instrument(s) … relating to intellectual property which will ensure the balanced and effective protection of genetic resources (GRs), traditional knowledge (TK) and traditional cultural expressions (TCEs).

3 Traditional Cultural Expressions in Australia

In the Australian context, the traditional cultural expressions of Aboriginal and Torres Strait Islander peoples may be protected to an extent under the Copyright Act 1968 (Cth) as a literary, dramatic, musical or artistic work, or subject matter other than works, such as sound recordings and films, provided the traditional cultural expression in question meets the requirements set out in the legislation including requirements as to originality. For example, contemporary original artwork depicting culturally significant images may satisfy the criteria for

20   Patricia Adjei and Natalie P Stoianoff 'The World Intellectual Property Organisation (WIPO) and the Intergovernmental Committee: Developments on Traditional Knowledge and Cultural Expressions' (2013) 92 Intellectual Property Forum 37.

21   Natalie Stoianoff 'The Recognition of Traditional Knowledge under Australian Biodiscovery Regimes: Why Bother with Intellectual Property Rights?' in Christoph Antons (ed) *Traditional Knowledge, Traditional Cultural Expressions and Intellectual Property Law in the Asia-Pacific Region* (Kluwer Law International, 2009) 293 at 294. For the latest draft agreements see above n 7.

22   Matters Concerning the Intergovernmental Committee on Intellectual Property and Genetic Resources, Traditional Knowledge and Folklore, Assemblies of Member States of WIPO LV (2–11 October 2017) Agenda Item 18 Decision www.wipo.int.

copyright protection as seen in the case of *Bulun Bulun*.[23] Copyright law vests ownership of a work in the author of that work; however, in the case of traditional cultural expressions, this fails to recognise the rights of the Aboriginal or Torres Strait Islander community to which the author belongs and the obligations that the author owes to their community. Australian courts have recognised the obligations that an author may owe to their community and have sought to characterise this obligation to community as a fiduciary duty:[24]

> The relationship between Mr Bulun Bulun as the author and legal title holder of the artistic work and the Ganalbingu people is unique. The 'transaction' between them out of which fiduciary relationship is said to arise is the use with permission by Mr Bulun Bulun of ritual knowledge of the Ganalbingu people, and the embodiment of that knowledge within the artistic work. That use has been permitted in accordance with the law and customs of the Ganalbingu people …

This approach is insufficient to fully reflect the rights and responsibilities of a creator or author and their respective Aboriginal or Torres Strait Islander community to traditional cultural expressions. Characterising the relationship as a fiduciary duty does not recognise the rights and obligations that the Aboriginal or Torres Strait Islander community has as the custodian or holder of such traditional cultural expressions:[25]

> Whilst the nature of the relationship between Mr Bulun Bulun and the Ganalbingu people is such that Mr Bulun Bulun falls under fiduciary obligations to protect the ritual knowledge which he has been permitted to use, the existence of those obligations does not, without more, vest an equitable interest in the ownership of the copyright in the Ganalbingu people. Their primary right, in the event of a breach of obligation by the fiduciary is a right in personam to bring action against the fiduciary to enforce the obligation.

---

23   *Bulun Bulun v R & T Textiles Pty Ltd* [1998] FCA 1082.
24   *Bulun Bulun v R & T Textiles Pty Ltd*, above n 23. For analyses of this decision, see Colin Golvan 'The protection of At the Waterhole by John Bulun Bulun: Aboriginal Art and the Recognition of Private and Communal Rights' in Andrew T Kenyon, Megan Richardson, Sam Ricketson (eds) *Landmarks in Australian Intellectual Property Law* (Cambridge University Press, New York, 2009) 191; and Kathy Bowrey 'The Outer Limits of Copyright Law – Where Law Meets Philosophy and Culture' (2001) 12(1) Law and Critique 75 at 78–84.
25   *Bulun Bulun v R & T Textiles Pty Ltd*, above n 23.

Both the Aboriginal or Torres Strait Islander community and the author or creator hold the responsibility for maintaining and protecting traditional cultural expressions and therefore the community has a particularly important role to play in the context of making decisions as to how traditional cultural expressions may be used and who may provide consent to such use. In his analysis of Yolngu art, Howard Morphy noted:[26]

> Yolngu art is part of a system of restricted knowledge in that not all people appear to have equal access to the knowledge contained within it. Secrecy appears to intervene to affect who can learn what.

This aspect of cultural law has implications for the application of fair use provisions under copyright and will be considered below.

Various other elements of copyright protection also fail to adequately protect traditional cultural expressions. For example, the term of copyright protection limits protection to a specific time frame, whereas the obligations and responsibilities that an Aboriginal or Torres Strait Islander community has with regards to the protection of traditional cultural expressions extend in perpetuity.[27]

Copyright must balance the interests or rights of an author or creator with the rights of users to access and use a copyright work. However, in the context of traditional cultural expressions, this issue moves beyond the economic or commercial considerations and requires an understanding of the cultural and spiritual obligations that inform the creation and use of traditional cultural expressions. As observed by the Australian Law Reform Commission (ALRC) in its report on Copyright and the Digital Economy: 'Moral rights and cultural considerations, in particular issues relating to Indigenous culture and cultural practices, need always to be considered, alongside economic rights'.[28]

The potential conflict between the exceptions and limitations established under the copyright system and the rights of Aboriginal and Torres Strait Islander peoples to control the use of copyright material is of concern. This is particularly the case with regards to proposed fair use exceptions to copyright infringement. Fair use provisions are intended to ensure that users have fair access to copyright content while ensuring

---

26   Morphy, above n 2.
27   See Copyright Act 1968 (Cth), ss 33, 34, 93, 94, 95 and 96, setting out the duration of copyright. For further discussion, see Lai, above n 18, at 78–85.
28   Australian Law Reform Commission (ALRC) *Copyright and the Digital Economy* (ALRC Report 122, November 2013) at 42 [2.7].

that copyright still provides sufficient protection and incentives for the creators of copyright works. In 2013, the ALRC recommended the introduction of a fair use exception into copyright law that would operate with reference to certain fairness factors. The introduction of a fair use exception has more recently been endorsed by the Productivity Commission in their report into Intellectual Property Arrangements.[29] The Australian Government response to the report on this issue was to acknowledge the need for further consultation while confirming the aim 'to create a modernised copyright exceptions framework that keeps pace with technological advances and is flexible to adapt to future changes'.[30] This paper will now consider the proposed fair use exception and the impact of such a provision on the creation and use of traditional cultural expressions in Australia.

4 Fair Use and Traditional Cultural Expressions in Australia

Copyright law in Australia currently has limited fair dealing exceptions to infringement and these exceptions do not apply consistently across all forms of copyright material. The ALRC has proposed the introduction of a fair use exception to copyright infringement in their report Copyright and the Digital Economy on the grounds that a broad, flexible exception would encourage innovation and provide a flexible standard that could easily 'adapt to new technologies and new commercial and consumer practices'.[31] The proposed fair use exception would be subject to consideration of certain fairness factors, and a non-exhaustive list of proposed fairness factors are identified by the ALRC in their report as:[32]

a.   the purpose and character of the use;

b.   the nature of the copyright material;

c.   the amount and substantiality of the part used; and

d.   the effect of the use upon the potential market for, or value of, the copyright material.

---

29   See Productivity Commission *Intellectual Property Arrangements* (Inquiry Report No. 78, Canberra, 2016) Recommendation 6.1.
30   'Australian Government Response to the Productivity Commission Inquiry into Intellectual Property Arrangements' (August 2017) at 7.
31   ALRC, above n 28, at 95 [4.39].
32   ALRC, above n 28, at 144 [Recommendation 5-2].

The ALRC has also provided a non-exhaustive list of examples of fair use including use for the purpose of research or study; education; criticism or review; parody or satire; reporting the news; professional advice; quotation; non-commercial private use; access for people with disability; incidental or technical use; and library or archive use.[33]

The introduction of a fair use exception to replace the existing fair dealing provisions has also received support from the Productivity Commission. In its Inquiry Report on Intellectual Property Arrangements, the Productivity Commission argued that the current fair dealing exceptions are 'too narrow and prescriptive, do not reflect the way people today consume and use content in the digital world, and do not accommodate new legitimate uses of copyright material'.[34] Reflecting the arguments previously raised by the ALRC, the Productivity Commission observed that an important and positive feature of fair use is its flexibility when compared to the prescriptive nature of the current fair dealing exceptions.[35]

While the proposed fair use exception is intended to encourage fair use while balancing the rights of creators of copyright material, consideration must be given to whether the application of fair use exceptions to the infringement of copyright material is appropriate in the context of traditional cultural expressions. Any fair use exception needs to take into account the special relationship between Aboriginal and Torres Strait Islander communities and their cultural production, as any use by a third party may be considered an affront to, or inconsistent with, that community's culture and law. Given that the proposed fair use provisions are intended as a flexible defence, the application of fair use provisions to use of traditional cultural expressions should be subject to the rights and interests of the relevant Aboriginal or Torres Strait Islander community.

The second fairness factor proposed by the ALRC provides the opportunity to factor in the nature of the copyright work in determining whether a proposed use is 'fair use' for the purpose of the exception to infringement. This second fairness factor may therefore be utilised to provide guidance on dealing with Aboriginal and Torres Strait Islander cultural production including traditional cultural expressions. The application of fair use exceptions to traditional cultural expressions should be subject to broad

---

33   ALRC, above n 28, at 150–151 [Recommendation 5-3].
34   Productivity Commission, above n 29, at 165.
35   Productivity Commission, above n 29, at 165.

consultation with Aboriginal and Torres Strait Islander communities to determine the principles that should inform any determination as to fair use.

In addition, the application of fair use exceptions should not erode the moral rights of the author as established under Part IX of the Copyright Act 1968 (Cth). Moral rights accrue to the author (or performer) of copyright material and provide for the right of attribution of authorship; the right not to have authorship falsely attributed and, most importantly for the purpose of this paper, the right of integrity of authorship. The right of integrity is the 'right not to have the work subjected to derogatory treatment' and this includes any material distortion, mutilation, material alteration or other act that is prejudicial to the author's honour or reputation.[36] Indeed, it may be argued that respect for Aboriginal and Torres Strait Islander peoples' works is a subset of the broader right of integrity of authorship. Despite this, moral rights do not provide sufficient rights to protect traditional cultural expressions from culturally or spiritually inappropriate use. As noted above, moral rights accrue to the author or performer and the Aboriginal or Torres Strait Islander community does not have any right to assert in the case of inappropriate use of their traditional cultural expressions. Rather, the community must rely on the relevant author or performer to assert the rights in relation to the traditional cultural expression.

There are a number of existing protocols that may provide guidance in determining the principles that would inform the application of fair use exceptions to traditional cultural expressions. These protocols are typically framed in ethical and moral conduct, and apply to using and working with Aboriginal and Torres Strait Islander cultural production, including traditional cultural expressions. For example, these include the Museums Australia protocol titled 'Continuous Cultures, Ongoing Responsibilities: Principles and Guidelines for Australian Museums Working with Aboriginal and Torres Strait Islander Cultural Heritage';[37] and the Aboriginal and Torres Strait Islander Library, Information and Resource Network protocols, most recently published in 2010 but originally published in 1995 by the Australian Library and Information

---

36 Copyright Act 1968 (Cth), ss 195AI, 195AJ, 195 AK and 195 AL.
37 Museums Australia 'Continuous Cultures, Ongoing Responsibilities: Principles and Guidelines for Australian Museums Working with Aboriginal and Torres Strait Islander Cultural Heritage' (February 2005) www.nma.gov.au.

Association.[38] The Australia Council has also developed protocols that provide guidance for working with Aboriginal and Torres Strait Islander artists in the production of music, writing, visual arts, media arts and performing arts.[39] A number of common elements inform these existing protocols, including the principles of respect; Aboriginal or Torres Strait Islander control; communication, consultation and consent; interpretation, integrity and authenticity; secrecy and confidentiality; attribution and copyright; proper returns and royalties; continuing cultures; and recognition and protection.[40]

The reviews of the copyright system in Australia described above, as well as the proposed Asian Pacific Copyright Code,[41] provide an opportunity to address the treatment of traditional cultural expressions within a copyright framework. Any reform to the copyright system would require consideration of special provisions to address issues specific to the protection of traditional cultural expressions, including communal rights to authorship; the duration of rights; and the applicability of originality requirements. However, amendments to the copyright system can only go so far and despite the best intentions may not provide adequate protection for the rights of Aboriginal and Torres Strait Islander peoples. As discussed above, Indigenous knowledge is a holistic concept and covers both traditional knowledge and traditional cultural expressions.[42] Any attempt to protect traditional cultural expressions as distinct from traditional knowledge fails to recognise the holistic nature of Indigenous knowledge systems where, as observed by Morphy above, traditional knowledge is often expressed in traditional cultural expressions.[43] This raises the question: how do we separate the expression and the knowledge when Indigenous communities do not? It is surely inadequate to keep layering requirements, guidelines and protocols as a means of providing

---

38   Aboriginal and Torres Strait Islander Library, Information and Resource Network 'Aboriginal and Torres Strait Islander Protocols for Libraries, Archives and Information Services' (2010) atsilirn. aiatsis.gov.au.

39   Australia Council 'Protocols for Working with Indigenous Artists' (2007) www.australiacouncil. gov.au. Music: 'Protocols for Producing Indigenous Australian Music' (2007); Writing: 'Protocols for Producing Indigenous Australian Writing' (2007); Visual Arts: 'Protocols for producing Indigenous Australian Visual Arts' (2007); Media Arts: 'Protocols for Producing Indigenous Australian Media Arts' (2007); Performing Arts: 'Protocols for Producing Indigenous Australian Performing Arts' (2007).

40   Australia Council for the Arts 'Protocols for Producing Indigenous Australian Visual Arts' (2007).

41   Adrian Sterling 'Asian Pacific Copyright Code' in this volume.

42   WIPO 'Intellectual Property Needs and Expectations of Traditional Knowledge Holders', above n 3, 86.

43   See also WIPO 'Intellectual Property Needs and Expectations of Traditional Knowledge Holders', above n 3, at 86.

protection when existing intellectual property regimes fall short. Given this inadequacy on the part of western intellectual property systems, a sui generis approach may prove a better alternative. The following section of this chapter focuses on a particular project, which approached the protection of Indigenous knowledge systems and their cultural expression in a more holistic manner.

5 A Sui Generis Regime for the Protection of Traditional Cultural Expressions?

Given the inadequacy of the western intellectual property system to provide protection for Indigenous knowledge systems, there is scope to establish a sui generis framework that may address the issues raised above.[44] This was the focus of the 2014 White Paper, 'Recognising and Protecting Aboriginal Knowledge associated with Natural Resource Management', prepared for the Office of Environment and Heritage New South Wales (NSW) (the White Paper).[45] While focused on Aboriginal knowledge systems in relation to the natural environment, the White Paper provides a potential blueprint for protecting cultural knowledge and expressions, together with a governance framework for managing access and benefit sharing arrangements over such knowledge and expressions. Commissioned by the Namoi Catchment Management Authority (now North West Local Land Services), under the NSW Office of Environment and Heritage, the White Paper represents the efforts of an extensive Working Party comprising both Indigenous and non-Indigenous experts, brought together under the umbrella of the University of Technology Sydney (UTS) Indigenous Knowledge Forum to:[46]

1. identify key elements of a regime that would recognise and protect Indigenous knowledge associated with natural resource management;

2. facilitate Aboriginal community engagement in the process of developing a regime;

---

44   See also Lida Ayoubi, 'Copyright Harmonisation in the Asian Pacific Region: Weaving the Peoples Together?' in this volume.
45   Stoianoff and others, above n 4.
46   Indigenous Knowledge Forum 'Recognising and Protecting Indigenous Knowledge Associated with Natural Resource Management' www.indigenousknowledgeforum.org.

3. develop a draft regime that not only accorded with the aims and goals of North West NSW Aboriginal communities but would be a model for implementation in other regions in NSW;

4. produce a Discussion Paper through which the draft regime could be distributed for comment; and

5. conduct community consultations to refine the draft regime into a model that may be implemented through NSW legislation by finalising a White Paper to be delivered by the UTS Indigenous Knowledge Forum and North West Local Land Services to the NSW Office of Environment and Heritage.

Terri Janke encapsulates succinctly the reason for embarking upon such a project:[47]

> A major concern of Indigenous people is that their cultural knowledge of plants, animals and the environment is being used by scientists, medical researchers, nutritionists and pharmaceutical companies for commercial gain, often without their informed consent and without any benefits flowing back to them.

In order to fill the gap in NSW legislation for the recognition and protection of Aboriginal knowledge, this project was carried out in three stages, utilising the experience of other jurisdictions, Australia's international obligations, and the active participation of Aboriginal communities to develop a model law that addresses the concern identified by Terri Janke.

Stage 1 comprised developing a comparative framework, commencing with collecting and analysing legislative and policy regimes already in existence in other parts of the world. Key criteria in each regime were identified and then compared to international obligations and instruments.[48] This provided the comparative framework upon which a standard-setting model could be developed to ensure the recognition and protection of Indigenous knowledge as part of a living culture. This comparative study considered the countries of Afghanistan, Angola, Argentina, Brazil, Chile, China, Costa Rica, Ecuador, Ethiopia, Hong Kong, India, Kenya, Malaysia, Peru, Philippines, South Africa and Vanuatu, whose laws relating to traditional knowledge, cultural expressions and genetic resources provided useful examples upon which

---

47 Terri Janke 'Biodiversity, Patents and Indigenous Peoples' (26 June 2000).
48 Including the CBD, Nagoya Protocol, UNDRIP and the Draft Articles of the Intergovernmental Committee of the WIPO; above n 7 and 12.

an Australian model could draw. In particular, the laws of Brazil, Costa Rica, Ethiopia, Peru, India, Kenya and South Africa provided relevant alternatives to inform the Working Party in developing the model law.

In Stage 2, the Working Party utilised the comparative study to develop a draft regime that meets the elements of supporting a living Aboriginal culture with improved access to Country through recognition and protection of Indigenous knowledge about Country. The resulting Discussion Paper identified 14 provisions that were necessary for the model law:[49]

1. Subject matter of protection – traditional knowledge, traditional cultural expressions, genetic resources;

2. Definition of terms – key terms used in the draft;

3. Scope – what is covered, respect for traditional ownership, respect for sovereignty over genetic resources, moral rights;

4. Beneficiaries – who should benefit;

5. Access – who speaks for Country, process for granting or refusing access including:

    a. Prior informed consent – ensuring traditional owners are aware of their rights and significance of agreements made;

    b. Mutually agreed terms – ensuring the bargaining process is fair and equitable;

6. Benefit sharing – how are benefits shared, what types of benefit, dealing with technology transfer, capacity building;

7. Sanctions and remedies – dealing with breaches;

8. Competent authority – establishment of a body to administer the legislation, deal with education, model clauses, codes of conduct, databases;

9. No single owner – addressing situations where traditional knowledge, cultural expressions, genetic resources are common to more than one group;

10. Exceptions – emergencies, traditional use, conservation;

---

49   Indigenous Knowledge Forum & North West Local Land Services (formerly Namoi CMA) *Recognising and Protecting Aboriginal Knowledge Associated with Natural Resource Management* (Discussion Paper 1, 2014) www.indigenousknowledgeforum.org/indigenous-knowledge-natural-resour at 9–10.

11. Disclosure – permits, databases, disclosure in intellectual property applications;

12. Interaction with existing laws – avoiding conflict with other laws;

13. Recognition of requirements of other nations – mutual recognition of rights and ensuring compliance;

14. Transitional provisions – existing uses.

Stage 3 involved distributing the Discussion Paper through North West Local Land Services to the Aboriginal communities of the North West NSW region and other interested parties. Then, consultation sessions were organised to meet with Aboriginal communities in key locations in the North West region, including Tamworth, Gunnedah, Walgett and Narrabri, in order to explain the proposed model and enable frank discussion. These focus group sessions enabled the draft regime to be refined into a model that could be implemented through legislation. To this end, a draft White Paper proposing the legislation was prepared and refined with the assistance of the Working Party. At the Second Indigenous Knowledge Forum, held in Sydney on 2 and 3 October 2014, the White Paper was delivered to the chief executive officer of the Office of Environment and Heritage. In a recent communication from the Office of the Minister for Environment, Planning and Heritage, the White Paper has been taken into account in the development of a proposed new system for managing and conserving Aboriginal cultural heritage in NSW.

The model presented in the White Paper provides draft legislation that aims to protect the knowledge held by Aboriginal communities in NSW. The language of the draft legislation avoids reference to 'property rights' in the knowledge and cultural expressions, as communities view their rights as custodial rights. The important aspect of this legislation is the recognition that Aboriginal communities have the right to control the knowledge they hold in accordance with customary law, now more frequently referred to as 'First law' in recognition of the First Nations of Australia. This means that others can only use that knowledge or cultural expression with the prior informed consent of the relevant Aboriginal community. In addition, the draft legislation ensures that where others are given permission to use the knowledge or cultural expression, the relevant Aboriginal communities get benefits for sharing their knowledge and cultural expressions.

This could be perceived as a counterpoint to the concept of fair use. As discussed above, exercise of a fair use exception would enable any third party to utilise Aboriginal cultural production without obtaining permission from the authors, let alone the relevant community, provided the use is in line with the fairness factors. However, 'fair use' is intended to be a flexible defence, and so a copyright work that is a cultural expression emanating from an Aboriginal community could have the requirement that permission be first sought from the community before the expression can be utilised by a third party.

It should be noted that the model proposed in the White Paper is a principles-based framework designed to address the following questions:

- What is knowledge?
- Who should speak for the knowledge?
- Who should benefit from the knowledge being shared with others?
- Should there be particular types of benefit?
- What should happen if there are disagreements?
- What sort of organisation should look after these matters?
- What sort of databases (if any) are appropriate?
- What should happen if knowledge is owned by more than one community?

It was recognised that there would be gaps in the draft legislation that would require regulations to ensure the proper operation of the legal regime: even so, the White Paper provides a case study to demonstrate how the draft legislation is intended to operate.[50]

An issue of particular concern to the communities consulted in the White Paper process related to the competent authority necessary to manage the access and benefit sharing regime created by the draft legislation. The proposed legislative competent authority would provide the governance framework for administering a legal regime covering the creation, maintenance and protection of Aboriginal community knowledge databases. However, community consultation raised concerns about the form such an authority would take, its independence from government, how it would be funded and wound up, local Aboriginal representation and engagement.

---

50   Stoianoff and others, above n 4, at 83–91.

Back in 2009, Terri Janke proposed an independent National Indigenous Cultural Authority as the appropriate form of a competent authority.[51] This was reinforced in 2013 by the National Congress of Australia's First Peoples espousing such a regime, and identifying various characteristics whereby the Authority should be independent from government, with its own legal status, board of governance, constitution and representing members.[52] The board would be elected from its grassroots membership base but also allow for the necessary skills based director representation. The Congress recognised a need for further research, funding and support to investigate how to best establish an Authority with these characteristics. This is the focus of the Australian Research Council Linkage Project called 'Garuwanga: Forming a Competent Authority to Protect Indigenous Knowledge', representing the follow-on project from the White Paper.

The community consultations undertaken for the White Paper revealed some important considerations: support for an entity to administer the proposed regime; importance of the independence of such an entity; 'concern regarding the functions of this entity being administered by one or more existing agencies' while acknowledging 'the need for the Competent Authority to include a local or regional community agency to administer the Knowledge Holder registers and provide for Community Knowledge databases'; a 'need for confidential information to be protected'; that an appeal process be established as well as 'a process for ensuring benefits under the control of the Competent Authority are applied and are not lost if the Authority is wound up'.[53] The consultations revealed community mistrust of government-based organisations, and the failings of past Indigenous bodies to fulfil community expectations.[54] Accordingly, the Garuwanga project builds on the White Paper, aiming to recommend a legal structure for the competent authority while addressing the issues raised in the community consultations.[55] It follows a similar methodology to that of the White Paper, adding:

---

51   Terri Janke *Beyond Guarding Ground: A Vision for a National Indigenous Cultural Authority* (Terri Janke and Co, Rosebery, NSW, 2009).

52   National Congress of Australia's First Peoples *The Call for a National Indigenous Cultural Authority* (position paper on National Indigenous Cultural Authority, 2013).

53   Stoianoff and others, above n 4, at 33–52.

54   Ibid.

55   Examples of relevant legal structures include Aboriginal and Torres Strait Islander corporations, and corporations under s 57A of the Corporations Act 2001, including incorporated and unincorporated associations, trust arrangements involving such organisations, statutory bodies and Aboriginal Land Councils.

- identifying the key features of the variety of legal structures utilised by other nations employing a competent authority governance framework;
- evaluating those legal structures through a research roundtable;
- proposing a workable model; and
- obtaining feedback through community consultation.

6 The Opportunity of an Asian Pacific Copyright Code

Adrian Sterling's 2015 proposal for an Asian Pacific Copyright Code brings to light the need to consider the issues and concerns of the nations located within the region. We would go so far as to say that any regional copyright code must heed the cultural expectations of the member states in that region. The Asian Pacific region is replete with rich traditional and/or Indigenous cultures, each with their own customary laws and protocols. These need to be at least acknowledged and in some way incorporated into such a plurilateral instrument, even though that instrument is grounded in western intellectual property law:[56]

> Two general aims of the Code principles are firstly, to incorporate the principles recognised in the relevant international copyright and related rights instruments, and secondly, to incorporate on particular points higher standards of protection than in these instruments.

Specifically, Part II Section C Rights provides a perfect opportunity to introduce the rights of traditional or Indigenous communities to their knowledge and cultural expressions. This could be achieved by reference to sui generis legislation that is already in place in the region or by a specific provision. Under Section D Limitations and exceptions, it would be important to note that an exclusion such as fair use should have some form of specific operation when dealing with traditional or Indigenous knowledge and cultural expression. The fairness factors could have a separate category for such cultural production which would enable reference to sui generis legislation or to a particular protocol or set of protocols in order to achieve a result regarding use by third parties. Equally, improving the nature of moral rights could serve to provide another layer

---

56   Sterling, above n 41.

of protection of the Indigenous knowledge and culture. Certainly, the most effective form of protection would be through sui generis legislation where non-compliance could result in sanctions and thereafter the use of protocols, which tend to be non-compulsory unless they are tied to funding schemes.

7 Conclusion

This chapter considered the place held by Indigenous cultural production in the sphere of copyright and the benefit of employing sui generis legislation to deal with the nuances of protection and use of that production. A potential blueprint for such a legal regime has been provided by the White Paper and appears to be gaining traction in NSW at present. Specifically, this chapter has addressed the issue of fair use in the context of the recommendations of the ALRC and the Productivity Commission, respectively. This is contrasted with the need for Aboriginal communities to have the right to control the use of that cultural production and to receive a fair level of compensation for such use. The proposed Asian Pacific Copyright Code provides an opportunity to consider how traditional or Indigenous cultural production in the region can be protected and how the specific exception of fair use can be moderated in this context.

Part 2: Norm-taking?

4

Copyright Reform in the 21st Century: Adding Privacy Considerations into the Normative Mix

Doris Estelle Long[1]

1 Introduction

There is no question that copyright norms have undergone a foundational shift over the past 20 years. From the advent of the 'Information Superhighway' in the 1990s to the 'Internet of Things' today, digital communications media have revolutionised the creation, dissemination and infringement of copyrightable works. As the hard goods world of books, films, records, painting and sculpture has been transformed into a digital one, the scope of protection for authorial rights has come under increasing scrutiny.

The new technology of the 'Digital Age' has led to the creation of potentially new copyrightable forms of works that do not automatically fit within existing paradigms based on a hard goods world. These new forms are as diverse as online video games, smart phone apps, streaming video and personal health monitors. The former lock on the distribution

---

1   Copyright © 2018 Doris Estelle Long. Professor Emeritus of Law, The John Marshall Law School (Chicago).

of new works by large corporate content providers has disappeared as amateur authors increasingly create and distribute their own digital content. As cross-border communications replace former, geographically restricted, telecommunications media, territorially based, collective rights licensing agreements are more out of step with present business models. Similarly, as streaming media, public performance and broadcast rights replace old reproduction-based models of uploads and downloads of digital files, gaps and missteps in coverage have become increasingly apparent. Perhaps most notably, enforcement in the digital environment has become glaringly problematic.

All of these changes have led to copyright reform efforts in jurisdictions as diverse as Australia, China, New Zealand, Singapore, South Korea, the European Union (EU), Hong Kong, Japan, Canada and the United States. These efforts have been triggered by the unique challenges the digital environment has posed to the hard goods–based regimes of the Berne Convention for the Protection of Literary and Artistic Works (Berne Convention),[2] and the Agreement on Trade-Related Aspects of Intellectual Property Rights (TRIPS).[3] Neither treaty limited its application to the hard goods world, in fact. But their application over time has only demonstrated the gaps and inadequacies they share in facing the copyright challenges of the 21st century. These inadequacies have been exacerbated by the failure to deal with the myriad personal and data privacy issues that increasingly arise as a direct result of the new technologies used to create and distribute copyrighted works in the digital environment. This chapter is not intended as detailed analysis of present reform efforts, but will use examples of potential reforms incorporating critical new privacy-based considerations that could be followed to create a workable, harmonised 'code' of future norms that would allow Asian Pacific countries to take full advantage of the opportunities presented by the global digital environment, while retaining protections for personal privacy and human dignity.

The present movement for domestic reforms internationally has been matched by a rise in new copyright-related treaties, such as the Marrakesh Treaty to Facilitate Access to Published Works for Persons Who Are Blind,

---

2   Berne Convention for the Protection of Literary and Artistic Works 1161 UNTS 31 (opened for signature 9 September 1886, entered into force 5 December 1887), art 15(4) [Berne Convention].
3   Agreement on Trade-Related Aspects of Intellectual Property Rights 1869 UNTS 299 (adopted 15 April 1994, entered into force 1 January 1995) [TRIPS].

Visually Impaired or Otherwise Print Disabled (Marrakesh Treaty).[4] Numerous draft treaties are currently in discussion before the World Intellectual Property Organization (WIPO), including the Draft WIPO Archive Treaty,[5] the Draft Broadcast Treaty,[6] and a Draft Treaty for the Protection of Traditional Cultural Expressions,[7] that are considering fundamental normative changes in international copyright limitations and exceptions based on a perceived gap between present treaties and new technologies, including, respectively, practices that threaten access to information and content rights in broadcast signals, and indigenous peoples' rights to control their own heritage.

The major copyright multinational treaties dealing with the 'new' phenomenon of the internet, the WIPO Copyright Treaty (WCT)[8] and its related-rights companion, the WIPO Performances and Phonograms Treaty (WPPT),[9] were executed over 20 years ago. Although the Beijing Treaty on Audiovisual Performances (Beijing Treaty),[10] dealing with related rights for audiovisual performers and producers, was executed more recently in 2012, it largely followed the foundational norms for performances set forth in the WPPT.[11] Major domestic reforms, such as the Digital Millennium Copyright Act (DMCA)[12] in the United States and the EU Directive on the harmonisation of certain aspects of

---

4   Marrakesh Treaty to Facilitate Access to Published Works for Persons Who Are Blind, Visually Impaired or Otherwise Print Disabled (adopted 27 June 2013, entered into force 30 September 2016) [Marrakesh Treaty].

5   See WIPO *Working Document Containing Comments on and Textual Suggestions Towards an Appropriate International Legal Instrument (In Whatever Form) on Exceptions and Limitations for Libraries and Archives* SSCR/ 26/3 (15 April 2013); see also Eve Woodberry *Treaty Proposal on Limitations and Exceptions for Libraries and Archives* (International Federation of Library Associations, 6 December 2013).

6   WIPO *Working Document for a Treaty on the Protection of Broadcasting Organizations* SCCR/27/2 REV (25 March 2014); see also WIPO *Revised Consolidated Text on Definitions, Object of Protection, Rights to be Granted and Other Issues* SCCR/34/3 (13 March 2017).

7   WIPO *Draft Articles for the Protection of Traditional Cultural Expressions* WIPO/GRTKF/ IC/34/6 (14 March 2017).

8   WIPO Copyright Treaty 2186 UNTS 121 (opened for signature 20 December 1996, entered into force 6 March 2002), art 1(4) [WCT].

9   WIPO Performances and Phonograms Treaty 2186 UNTS 203 (adopted 20 December 1996, entered into force 20 May 2002) [WPPT].

10   Beijing Treaty on Audiovisual Works (adopted 24 June 2012, not yet in force) [Beijing Treaty].

11   These norms included reliance on the performers' making available right for exclusive control; compare WPPT, above n 9, arts 8 and 10 with Beijing Treaty, above n 10, arts 8 and 10; on the three-step test for exceptions and limitations; compare WPPT, above n 9, art 16 with Beijing Treaty, above n 10, art 13; and on technological protection measures to combat piracy; compare WPPT, above n 9, art 18 with Beijing Treaty, above n 10, art 15. Efforts to deal with new 'environmental' issues such as webcasting were basically tabled.

12   Digital Millennium Copyright Act 17 USC §§ 512, 1201, diverse [DMCA].

copyright and related rights in the information society (InfoSoc)[13] also date from approximately the same period as the WCT and the WPPT.[14] They have not been significantly altered since their respective dates of enactment. Perhaps even more notable, for the purposes of our analysis of the relevance of privacy issues to copyright reform for the digital environment, is that none of these instruments, including the Beijing Treaty,[15] addressed the issue of the interrelationship between copyright and privacy on the internet. Neither have subsequent efforts, such as the Asian Pacific Copyright Code.[16]

The necessary question arises: why now? What is different about today's digital environment that has suddenly sparked this long-overdue evaluation of copyright boundaries? Part of the explanation is necessarily based on the need for sufficient experience with the reality of the altered circumstances of copyright utilisation in the digital environment. Copyright reform always evolves more slowly than the technological changes in communications media it must address. For example, in the United States, the first photographs (daguerreotypes) were created in the late 1830s. Yet copyright law was not altered to acknowledge that works created using this new medium qualified for protection as original works until the Supreme Court decision, *Burrow-Giles Lithographic Co v Sarony*, in 1884.[17]

But I believe the most significant reason for the explosion in reform efforts currently is because technology has not resolved the challenges faced by copyright owners in the digital environment. Early hopes that anti-circumvention regimes would provide adequate protection for technological solutions to the unauthorised use of copyrighted works have proven evanescent, as pirate websites have grown exponentially.[18] The increased success of third parties in hacking technological protection measures, the rise of virtual private networks and dark nets that utilise

---

13   Directive 2001/29/EC on the Harmonisation of Certain Aspects of Copyright and Related Rights in the Information Society [2001] OJ L 167/10 [InfoSoc].
14   WCT, above n 8; WPPT, above n 9.
15   Beijing Treaty, above n 10.
16   Adrian Sterling 'Asian Pacific Copyright Code' in this volume.
17   *Burrow-Giles Lithographic Co v Sarony* 111 US 53 (1884).
18   See Susan Corbett 'Free Trade Agreements with the United States, Rulemaking and TPMs: Why Asian Pacific Nations Should Resist Increased Regulation of TPMs in their Domestic Copyright Laws' in this volume.

encryption to protect infringing activity, and the proliferation of pirated works due to even newer reproductive technologies, such as 3D printers, have created a renewed urgency for reform.

Yet, as we deal with the new realities of copyright in the global digital environment, it is critical that we avoid the mistakes of the past. We must acknowledge that there are new inputs that must be considered as we create the normative foundations for copyright protection in the 21st century.[19] One of those critical new inputs concerns both personal and data privacy. Such concerns are no longer adjuncts to issues of copyright protection but instead argue for new normative values as we reconfigure the boundaries of authorial control in this new era of access and transformation.

2 What Privacy?

Privacy has no single definition internationally. The concept of privacy can include everything from the right to be left alone or 'forgotten'; to the right to associational privacy; the right to avoid unwanted surveillance of either physical space or data; the right to a private space in one's own physical surroundings or in one's own mind (access to information); the right to control the dissemination of one's unpublished works or images of private lawful activities; or the right to control the disclosure and use of personal identifying information and personal information.[20]

This last category of 'privacy' has received the most attention in recent years. As used here, the term 'personal identifying information' is meant to include any information that can be used to identify an individual, directly or indirectly. Such information includes traditional categories, such as a name, address and social security number, as well as newer methods of source identification such as DNA and other biometric information, digital footprints, aggregated data and other aspects of so-called 'big data' that can be used to determine identity. This broad definition of privacy is intended to be co-extensive with, but not necessarily limited by, the definition for 'personal data' contained in the EU General Data Protection

---

19   See Lida Ayoubi 'Copyright Harmonisation in the Asian Pacific Region: Weaving the Peoples Together?' in this volume.
20   See generally Samuel D Warren and Louis D Brandeis 'The Right to Privacy' (1890) 4 Harv L Rev 193; see also Doris Estelle Long 'Is a Global Solution Possible to the Technology/Privacy Conundrum?' (2005) 4 J Marshall Rev Intell Prop L 6.

Regulation (GDPR),[21] in South Korea's Personal Information Protection Act (PIPA)[22] and for 'personal information' contained in China's 2016 Cybersecurity Law.[23]

Under the GDPR, protected 'personal data' includes 'any information relating to an identified or identifiable natural person ("data subject")'.[24] An 'identifiable natural person' is:[25]

> one who can be identified, directly or indirectly, in particular by reference to an identifier such as a name, an identification number, location data, an online identifier or to one or more factors specific to the physical, physiological, genetic, mental, economic, cultural or social identity of that natural person.

South Korea's PIPA defines 'personal data' even more broadly to also include:[26]

> information pertaining to any living person that makes it possible to identify such individual by his/her name and resident registration number, image, etc. (including the information which, if not by itself, makes it possible to identify any specific individual if combined with other information).

China's definition of 'personal information', under its new Cybersecurity Law, reflects a similarly open-ended approach by including:[27]

---

21 Regulation 2016/679 General Data Protection Regulation [2016] OJ L119/1 art 4(1) [GDPR].

22 Personal Information Protection Act 2011 (South Korea) [PIPA].

23   Cybersecurity Law 2016 (China), art 76(5). Under art 79, the effective date of China's Cybersecurity Law was 1 June 2017. Due to strong criticism, the enactment of the provisions regarding cross-border transfer and data retention was delayed until 31 December 2018. The effective date for the remaining provisions, including the notice and takedown (NTD) provisions, however, remained unchanged; see Joe McDonald 'China postpones portion of cybersecurity law' *Associated Press* (online ed, New York, 31 May 2017). Additional regulations will undoubtedly be issued prior to this date to clarify the data localisation issues raised by these provisions.

24   GDPR, above n 21, art 4.

25   Article 4.

26   PIPA, above n 22, art 2(1).

27   Cybersecurity Law 2016 (China), art 76(5). A Personal Information Security Specification was published in January 2018, with an effective date of 1 May 2018, which defined a new category of 'sensitive personal information' that should receive heightened protection. Information Technology-Personal Information Security Specification GB/T 35273-2017 (2018) (China) Center for Strategic and International Studies www.csis.org [Personal Information Security Specification]. Although the Personal Information Security Specification is voluntary, it will likely be applied as a guide to measure compliance. It is discussed in greater detail below in Part 4.4.

all kinds of information, recorded electronically or through other means, that taken alone or together with other information, is sufficient to identify a natural person's identity, including, but not limited to, natural persons' full names, birth dates, identification numbers, personal biometric information, addresses, telephone numbers, and so forth.

Yet in the interstices between copyright and privacy and, in particular, in the normative spaces addressed in this chapter, 'privacy' is not simply limited to identifying data, no matter how broadly defined. To the contrary, other aspects of 'privacy' that relate to a sense of personal control over one's space and actions (surveillance) or to one's image or works (unauthorised publication or dissemination) are equally relevant in creating viable copyright norms for the 21st century. Such spatial or informational privacy includes considerations regarding the unauthorised dissemination of private correspondence or images of private sexual activity. In the context of the internet, it also includes the right to avoid the collection of personal information about one's web viewing or reading habits.[28]

In addition, corollaries to securing spatial and informational privacy are also relevant in the creation of copyright norms. These corollaries include the protection of encryption and other technological methodologies to secure privacy rights in the 'Digital Age' and their unauthorised breach through such efforts as hacking, phishing and cyber espionage. They also include content-based privacy concerns from other legal regimes such as protection against 'sexting' and 'revenge porn'.

The purpose of this wide-ranging definition is not to provide an all-inclusive list of topics to be covered within the context of copyright reform. Instead, it is to underscore the need for an approach that welcomes and actively seeks other normative inputs in creating the next generation of global copyright regimes. It is only through a fluid and more flexible approach that we can assure a more appropriate and sustainable future copyright regime for the 'Digital Age', and beyond.

---

28 Unlike other jurisdictions – such as Australia, China, Japan, the Philippines, Singapore and the EU, which provide relatively strong protection regarding data collection practices – in the United States, such considerations may be more difficult to bring into present copyright reform discussions given recent Congressional action overturning such protections imposed by regulations passed by the Federal Communications Commission, see Joint Resolution Pub L No. 115-22, 131 Stat 88 (2017). Although there are other laws and regulations that provide partial protection for these activities, this recent legislative action undoubtedly makes the inclusion of such considerations as part the United States copyright reform highly problematic.

3 Breaching the Copyright/Privacy Wall

Even in the pre-digital era, the wall between copyright and privacy regimes was not an absolute one. To the contrary, data privacy concerns often arose in the context of securing information regarding the identity of the manufacturers and distributors of pirated goods. Courts routinely balanced the need for such disclosure as a matter of legal relevance with an individual's right of privacy. The need for identity disclosure became even more severe with the explosion of pirated works distributed through early peer-to-peer networks such as Napster and Kazaa.[29] It has continued apace as anonymiser technologies have made the securing of such information even more difficult. As requests for end-user identities increased, privacy considerations were initially given relatively short shrift.[30] For example, under the DMCA, the United States originally mandated end-user identity disclosures by affected online service providers (OSPs) without judicial oversight.[31] Over time, however, even in the United States, with its relatively limited protections for end-user privacy generally, privacy protections have played an increasingly significant role in controlling such disclosures.[32]

The interconnections between copyright and personal privacy regimes are no longer limited to issues of identity disclosure. To the contrary, data privacy issues now affect such critical questions as the admissibility of evidence of infringing activity secured through the use of website scraper technologies and automatic takedown bots. In *Arista Records LLC v DOE 3*,[33] for example, the Court expressly held that the right to anonymity in internet communications could outweigh copyright interests in identity disclosure (although, in this particular instance, privacy interests did not outweigh those of the copyright owner).

---

29   Napster www.napster.com; the Kazaa website is no longer active.
30   See DMCA, above n 12, § 512(h) (establishing an identity disclosure subpoena process that mandated disclosure on good faith request).
31   § 512(h). See discussion below.
32   See *London-Sire Records Inc v Doe 1 Et Al* 542 F Supp 2d 153 (D Mass 2008); *BMG Canada Inc v John Doe* 2004 FC 448, [2004] 3 FCR 241; Case C-461/10 *Bonnier Audio AB v Perfect Communication Sweden AB* [2012] ECR I-219.
33   *Arista Records LLC v DOE 3* 604 F 2d 110 (2d Cir 2010). See also *Forman v Henkin*, Slip Op 01015 (NY Ct.App 2018) (acknowledging that private information on Facebook may be discoverable by 'balancing the potential liability of the information sought against any specific "privacy" or other concerns raised by the account holder').

Similarly, the enforceability of injunctions blocking end-user access to identified pirate websites is frequently decided by balancing personal privacy interests against copyright protections.[34] In brief terms, website blocking is achieved by a technological impediment, imposed by an OSP, that prevents end users from accessing designated pirate websites. Such blocks include 'IP blocks' that prohibit access to specific internet protocol addresses, 'DNS blocks' that block access to specified domain names and 'proxy blocks' that route the traffic on a site through a proxy server for filtering. The EU, for example, has insisted on 'proportionality' in balancing copyright and privacy interests when seeking to impose website blocking solutions to digital piracy.[35] Such proportionality does not prevent the enforcement of website blocking injunctions,[36] but it does make such relief more difficult to secure.[37] By contrast, in Australia, privacy issues are not expressly considered in determining whether a block should issue.[38] This approach may change, however, as Australia's efforts to establish broader rights to protect personal privacy continue.[39]

Finally, even decisions allowing filtering to remove infringing content are impacted by privacy considerations.[40] Recent attempts to impose filtering obligations on OSPs through government or private regulation have been challenged because their application directly impacts end-user privacy rights.[41]

Even activities perceived to be related to the traditional domain of privacy law, such as hacking and surveillance, have increasingly intruded into the arena of copyright.[42] From the heightened surveillance possibilities

---

34   See Case C-70/10 *Scarlet Extended v Société belge des auteurs, compositeurs et éditeurs SCRL (SABAM)* [2011] ECR I-771.
35   *Scarlet Extended*, above n 34, at [36].
36   See *EMI Records Ltd & Ors v British Sky Broadcasting Ltd & Ors* [2013] EWHC 379 (Ch).
37   See *Scarlet Extended,* above n 34.
38   See *Roadshow Films Pty Ltd v Telstra Corporation Ltd* [2016] FCA 1503; *Foxtel Management Pty Limited v TPG Internet Pty Ltd* [2017] FCA 1041.
39   See Narelle Smythe and Morgan Clarke 'A statutory cause of action for serious invasions of privacy on the way for New South Wales?' (17 March 2016) Clayton Utz www.claytonutz.com; see also Commonwealth of Australia *Issues Paper: A Commonwealth Statutory Cause of Action for Serious Invasion of Privacy* (September 2011).
40   See Case C-360/10 *Belgische Vereniging van Auteurs, Componisten en Uitgevers CVBA (SABAM) v Netlog* [2012].
41   Jeremy Malcolm 'Upload Filtering Mandate Would Shred European Copyright Safe Harbor' (12 October 2016) Electronic Frontier Foundation www.eff.org (contending such regulations violate personal privacy and access to information provisions of the European Charter of Fundamental Rights).
42   See Susy Frankel 'The Copyright and Privacy Nexus' (2005) 36(3) VUWLR 507 (analysing connections between privacy and, inter alia, unauthorised distribution of personal photographs).

of drone photography to the rapid unauthorised dissemination of personal information through the digital posting of leaked documents and personal sexting images, privacy has become inextricably linked with copyright. The first attempts to remove leaked information regarding membership in a website that promoted marital infidelity in the United States, Ashley Madison,[43] was based on its purported violation of the copyright in the membership list.[44] Early efforts to remove photos of private consensual sexual activity, distributed without the participant's consent in cases of 'sexting' or 'revenge porn' in the United States have similarly focused on copyright and the ability to take down infringing works.[45] In fact, such efforts have proven so popular that companies, such as DMCA Defender,[46] have been created to help victims remove such items from the diverse array of internet sites, including Twitter, on which they can appear. New Zealand even has a specific provision in the Copyright Act 1994, under its moral rights part,[47] giving the subject of photos commissioned for private or domestic purposes the right to prevent their unauthorised public distribution, exhibition or communication.[48]

4 How Privacy Considerations Can Impact Copyright Reform

4.1 Reforming Notice and Takedown Regimes and Other Digital Enforcement Mechanisms

One of the most contentious issues facing copyright owners and the public today is the method used to remove infringing content from digital networks.[49] Regardless of the precise economic impact of digital piracy, there is no question that the proliferation of illegal content on the internet

---

43 Ashley Madison www.ashleymadison.com.

44 Hope King 'Ashley Madison tries to stop the spread of its leaked data' (21 August 2015) CNN money.cnn.com.

45 See 17 USC § 512(c). See also Ian Sherr 'Forget being a victim: What to do when revenge porn strikes' (13 May 2015) CNET www.cnet.com.

46 dmcadefender.com.

47 Part 4.

48 Section 105.

49 In fact the NTD provisions of the DMCA, above n 12, have already been the subject of four days of public roundtables and an ongoing study by the United States Copyright Office, including two requests for public comments that have generated over 92,000 submissions to date. United States Copyright Office 'Section 512 Study' www.copyright.gov.

and on other digital platforms is the greatest challenge facing content owners. Most countries that have considered some form of a notice and takedown (NTD) regime to alleviate the problem have achieved less than stellar results. Privacy considerations would not only place such takedown techniques in a different light, they would also provide unique insights into how NTDs can be reformed to achieve the balanced approach to protection between authors' and end users' rights they were originally designed to achieve.

Internationally, NTD procedures have evolved from the original NTD procedures of the DMCA,[50] to the 'three strikes' rule of the French Haute Autorité pour la diffusion des oeuvres et la protection des droits sur internet (Hadopi),[51] to the Notice and Notice provisions of the Canadian Copyright Modernization Act (CMA)[52] and variations of this new iteration of the 'graduated response' to online piracy, including the 'six strikes plus' rules of current private initiatives.[53] None has proven wholly satisfactory.

Under the DMCA,[54] on receipt of an appropriate notice of infringement from a copyright holder, the OSP must take down the identified material or lose its safe harbour. Such takedown can occur either by actual removal of the identified material from the website or by disabling access to it. To secure content takedowns, copyright owners must provide a written notice containing identification information regarding the infringing material, including name and locational data,[55] along with a statement

---

50   DMCA, above n 12, § 512(c). Other jurisdictions that have adopted a similar NTD process include: South Korea (Copyright Act 1957, art 103); Singapore (Copyright Act 1987 (revised edition 2006), art 193D); and the EU Directive 2000/31/EC on Electronic Commerce [2000] OJ L178/1, art 14. The efficacy of this process, particularly where it lacks a stay-down requirement, has been severely criticised. See Devlin Hartline 'Endless Whack-A-Mole: Why Notice-and-Staydown Just Makes Sense' (14 January 2016) Centre for the Protection of Intellectual Property www.cpip.gmu.edu; but see Elliot Harmon '"Notice-and-Stay-Down" Is Really "Filter-Everything"' (21 January 2016) Electronic Frontier Foundation www.eff.org.

51   Code de la Propriété Intellectuelle 1992 (France), art L-331-25. Other countries that have adopted a similar 'three strikes' graduated response include New Zealand (Copyright Act 1994, s 122B) and South Korea (Copyright Act 1957 (South Korea) art 133*bis*).

52   Copyright Act RSC 1985 c C-42, art 41.25. Other countries have adopted a graduated response requiring notice and notice with no obligation of takedown absent a court order, and no limit on the number of notices (unlike the 'three-strikes' rule), see Digital Economy Act 2010 (UK), s 3, inserting s 124A into the Communications Act 2003.

53   See discussion below.

54   DMCA, above n 12.

55   § 512(c)(3).

of good faith on the part of the copyright holder.[56] Where an OSP acts in good faith in response to a notice of infringement, it will not be liable so long as it promptly notifies the subscriber of its actions, provides the complaining party with any counter notifications it receives from the end user and replaces any removed material subject to a proper counter complaint within 10 to 14 days of receipt of the counter notice, unless the OSP receives notice from the original complaining party that it has filed a lawsuit regarding the material in question.[57] Similar NTD provisions have been adopted by a variety of countries, including China, New Zealand, Singapore and South Korea; however, the precise timing of such takedowns has varied.[58]

The efficacy of these takedown procedures has been hotly contested. Content owners criticise this process because there is no general obligation for OSPs to monitor content to assure that removed material is not reposted. OSPs criticise the process because compliance has become extremely costly. According to Google's Transparency Report, it responds to over two million takedown requests a day.[59] End users criticise the process because it is frequently abused by copyright owners who seek to remove lawful material. Such removal is increasingly secured through the use of automated bots, which do not examine the material to determine if the use at issue qualifies as a fair or permitted one despite the legal obligation to do so in some countries.[60] Although, similar to other countries,[61] the NTD process under the DMCA allows end users

56 § 512(c)(3) (they must also include an affirmation of accuracy).
57 § 512(g).
58 Regulation on Protection of the Right to Network Dissemination of Information (State Council Order No. 468, 18 May 2006, amended in accordance with the Decision of the State Council on Amending the Regulation on Protection of the Right to Network Dissemination of Information on 30 January 2013) (China), art 15 (takedown must occur 'promptly') [Network Regulations (China)]; Copyright Act 1994 (NZ), s 92C (takedown 'as soon as possible'), Copyright Act 1987 (Singapore), art 193D(2)(b)(iii) (OSP 'expeditiously takes reasonable steps to remove or disable access'); Copyright Act 1957 (South Korea), art 103(2) (OSP must 'immediately suspend the reproduction and interactive transmission'); but see art 133bis (establishing a three strikes graduated response in certain cases); but see Copyright Act 1994 (NZ) s 122B (establishing three strikes graduated response for the issuance of enforcement notices intended to result in OSP account suspensions for alleged infringing file sharing).
59 See Google 'Transparency Report' (10 March 2011 – 7 July 2017) Google www.google.com.
60 See *Lenz v Universal Music Corp* 572 F Supp 2d 1150 (ND Cal 2008). For a further discussion of the relationship between fair use and NTDs, see below.
61 Network Regulations (China), above n 58, arts 16 and17; Copyright Act 1987 (Singapore), art 193DA.

to challenge unauthorised takedowns. Incomplete studies and anecdotal evidence seems to indicate that only a small percentage of end users actually utilise the process.[62]

While the first generation of NTD regimes allowed for relatively rapid removal of infringing material, they did not end the cycle of notice, removal, repost that these regimes created (often referred to as a game of 'whack a mole').[63] The 'three strikes' rule of the French Hadopi,[64] established in 2009,[65] arguably resolved this problem by providing that end users who engaged in three instances of online copyright infringement within a specified period of time could have their internet access suspended for a period of up to one year.[66] Infringing acts were broadly defined to include the unauthorised reproduction, representation, distribution or communication to the public.[67] As opposed to a single notice, three notices were required before the potential suspension penalty could attach.[68] Ultimately, the threat of so draconian a penalty, along with the practical realities in effectuating an actual suspension of access to the internet (as opposed to a single OSP), doomed the three strikes approach of Hadopi.[69] In contrast to Hadopi's internet suspension approach, however, New Zealand's, South Korea's and Taiwan's three strikes approach were directed to suspension from a particular OSP's account.[70] In addition, New Zealand's law was directed expressly to instances of infringement based on 'communication to the public'.[71] By narrowing the scope of the access denial penalties, these laws arguably provided a more workable version of the three strikes regime.

---

62   Daphne Keller and Annemarie Bridy 'DMCA Counter-Notice: Does It Work To Correct Erroneous Takedowns?' (17 January 2017) Stanford Law School: The Centre for Internet and Society cyberlaw.stanford.edu.
63   'Whack-a-mole' refers to the general ineffectiveness of the present process. You may try to hit a mole but it moves so quickly and disappears down holes so rapidly you cannot really hit one.
64   Code de la Propriété Intellectuelle 1992 (France), above n 51.
65   Established by Loi favorisant law diffusion et law protection de la création sur Internet 2009 (France).
66   Code de la Propriété Intellectuelle 1992 (as at 2009) (France), above n 51, art L-331-25.
67   Article L-336-3.
68   Article L-331-26.
69   Code de la Propriété Intellectuelle 1992 (France), above n 51.
70   Code de la Propriété Intellectuelle 1992 (France), above n 51; Copyright Act 1994 (NZ), s 122P; Copyright Act 1957 (South Korea), art 133*bis*; Copyright Act 2016 (Taiwan), art 90*quinquies*. To date, the suspension provisions of the Copyright Act 1994 (NZ) under s 122P have not yet been brought into force: s 122R requires enactment 'by Order in Council' from the Governor-General, which has not yet occurred.
71   Copyright Act 1994, s 122P. Unfortunately s 122P has yet to be brought into force, above n 69.

In the next iteration of the graduated response NTD, Canada enacted art 41.25 of the CMA,[72] establishing a 'Notice and Notice' approach that further extended the time for removal of infringing material. The CMA does not require OSPs to remove identified infringing material. Instead, it obligates them to forward notices of infringement from copyright owners and retain end-user identity information to turn over on court order to the copyright owner for subsequent legal action.[73] While this process improves end-user education and eliminates the problem of abusive removals, its graduated response does not contain any rapid removal obligations, even at the end of the Notice cycle, without court action. The 'Notice and Notice' approach has proven extremely popular. Subsequent private arrangements between content providers and OSPs, such as the 'six strikes' agreement (Copyright Alert System), established in 2011 between various OSPs and content owners in the United States, including Verizon, AT&T, the Motion Picture Association of America and the Recording Industry Association of America,[74] and the Creative Content program in the United Kingdom,[75] have followed a similar approach. In fact, the phrase 'six strikes' appears a misnomer since there is no required takedown or account suspension after receipt of six notices of infringing conduct. As with the Notice and Notice approach of the CMA, content owners would have to seek takedown relief through the courts.[76]

---

72   Copyright Act RSC 1985 c C-42, art 41.25.
73   Article 41.26. Similar identity disclosure obligations on court order exist under New Zealand's copyright law. See Copyright Act 1994, ss 122J and 122Q (identity disclosure on Tribunal and Court order, respectively). The identity disclosure provisions by court order under s 122Q are not yet in force: see s 122R (requiring enactment by 'Order of the Council' for this provision that has not yet occurred).
74   In 2017, the Copyright Alert System was 'concluded' with the statement that it 'succeeded in educating many people about the availability of legal content, as well as about issues associated with online infringement' Centre for Copyright Information 'Statement on the Copyright Alert System' (press release, 27 January 2017). Others suggested its 'conclusion' was not the result of educational success, but of its failure to deal effectively with persistent infringers: see Jacob Kastrenakes 'Six strikes' anti-piracy initiative ends after failing to scare off "hardcore" pirates' (30 January 2017) The Verge www.theverge.com. This system is slowly being replaced by a series of private Trusted Notifier Agreements between copyright holders and domain name registrars in which the registrars require domain name owners to remove content identified by the copyright holder as infringing or lose their domain names. The effective impact of these private arrangements remain hotly contested. Compare Anne Marie Bridy 'Notice and Takedown in the Domain Name System: ICANN's Ambivalent Drift into Online Content Regulation' (2017) 17 Wash & Lee L Rev 1345 with Paul Vixie 'Notice, Takedown, Borders and Scale' (1 March 2017) Circle ID circleid.com.
75   This program is currently known as 'Get It Right from a Genuine Site': see Get It Right From a Genuine Site www.getitrightfromagenuinesite.org. Notices under the 'Get It Right' program reportedly were first issued in February 2017. See also Andy 'UK Piracy Alerts: The First Look Inside the Warning System' (10 February 2017) Torrent Freak torrentfreak.com.
76   Copyright Act RSC 1985 c C-42.

The trend toward delayed removal of infringing material from the internet in the most recent iterations of NTDs is problematic, given the rapidity with which material spreads in the digital environment. One of the reasons for the continued popularity of the NTD process under the DMCA in the United States[77] has been its utility in dealing with non-copyright issues, such as removing fake mirror websites that mislead consumers including shadow bank and consumer products sites. These shadow websites are often used to support phishing attacks, by securing personal information from unsuspecting consumers that can then be used in various criminal and fraudulent activities, including identity theft. NTD processes allow for a quick removal of such websites while investigations and court actions based on the fraudulent activity proceed along a separate track. As noted above, DMCA NTD processes have also proven popular in removing sites that disseminate materials that violate individual privacy, such as the membership list from the Ashley Madison website.[78] Although other claims based on the illegal conduct that secured these lists, including violation of anti-hacking provisions under the Computer Fraud and Abuse Act,[79] might be used to secure similar relief, it would not be so quickly achieved.

While the need for swift removal of content based on its copyrighted nature might be subject to dispute, when privacy considerations are added into the normative mix swift removal becomes a viable and arguably even a necessary solution. But privacy issues also require a more nuanced approach to takedown, since abuse could have serious effects beyond chilling free speech. Moreover, coverage decisions would not be made solely on the existence of copyright.

Where the subject matter or the circumstances surrounding dissemination raise privacy issues in connection with copyrighted materials, rapid takedowns serve a critical role in protecting personal rights. Pirated works generally cause monetary harm. By contrast, private diaries, surveillance videos, child pornography, cyberbullying, sexting and other content whose unauthorised dissemination violates personal privacy cause emotional harm. In some cases, such as revenge porn and cyberbullying, emotional harm is so severe that some subjects have committed suicide as a result of such unauthorised communications. The longer such content

---

77 DMCA, above n 12.
78 See discussion above, Part 3; DMCA, above n 12; Ashley Madison, above n 43.
79 18 USC § 30.

remains available on the internet, the greater the emotional harm. Rapid takedown may not fully eliminate emotional harm, but it certainly helps stop its growth.

Even under the takedown procedures that obligate removal of infringing material, rapid takedowns are not so rapid. Removal under Singapore's Copyright Regulations must occur within 14 days.[80] Other countries, such as China, Australia and the United States, require 'prompt' or 'expeditious' removal.[81] New Zealand requires removal 'as soon as possible'.[82] None of these set forth a specific time frame for action.

In contrast, the New Zealand Harmful Digital Communications Act 2015 (HDCA) requires takedown by the OSP within 48 hours of receipt of appropriate notice from the affected subject.[83] The HDCA applies to 'digital communications' that 'cause serious emotional distress'.[84] It is not a copyright statute, but it serves as a useful model for the types of privacy concerns that would be implicated if privacy considerations were included in the reformation of present NTD processes for copyrighted works. Among the harmful communications covered by the HDCA are cyberbullying, sexting and the unauthorised dissemination of 'intimate visual recordings' made 'without the knowledge or consent of the individual who is the subject'.[85] To qualify as an 'intimate visual recording' under the HDCA, the image must have been made in 'a place which, in the circumstances, would reasonably be expected to provide privacy'.[86] A covered 'digital recording' includes depictions and accompanying text concerning private sexual activity.[87]

The HDCA, similar to the DMCA, requires OSPs to forward copies of complaints to the end user and allows for counter notification to prevent removal or secure reposting of the affected work.[88] Either party can also seek quick relief from Netsafe, the approved agency for reviewing complaints,

80   Copyright (Flagrantly Infringing Online Location) Regulations 2014 (Singapore), s 3.
81   Network Regulations (China), above n 58, art 15 ('promptly'); Copyright Regulations 1969 (Cth), r 20J ('expeditiously'); DMCA, above n 12, § 512(c)(1)(C) ('expeditiously').
82   Copyright Act 1994, s 92C.
83   Harmful Digital Communications Act 2015, s 24 [HDCA]. See discussion below, at 4.2, for an examination of the shift from author to subject ability to take down violating materials.
84   HDCA, above n 83, s 24(2).
85   Section 4.
86   Section 4.
87   Section 4.
88   Section 4.

and from the courts (after the required agency review).[89] This allows for a necessary safety net in cases of abusive or improper requests or OSP reluctance to remove end-user content.

Privacy considerations would undoubtedly support the institution of some form of rapid takedown in copyright reforms at least for certain works. Given the content-specific nature of the covered works – they must violate the requisite privacy interests – actual review prior to a subject's issuing a takedown request would likely be mandated. Yet in some NTD processes, such content review is already required. For example, although the DMCA only requires that copyright owners make a 'good faith declaration that use of the material in the manner complained of is not authorised by the copyright owner, its agent, or the law',[90] recent decisions have indicated that such 'good faith' basis does not eliminate the obligation to review identified content for fair use exceptions. In *Lenz v Universal Music Corp*,[91] the OSP had taken down a 29-second video containing the defendant's young children dancing in the family's kitchen while a poor-quality sound track of 'Let's Go Crazy' by Prince and the Revolution played in the background. The trial court found that Universal was obligated to consider whether Lenz's use of the song qualified as a fair one before seeking its takedown:[92]

> Undoubtedly, some evaluations of fair use will be more complicated than others. But in the majority of cases, a consideration of fair use prior to issuing a takedown notice will not be so complicated as to jeopardize a copyright owner's ability to respond rapidly to potential infringements. The DMCA already requires copyright owners to make an initial review of the potentially infringing material prior to sending a takedown notice; indeed, it would be impossible to meet any of the requirements of Section 512(c) without doing so. A consideration of the applicability of the fair use doctrine simply is part of that initial review … . [A] full *investigation* to verify the accuracy of a claim of infringement is not required.

---

89   Section 8; Harmful Digital Communications (Appointment of Approved Agency) Order 2016.
90   DMCA, above n 12, § 512(c)(3).
91   *Lenz v Universal Music Corp* 801 F 3d 1126 (9th Cir 2015).
92   *Lenz v Universal Music Corp* 572 F Supp 2d 1150 at 1155–1156 (ND Cal 2008) aff'd 801 F 3d 1126 (9th Cir 2015) (emphasis added).

By using a 'good faith' standard,[93] the DMCA allows content owners to make good faith judgments about fair use without penalty. Leniency in harmful communications reviews would similarly give breathing space to subjects who seek good faith removal of such communications.

One of the difficulties with NTDs has been the potential for abuse. In response to a recent roundtable on reform held by the United States Copyright Office,[94] Google identified several recent instances of abuse, including flooding an OSP with demands to remove non-existent websites to ensure that all copies of an identified infringing work are removed from all potential locations and a demand by a lawyer seeking removal of a blog post criticising the lawyer for plagiarising content on his website.[95] There are also countless examples of clearly acceptable instances of fair use/fair dealing that have been removed inappropriately.[96] The potential for abusive complaints could be even greater where the basis for takedown is its 'harmful' nature. Allegations that an internet provider hosts such content could create significant reputational harm that is not generally present even in cases of pirate websites. To reduce such abuses, NTD reform would require strong penalties for knowingly making wrongful requests for takedowns.

Section 512(f) of the DMCA, for example, imposes damages, including costs and attorneys' fees, against 'any person who *knowingly materially misrepresents* ... that material or activity is infringing'.[97] The damages include those: [98]

> incurred by the alleged infringer, by any copyright owner or copyright owner's authorized licensee, or by a service provider, who is injured by such misrepresentation, as the result of the service provider relying upon such misrepresentation in removing or disabling access to the material or activity claimed to be infringing, or in replacing the removed material or ceasing to disable access to it.

---

93   DMCA, above n 12, § 512(c)(3).
94   'Section 512 Study: Announcement of Public Roundtable' (18 March 2016) 81(53) *Federal Register* 14896 at 14896.
95   Letter from Google Inc to Karyn Temple Claggett (Acting Register of Copyrights) regarding Section 512 Study: Request for Additional Comments (21 February 2017).
96   See *Online Policy Group v Diebold Inc* 337 F Supp 2d 1195 (ND Cal 2004); *Lenz v Universal Music Corp*, above n 92. See generally Jennifer Urban, Joe Karaganis and Brianna L Schofield 'Notice and Takedown In Everyday Practice' (Public Law Research Paper No. 2755628, UC Berkley, March 2017) [Takedown Report].
97   DMCA, above n 12, § 512(f) (emphasis added).
98   § 512(f).

Although Section 512(f) has been underutilised,[99] it represents an example of the type of penalty assurance required to reduce abuse of takedown rights.

While adding privacy concerns into copyright reform should give rise to a reconsideration of the importance of rapid takedowns, combined with penalties against abuse of such processes, the normative values derived from this exercise are not so circumscribed. To the contrary, by establishing a process that recognises a content-based approach to rapid takedown, the use of this differential approach does not have to be so narrow. Rapid takedown could also be established for works for which the economic harm of its unauthorised communication to the public is significantly greater than for other works. The clearest example would be commercial works that are in their pre-release periods, when the unique harm caused by their unauthorised release causes a special type of artistic harm. In support of the Family Entertainment and Copyright Act of 2015 (US), which established specific criminal penalties for the unauthorised distribution of copyrighted works 'being prepared for commercial distribution',[100] Congressman Howard Berman of the United States House of Representatives recognised that:[101]

> Unauthorized prereleases are unfair to an artist because his or her song is circulating even before it is in its final form. Just as we edit letters and speeches, we must allow songwriters to tweak and refine their works. They deserve to have the tools to penalize those who thrive on the ability to leak a song or CD before it is available in stores or other legitimate avenues of commerce.

In a similar vein, during the initial premiere (public release) stage of motion pictures and other works, income potential is at its highest and pirated copies can cause their greatest direct economic harm to the bottom line.[102] This unique status would also argue for rapid NTD of pirated versions of such works.

---

99 See Takedown Report, above n 96.
100 DMCA, above n 12, § 506(a)(1)(C).
101 (19 April 2005) 151(47) Cong Record 109/1 at H2118 (statement of Howard Berman).
102 At H2118: 'Distributing a film before final edits are made can undermine artistic integrity and can also harm the film's commercial prospects because the release is typically coordinated with a marketing effort.'

4.2 The Author/Subject Dichotomy

As is clear from the HDCA,[103] one of the critical distinctions between copyright- and privacy-focused takedown regimes is the identity of the person whose rights are at issue. Copyright at its heart is focused on authors, who, by definition, are the creators of the material sought to be removed. By contrast, those who seek takedowns of 'harmful communications', including in particular those that violate personal privacy, are the subjects of such materials. With the exception of private works distributed without authorisation, in most cases, the individuals seeking takedown do not presently own any copyright interest in such materials. This shift in identity of the protected rights holder does not eliminate the relevancy of privacy considerations. However, it admittedly makes them a secondary factor in NTD reforms, unless privacy considerations are also used to redefine authorial rights.

Despite the critical role that authorship plays in the control of rights under copyright, the term is undefined in governing multilateral treaties. With some noted exceptions based on the unique collaborative nature of films and sound recordings,[104] 'authors' are generally defined as the human originators of a particular work. Even for countries such as the United States,[105] South Korea[106] and Japan,[107] which recognise non-human authorship in the form of a 'work for hire', the entity may be non-human, but the actual creators of the work are still human. In today's digital environment, new technologies have created truly potential non-human 'authors', including works created by artificial intelligence.

From the copyright ownership of buildings and light displays reproduced in panoramic photos,[108] to the authorship of selfies taken by a monkey,[109] and oil paintings created by Artificial Intelligence,[110] the contours

---

103 HDCA, above n 83.

104 See Directive 2006/116/EC on the term of protection of copyright and certain related rights OJ L372/12, art 2(1) (establishing that the 'principal director' of a cinematographic or audio visual works shall be considered an author) [Copyright Directive]; Copyright Act 1968 (Cth), s 98 (establishing the 'maker' of a cinematographic work as the copyright holder and specifying such 'maker' can be the 'director' where the film is not a commissioned work); *16 Casa Duse, LLC v Merkin* 791 F 3d 247 (2d Cir 2015) (holding producer was author of film).

105 DMCA, above n 12, § 201(b).

106 Copyright Act 1957 (South Korea), art 9.

107 Copyright Act 2010 (Japan), art 15(1).

108 Doris Estelle Long 'World Finds Itself in Quandary Over "Panorama Photos"; Now Come Drones' (2015) 161 Chi Daily L Bull 241.

109 *Naruto v Slater* 2016 WL 362231 (ND Cal 28 January 2016).

110 'The Next Rembrandt' J Walter Thompson www.jwt.com.

of authorship remain in flux. As countries reconsider the authorial boundaries to be drawn in the face of such new technologies, there is room to reconsider the relationship between the photographer and his subject that lie at the heart of privacy-based copyright norms.[111] Even in cases where the subject has consented to having his photo taken, subjects are increasingly seeking control over the use of those images. In the United States, in *Natkin v Winfrey*,[112] the well-known celebrity Oprah Winfrey sued for copyright in her images taken by freelance photographers authorised by her to take such images. The court ultimately rejected the claim because:[113]

> … the subject matter of the photographs is not copyrightable … To qualify as an author, one must supply more than mere direction or ideas. An author is the party who actually creates the work, that is, the person who translates an idea into a fixed, tangible expression.

Neither Winfrey's 'facial expressions, her attire, the "look" and "mood" of the show, the choice of guests [or] the staging of the show'[114] qualified as a copyrightable work.

If privacy issues are considered, at least in cases of unauthorised photography, however, countries might determine that the unwilling subjects have the right to control the future use of their image as, at least, a joint author. Such authorship would not only resolve the issue of the right to control dissemination of private images of sexual conduct, and drone and other forms of unauthorised surveillance images (discussed below), but could also have applications with regard to so-called paparazzi photography, at least where such photographs intrude into the subject's private spaces. One useful example of this approach is New Zealand's grant of a moral right to '[a] person who, for private and domestic purposes, commissions the taking of a photograph or the making of a film' to prevent the public exhibition, communication to the public or issuing of copies, even if the copyright is owned by another.[115] The right of control under this provision would not cover unauthorised photos created by drones or the paparazzi since it is limited to 'commissioned'

111 See Susan Corbett 'The Case for Joint Ownership of Copyright in Photographs of Identifiable Individuals' (2013) 18 MALR 330.
112 *Natkin v Winfrey* 111 F Supp 2d 1003 at 1011 (ND Ill. 2000).
113 At 111, citing *Erickson v Trinity Thirty Theatre Inc* 13 F 3d 1061 at 1071 (7th Cir 1994), which cited *Community for Creative Non-Violence v Reid* 490 US 730 at 737 (1989).
114 *Natkin v Winfrey*, above n 112, at 111.
115 Copyright Act 1994, s 105 (as amended by the New Technologies Amendment Act 2008, s 62(1)).

works. But it provides a useful starting place for reconfiguring the rights of photographed subjects (regardless of the medium used to create the image) to prevent the distribution/public communication of hidden photography that is violative of personal privacy.[116]

Given that numerous countries are already considering the lines between authorship and technology, including revisions to the definitions of joint authorship in cases of collaborative works, privacy considerations could rewrite the landscape of such rights. The primary focus on authorship premised on creative contributions could still be maintained. But creative contribution would not need to be constrained to those who knowingly contributed to the work. Instead, privacy considerations could push normative contribution tests so that even unconsented-to poses, facial expressions and the like would give rise to sufficient creativity to qualify for joint authorship.[117] Where the unconsented-to image violates personal privacy, privacy considerations would argue for the subject having the right to prevent its public distribution/exhibition/communication to the public. Such right to prohibition could be based on an expanded moral right, such as that contained in New Zealand's copyright law,[118] or on a redefined right of control as a joint author.

4.3 Drones, Surveillance and Data Collections

From drones, whose cameras can peek over privacy hedges and into second-storey windows, to panoramic drones, which create beautiful cinematography, the advance of drone technology has raised the connections between copyright and privacy to new levels of concern. While drones can be used for diverse purposes, including as machines to transport balloons in parades,[119] their use as aerial camera platforms also invite paparazzi, nosy neighbours and law enforcement to take invasive photos and post them before the subject knows he has been under observation.

---

116 See also Anti-Photography and Video Voyeurism Act 2009 (Philippines), ss 3(d) and 4 (providing criminal penalties for 'selling, copying, reproducing, broadcasting, sharing, showing or exhibiting' photos, videos or recordings capturing specified private sexual acts or 'similar' activity 'without the written consent of the person/s involved, notwithstanding that consent to record or take photo or video coverage of same was given by such persons').

117 See Corbett, above n 111.

118 Copyright Act 1994, s 105.

119 Jordan Crook 'Disney Files Patents to Use Drones in Park Shows' (27 August 2014) Tech Crunch techcrunch.com.

Combined with new biometric identification techniques, drone photography eliminates the anonymity crowds or personal property fences might otherwise provide. Yet the current focus on regulating drones as aerial devices by the United States, the EU and diverse Asian Pacific countries often ignores the reality of their use for civil surveillance. To the contrary, present regulations largely focus on the control of air space above 400 feet, and have relatively few have provisions regarding personal privacy. One notable exception is an Ordinance specifically enacted in 2015 by the City of Chicago (Chicago Ordinance), Illinois, to address, among other issues, the threat to privacy posed by unregulated civilian drone activity. The Preamble expressly recognised that 'drones can be equipped with highly sophisticated surveillance technology that threatens privacy'.[120]

To combat this threat the Chicago Ordinance provides that no one 'shall operate … any small unmanned aircraft in city airspace … for the purpose of conducting surveillance, unless expressly permitted by law'.[121] It further provides an expanded definition of 'surveillance' designed to reach all potential intrusions:[122]

> 'Surveillance' means the gathering, without permission and in a manner that is offensive to a reasonable person, of visual images, physical impressions, sound recordings, data or other information involving the private, personal, business or familial activities of another person, business or entity, or that otherwise intrudes upon the privacy, solitude or seclusion of another person, business or entity, *regardless of whether a physical trespass onto real property* owned, leased or otherwise lawfully occupied by such other person, business or other entity, *or into the airspace above real property* owned, leased or otherwise lawfully occupied by such other person, business or other entity, occurs in connection with such surveillance.

The Chicago Ordinance also prohibits operating small, unmanned aircraft 'directly over any person who is not involved in the operation of the small unmanned aircraft, without such person's consent'[123] or 'over property

---

120 Office of the City Clerk, City of Chicago 'Amendment of Municipal Code Title 10 by adding new Chapter 10-36 to regulate use of small unmanned aircraft in City airspace' (29 July 2015) SO2015-5419 at 2; Chicago, Illinois, Municipal Code, art 1036-400.
121 Article 1036-400(b)(12).
122 Article 1036-400(a) (emphasis added).
123 Article 1036-400(b)(2).

that the operator does not own, without the property owner's consent, and subject to any restrictions that the property owner may place on such operation'.[124] A 'small unmanned aircraft' is defined as:[125]

> an aircraft that (1) is operated without the possibility of direct human intervention from within or on the aircraft, and (2) weighs less than 55 pounds at the time of the operation, including the weight of any payload or fuel.

Gliders and small aircraft tethered by a wire or rope are expressly excluded from the Ordinance.[126]

New Zealand has created a similar Civil Aviation Rule, requiring persons operating a 'remotely operated aircraft' to:[127]

> avoid operating in airspace above persons who have not given consent for the aircraft to operate in that airspace; and above property unless prior consent has been obtained from any persons occupying that property or the property owner.

Similar to the Chicago Ordinance, the Rule defines the covered aircraft as 'radio controlled' ones and excludes 'model aircraft' and 'free flight aircraft'.[128]

Although Chicago's Ordinance and New Zealand's Civil Aviation Rule prohibit unauthorised flights over people and property, similar to other civilian drone regulations that include privacy concerns within their scope,[129] they do not provide remedies if the results of an authorised overflight are posted on the internet or otherwise published. Some countries may provide some, but not complete, relief under privacy or related laws.[130] Fortunately, the outputs of drones and other surveillance technologies include photographic images and audio recordings that are potentially regulatable under copyright regimes. Thus, their takedown

---

124 Article 1036-400(b)(3).

125 Article 1036-400(a).

126 Article 1036-400(a). Penalties for violating the Ordinance include fines from US$500 to US$5,000 for each offense, and/or incarceration for a term not to exceed 180 days: art 1036-400(d).

127 Civil Aviation Rules 1990, r 101.207.

128 Rule 101.1.

129 See European Aviation Safety Agency '"Prototype" Commission Regulation on Unmanned Aircraft Operations' (22 August 2016) EASA www.easa.europa.eu.

130 See HDCA, above n 83, s 24(2) (allowing quick takedown of images that 'cause serious emotional distress'); Standing Committee on Social Policy and Legal Affairs *Eyes in the Sky* (The Parliament of the Commonwealth of Australia, July 2014) at n 10 (detailing state laws governing surveillance that might be used to challenge such images).

might be possible under a reformed NTD regime discussed above, applying the same normative principles for removal of photographic images that invade personal privacy. Where the invasive materials consist of audio recordings, the normative rules would be different. Assuming that the recorded sounds consist of words, and not just ambient sounds, there is little doubt that such recordings by a drone could be copyright protectable. But there would be less need to reconfigure creativity or authorship norms per se. Instead, the recording by drones could be considered merely a mechanical act, recording without creative input, so that the owner/operator of the drone would have no authorship rights. Instead, the speakers would be the authors of any captured recording.[131]

4.4 Fair Use, Fair Dealing and the Public Interest in Privacy

Fair use or fair dealing considerations based on unauthorised uses of copyrighted works represent the most obvious normative alteration that the inclusion of privacy considerations would present. Privacy considerations have already begun to be recognised as a viable third-party interest to be protected against overzealous protection of copyrighted works in the heightened scrutiny applied to requests for end-user identity subpoenas[132] and to efforts applied to combat pirated works on the internet.[133] However, in the context of fair use or fair dealing considerations, privacy concerns might militate against the application of such exceptions, particularly where the underlying work at issue also breaches certain privacy rights. In such cases, privacy concerns would not be the sole factor in determining whether any particular work qualified for an exception under copyright. To the contrary, other factors currently considered in determining whether a particular use is fair, including categorical exceptions for such diverse categories as satire or parody, research, scholarship, current news, security

---

131 In the United States, the present obligation that a work be 'fixed' to qualify for copyright protection, and that such fixation is 'by or under the authority of the author', DMCA, above n 12, §§ 101–102, would need to be altered for this result to apply.

132 See *Sony Music Entertainment Inc v Does* 1-40, 326 F Supp 2d 556, 564-65 (2d Cir 2004) (requires evaluation of the 'concrete[ness of the plaintiff's] showing of a prima facie claim of actionable harm', consideration of 'alternative means' to secure the requested identity disclosure and an express evaluation of the objecting party's expectation of privacy); *BMG Canada, Inc v John Doe*, above n 31 (similar requirements for disclosure); Case C-275/06 *Promusicae v Telefonica de Espana SAU* [2008] ECR I-54 (similar requirements for disclosure).

133 Case C-275/06 *Promusicae v Telefonica de Espana SAU* [2008] ECR I-54, at 70 ('[Relevant] Directives … do not require the Member States to lay down … an obligation to communicate personal data in order to ensure effective protection of copyright in the context of civil proceedings').

testing and the like, would remain critical factors. But privacy interests would represent a strong 'thumb' on the copyright fair use/fair dealing balance. The strength of this factor could be balanced by the same types of considerations that currently regulate the protections given personal data.

We already have examples in numerous regimes aimed at protecting personal data privacy in which special categories of information have been granted heightened protection. For example, under art 8 of the EU Directive on Data Privacy, sensitive personal information relating to the following categories are subject to extremely narrow processing rights:[134]

1. racial or ethnic origin;
2. political opinions;
3. religious or philosophical beliefs;
4. trade-union membership;
5. data concerning health or sex life; and
6. data relating to offenses, or criminal convictions.

Article 9 of the GDPR provides greater detail about these protected data categories and includes genetic data, biometric data for the purpose of uniquely identifying a natural person and sexual orientation.[135] Other countries in the Asia Pacific that provide heightened protection for 'personal sensitive information' have included additional categories, reflecting expanded norms for such protection. For example, Australia includes 'membership of a political association', sexual orientation or practices and biometric templates.[136] Japan includes a crime victim's history and contains a catch-all category 'other sensitive information that may lead to social discrimination or disadvantage'.[137] The Philippines includes 'age' and 'philosophical affiliations' and expands sensitive information regarding 'offenses' to specifically include those that have only been 'alleged'.[138] China includes 'biometric information', 'personal financial and real estate information', 'health and physiological information', 'sexual orientation', 'undisclosed criminal records' and all personal information about minors (under the age of 14).[139]

---

134 Directive 95/46/EC on the protection of individuals with regard to the processing of personal data and on the free movement of such data [1995] OJ L 281/31, art 8 [Data Privacy Directive].
135 GDPR, above n 21, art 9.
136 Federal Privacy Act 1988 (Cth), s 6(1).
137 Act on the Protection of Personal Information and Amendments 2015 (Japan), art 2(3).
138 Data Privacy Act 2012 (Philippines), s 3(l)(1).
139 Personal Information Security Specification, above n 27, at Appendix B.

While personal data privacy in these instances focuses on categories of *data* for heightened protection,[140] the California State 'Online Eraser' Statute establishes a protected class of subjects entitled to greater protection.[141] Chapter 22.1(a) of the California Business and Professions Code obligates the OSP of a site or application 'directed to minors' or who has 'actual knowledge' that a minor is using its services to remove content posted by the minor on the minor's request.[142] A minor is defined as any California resident under the age of 18.[143] There is no obligation that the content be created by the minor, or that the content breach the minor's privacy or otherwise cause any type of embarrassment or emotional harm. To the contrary, the purpose for the Online Eraser Statute is to allow those who are underage to remove whatever they might have posted that they now regret for whatever reason. The removal right is not an absolute one. It does not obligate the OSP to remove copies of the posting that appear on other websites. But it does recognise that minors should be subject to special protections given their age and general immaturity of judgment regarding personal privacy boundaries.

These nuanced considerations could be added into an expanded fair use or fair dealing balance that considers the public interest, including the public interest in privacy. Thus, for example, where the original work is an unauthorised image of a minor engaged in sexual activity, the heightened interest in protecting minors against the embarrassment and harm that such privacy violations could cause might well argue against any fair use.

Privacy considerations could also alter the balance in the ability to use unpublished, private works under a fair use or fair dealing exception. Privacy considerations do not necessarily prohibit fair use accommodations for the use of unpublished works. But they do suggest that, just as the nature of the data at issue receives variable protection under privacy regimes, the nature of the work under fair use should be considered. Where that nature is 'private', in the sense that it has not been published or otherwise distributed or communicated publicly, or where it deals with subject matter of an extremely private personal nature (perhaps as represented

---

140 Children's Online Privacy Protection Rule 16 CFR 312; Children's Online Privacy Protection Act of 1988, 15 USC 6501–6505.
141 California Business and Professions Code, ch 22.1.
142 § 22581.
143 § 22580(f).

by the categories of sensitive data contained in data privacy collection laws discussed above), then personal privacy issues should be given greater consideration.

For those countries with strong moral rights that include the right of divulgation (first publication), such as France,[144] or some variation such as New Zealand's special moral rights for photographs,[145] unpublished works are already prevented from unauthorised publication. However, since the right of divulgation is not included in the obligatory moral rights protections under the Berne Convention,[146] such protection is not required. Indeed, this right may not even be protectable under the relatively flexible 'balancing test' for fair use utilised by the United States,[147] the Philippines,[148] Taiwan[149] and South Korea,[150] among others.

The United States fair use provision has provided the template for the fair use balancing test internationally. Under this balancing test, the question of whether any use is considered a 'fair' one under copyright is determined by balancing four statutory factors. They are:[151]

1. The purpose and character of the use, including whether such use is of a commercial nature or is for nonprofit educational purposes;

2. The *nature of the copyrighted* work;

3. The amount and substantiality of the portion used in relation to the copyrighted work as a whole;

4. The effect of the use upon the potential market for, or value of, the copyrighted work.

Although the 'nature' of the work is considered, presently such consideration is generally limited to the factual nature of the work. Where a work is considered more factual in nature, such as directories, software codes and

---

144 Code de la Propriété Intellectuelle (France), art L-121-2 ('The author alone has the right to disclose his work'); Copyright Act 2016 (Taiwan), art 15 ('The author shall enjoy the right to publicly release the work').

145 Copyright Act 1994, s 105.

146 Berne Convention, above n 2, art 6*bis* (limiting obligatory moral rights to integrity and patrimony).

147 DMCA, above n 12, § 107; see *Swatch Group Management Services Ltd v Bloomberg LP* 756 F 3d 73 (2d Cir 2014) where an injunction was denied to halt distribution of private recording due to public interest in access to financial information.

148 Intellectual Property Code, Republic Act No. 8293 (Philippines), s 185.

149 Copyright Act 2016 (Taiwan).

150 Copyright Act 1957 (South Korea), art 35*ter*(2).

151 DMCA, above n 12, § 107 (emphasis added).

the like, an end user can use a greater portion of it and still have such use qualify as a fair one. By adding privacy as a consideration in fair use determinations, the nature of the work would go beyond a simple question of whether the work was more fictive or factual in nature. It would also consider the personal nature of the work and any indicia of the author's desire for its continued secrecy. Like other factors, the unpublished nature of the work or its private or unconsented nature would not be an absolute bar to a fair use/fair dealing exception. But such private nature would not be given such short shrift as it receives currently in some countries, including the United States.[152] Although including privacy considerations would not automatically lead to a finding against fair use, it would at least require more than outright dismissal of an author's interest in maintaining such privacy. For those countries that utilise a fair dealing approach, care in assuring that categories of acceptable uses do not implicitly permit the use of private works, in publication status or its private subject matter, should achieve the same result.

The normative inclusion of the private nature of the subject matter at issue in a case of fair use or fair dealing would represent a contrary trend toward the current international push to secure greater flexibility in the rights of the public to utilise others' works. This trend is strongly represented by the current trend in the United States to recognise fair use for 'transformative' uses that have included the unauthorised digitisation of copyrighted works.[153] Including privacy considerations as part of a fair use or fair dealing norm, however, would assure that determinations reflect a careful balance between public access to information and personal dignity represented by increased protection against unauthorised uses that implicate sensitive private information.

4.5 Resolving the Technical Protection Measures Debate: Considerations of Personal Data Privacy in Access Debates

Since the earliest days of digital media, content owners have attempted to shield their copyrighted works from unauthorised uses through technology. From debates over the requirements of copy controls on digital audio players to the present arms race in encryption and other

---

152 § 107 (The private unpublished nature of the work 'shall not itself bar a finding of fair use').
153 *Authors Guild v Google Inc* 804 F 3d 202 (2d Cir 2015).

technologies to prevent unauthorised access, technology has always been perceived, rightly or wrongly, as a potential solution to digital piracy.[154] Even the first multilateral treaty to deal with copyright protection in the 'Digital Age', the WCT, set forth a positive obligation on signatories to 'provide adequate legal protection and effective legal remedies against the circumvention of effective technological measures that are used by authors in connection with the exercise of their rights'.[155] This obligation has been reiterated in all subsequent WIPO-administered Treaties dealing with copyrighted content.[156]

The protection of technological protection measures (TPMs) remains a contested issue. Two major areas of contention are the scope of rights to be protected by such TPMs and the application of fair use/fair dealing exceptions to circumvent such measures. Consideration of privacy issues could significantly alter the analysis in both areas.

As noted above, under art 11 of the WCT, only TPMs erected to protect 'the exercise of [author's] *rights*' are covered.[157] This language undeniably includes encryption and other technological measures designed to prohibit unauthorised reproduction or performance of a streamed or downloaded work. It does not, however, mandate protection of TPMs that restrict *access* to copyrighted works. Copyright owners are not granted the express right to prohibit 'access' to their works under either international or domestic regimes. Such right of access implies a right to prohibit the 'use' of a work. But such 'use' right is not, per se, a recognised one under copyright.[158] To the contrary, if a work is publicly available, the copyright owner cannot lawfully stop an end user from reading a lawfully acquired copy of the work, or from using the *information* in that work.

In art 6 of the EU's InfoSoc Directive, protected technological measures were defined as:[159]

---

154 See Corbett, above n 18.
155 WCT, above n 8, art 11.
156 WPPT, above n 9, art 18; Beijing Treaty, above n 10, art 15.
157 WCT, above n 8, art 11 (emphasis added).
158 Doris Estelle Long 'When Worlds Collide: The Uneasy Convergence of Creativity and Innovation' (2009) 25 J Marshall J Computer & Info L 653.
159 InfoSoc, above n 13, art 6 (emphasis added).

any technology, device or component that, in the normal course of its operation, is designed to prevent or restrict acts, in respect of works or other subject matter, which are not authorised by the rightholder of any copyright or *any right related to copyright as provided for by law* or the sui generis right provided for in the [Database Protection Directive].

Similar to the language of art 11 of the WCT, access or use rights are not included among the rights expressly protected under these measures. Section 226(a) of New Zealand's Copyright Act similarly defines a TPM as 'any process, treatment, mechanism, device, or system that in the normal course of its operation prevents or inhibits *the infringement of copyright* in a TPM work'.[160] China also prohibits the intentional circumvention of TPMs 'adopted by a copyright owner … to protect the copyright or the rights related to the copyright in the work to protect the copyright'.[161] The rights defined under New Zealand's copyright laws do not include 'access' or 'use' rights.[162] Neither do those under China's copyright laws.[163]

By contrast, s 1201 of the United States DMCA expressly prohibits the circumvention of TPMs designed to 'control access' to a copyrighted work[164] or to protect 'a *right* of a copyright owner'.[165] Several Asian Pacific countries provide for similar protection for access control measures, including Australia,[166] Singapore,[167] South Korea[168] and Taiwan.[169] The United States, however, provides potentially the strongest protection for such access measures because it rejects any fair use exceptions to permit circumvention of access protection TPMs. Section 1201(a)(1)(A) expressly provides: 'No person shall circumvent a technological measure that

---

160 Copyright Act 1994, s 226(a) (emphasis added). But see Trans Pacific Partnership Amendment Act 2016, s 226AC (establishing anti-circumvention protection for an 'access control TPM'). The Amendment does not come into force until the Trans Pacific Partnership comes into force in New Zealand (see s 44); The Comprehensive and Progressive Agreement for the Trans-Pacific Partnership (CPTPP) (signed 8 March 2018, not yet entered into force), however, expressly suspended art 18.68 which covers anticircumvention measures: at art 2. It is uncertain whether this provision will become effective; see Corbett, above n 18.

161 Copyright Law of the Peoples Republic of China (China), art 48(6).

162 Copyright Act 1994, ss 29–39.

163 Copyright Law of the Peoples Republic of China (China), arts 10 and 48.

164 DMCA, above n 12, § 1201(a).

165 § 1201(b).

166 Copyright Act 1968 (Cth), s 116AN.

167 Copyright Act 1987 (Singapore), art 261B.

168 Copyright Act 1957 (South Korea), art 2(28).

169 Copyright Act 2016 (Taiwan), art 80*ter*. For a discussion of the potential expansion to protection for access control TPMs in New Zealand, see Corbett, above n 18.

effectively controls access to a work protected under this title.'[170] As the United States Copyright Office recognised in its Executive Summary of the DMCA:[171]

> [S]ince the fair use doctrine is not a defense to the act of gaining unauthorised access to a work, the act of circumventing a technological measure in order to gain access is prohibited.

The ultimate impact of this distinction was to make protection for access-restrictive measures stronger than those for rights-restrictive ones.[172]

One of the sharpest debates to date remains the balance to be struck between protection of technological measures to reduce piracy and access rights, particularly those supported by fair use or fair dealing considerations. Privacy considerations would undoubtedly impact the normative balance struck between protection and access. Similar to its impact on other fair use or fair dealings discussed above, privacy considerations could have a strong impact on the categories of materials to be excluded from any fair use exceptions to circumvention controls. For instance, greater protection for TPMs might be desirable where they are used to protect copyrighted works that also pose serious privacy threats if breached. For the same reason, however, privacy issues might resurrect the desirability of expanding protected TPMs from rights-based to access-restrictive ones at least for certain types of private information whose dissemination should remain in the hands of the copyright owner.

The normative inclusion of the private nature of the subject matter at issue with regard to TPMs would represent a contrary trend toward the current international push to secure greater flexibility in the rights of the public to access TPM-protected works in certain cases. But it could also be used to draw a clearer normative line between works that are deserving of heightened protection (because of their sensitive subject matter) and those for which fair use/fair dealing rights should be allowed. Such addition, however, would not fully answer the issue of how to secure fair

---

170 DMCA, above n 12, § 1201(a)(1)(A); see also *Universal City Studios Inc v Corley* 273 F.3d 429 (2d Cir 2001).

171 United States Copyright Office *The Digital Millennium Copyright Act of 1998: US Copyright Office Summary* (December 1998).

172 See *The Chamberlain Group Inc v Skylink Technologies Inc* 381 F 3d 1178, 1201 (Fed Cir 2004), which held that only access-restrictive TPMs that 'bear a reasonable relationship to the protections that the Copyright Act otherwise affords copyright owners' fell within the scope of the DMCA § 1201 protections.

use/fair dealing access while maintaining anti-circumvention measures as a viable method for protecting copyrighted works. It could, however, provide needed illumination on why this issue still matters.

4.6 Distributional Controls, Transformations and Injunctive Relief

As noted above, privacy considerations could significantly alter the normative scope of NTD processes designed to assist in the protection of copyright interests in the 'Digital Age'. Yet the impact of such considerations on enforcement mechanisms would not be limited solely to this admittedly critical issue. To the contrary, adding privacy issues into normative reforms in copyright could directly impact critical questions regarding the scope of relief available for infringing uses. In short, it could impact the extent to which copyright owners would be entitled to injunctions against the continued unauthorised use of copyrighted materials.

One of the most consistent debates over the scope of protection afforded copyrighted works is whether such works represent property rights for which injunctive relief against unauthorised uses should be available or whether liability rules that impose money damages are sufficient.[173] Even in the United States, injunctive relief is no longer always granted in cases of copyright infringement. Instead, courts examine whether irreparable harm will occur to the copyright owner.[174] Historically, such harm was presumed to occur. Currently, courts not only require that copyright owners 'show that, on the facts of their case, the failure to issue an injunction would actually cause irreparable harm'.[175] Courts must also consider the public interest:[176]

> The object of copyright law is to promote the store of knowledge available to the public. But to the extent it accomplishes this end by providing individuals a financial incentive to contribute to the store of knowledge,

---

173 See Tracy Lewis and JH Reichman 'Using Compensatory Liability Rules to Stimulate Innovation in Developing Countries' in Keith Maskus and JH Reichman (eds) *International Public Goods and Transfer of Technology under a Globalized Intellectual Property Regime* (Cambridge University Press, Cambridge, 2005).
174 See *eBay Inc v MercExchange LLC* 547 US 388 at 392–393 (2006) ('This Court has consistently rejected invitations to replace traditional equitable considerations with a rule that an injunction automatically follows a determination that a copyright has been infringed').
175 *Salinger v Colting* 607 F 3d 68 at 82 (2d Cir 2010).
176 At 82.

the public's interest may well be already accounted for by the plaintiff's interest. The public's interest in free expression, however, is significant and is distinct from the parties' speech interests … Every injunction issued before a final adjudication on the merits risks enjoining speech protected by the First Amendment.

If privacy considerations were added into the irreparable harm/public interest balance, depending on the subject matter of the work at issue, injunctive relief might become more readily available. 'Liability rules' that favour the imposition of what amounts to a compulsory licence for the use of the infringed work might be preferable where a work has a non-speculative commercial value that can be readily calculated. But if the work also poses a serious threat to the public's interest in personal privacy, such compulsory licences would be wholly inappropriate. For example, the public interest in limiting the harm caused by the dissemination of works that qualify as sexting or revenge porn would support injunctions against their further distribution.

Alternatively, depending on their subject matter, privacy considerations could well be used to deny enforcement to the holders of copyright in such works. Many countries, including the United States, refuse to enforce copyright in works that are considered obscene or pornographic.[177] Similar denials of enforcement could be extended to works such as surveillance videos or depictions of private sexual activity that represent a serious violation of personal privacy rights. At its most extreme, revised copyright norms might even deny subject matter eligibility to works that present the greatest threat to personal privacy.

Adoption of enforcement norms that decline enforcement on the grounds of the private nature of the materials could serve as a useful adjunct to other normative protections discussed previously. At a minimum, they would prevent aggressive cyberbullies and revenge porn posters from securing relief under declaratory relief actions when their posts are challenged. But these provisions are only supplementary and should not take the place of NTDs and other methods for reforming copyright to protect personal privacy.

---

177 *Devil's Films Inc v Nectar Video* 29 F Supp 2d 17 (SDNY, 1998).

5 Conclusion

The rapid change in technology over the past several decades has rewritten the practical realities of the role of copyright in today's global digital environment. As countries struggle to reform present norms, derived largely from an older hard goods–focused world, new inputs are needed to assure that the reconfigured regimes created today accurately reflect present realities and future possibilities. Among those 'new' inputs should be a consideration of the interrelationship between copyright and personal and data privacy.

There has always been a tangential relationship between copyright and personal privacy regimes in connection with identity disclosures of potential infringers. Yet over time, this relatively slight relationship has expanded to the point where privacy considerations are beginning to influence international copyright norms. Such considerations have already begun to change the boundaries of authorial rights in the 21st century. Their formal inclusion as part of the normative background for present efforts at copyright reform is long overdue and could add clarity and even new paradigms for the future. Privacy norms have the possibility of significantly changing present copyright norms by adding new issues and new points of view.

Yet simply adding privacy issues into the copyright reform 'mix' and adopting some of the norms discussed in this chapter is only the first step in creating a normative framework for copyright that avoids the empty promises of the 1990s. To create copyright laws that will survive the next technological revolution, we must create a harmonised reformation, a code, that will assure that these critical normative changes are incorporated across borders. Merely creating a patchwork of reformed laws in some countries based on new privacy-informed regimes may be better than making no change at all, but it disserves the borderless realities of the digital environment. Fortunately, the task is made easier in the Asia Pacific because a draft Copyright Code for the region has already been created by Professor Adrian Sterling.[178] This Code provides the critical framework of foundational norms that could be examined and potentially strengthened through a reconsideration of the current separation between copyright and privacy laws. If we truly want to create copyright laws for

---

178 Adrian Sterling 'Asian Pacific Copyright Code' in this volume.

the 21st century, we must be brave enough to complete the entire task. Anything less will simply leave the work for another generation. Given how quickly technology moves, I am not certain we can wait that long.

5

Free Trade Agreements with the United States, Rulemaking and TPMs: Why Asian Pacific Nations Should Resist Increased Regulation of TPMs in their Domestic Copyright Laws

Susan Corbett[1]

1 Introduction

The draft Asian Pacific Copyright Code (draft Code)[2] draws on international copyright treaties and agreements (the most recent of which were drafted in the 1990s and brought into force in the early 2000s)[3] to provide guidance on the minimum standards to be achieved in the copyright laws in the region. The draft Code is brief, however, and there is much potential for extending its scope to cover important areas of

---

1   Copyright © 2018 Susan Corbett. Associate Professor of Law in the School of Accounting and Commercial Law, Victoria University of Wellington and founder member and President of the Asian Pacific Copyright Association.
2   See Adrian Sterling 'Asian Pacific Copyright Code' in this volume.
3   WIPO Copyright Treaty 2186 UNTS 121 (opened for signature 20 December 1996, entered into force 6 March 2002) [WCT] and the WIPO Performances and Phonograms Treaty 2186 UNTS 203 (adopted 20 December 1996, entered into force 20 May 2002) [WPPT].

copyright that have increased in international significance since the 1990s. Accordingly, this chapter considers how copyright laws in the Asian Pacific region should regulate the use of anti-circumvention technologies – that is, technological measures that permit users to access copyright works that are protected by technological protection measures (TPMs).

A more conceptual question is whether it is appropriate or necessary to provide additional protections by way of anti-circumvention regulation in copyright law to the owners of all works that are already physically protected by TPMs. An alternative suggestion is that the anti-circumvention provisions in copyright law should be limited in their application. Anti-circumvention provisions should apply only to those TPM-protected works in regard to which the copyright owners have formally agreed to facilitate TPM circumvention for users who provide written confirmation that their proposed use of the work falls within one of the permitted exceptions in the relevant copyright legislation. Thus, similarly to inventors who choose to keep their invention a trade secret and thereby reject the temporary legal monopoly provided by the patent system, the copyright owner of a TPM-protected work who is not willing to instruct the manufacturer of the work to facilitate circumvention for legitimate purposes must accept the possibility that a third party might reverse-engineer or 'circumvent' the TPM. Unfortunately, however, due to the requirements of extant free trade agreements (FTAs) that have mandated strong anti-circumvention measures for TPM-protected works, this suggestion may not be tenable, at least for the present.

Members of the legal academy have recently begun to question the appropriateness of international copyright agreements and treaties created in a pre-digital era.[4] Some call for a new paradigm for copyright laws. Others argue that new business models must be developed alongside changes in copyright laws.[5] The regulation of TPMs, I suggest, should be a particular target of these proposals and would perhaps encourage renegotiation of the relevant terms in FTAs.

---

4   See Peter K Yu 'The Copy in Copyright' in Jessica C Lai and Antoinette Maget Dominicé (eds) *Intellectual property and access to im/material goods* (Edward Elgar, UK, 2016) at ch 3; Alpana Roy 'Copyright: a Colonial Doctrine in a Postcolonial Age' (2008) 26(4) Copyright Reporter 112; and *What if we could re-imagine Copyright?* Kimberlee Weatherall and Rebecca Giblin (eds) (ANU Press, Canberra, 2017).

5   See Ian Hargreaves *Digital Opportunity: A Review of Intellectual Property and Growth* (UK Department for Business, Innovation and Skills, Independent Report, May 2011) [the Hargreaves Report]; and Nicola Searle *Changing Business Models in the Creative Industries: The cases of Television, Computer Games and Music* (UK Intellectual Property Office, October 2011).

Meanwhile, noting that some countries in the Asian Pacific region are already bound by, or are considering entering into FTAs with the United States (a net copyright-exporting country),[6] this chapter warns that countries that are net importers of copyright works should be wary of amending their laws in ways that will result in their citizens being placed at a disadvantage compared to United States' citizens.

Focusing on New Zealand as an example, this chapter describes the anti-circumvention provisions that New Zealand had proposed to introduce into its copyright law to comply with the Trans-Pacific Partnership (TPP) (now replaced by the Comprehensive and Progressive Trans-Pacific Partnership (CPTPP)).[7] The chapter contrasts New Zealand's proposed amendments to comply with the TPP and their impact on copyright users in New Zealand with the Digital Millennium Copyright Act (DMCA), the outcome of the 2015 rulemaking process and the effect on copyright users in the United States.[8] Fortuitously for users in the Asian Pacific region more generally, the CPTPP suspends the requirements for Parties to provide more extensive protections to TPMs, pending further agreement.[9] Nevertheless, the discussion in this chapter remains pertinent, since the influence of United States law on international copyright is pervasive and may well form part of further discussions when Parties to the CPTPP renegotiate the suspended provisions.

The chapter is structured as follows: the next part explains the nature of, and the debate around, TPMs as well as the important role played by circumvention devices and the influence of copyright clauses in FTAs with the United States on increasingly draconian anti-circumvention laws

---

6   Existing FTAs with the United States are in place in Australia, Korea, Myanmar and Singapore. Negotiations are underway for FTAs with the United States in Malaysia, while in Thailand negotiations for a Thailand – United States FTA are currently suspended: see 'Free Trade Agreements' Asian Regional Integration Center aric.adb.org.

7   Trans-Pacific Partnership (signed 4 February 2016, version 26 January 2016) [TPP]. The official signed version is not yet public. The 26 January 2016 version is the 'legally verified text' that can be found on the website of the Ministry of Foreign Affairs and Trade (MFAT) 'Text of the Trans-Pacific Partnership' (26 January 2016) New Zealand Trans-Pacific Partnership www.tpp.mfat.govt.nz. For the legally verified text of the Comprehensive and Progressive Trans-Pacific Partnership (signed 8 March 2018, not yet in force), released on 21 February 2018, see www.mfat.govt.nz/en/trade/free-trade-agreements/free-trade-agreements-concluded-but-not-in-force/cptpp/comprehensive-and-progressive-agreement-for-trans-pacific-partnership-text/ [CPTPP].

Following the withdrawal of the United States from the TPP the remaining 11 countries – Australia, New Zealand, Brunei Darussalam, Canada, Chile, Japan, Malaysia, Mexico, Peru, Singapore and Vietnam – have now signed the CPTPP.

8   Digital Millennium Copyright Act 17 USC § 1201 [DMCA].

9   See CPTPP, art 2 and Annex 7(h) suspending TPP, art 18.68.

that are being introduced into domestic legislation. Part 3 describes the current anti-circumvention provisions in the New Zealand Copyright Act 1994[10] and summarises the proposed amendments to those provisions that were intended to comply with the TPP. In Part 4, the equivalent provisions in United States copyright law that were introduced by the DMCA and the role of the rulemaking process are described.[11] Noting that the rulemaking process, which occurs every three years, increasingly moderates the impact of the DMCA for United States copyright users, I argue that, absent similar rulemaking processes, New Zealand and other Asian Pacific countries should be wary of introducing DMCA-compliant provisions into their respective copyright laws. Part 5 concludes by describing possible interim measures (that is, pending an eventual development of a new paradigm for copyright) that could be adopted by the Asian Pacific region to ensure its citizens are not disadvantaged by anti-circumvention laws.

2 TPMs and Circumvention Devices

2.1 Context

In the digital age, many authors and publishers argue (with some justification) that traditional copyright law is not adequate to protect their economic interests.[12] Although digital entities may be superficially indistinguishable from traditional analogue cultural entities, their underlying structure is very different. The high-level language program ('source code') for each digital entity varies depending upon both the programming language chosen and the unique characteristics of the particular entity but the machine-readable computer code ('object code') is always some form of combination of binary numbers. This characteristic means that digital entities can be easily and rapidly duplicated, combined with one another, adapted, transformed and distributed on the internet.[13]

---

10   Copyright Act 1994, ss 226–226E.
11   DMCA, above n 8.
12   See, for example, Peter K Yu 'Digital Copyright and Confuzzling Rhetoric' (2010–2011) 13 Vand J Ent & Tech L 881 at 918–939; Jessica A Wood 'The Darknet: A Digital Copyright Revolution' (2010) 16 JOLT 1 at 19.
13   For a detailed explanation of the technicalities of digitisation and its versatility in relation particularly to copyright works, see Peter S Menell 'Envisioning Copyright Law's Digital Future' (2002–2003) 46 NYL Sch Rev 63 at 108 and 114.

The opportunities for copyright infringement of digital works are almost unlimited and can take a plethora of forms, including using peer-to-peer (P2P) file-sharing technology to distribute and share digital media, cloud storage services allowing uploading of potentially infringing works and virtual private networks that allow users to hide their physical location and access geo-blocked copyright works. In essence, the widespread sharing of digital media files has weakened the effective strength of copyright law worldwide. Indeed, it is arguable that copyright law's traditional ex post provisions are largely ineffective in the digital environment. For example, P2P websites such as The Pirate Bay[14] and kickasstorrents[15] regularly switch domain names to avoid court orders requiring local internet service providers (ISPs) to block access to their original websites. Frequently the P2P sites display news of one another's re-emergence, thereby allowing their users to participate in the uninterrupted illegal sharing of digital media. Furthermore, users of the sites are able to circumvent blocked access, by using methods such as reverse proxies.[16] A recent example of exactly this situation is *Roadshow Films Pty Ltd v Telstra Corporation Ltd*,[17] in which the Federal Court of Australia applied a new provision of the Copyright Act 1968,[18] ordering Australia's largest ISPs[19] to block customer access to four movie torrent sites[20] but refusing to grant a rolling injunction that would have required the ISPs to also block mirror domains set up by the torrent sites.[21]

The very real fears of creators and distributors of digital works can be likened to the fears of authors and publishers when the use of photocopying became widespread and to those of the music publishers on the advent of the tape recorder. Producers of digital works have therefore increasingly turned to TPMs in an attempt to physically prevent unauthorised access to the underlying computer software.

---

14   The Pirate Bay thepiratebay.org (note: the URL changes frequently).

15   kickasstorrents kickasstorrents.to (note: the URL changes frequently).

16   Ernesto Van Der Sar 'Pirate Sites Remain Popular in the UK, Despite Website Blockades' (2016) Torrent Freak torrentfreak.com.

17   *Roadshow Films Pty Ltd v Telstra Corporation Ltd* [2016] FCA 1503, (2016) 122 IPR 81.

18   Copyright Act 1968 (Cth), s 115A.

19   Telstra, Optus, TPG and M2.

20   The Pirate Bay thepiratebay.org; Torrentz torrentz.eu; TorrentHound www.torrenthound.com; and IsoHunt isohunt.to. Note: all URLs change frequently.

21   Instead, the ISPs must apply separately for injunctions against mirror sites: see *Roadshow Films Pty Ltd v Telstra Corporation Ltd*, above n 17, at [13].

2.2 TPMs

The term TPM describes various types of digital technologies used by copyright owners to provide them with physical (ex ante) control over their copyright works, as opposed to relying on the unsatisfactory (ex post) prohibitions in copyright laws.

TPMs provide two categories of physical control: the first is intended to prevent unauthorised persons obtaining access to a work (access control TPMs), the second is intended to prevent acts protected by copyright (copy control TPMs). Typical TPMs include encryption (which allows only persons with the appropriate 'key', or code, to access a work) and technological copy controls (which allow authorised users to access a work but not to make copies). Due to the prevalence of computer software-driven devices and products in modern life, TPMs are ubiquitous and can be found in such diverse products as cars, medical devices, ebooks, toys and domestic appliances.

TPMs have been strongly criticised by the academy and the community for preventing legitimate 'permitted uses' of copyright works, such as fair use and fair dealing,[22] and for also preventing uses that are not rights pertaining to copyright, such as facilitating the avoidance of consumer protection laws.[23] A TPM can be used to support non–copyright related activities that are anti-competitive by, for example, locking protected products to a particular manufacturer or service provider.[24] Privacy concerns are also linked to some TPMs, which are used by businesses to collect data about their customers – often unbeknownst to the customer due to the activity taking place at a very deep level of the product.[25] Furthermore, a TPM is capable of protecting a copyright work for an infinite time, rather than being limited to the finite term of copyright provided by legislation, thereby potentially preventing copyrighted material from entering the public domain. TPMs thus present a challenge

---

22   See Louise Longdin 'Copyright and Fair Use in the Digital Age' (2004) 6(1) UABR 1; and Gideon Parchomovsky and Philip J Weiser 'Beyond Fair Use' (2010) 96 Cornell L Rev 91.

23   See Pamela Samuelson and Jason Schulz 'Should Copyright Owners Have to give Notice of their Use of Technical Protection Measures?' (2007) 6 JTHTL 41; Lucie Guibault and Natali Helberger *Copyright Law and Consumer Protection* (European Consumer Law Group, 2005).

24   Dan L Burk 'Anticircumvention misuse' (2003) 50(5) UCLA L Rev 1095; Dan L Burk 'Legal and Technical Standards in Digital Rights Management Technology' (2005–2006) 74 Fordham L Rev 537; Maryna Koberidze 'The DMCA Rulemaking Mechanism: Fail or Safe?' (2015) 11(3) Wash J of L Tech & Arts 213 at 225.

25   See Samuelson and Schulz, above n 23, at 50.

to users of copyright works, who argue that they are an overreaction by copyright owners, that they represent an unjustifiable restriction of users' rights and that the use of TPMs will inevitably lead to a reduction of the public domain of creative works and information.[26] Such arguments have driven the development of competing technological devices that are able to overcome or circumvent the TPMs put in place by copyright owners. These devices are termed 'circumvention devices'.

2.3 Circumvention Devices

Just as the TPM is capable of preventing both infringing and non-infringing uses of a copyright work, the potential use of a circumvention device is not confined to non-infringing uses: such a device can also provide the means for infringing copyright in a digital work. Common examples involve the circumvention, using mod chips,[27] of key encryption or scrambling technology installed to prevent the illegal copying of computer games.[28] Moreover, it takes only one person to successfully circumvent a TPM on a digital work, such as a movie on a DVD, for that unprotected movie to be distributed to thousands or millions of other users via P2P sharing.

The World Intellectual Property Organization's (WIPO) economic report on anti-piracy enforcement notes that in the 10 years following the creation of Napster in 1999,[29] sales of recorded music decreased globally by 50 per cent.[30] Similarly, after BitTorrent was created,[31] sales of DVDs and VHS (that had risen between 2000 and 2003) dropped by 27 per cent.[32] The report notes a general consensus among economists (based on synthesis of 21 studies in peer-reviewed journals)[33] that piracy negatively impacts sales across all media (to different degrees according

---

26   See, for example, Séverine Dusollier 'Electrifying the Fence: Legal Protection of Technological Measures for Protecting Copyright' (1999) EIPR 285; and Burk 'Anticircumvention Misuse', above n 24, at 1103.

27   Mod chips are devices that, when fitted to a games console, enable the user to play pirated games: see David Cran 'The modchips are down – Nintendo obtains summary judgment for circumvention of copyright protections' (2010) 21(8) Ent LR 315.

28   See *Nintendo Co Ltd and Nintendo of Europe GmbH v Playables Ltd and Wai Dat Chan* [2010] EWHC 1932 (Ch); *Stevens v Kabushiki Kaisha Sony Computer Entertainment* [2005] HCA 58.

29   Napster us.napster.com.

30   See Brett Danaher, Michael Smith and Rahul Telang *Copyright Enforcement in the Digital Age: Empirical Economic Evidence and Conclusions* WIPO/ACE/10/20 (2015) at 4 (citing Stan Liebowitz, *The Economics of Copyright* (Edward Elgar, UK, 2014)).

31   BitTorrent www.bittorrent.com.

32   Danaher, Smith and Telang, above n 29, at 4.

33   At 4.

to geographic regions, time periods, distribution and media).[34] Reports, such as the foregoing, have encouraged the creative industries to lobby strenuously for amendments to copyright laws that would prevent the use of circumvention devices.[35]

Although earlier research reported by Nicola Searle suggested that new business models in the creative industries appeared to have led to a reduced reliance on copyright laws,[36] Searle's latest research suggests otherwise.[37] In a recent posting on the IPKat law blog,[38] Searle describes her surprise at finding that, 'while the creative industries have lobbied against changes to copyright, very little has changed by way of business models'.[39] The seeming lack of initiatives taken by the creative industries to develop new business models in the face of challenging new technologies is puzzling. Seemingly, it indicates that the industries are content to continue their reliance on copyright law, despite the certain knowledge that developments in the law will always lag behind technological developments.

As early as 1996, confronted with an increasing desire by publishers to make use of digital technology to distribute copyright works, WIPO held a diplomatic conference to consider how the law might be developed to provide adequate and effective protection for digital copyright works. The outcome of that meeting was the WIPO Copyright Treaty (WCT).[40] Article 11 of the WCT addresses TPMs and their circumvention:[41]

> Contracting Parties shall provide adequate legal protection and effective legal remedies against the circumvention of effective technological measures that are used by authors in connection with the exercise of their rights under this Treaty or the Berne Convention and that restrict acts, in respect of their works, which are not authorized by the authors concerned or permitted by law.

---

34   At 4.
35   See Publishers Association of New Zealand 'Submission to Foreign Affairs, Defence and Trade Committee on consultation document: Implementation of the Trans- Pacific Partnership Intellectual Property Chapter'; see also Barry B Sookman and Daniel G C Glover 'TPMs are Alive and Well: Canada's Federal Court Awards Nintendo $12.57-million in Damages' (March 2017) Lexology www.lexology.com.
36   Searle, above n 5.
37   Nicola Searle 'A Tale of Stability – Business Models in the Creative Industries' (15 June 2017) The IPKat ipkitten.blogspot.co.nz.
38   IPKat ipkitten.blogspot.co.nz.
39   Searle, above n 37.
40   WCT, above n 3.
41   Article 11.

The objective of art 11 is clear: the rights of copyright authors (or owners) must be protected, while those of copyright users, art 11 implies, are of lesser importance. Indeed, the final words of art 11 suggest that authors have far-reaching 'rights' worthy of protection by TPMs and that their 'rights' are not confined to 'rights protected by law'. Unfortunately, however, many countries that have introduced TPM regulation into their domestic laws have implicitly taken the emphasis of art 11 on the rights of owners to extreme levels, sometimes of their own accord, but more often due to the requirements of the United States as a condition of its entering into an FTA with that country.

The importance of intellectual property to the global economy is reflected by the inevitable presence of an intellectual property chapter in bilateral and multilateral FTAs. The United States, a net exporter of copyright works, leads many such agreements and requires contracting states, many of which are copyright importers, to strengthen their intellectual property laws to be equivalent to the United States' laws.[42] The strengthened anti-circumvention laws required by the United States in its FTAs with other states generally conform to the equivalent provisions in the DMCA.[43] However, such requirements do not explicitly acknowledge the outcomes of the rulemaking process that moderates the anti-circumvention provisions of the DMCA for specific classes of users of certain copyright works every three years.[44]

An example is the TPP, a free trade agreement that was intended[45] to facilitate free trade and investment between 12 countries, including the United States, New Zealand and five other countries from the Asian Pacific region.[46] Notably, once the United States joined the TPP

---

42 This situation is well-traversed in academic literature. See, in regard to Thailand, Noppanun Supasiripongchai 'The development of the provisions on the protection of technological protection measures (TPMs) in the light of the prospective Thailand – United States Free Trade Agreement (FTA) and its possible impacts on non-infringing uses under copyright exceptions in Thailand: what should be the solution for Thailand?' (2013) 19(1) CTLR 21. In regard to the Australia – United States Free Trade Agreement (AUFSTA), see Susan Corbett 'Copyright law in Australia: What price free trade?' (2004) 4(1) NZIPJ 5. In regard to the Korea – United States Free Trade Agreement (KORUS), see Dae-Hee Lee 'KORUS FTA and Copyright Protection in Korea' in C Antons and R M Hilty (eds) *Intellectual Property and Free Trade Agreements in the Asia-Pacific Region* (Springer, New York, 2015).

43 DMCA, above n 8.

44 DMCA, above n 8, § 1201.

45 The TPP did not come into force following withdrawal of the United States, but has been replaced by the CPTPP – see text to n 7 above.

46 TPP, above n 7; the other 10 countries are Australia, Brunei Darussalam, Canada, Chile, Japan, Malaysia, Mexico, Peru, Singapore and Vietnam.

negotiations,[47] it assumed a leadership role and demanded changes to the intellectual property laws of the other 11 countries to provide parity with its own intellectual property laws.[48] However, a few months prior to the signing of the TPP, the United States Register of Copyrights released her recommendation to the Librarian of Congress relating to the sixth round of rulemaking on exemptions from the anti-circumvention provisions of the DMCA.[49] The rule, which came into force on 28 October 2015, permits exemptions from the anti-circumvention provisions for 10 additional classes of copyright works – the highest number to date.[50]

In essence, by its use of the rulemaking process, the United States provides a more user-friendly copyright environment than appears in the DMCA for its own citizens.[51] Conversely, the United States requires, in the form of intellectual property chapters in its negotiated FTAs, rigorous protections for TPMs in the domestic copyright laws of other jurisdictions, most of which are copyright-importing nations.[52]

The following Part describes the anti-circumvention provisions in the New Zealand Copyright Act 1994 (the Copyright Act) and the proposed changes to that Act that were intended to comply with the requirements of the TPP.[53]

3 New Zealand Anti-Circumvention Law

3.1 Background

In 2008, following a review of the Copyright Act, new provisions were inserted to address the issue of TPMs and to implement the requirements of the WCT.[54] Although New Zealand had not formally acceded to

---

47   The United States joined the negotiations in February 2008 but withdrew from the TPP Agreement on 23 January 2017; see David Smith 'Trump withdraws from Trans-Pacific Partnership amid flurry of orders' *The Guardian* (online ed, UK, 23 January 2017).
48   The TPP was signed by the then 12 participating countries on 4 February 2016.
49   Jacqueline C Charlesworth *Exemption to Prohibition on Circumvention of Copyright Protection Systems for Access Control Technologies* (Library of Congress, US Copyright Office, 37 CFR 201, 28 October 2015); DMCA, above n 8, § 1201.
50   § 1201.
51   DMCA, above n 8.
52   See Steven Seidelberg 'US perspectives: TPP's Copyright Term Benefits US, Burdens Others' (23 March 2015) Intellectual Property Watch www.ip-watch.com.
53   Copyright Act 1994; TPP, above n 7.
54   Copyright Act 1994, ss 226, 226A–226E; WCT, above n 3.

the WCT, the Ministry of Economic Development (MED), which led the review process, had stated its intention to adopt a deliberate policy of taking into account the provisions of the WCT, while 'addressing particular concerns for New Zealand copyright stakeholders'.[55]

The new provisions expanded the prohibition formerly contained in s 226 of the Copyright Act ('copy-protection'), to cover not just unauthorised copying, but all the exclusive rights of the copyright owner and replaced the term 'copy-protection' with 'technological protection measure (TPM)'.[56] This term is described in the amended s 226, in very broad language, as 'any process, treatment, mechanism, device, or system that in the normal course of its operation prevents or inhibits the infringement of copyright in a TPM work'.[57] However a process, treatment, mechanism, device or system that controls access for non-infringing purposes such as geographic market segmentation is not a TPM.[58]

A TPM circumvention device is defined as a device or means that is primarily designed, produced or adapted for the purpose of enabling or facilitating the circumvention of a TPM and that has only limited commercially significant application, except for its use in circumventing a TPM.[59] Trafficking in circumvention devices, or information about circumvention devices, is prohibited if the trafficker knows or has reason to believe that the device, service or information will be, or is likely to be, used to infringe copyright in a TPM work.[60] Notably, because the definition of TPM does not include access control, anti-circumvention provisions have no bearing on devices that assist with access.

It is noteworthy that the actual *use* of a circumvention device is not prohibited (although if the device should be used to make infringing copies, that activity would of course be actionable by the copyright owner or licensed issuer of the work). Indeed, if a person has a device or means specifically designed to circumvent copy-protection in his or her possession and a licensed issuer of TPM works believes that the person is

---

55   Ministry of Economic Development *Digital Technology and the Copyright Act 1994 Position Paper* (December 2002).
56   Copyright Act 1994, s 226; Copyright (New Technologies) Amendment Act 2008, s 90.
57   Copyright Act 1994, s 226(a).
58   Section 226(b).
59   Section 226.
60   Sections 226A(1), (2) and (3).

intending to use the device to make infringing copies, then the issuer may seek an order for delivery up of the device in the same way as a copyright owner may apply for delivery up in relation to an infringing copy.[61]

The Copyright Act provides limited exceptions in that the rights of issuers of TPM works do not 'prevent or restrict the exercise of a permitted act' or:[62]

> the making, importing, sale, or letting for hire of a circumvention device to enable a qualified person to exercise a permitted act on behalf of a user of a TPM work, or to undertake encryption research.

'Qualified person'[63] means the librarian of a prescribed library,[64] the archivist of an archive[65] or an educational establishment.[66]

Finally, the current TPM provisions provide options for a person who wishes to exercise a permitted act but is prevented from doing so by a TPM – they are instructed to apply for assistance from the copyright owner or licensee. If the assistance is not forthcoming in a reasonable time, they may engage a qualified person to exercise the permitted act on their behalf.[67]

Contrary to MED's stated position, the anti-circumvention provisions place an extraordinary amount of power in the hands of issuers of TPM works at the expense of the public good side of the traditional copyright balance. Without the ability to obtain circumvention devices or information about how to circumvent a TPM, the average citizen has no practical way of making use of the provision that allows them to exercise a permitted act.[68] It seems impractical and complex, to say the least, for each person who wishes to exercise a permitted act (assuming that 'permitted act' is intended to refer to all activities described in Part 3 'Acts permitted in relation to copyright works')[69] to try to get assistance from the issuer and then to 'engage a qualified person to exercise the act on their behalf',[70] particularly when the categories of 'qualified person' are so restricted.[71]

---

61 Section 226B(3).
62 Section 226D.
63 Section 226D.
64 For 'prescribed library' see s 50(1).
65 For 'archive' see s 50(1).
66 For 'educational establishment' see s 2(1).
67 Sections 226E(1) and (2). Encryption researchers have an additional exemption: s 226E(3).
68 Section 226D.
69 Part 3; s 226D.
70 Section 226E(2)(b).
71 Section 226D.

Somewhat surprisingly, however, the anti-circumvention provisions presently in the Copyright Act have not, to date, been controversial – there has been no outcry by New Zealanders about the anti-trafficking provisions, for example. There have been no recorded disputes or judicial hearings. However, this situation may change, if and when the TPP Agreement Amendment Act 2016 (TPPA Act) comes into force.[72]

3.2 Proposed Amendments – The TPP Agreement Amendment Act 2016

On 12 May 2016, the Trans-Pacific Partnership Agreement Amendment Bill 2016,[73] described as 'an omnibus bill that amends New Zealand law as part of the implementation of the free trade agreement named the Trans-Pacific Partnership Agreement', was introduced to the New Zealand Parliament.[74] The Bill passed through all stages of the legislative process and is listed as the Trans-Pacific Partnership Agreement Amendment Act 2016 (the TPPA Act),[75] although it states that it will not come into force until the date on which the TPP enters into force for New Zealand.[76]

The New Zealand legislature moved swiftly to draft the TPPA Act, which proposes changes to the Copyright Act to comply with the requirements of the TPP.[77] Many of the proposed amendments are contentious and worthy of debate (but may have been suspended following the abandonment of the TPP and the uptake of the CPTPP in its place). This chapter, however, focuses on the provisions of the TPPA Act that were intended to introduce new anti-circumvention measures into the existing Copyright Act.[78] For simplification, from here on in this chapter these proposed anti-circumvention measures are referred to as the 'suspended TPM amendment provisions'.

---

72 At the date of writing, the Act is not in force.

73 Now the Trans-Pacific Partnership Agreement Amendment Act 2016 [TPPA Act] – which will come into force on 'the date the TPP Agreement enters into force for New Zealand': s 2.

74 Trans-Pacific Partnership Agreement Amendment Bill 2016 (133-3); 'Trans-Pacific Partnership Agreement Amendment Bill' New Zealand Parliament www.parliament.nz.

75 TPPA Act 2016; TPP, above n 7.

76 TPPA Act 2016, s 2. At the time of writing, the situation is not clear. One presumes that the TPP Act will be extensively amended to take account of the failure of the TPP to come into force and its recent replacement by the CPTPP (see text to n 7 above).

77 TPPA Act 2016; Copyright Act 1994; TPP, above n 7.

78 TPPA Act 2016, ss 38–43, (implementing the TPP, art 68, which is now suspended by the CPTPP); Copyright Act 1994; see also Jessica C Lai 'The Development of Performers' Rights in New Zealand: Lessons for the Asian Pacific Region?' in this volume.

Article 18.68 of the TPP required Parties to introduce strict restrictions on the trafficking of TPMs and the use of access control TPMs and to provide increased penalties for activities that are carried out in disregard of those restrictions.[79]

Parties were, however, permitted to provide exceptions from criminal and civil liability for breach of the TPM provisions by non-profit libraries, museums, archives, educational institutions and public non-commercial broadcasting entities, provided the activities were carried out in good faith and without knowledge that the activity was prohibited.[80] Finally, the TPP allowed parties to create limitations and exceptions to the new TPM provisions to enable 'non-infringing uses' but only where there was an actual or likely adverse impact on those non-infringing uses and after considering whether there were means of making non-infringing uses without circumventing TPMs.[81] Furthermore, additional exceptions were not permitted to undermine the protection of TPMs or the effectiveness of remedies against TPM circumventors.[82]

The circumvention activities that would be permitted for New Zealand users, if the TPPA Act had come into force in its unamended form,[83] are similar to but in some instances exceed those afforded to United States' copyright users by the DMCA itself (ignoring the rulemaking amendments to the DMCA).[84] Nevertheless, the suspended TPM amendment provisions in the TPPA Act are onerous and exceed the requirements of both the WCT and the TPP.[85]

The TPPA Act, in its current form, also proposes to extend the application of the TPM provisions to include TPM-protected performers' rights[86] (a performer will be treated as an issuer of a TPM work if their performance is fixed in a TPM sound recording).[87]

---

79   TPP, above n 7, art 18.68 paras 1(a) and (b). Note that the CPTPP suspends the implementation of the TPP, art 18.68.

80   Article 18.68 para 1(b). Confusingly, exceptions from civil liability for these institutions are required to be subject to a proviso that the activities 'are carried out in good faith without knowledge that the conduct is prohibited'.

81   Article 18.68 paras 4(a) and (b).

82   Article 18.68 para 4(c).

83   TPPA Act 2016; see also TPP above n 7.

84   DMCA, above n 8; see also Supasiripongchai, above n 42.

85   TPPA Act 2016; WCT, above n 3; TPP, above n 7; however the TPPA Act 2016 is likely to be extensively amended to take account of the CPTPP, see above n 76.

86   TPPA Act 2016, s 38, which proposes replacing the Copyright Act 1994, s 226.

87   TPPA Act 2016, s 40, which proposes amending the Copyright Act 1994, s 226B and inserting new s 226B(6). See further Lai, above n 78.

Finally, and more significantly, the TPPA Act in its current form exceeds the requirements of the TPP, as its provisions are clearly intended to apply to both *access* control and *copy* control TPMs.[88]

In order to ensure that the proposed new TPM regime will apply to both physical and online distribution, the definition of 'issuer of a TPM work' will be amended to include a copyright owner or a person licensed by the copyright owner who issued a copy to the public, or who communicated the TPM work to the public.[89]

The TPPA Act includes a new definition of an 'access control TPM' and defines 'TPM' as:[90]

> an access control TPM, or a technology, device, or component that, in the normal course of its operation, prevents or inhibits the infringement of copyright in a TPM work or of any specified performers' rights (other than a technology, device, or component that can, in the normal course of its operation, be circumvented accidentally).

Under the existing Copyright Act, one is not permitted to provide a circumvention device or service knowing that it will be used 'to infringe copyright' in a TPM work.[91] The suspended TPM amendment provisions (should they come into force) will explicitly allow providers of circumvention devices and of services to circumvent a TPM to make them available to users for non-infringing purposes.[92] This proposed change is a positive step, as it resolves the situation created by the original provision that had prevented the ordinary user from being able to access circumvention devices for non-infringing purposes. A similar provision is proposed that will permit a person to circumvent an access control TPM for non-infringing purposes.[93]

---

88 TPPA Act 2016, s 38, which proposes replacing the Copyright Act 1994, s 226A and inserting new s 226AAA; TPP, above n 7.

89 TPPA Act 2016, s 38, which proposes replacing the Copyright Act 1994, s 226.

90 Proposed new s 226(1) of the Copyright Act 1994 (see TPPA Act 2016, s 38). The bracketed exception aligns with the definition of the word 'effective' in the TPP text, above n 7: both the DMCA, above n 8, and TPP, above n 7, limit their definitions of TPM as one that provides 'effective' control. Arguably, the TPPA Act 2016 is overly complex and in addition it is not clear whether the exception applies to the whole of the definition of TPM or only to the phrase 'specified performers' rights'.

91 Copyright Act 1994, s 226A.

92 TPPA Act 2016, s 39 which proposes replacing the Copyright Act 1994, s 226A with new ss 226A, 226AB and 226AC.

93 TPPA Act 2016, s 39 which proposes replacing the Copyright Act 1994, s 226A.

The TPPA Act in its current form proposes to insert new permitted exceptions into the Copyright Act that roughly align with the existing exceptions in the DMCA, though they are described in broader terms.[94] In addition, the TPPA Act proposes to explicitly permit circumvention of a TPM for acts permitted under Part 3 of the existing Copyright Act 1994 and for any act that 'otherwise does not infringe copyright in the TPM work and does not infringe any specified performers' rights in the TPM work'.[95]

The TPPA Act will permit circumvention of a TPM that controls geographic market segmentation.[96] In this regard, New Zealand has chosen not to follow the route of the United States, the United Kingdom and Australia, where producers such as Sony have relied on anti-circumvention provisions in copyright legislation to prevent the circumvention of equipment fitted with regional zone coding TPMs, despite there being no copyright infringement.[97] The New Zealand Government, however, considers that this prohibition would be inconsistent with its parallel importing policy.[98]

The proposed TPPA Act in its current form provides for the making of regulations for new exceptions and the modification or removal of any existing TPM exceptions, but does not describe any mandatory considerations, the review process or the timing.[99] These provisions will be reinforced by minor amendments to s 234 of the Copyright Act 1994, which already provides for the Governor-General, by Order in Council, to make regulations for various purposes.[100] The Select Committee considering the TPP Amendment Bill stated:[101]

---

94   TPPA Act 2016, s 41 which proposes inserting new ss 226F to 226L into the Copyright Act 1994; Copyright Act 1994; DMCA, above n 8.

95   TPPA Act 2016, s 41, which proposes inserting new s 226E into the Copyright Act 1994.

96   TPPA Act 2016, s 41, which proposes inserting new s 226F into the Copyright Act 1994.

97   For example, in Australia see *Kabushiki Kaisha Sony Computer* Entertainment v Stevens (2003) 57 IPR 161.

98   TPPA Act 2016; see 'Parallel Importing in New Zealand' (22 September 2016) Ministry of Business, Innovation and Employment www.mbie.govt.nz. Other provisions include circumvention by the Crown for the purposes of law enforcement and national security, for encryption research, circumvention of embedded software in relation to goods and services (thereby enabling consumer self-help) provided the circumvention does not infringe copyright and enabling circumvention of TPM-protected computer programs that are no longer supported by a remote server: see TPPA Act 2016, s 39, which proposes inserting new ss 226G, 226H and 226I into the Copyright Act 1994.

99   TPPA Act 2016, s 44, which proposes inserting new ss 226K and 226L into the Copyright Act 1994.

100 Copyright Act 1994, s 234; see new ss 234QA and 226QB (Trans-Pacific Partnership Agreement Amendment Bill 2016 (133-3), cl 44).

101 Trans-Pacific Partnership Amendment Bill (133-2) (select committee report) at 2.

This regulation-making power would future-proof the regime as technology can change very quickly. We recommend amending section 234(c) to include two factors that the Minister must consider when recommending regulations under section 234(1)(qa) and (qb). Those factors are the proposed effect on the dissemination of works and the use of non-infringing works. We also recommend inserting section 234(6) to ensure that regulations made under this power would be subject to confirmation by Parliament. This would mean that the regulations would have a temporary effect unless confirmed by Parliament through a confirmation bill.

Section 234 of the Copyright Act, with the amendments proposed by the TPPA Act, may well be intended to approximate to the rulemaking provision contained in the DMCA.[102] Clearly, however, a *power* to make regulations, which has no specific timeline attached, is a much weaker regulatory mechanism than the *requirement* to review every three years that is mandated in the DMCA.[103] Should the TPPA Act come into force in its current form, thereby introducing TPM access control provisions into New Zealand copyright law, it is essential to re-evaluate the existing TPM exemptions and to equate the abilities of New Zealand citizens to circumvent certain TPM access controls with those permitted by the rulemaking provisions to United States citizens.[104]

In the following Part, I examine the existing permanent exceptions to the anti-circumvention provisions set out in the DMCA and the outcome of the most recent rulemaking, which has considerably extended those exceptions.[105]

4 United States Anti-Circumvention Law

The United States gave domestic effect to the WCT by means of the DMCA.[106] The DMCA, however, goes far beyond the requirements of the WCT (which requires only that countries provide 'adequate

---

102 Copyright Act 1994, s 234; DMCA, above n 8.
103 DMCA, above n 8.
104 TPPA Act 2016; see Table in Part 4.1 of this chapter for a comparison between United States Copyright Office *Section 1201 Rulemaking: Sixth Triennial Proceeding to Determine Exemptions to the Prohibition on Circumvention* (8 October 2015) [2015 Rules] and the proposed changes to be made by the TPPA Act 2016, should it come into force.
105 DMCA, above n 8; 2015 Rules, above n 104.
106 DMCA, above n 8, § 1201; WCT, above n 3.

protection' against the circumvention of TPMs),[107] in that it prohibits both the act of circumventing technological access controls and also that of manufacturing or distributing (perhaps even creating and making available) technologies whose primary use is to enable circumvention of technological protection systems.[108] Pamela Samuelson warns that the DMCA anti-circumvention provisions contain language very close to that 'rejected by the WCT's Diplomatic conference as overbroad and detrimental to the public domain'.[109] Since its inception, the DMCA's anti-circumvention provisions have been criticised as 'fiendishly complicated',[110] over-broad and unclear, 'creating new rights that are expansive and unprecedented',[111] thereby offering too much protection to authors and publishers at the expense of users of copyright works and constituting a threat to the public domain.[112] In particular, the DMCA prohibits circumventing a TPM that prevents access to a work – which is not a right protected by traditional copyright law.[113] The 'rights' of a copyright owner include copying a work, issuing it to the public, playing, showing or communicating a work to the public, or making an adaptation of a work.[114] They do not include a right to restrict access to the work per se (that is, once it has been released or communicated to the public).

Nevertheless, the DMCA does include certain permanent exceptions to each of the prohibitions.[115] Further, the act of circumventing a TPM that protects the rights of a copyright owner in a work or part of a work ('copy control') is not explicitly prohibited by the DMCA.[116] The reason for this different treatment is, in part, because Congress believed that to prohibit the conduct of circumventing copy controls would penalise certain non-infringing conduct, such as fair use. Indeed, the DMCA affirms that fair use and other existing defences to copyright infringement

---

107 WCT, above n 3, art 11.
108 Pamela Samuelson 'Intellectual Property and the Digital Economy: Why the Anti-Circumvention Regulations Need to be Revised' (1999) 14(2) Berkeley Tech L J 519 at 521.
109 Pamela Samuelson 'The US Digital Agenda at WIPO' (1997) 37 Va J Intl L 369 at 413 (cited in Burk 'Anticircumvention Misuse', above n 24, at 1103).
110 David Nimmer 'Riff on Fair Use in the Digital Millennium Copyright Act' (2000) 148(3) U Pa L Rev 673 at 675.
111 Burk 'Anticircumvention Misuse', above n 24, at 1103.
112 See Samuelson, above n 108, at 519.
113 DMCA, above n 8, § 1201(a)(1)(A).
114 Copyright Act 1994, s 16.
115 DMCA, § 1201.
116 DMCA, above n 8.

will not be affected by the anti-circumvention provision.[117] (Notably, however, in several decisions the United States courts have denied that fair use is an adequate rationale for circumvention of a TPM.)[118]

Other specific exceptions to the anti-circumvention provision in the DMCA are non-profit libraries that are open to the public, archives and educational institutions (for the limited purpose of making a decision whether or not to purchase a copy of the digital work for that institution's non-infringing purposes);[119] law enforcement, intelligence and other government activities;[120] the reverse engineering of a lawfully acquired computer program by the owner for the purpose of achieving interoperability with other programs;[121] encryption research;[122] protection of minors from internet materials (for example, safe search);[123] removal of capacity to collect or disseminate personally identifying information;[124] and security testing.[125]

However, there is another route by which the permanent exemptions in the DMCA may be expanded to include other classes of works and users. This route is the 'Section 1201 Rulemaking'.[126]

4.1 Background to the DMCA Rulemaking

In the face of widespread opposition to the DMCA's anti-circumvention provisions, the 1998 Report of the House Committee on Commerce on the DMCA[127] recommended that certain exceptions should be provided that would continue for three years from the coming into force of the provisions and that would ensure that the public would have continued ability to engage in non-infringing use of copyrighted works, such as fair use.[128]

---

117 DMCA, above n 8, § 1201(c)(1).
118 See *Universal City Studios Inc v Reimerdes* 111F Supp 2d 346 (SDNY 2000), affd 273 F 3d 429 (2d Cir 2001) at 457–458; and *MDY Indus LLC v Blizzard Entertainment Inc* 629 F 3d 928 (9th Cir 2010), 948–950.
119 DMCA, above n 8, § 1201(d).
120 § 1201(e).
121 § 1201(f).
122 § 1201(g).
123 § 1201(d).
124 § 1201(i).
125 § 1201(j).
126 § 1201.
127 Digital Millennium Copyright Act of 1998 (105-551) (Report of the Committee of Commerce) at 36.
128 Despite the fact that it is unclear whether DMCA, above n 8, § 1201 would in fact allow the development of technologies for such non-infringing use.

Congress therefore directed the Register of Copyrights to conduct a rulemaking proceeding, soliciting public comment and consulting with the Assistant Secretary for Communications and Information, during the two years between the enactment of the DMCA, on 28 October 1998, and the effective date of the anti-circumvention provisions. The specific areas to be examined by the Register are set out in the DMCA:[129]

i.   the availability for use of copyrighted works;

ii.   the availability for use of works for non-profit archival, preservation and educational purposes;

iii.   the impact that the prohibition on the circumvention of technological measures applied to copyrighted works has on criticism, comment, news reporting, teaching, scholarship or research;

iv.   the effect of the circumvention of technological measures on the market for or value of copyrighted works; and

v.   such other factors as the Librarian considers appropriate.

After reviewing all submissions, the Register concluded that a case had been made for granting exemptions in respect of only two classes of works, each of which, she explained, satisfied the statutory requirements that exceptions be granted only to 'particular classes of copyrighted works' and only where 'genuine harm to the ability to engage in non-infringing activity has been demonstrated'.[130] These classes were:

> compilations, consisting of lists of websites blocked by filtering software applications; and

> literary works, including computer programs and databases, protected by access control mechanisms that fail to permit access because of malfunction, damage or obsoleteness.[131]

Every three years the Register is required by the legislation to make a determination on potential new exemptions, followed by recommendations to the Librarian of Congress (the Librarian).[132]

---

129 §§ 1201(a)(1)(C)(i)–(v).

130 United States Copyright Office, Library of Congress 'Digital Millennium Copyright Act: Circumvention of copyright protection systems for access control technologies: exemption to prohibition' (27 October 2000) 65(209) *Federal Register* 64555 at 64563.

131 At 64562.

132 The Librarian is senior to the Copyright Register and as such is required to approve or not allow the Register's recommendations in regard to rulemaking.

The most recent (sixth) rulemaking proceeding was completed in October 2015 and was described by the Register as 'the most extensive and wide-ranging to date'.[133]

The exemptions granted by the 2015 rulemaking are summarised in the table below, which also shows proposed changes to be made to the Copyright Act 1994 by the TPPA Amendment Act (should it come into force):

Table 1: Summary of proposed changes to the Copyright Act 1994.

Exemptions granted in the Library of Congress DMCA 1201 Rules[1] (permitting circumvention of access control TPMs for non-infringing uses of copyrighted works)	TPPA Amendment Act 2016 (NZ) proposed comparable provisions to be introduced into the Copyright Act 1994[2] (permitting circumvention of access control TPMs for non-copyright infringing uses and non-performers' rights infringing uses)
Literary works distributed electronically (i.e. ebooks), for use with assistive technologies for persons who are blind, visually impaired or have print disabilities.	
Computer programs that operate the following types of devices, to allow connection of a used device to an alternative wireless network ('unlocking'): Cell phones, tablets, mobile hotspots, wearable devices (e.g. smartwatches).	Circumventing a TPM work that is a computer program embedded in a machine or device that restricts the use of goods or services [proposed new s 226I].
Computer programs that operate the following types of devices, to allow the device to interoperate with or to remove software applications ('jailbreaking'): Smartphones, tablets and other all-purpose mobile computing devices, smart TVs.	
Computer programs that control motorised land vehicles, including farm equipment, for purposes of diagnosis, repair and modification of the vehicle (effective in 12 months).	

133 The 2015 Recommendation of the Register of Copyrights to the Librarian of Congress comprised 400 pages: 2015 Rules, above n 104.

Exemptions granted in the Library of Congress DMCA 1201 Rules[1] (permitting circumvention of access control TPMs for non-infringing uses of copyrighted works)	TPPA Amendment Act 2016 (NZ) proposed comparable provisions to be introduced into the Copyright Act 1994[2] (permitting circumvention of access control TPMs for non-copyright infringing uses and non-performers' rights infringing uses)
Computer programs that operate the following devices and machines, for purposes of good-faith security research (effective in 12 months or, for voting machines, immediately): Devices and machines primarily designed for use by individual consumers, including voting machines, motorised land vehicles, medical devices designed for implantation in patients and corresponding personal monitoring systems.	
Video games for which outside server support has been discontinued, to allow individual play by gamers and preservation of games by libraries, archives and museums (as well as necessary jailbreaking of console computer code for preservation uses only).	Enabling functionality of computer programs that are no longer supported by a remote server (provided that the use of the goods or services does not infringe copyright in the program or any specified performers' rights) [new s 226J].
Computer programs that operate 3D printers, to allow use of alternative feedstock.	
Literary works consisting of compilations of data generated by implanted medical devices and corresponding personal monitoring systems.	
Motion pictures (including television programs and videos): For educational uses by college and university faculty and students, K–12 instructors and students, in massive open online courses (MOOCs) and in digital and literacy programs offered by libraries, museums and other non-profits; for multimedia ebooks offering film analysis; for uses in documentary films; for uses in non-commercial videos.	

[1] United States Copyright Office, Library of Congress 'Exemption to Prohibition on Circumvention of Copyright Protection Systems for Access Control Technologies' (28 October 2015) 80(208) *Federal Register* 65944.

[2] TPPA Act 2016, now likely to be substantially amended; see above n 76.

Source: Author's summary.

The rigour of the rulemaking process is illustrated by the fact that the Register declined to recommend six proposed classes of works – for either 'lack of legal and factual support for exemption' (audiovisual works for space shifting and format shifting, computer programs in video game consoles for jailbreaking purposes) or 'because incomplete record presented' (ebooks for space shifting and format shifting, computer programs that operate ebooks, for jailbreaking purposes, computer programs that operate 'consumer machines', music recording software that is no longer supported to allow continued use of the software).[134]

There is no doubt that the rulemaking process is lengthy, complex and expensive. The 2015 Register's Recommendation included comments and criticisms about the time-consuming administrative process noting that:[135]

> During the course of the rulemaking, the Office received nearly 40,000 comments. The written submissions were followed by seven days of public hearings in Los Angeles and Washington, D.C., at which the Office received testimony from sixty-three witnesses. [footnotes omitted]

Furthermore, there are flaws in the legislative requirements with which the Register must comply. For instance, the rules are restricted to cases of direct circumvention by a specified class of user – this means the Librarian may not allow rules to include the possibility of third party assistance with circumvention of a TPM work.[136] As technology becomes more complex and less accessible by a layperson, this restriction is problematic and anti-competitive. A simple example is that the law in its current form does not permit car mechanics to carry out repairs on vehicles if the fault to be addressed requires circumvention of a TPM.

Each rule is very specific, as exemplified by the 2015 rule for video games,[137] which is clearly designed for the expert in the field, whereas the average citizen would likely find it almost incomprehensible and therefore unusable.

---

134 United States Copyright Office *Understanding the Section 1201 Rulemaking* (28 October 2015) at 5.
135 2015 Rules, above n 104.
136 DMCA, above n 8, § 1201(a)(1)(E).
137 Library of Congress, United States Copyright Office, above n 133, at 65963.

The rulemaking process itself is controversial and potentially inconsistent. For example, in 2010 the Register recommended against renewing the exception for text-to-speech software, even though no opposition to the renewal had been received. This recommendation was, however, overruled by the Librarian.[138] Even more controversially, in 2012, the Register refused to renew the exemption that had been in place since the 2006 rulemaking permitting the unlocking of mobile phones by consumers to allow them to change wireless network carriers without permission from the original carrier linked to their device.[139] This refusal proved to be highly contentious and an extraordinary numbers of complaints from consumers persuaded Congress to introduce legislation to allow the unlocking of mobile phones.[140]

The Register's Recommendation in 2015[141] also raised concerns in that, while some exceptions sought related to the ability to access and make non-infringing uses of works such as movies and video games (a purpose that was foreseen by Congress), many other proposals for exceptions related to access for functionality, not creative content:[142]

> Many of the issues that were raised in this proceeding would be more properly debated by Congress or the agencies with primary jurisdiction in the relevant areas. Indeed, the present record indicates that different parts of the Administration have varying views on the wisdom of permitting circumvention for security research or to enable modification of motor vehicles … . The Register appreciates and agrees with NTIA's view that such concerns have at best a very tenuous nexus to copyright protection.

Two more general legislative challenges to the DMCA were introduced to the Senate in 2015: the Unlocking Technology Act of 2015 (intended to make the rulemaking process redundant)[143] and the Breaking Down

---

138 The Register has very little autonomy as her decisions are subject to review by the Library of Congress – for arguments that this is unsatisfactory, see, for example, *US Copyright Office: Its Functions and Resources* Serial No. 114-4, Hearing, 26 February 2015 at 35.

139 See Recommendation of the Register of Copyrights 'Section 1201 Rulemaking: Fifth Triennial Proceeding to Determine Exemptions to the Prohibition on Circumvention' October 2012 at 81.

140 Unlocking Consumer Choice and Wireless Competition Act 2014 Pub L No. 113-114, 128 Stat 1751 (2014).

141 2015 Rules, above n 104.

142 At 2–3.

143 Unlocking Technology Act of 2015, HR 1587, 114th Cong (2015). Significantly, for this chapter, the Bill also 'directs the President to ensure that applicable bilateral and multilateral trade agreements are modified to be consistent with this Act' at § 4.

Barriers to Innovation Act of 2015 (intended to improve the rulemaking process and expand existing statutory exceptions in the DMCA).[144] However, neither has progressed since April 2015.[145]

Although wary of the DMCA in principle, even its strongest critics concede that the three-yearly review process, which culminates in specific exceptions to the anti-circumvention provisions, has proved to be a positive move towards providing a balance between the public interest in cultural and educational matters and the economic interests of authors and publishers of digital copyright works.[146]

For the countries of the Asian Pacific region, however, the introduction of a similar three-yearly rulemaking procedure is impracticable. These countries are mainly net copyright importers with fragile economies. They do not have the resources, expertise or indeed the political will to introduce such a demanding procedure into their copyright laws. While New Zealand (similarly to at least some other Asian Pacific countries) includes in its copyright legislation a ministerial power to make new regulations as required, there is no formal requirement for this to be actioned.[147] Other jurisdictions in the Asian Pacific region that have already introduced copy control and access control regulation into their copyright laws in order to enter into FTAs with the United States include Australia,[148] Singapore[149] and South Korea.[150] None of these jurisdictions included a compulsory rulemaking process in their copyright law. Instead, Australia and Singapore include a 'power to make regulations', while South Korea does not appear to include any regulation-making possibilities.[151]

---

144 Breaking Down Barriers to Innovation Act of 2015, S 990, 114th Cong (2015).
145 There is also an ongoing review of copyright in the United States, which began in 2013 and has generated much public interest. Although the review addresses many issues, including rulemaking, obstructive costs, antiquated search and record systems, lack of funding, structure and role and so on, the review has been aptly described as 'more talk than action': see Kerry Sheehan 'This Year in U.S. Copyright Policy: 2016 in Review' (2016) Electronic Frontier Foundation www.eff.org.
146 See Pamela Samuelson 'Towards a New Deal for Copyright in the Information Age' (2002) 100 Mich Law Rev 1488 at 1499 and Joseph P Liu 'Regulatory Copyright' (2004) 83(1) NCL Rev 87 at 123.
147 Copyright Act 1994, s 234.
148 Copyright Act 1968 (Cth), s 116AN.
149 Copyright Act 1987 (Singapore), s 261B.
150 Copyright Act 2006 (South Korea), art 2(28).
151 For Australia see the Copyright Act 1968 (Cth), s 249. For Singapore, see a power to make regulations in connection with TPM regulation: Copyright Act 1987 (Singapore), s 261D(2).

Therefore, the remaining Asian Pacific nations must ideally 'get it right' in their domestic copyright laws from the outset and should not automatically agree to United States demands to strengthen their laws to comply with the DMCA.[152]

5 Summary and Conclusion

There is no doubt that TPMs present a challenge to traditional copyright laws and policies. For copyright owners, the TPM provides a practical alternative to copyright laws that fail to address the vulnerability of digital copyright works to large-scale infringements. Conversely, for users of copyright works, TPMs facilitate avoidance of fair use and fair dealing provisions and encourage eternal copyright, by preventing works falling into the public domain. Although recent amendments to copyright laws appear to partially address this challenge by allowing circumvention of TPMs in strictly prescribed situations, in practice the complexity of these amendments means they are unlikely to provide any real support to the average user of a TPM-protected work. As is typical of an international treaty, the requirements of the WCT are broad; for example, there is no definition of the terms 'adequate legal protection' or 'effective remedies'.[153] Furthermore, the manner of implementation of the WCT in member countries is not prescribed. Commonalities, however, are that, while certain exceptions to the *use* of circumvention devices are generally provided in domestic copyright laws, the *trafficking* (variously described as advertising, publishing or sale) of circumvention devices by third parties is prohibited. The lack of exceptions for trafficking is a serious defect as, in practice, it limits the ability to take advantage of the exceptions for use of circumvention devices to technical experts in the field.[154] Copyright user organisations, such as the Electronic Frontier Foundation, argue that anti-circumvention laws have caused 'substantial harm to consumers, scientific research, competition and technological innovation'.[155] Moreover, the Electronic Frontier Foundation claims, the harms to developing countries

---

152 DMCA, above n 8.
153 WCT, above n 3, art 11.
154 Supasiripongchai, above n 42, at 267.
155 'Electronic Frontier Foundation Briefing Paper on Technological Protection Measures Prepared for the WIPO Inter-Sessional Intergovernmental Meeting on the Development Agenda Proposal & Fourth Session of the Permanent Committee on Cooperation Related to Intellectual Property Development April 11–15, 2005' Electronic Frontier Foundation www.eff.org at 1.

that are forced to incorporate anti-circumvention laws into their copyright law 'will result in a transfer of wealth from domestic economies to foreign rights holders, without any guarantee of reciprocal investment in the local cultural economy'.[156]

As a net exporter of copyright works, in 1998 the United States addressed the claims of copyright producers by providing strict anti-circumvention measures in the DMCA, with limited support for the rights of users to circumvent TPMs. Public outcry led to the inclusion of the rulemaking provision in the DMCA, which, despite its many flaws, has achieved some moderation of the anti-circumvention measures for selected users. However, when entering into FTAs, the United States tends to require partner countries to introduce anti-circumvention measures that are equivalent to the provisions of the DMCA, neglecting to mention any moderation of those provisions that may have been provided by the current rulemaking. For this reason (inter alia of course), the countries of the Asian Pacific region, all of which are mainly copyright importers, must be cautious when entering into FTAs with the United States.

New Zealand, as a typical example, was preparing to pass into law the TPPA Act, which complies with United States requirements for all TPP Member States and includes more complex anti-circumvention laws in the proposed amendments to the Copyright Act 1994. Although the current TPPA Act attempts to address and affirm many of the rights of users of copyright works by permitting circumvention of TPMs in a plethora of circumstances, there remain many problems. These include that the legislation is complex and unlikely to be understood by the average citizen, that there are few powerful lobby groups of users in New Zealand and that there is a lack of political interest in copyright law (since as a net importer the benefits to the economy are less visible).[157] Thus, although the TPPA Act provides that (inter alia) the circumvention measures can be permitted by regulations[158] made on the recommendation of the Minister 'after consultation with persons who will be substantially affected by the

---

156 At 1.
157 That is not to say there are no benefits – education (which leads directly to economic improvements) being one of the main beneficiaries of copyright imports.
158 TPPA Act 2016, ss 41 (inserting new s 226L into the Copyright Act 1994) and 43 (amending Copyright Act 1994, s 234) (not yet in force).

regulations',[159] this provision is weak and does not have the reassurance provided by the compulsory rulemaking provision in the DMCA. In short, a *power* to introduce regulations is not the same as a *requirement* to review.

Thanks to the detailed rulemaking provision in the DMCA, intended to allow 'lawmakers to amend the law in a faster and more efficient manner than the traditional legislative process or court proceedings',[160] the United States, whose fair use provisions have always been much more extensive than the fair dealing provisions in New Zealand copyright law, may further overtake New Zealand in its concessions to educational and cultural users of copyright works in the digital age.

Finally, with the foregoing warnings in mind, I recommend that although the draft Asian Pacific Copyright Code provides that authors have the rights 'granted to them by relevant international instruments' (thereby incorporating art 11 of the WCT),[161] specific amendments to the Code should be made, as permitted by Clause D2 of the draft Code,[162] to ensure the users of copyright works in the Asian Pacific region will not be disadvantaged by TPM anti-circumvention laws – particularly those regulating access control TPMs.

159 Section 43 (amending Copyright Act 1994, s 234) (not yet in force).
160 Koberidze, above n 24, at 214–215.
161 See Sterling, above n 2, at cl C1; WCT, above n 3.
162 Sterling, above n 2, at cl D2.

Part 3: Users and Access

6

Harmony and Counterpoint: Dancing with Fair Use in New Zealand and Australia

Melanie Johnson,[1] Robin Wright[2] and Susan Corbett[3]

1 Introduction

This chapter considers whether introducing a fair use provision into Australia's and New Zealand's copyright laws would be beneficial, in particular for facilitating technological developments and international trade in each country. Although Australia considered and rejected the possibility of introducing fair use, largely to reduce the impact of its harmonisation with United States copyright laws when negotiating entry into the Australia – United States Free Trade Agreement (AUSFTA), the issue has since been revived.[4] Conversely, New Zealand has not, to date,

---

1   Copyright Officer, Libraries and Learning Services, University of Auckland, New Zealand. Copyright © 2018 Melanie Johnson, Robin Wright and Susan Corbett.
2   Copyright Manager, Swinburne University of Technology, Australia.
3   Associate Professor of Commercial Law, School of Accounting and Commercial Law, Victoria University of Wellington.
4   See Copyright Law Review Committee *Simplification of the Copyright Act 1968. Part 1: Exceptions to the Exclusive Rights of Copyright Owners* (1998) at [1.03] [CLRC]; The Joint Standing Committee on Treaties (JSCOT)—Parliament of Australia *Report 61: The Australia–United States Free Trade Agreement* (Report No. 61, June 2004) Rec 17; and Australian Law Reform Commission (ALRC) *Copyright and the Digital Economy* (ALRC Report No. 122, November 2013); Australian Productivity Commission *Intellectual Property Arrangements* (Inquiry Report No. 78, 2017).

given much detailed examination to the possibility of introducing fair use into the Copyright Act 1994. Yet for such close trading partners, it is desirable that their copyright laws should be similar. Indeed, under the Australia – New Zealand Closer Economic Relations Trade Agreement (CER), which is intended, inter alia, to remove technical barriers to trade between the two countries, it has become essential – to reflect the increasing trading reliance on new technologies and other intellectual property goods. Moreover, although New Zealand has not yet entered into a free trade agreement (FTA) with the United States, it has recently signed such an agreement with Japan (among other states),[5] another powerful copyright-exporting nation. Should this agreement come into force, New Zealand may also be encouraged to consider the potential benefits of introducing a fair use defence.

The role of FTAs is significant in the copyright context, as FTAs routinely include intellectual property provisions, primarily aimed at harmonising laws between trading partners in order to facilitate trade.[6] Inevitably this means that protections are increased to ensure the parties' laws are consistent with those of the major exporters of intellectual property: the United States, Europe and Japan.[7] It was companies from these countries that campaigned for the inclusion of an agreement on intellectual property rights in the Uruguay Round of Multilateral Trade Negotiations.[8] Those negotiations resulted in the Agreement on the Trade-Related Aspects of Intellectual Property Rights (TRIPS), which adopted minimum standards for patent protection, raised the levels of protection for copyright and trade marks, extended coverage to trade secrets, design protection and geographical indications, and instituted enforcement obligations.[9] Many of the minimum standards provided in TRIPS, however, were subsequently extended by the net-exporting countries in their domestic

---

5   The Comprehensive and Progressive Agreement for Trans-Pacific Partnership (signed 8 March 2018, not yet in force) [CPTPP].

6   Agreement on Trade-Related Aspects of Intellectual Property Rights 1869 UNTS 299 (adopted 15 April 1994, entered into force 1 January 1995) [TRIPS Agreement]. See Susan Corbett 'Free Trade Agreements with the United States, Rulemaking and TPMs: Why Asian Pacific Nations Should Resist Increased Regulation of TPMs in their Domestic Copyright Laws' in this volume.

7   Peter Drahos 'Expanding Intellectual Property's Empire: the Role of FTAs' (November 2003) International Centre for Trade and Sustainable Development ictsd.net at 6.

8   Drahos, above n 7, at 2 (12 US corporations were primarily responsible for the lobbying that brought TRIPS into being), citing Susan Sell *Private Power, Public Law: the Globalization of Intellectual Property Rights* (Cambridge University Press, Cambridge, 2003); and Peter Drahos 'BITS and BIPS: Bilateralism in Intellectual Property' (2001) 4 JWIP 791 at 798–799.

9   TRIPS was negotiated at the end of the Uruguay Round of the General Agreement on Tariffs and Trade [GATT] in 1994 and is administered by the WTO.

intellectual property laws. Unable to use TRIPS to force other nations to similarly extend the minimum standards, these countries began using FTA negotiations as a lever.

In 2016, New Zealand and Australia (along with 10 other nations)[10] signed the Trans-Pacific Partnership (TPP) Agreement that mandated strong levels of copyright protections for Member States, including requiring that the term of copyright protection would be the life of the author plus 70 years. Although the Australian copyright term had, under the terms of the AUSFTA, already been extended to life of the author plus 70 years,[11] the term of copyright protection under New Zealand law is the minimum required by TRIPS – that is, life of the author plus 50 years.[12] New Zealand subsequently passed an Act (the TPP Agreement Amendment Act 2016) to implement the TPP,[13] to 'send a clear message that we see value in a common set of high quality rules across the Asia-Pacific'.[14] Although the original TPP will not be implemented, following the withdrawal of the United States from the agreement,[15] the remaining TPP partners have since signed up to a revised agreement: the Comprehensive and Progressive Agreement for Trans-Pacific Partnership (CPTPP).[16] The New Zealand TPP Agreement Amendment Act (which was based on the TPP and includes provisions intended to strengthen the Copyright Act 1994 in favour of rights owners) has thus far remained on the books and may be brought into force, albeit in amended form, to comply with the CPTPP. The CPTPP does not, for example, require the introduction of an increased term of copyright protection and has also suspended the introduction of several other copyright provisions in the TPP.[17]

Australia had already increased many copyright protections, and extended its term of copyright protection, in response to United States requirements when it entered the AUSFTA in 2005. Since that time, several official

---

10   The other nations are the United States (which has since withdrawn), Canada, Mexico, Japan, Brunei Darussalam, Chile, Malaysia, Peru, Vietnam and Singapore.

11   Copyright Act 1968 (Cth), s 33.

12   Copyright Act 1994 (NZ), s 22.

13   The Trans-Pacific Partnership (signed 4 February 2016, version 26 January 2016) [TPP].

14   Todd McLay 'McLay says TPP Ratification Keeps Options Open' (Beehive press release, 11 May 2017).

15   The White House Press Office 'Statements and Releases' (28 January 2017) www.whitehouse. gov; and Donald J Trump 'Withdrawal of the United States from the Trans-Pacific Partnership Negotiations and Agreement' (2017) 82 Fed Reg 8497 [Presidential Memorandum].

16   For discussion, see Peter K Yu 'TPP, RCEP and the Future of Copyright Norm-setting in the Asian Pacific' in this volume and Corbett, above n 6.

17   See text to below n 90 and n 91.

bodies have recommended that the government should introduce a broader United States–style fair use or expanded fair dealing exception to counterbalance the increased protections for rights owners and to provide greater flexibility in a rapidly changing digital environment.[18] While in New Zealand calls for such an exception have also been made by various stakeholder groups,[19] unlike in Australia, there have been no official recommendations to introduce such an exception.

Currently, copyright legislation in both New Zealand and Australia includes fair dealing permitted exceptions, which are based on the British model.[20] The prescriptive nature of fair dealing exceptions means they cannot readily adapt to developments in technology. In essence, in order to provide user rights in relation to a new technological development, Parliament must amend the law – a complex and time-consuming process.

If Australia should adopt a fair use–type exception, as has been recommended most recently by both the Australian Law Reform Commission (ALRC) in 2012[21] and the Australian Productivity Commission in 2017,[22] should New Zealand follow suit? New Zealand and Australia entered into the CER in 1983.[23] The commitment of CER was to unify policy, laws and regulatory regimes in both countries. To date, however, there has been no attempt to unify the copyright laws (other than potential strengthening of copyright protections to comply with the CPTPP), as proposed in New Zealand's TPP Agreement Amendment Act.

This chapter will first give a brief of overview of the existing fair dealing provisions in Australia and New Zealand copyright laws and will describe recent changes to the legislation in both countries. Parts 4 and 5 will contrast fair dealing more generally with the arguments for introducing a fair use exception. Parts 6 and 7 will explain how other Asian Pacific countries have approached implementing user exceptions to make them more open and flexible and, as Ariel Katz has suggested, 'closer to the

---

18   CLRC, above n 4, at [1.03]; JSCOT—Parliament of Australia, above n 4; ALRC, above n 4; Australian Productivity Commission, above n 4.

19   See submissions on the Trans-Pacific Partnership (TPP) Agreement Amendment Bill 2016 made by: LIANZA [Library and Information Association of New Zealand Aotearoa], InternetNZ, Trade Me, Electronic Frontier Foundation, Universities New Zealand, Google www.parliament.nz.

20   Copyright Designs and Patents Act 1988 (UK).

21   ALRC, above n 4.

22   Australian Productivity Commission, above n 4.

23   John Belton 'Documentary Filmmakers' Statement of Best Practices for Fair Use' (2007) 19(2) Film History: An International Journal 144.

origins of fair dealing'.[24] In considering whether harmonisation of the copyright law of Australia and New Zealand is possible, with particular regard to fair use, the chapter concludes by examining whether or not introducing fair use would be in the best interests of each country.

2 Background

2.1 Fair Dealing

Copyright law in both New Zealand and Australia originated from the United Kingdom Imperial Copyright Act 1911. The Imperial Copyright Act provided that 'any fair dealing with any work for the purpose of private study, research, criticism, review or newspaper summary' did not constitute copyright infringement.[25] Australia declared the Imperial Copyright Act to be in force in the Copyright Act 1912 (Cth). New Zealand enacted a similar provision in s 5 of the Copyright Act 1913. Both New Zealand and Australia have continued to enact narrow permitted exceptions that are limited to specific users. This has resulted in systems where:[26]

> Rigidity is the rule. It is as if every tiny exception to the grasp of copyright monopoly has had to be fought hard for, prized out of the unwilling hand of the legislature and, once conceded, defined precisely and confined within high and immutable walls.

The provision of prescriptive fair dealing provisions for users of copyright works in jurisdictions that have adhered to the United Kingdom's model has been described thus:[27]

> Tragically, what was supposed to be an exercise in the codification of a dynamic and evolving common-law principle, usually referred to as 'fair use', ended up – with a few notable exceptions – in a hundred years of solitude and stagnation. Misinterpreting the 1911 Act, some courts and commentators in many Commonwealth jurisdictions adopted a narrow and restrictive view of fair dealing.

24   Ariel Katz 'Fair Use 2.0: The Rebirth of Fair Dealing in Canada' in Michael Geist (ed) *The Copyright Pentalogy* (University of Ottoway Press, 2013) 93.
25   Section 2(1)(ii).
26   Justice Laddie 'Copyright: Over-strength, Over-regulated, Over-rated' in David Vaver (ed) *Intellectual Property Rights: Critical Concepts in Law* (Taylor & Francis, Oxford, 2006) vol 2 at 104.
27   Katz, above n 24. See also Alexandra Sims 'Strangling Their Creation: The Courts' Treatment of Fair Dealing Since 1911' (2010) 2 IPQ 192.

Fair dealing itself is not defined in Australian or New Zealand copyright legislation: instead fair dealing exceptions are included for the purposes of research and private study;[28] criticism and review;[29] reporting news;[30] and additionally, in Australia, for the provision of professional advice by the legal practitioner, registered patent attorney or registered trademarks attorney.[31] Following its entry into the AUSFTA, Australia further expanded the limits and exceptions to infringement by adding fair dealing for the purposes of parody and satire,[32] and provided expanded permitted exceptions for private use and archiving.[33] A 2017 amendment to the Australian Copyright Act added another fair dealing exception for the purpose of access by persons with a disability.[34] New Zealand copyright law also provides several specific 'permitted exceptions' that operate outside the fair dealing paradigm but are nonetheless very prescriptive in their application.

The fair dealing model in Australia and New Zealand requires a two-stage analysis: first, whether the intended use qualifies for one of the permitted purposes provided for in the legislation, and second, whether the use itself meets the fairness criteria. For example, the New Zealand Copyright Act provides more detailed guidance for the courts when considering whether the copying of a copyright work for research or private study is 'fair dealing'.[35] For the criteria to apply regarding other purported 'fair dealing' uses, the legislation is silent – implying that whether a particular use is fair must depend on the circumstances.[36] As Lord Denning observed in *Hubbard v Vosper*:[37]

> It is impossible to define what is 'fair dealing'. It must be a question of degree. You must consider first the number and extent of the quotations and extracts. Are they altogether too many and too long to be fair? Then you must consider the use made of them. If they are used as a basis for comment, criticism or review, that may be a fair dealing. If they are used to convey the same information as the author, for a rival purpose, that may be unfair. Next, you must consider the proportions. To take long

---

28   Copyright Act 1968 (Cth), ss 40(1) and 103C(1); Copyright Act 1994 (NZ), s 43.
29   Copyright Act 1968 (Cth), ss 41 and 103A; Copyright Act 1994 (NZ), s 42.
30   Copyright Act 1968 (Cth), ss 42 and 103B; Copyright Act 1994 (NZ), s 42(2) and (3).
31   Copyright Act 1968 (Cth), ss 43, 104.
32   Sections 41A and 103AA.
33   Sections 43C and 103AA.
34   Copyright Amendment (Disability Access and Other Measures) Act 2017 (Cth), s 113E.
35   Copyright Act 1994 (NZ), s 43(3).
36   ALRC, above n 4, at [5.25]–[5.27].
37   *Hubbard v Vosper* [1972] 1 All ER 1023 (CA) at 1027.

extracts and attach short comments may be unfair. But, short extracts and long comments may be fair. Other considerations may come to mind also. But, after all is said and done, it must be a matter of impression. As with fair comment in the law of libel, so with fair dealing in the law of copyright. The tribunal of fact must decide.

These prescriptive ad hoc exceptions are less than satisfactory, as Alexandra Sims has commented in relation to the New Zealand Copyright Act:[38]

> First, the legislature cannot keep pace with the need to create exceptions. … In respect to sound recordings, the delay between the realisation of the need to create such an exception and the implementation has arguably been even slower: the practice of copying sound recordings to make compilation tapes was many decades old by the time the exception was created in 2008. Experience shows that there is often a 'lengthy delay' between the time a new use emerges and the legislature even considering whether a new exception is required.

In some countries[39] the original categories of fair dealing, set out in the 1911 Act, have now been replaced with a non-exclusive list of examples – as provided in the United States fair use exception.[40] In Australia and New Zealand, as discussed above, and in certain other countries the legislature provides factors that their courts must consider when determining whether a dealing is fair.

The requirement to apply a complex two-stage analysis to ascertain whether a use falls within a fair dealing exception – coupled with the prospect that some new uses, facilitated by new technologies, that would arguably be in the public interest to permit, are likely to fail to qualify for one of the circumscribed purposes – has encouraged some 'fair dealing countries' to consider whether to adopt fair use provisions or expand their fair dealing criteria.[41] South Africa, Ireland and the European Union are in the process of reviewing their copyright laws and each is considering issues around the adoption of fair use–like regimes. Four nations in the Asian Pacific region have already implemented fair use–type exceptions: Singapore, South Korea, the Philippines and Taiwan. In a few countries, the term

---

38   Alexandra Sims 'The Case for Fair Use in New Zealand' (2016) 24(2) Int J Law Info Tech 176.
39   Jonathan Band and Jonathan Gerafi *Fair Use/Fair Dealing Handbook* (policybandwidth, 2015).
40   17 USC § 107 – Limitations On Exclusive Rights: Fair Use.
41   Association of Research Libraries 'Copyright Timeline: A History of Copyright in the United States' www.arl.org.

'fair dealing' has been replaced with 'fair use'. In some countries, such as Canada and Kenya, the courts have interpreted the fair dealing provision in such a way that it is increasingly similar to a fair use provision.[42]

The next part describes the development of fair use as a statutory defence that permits limited uses of a copyright work without the consent of the copyright owner and explains its application in United States copyright law.

2.2 Fair Use

Both 'fair use' and 'fair dealing' developed out of common law, following the enactment of the English Statute of Anne in 1710.[43] The formal title of the Statute of Anne is 'An Act for the Encouragement of Learning, by Vesting the Copies of Printed Books in the Authors or Purchasers of Copies, during the Times therein Mentioned'. The phrase in the title 'for the encouragement of learning' reminds us of the importance of allowing scholarly access to copyright works and has, arguably, led to the inclusion of permitted uses, fair dealing provisions and fair use provisions in modern copyright legislation.

Until 1976, fair use played little part in United States copyright law. In 1976, however, a new United States Copyright Act extended the term of copyright, abolished the registration requirement for copyright protection, and codified fair use in s 107:[44]

> … the fair use of a copyrighted work, including such use by reproduction in copies or phonorecords or by any other means specified by that section, for purposes such as criticism, comment, news reporting, teaching (including multiple copies for classroom use), scholarship, or research, is not an infringement of copyright. In determining whether the use made of a work in any particular case is a fair use the factors to be considered shall include—

---

42   See *Communications Commission of Kenya & 5 others v Royal Media Services Limited & 5 others* [2014] eKLR; *CCH Canadian Ltd v Law Society of Upper Canada* [2004] 1 SCR 339, 2004 SCC 13, discussed in Victor B Nzomo *In the Public Interest: How Kenya Quietly Shifted from Fair Dealing to Fair Use* (WIPO-WTO IP Colloquium Research Paper Series, 1 December 2016) papers.ssrn.com; Michael Geist *Fairness Found: How Canada Quietly Shifted from Fair Dealing to Fair Use, The Copyright Pentalogy* (University of Ottawa Press, Ottawa, 2013), citing *Society of Composers, Authors and Music Publishers of Canada v Bell Canada et al* [2012] 2 SCR 326 at [27].

43   Copyright Act 1710 (UK) 8 Ann c 21.

44   17 USC § 107 – Limitations On Exclusive Rights: Fair Use.

1. the purpose and character of the use, including whether such use is of a commercial nature or is for nonprofit educational purposes;

2. the nature of the copyrighted work;

3. the amount and substantiality of the portion used in relation to the copyrighted work as a whole; and

4. the effect of the use upon the potential market for or value of the copyrighted work.

The fact that a work is unpublished shall not itself bar a finding of fair use if such finding is made upon consideration of all the above factors.

Fair use provides an open-ended exception under which any use may qualify as a fair use provided that it satisfies four factors designed to establish reasonable limits.[45] The interpretation of these criteria, which have some similarities with the three-step test criteria set out in art 9 of the Berne Convention and art 13 of the TRIPS agreement, has been developed through extensive case law.

Although all four factors in s 107 must be 'explored' and 'weighed together',[46] they need not all be satisfied. It is the first of the fairness factors, requiring consideration of the 'purpose and character' of the use, which is regarded as the 'heart of the fair use enquiry'.[47] Accordingly, United States courts first consider 'whether and to what extent the new work is transformative' – that is, whether it merely 'supersedes the objects' of the original or 'instead adds something new, with a further purpose or different character, altering the first with new expression, meaning or message'.[48]

3 Fair Dealing in Australia and New Zealand

3.1 New Zealand Legislation

It was not until 2008 that the New Zealand Copyright Act 1994 (the Copyright Act) was updated 'to clarify the application of existing rights and exceptions in the digital environment … [and to] … create a more technology-neutral framework for the Act' (the 2008 digital

---

45   17 USC § 107 – Limitations On Exclusive Rights: Fair Use.
46   *Campbell v Acuff-Rose Music Inc* (1994) 510 US 569 at 578.
47   *Blanch v Koons* 467 F 3d 244 (2d Cir 2006) at 251.
48   *Campbell v Acuff-Rose*, above n 46, at 579.

amendments).[49] Key changes made by the 2008 digital amendments were to extend the definition of 'copying' to cover digital copying of works in all forms; a new right of communication to the public; and a new category of work, 'communication work', which covers the previous rights of broadcast and cable programs, as well as communication to the public via other technologies.[50] The 2008 digital amendments also made changes to many of the permitted exceptions in Part 3 of the Copyright Act, including clarifying that educational institutions and libraries and archives could create, store and communicate digital copies to authenticated users;[51] and allowing educational institutions to store and supply to authenticated users works made available on websites or other electronic retrieval systems.[52] Copyright owners could now take action against anyone who dealt in circumvention devices or provided a service which assisted in circumventing technological protection measures (TPMs), or removed or altered copyright management information that protected any of the copyright owner's exclusive rights.[53] The provisions were designed to prevent commercial dealing and introduced criminal liability for such dealing (attracting fines of up to NZ$150,000 or imprisonment of up to five years, or both).[54] A very constrained exception was enacted to allow format shifting of sound recordings for personal use onto digital playback devices, such as iPods and mp3 players owned by the user.[55] The 2008 digital amendments also introduced new limited exceptions for decompilation and error correction of software.[56]

While the amendments to the Copyright Act were designed to facilitate the uptake of technology, the prescriptive nature of the exceptions combined with the continued rapid changes in technology and in the means of delivering content to users has meant that many potential new uses now fall outside the permitted exceptions.[57]

---

49   Copyright (New Technologies and Performers' Rights) Amendment Bill (NZ), explanatory note at 2.
50   Copyright Act 1994 (NZ), s 2(1).
51   Sections 48, 51(5), 52(4), 53(5), 54(5), 55(3)–(4), 56(6) and 56A.
52   Section 44A.
53   Sections 226A–226E.
54   Section 226C.
55   Section 81A.
56   Sections 80A–80D.
57   Alexandra Sims 'A Law for Fair Use is not a Pirate's Charter' *New Zealand Herald* (online ed, Auckland, 23 February 2017), stating: 'Educational establishments here, despite paying tens of millions of dollars a year to copyright owners, are short-changing their students as they cannot use some materials protected by copyright in their teaching as teachers in the US can do.'

At the time of the 2008 digital amendments, the New Zealand Government agreed the Copyright Act would be reviewed in 2013 to assess its effectiveness for digital technology.[58] The Government delayed this review until negotiations for the TPP were concluded.[59] Following the signing of the TPP (now defunct and replaced by the CPTPP) and the potential introduction of legislation further strengthening copyright protections,[60] the Government has now given notice of a forthcoming review of the Copyright Act.[61]

The New Zealand Government will be taking a new approach to reform of the Copyright Act. As a first step, rather than commissioning an independent report, it has undertaken a study of the role of copyright and registered designs in the creative sector. The purpose of the study was to better understand how copyright is used in practice and in context, and to inform officials advising Ministers about the scope and timing of the review of the Copyright Act.[62] This resulted in the New Zealand government releasing the terms of reference for a review of the Copyright Act in 2018. These indicate that the government intends to take an evidence-based approach to the review.[63]

3.2 Australian Legislation

The most recent significant changes to exceptions in the Copyright Act 1968 (Cth) (Australian Act) were introduced in 2006 following AUSFTA coming into effect on 1 January 2005. The implementation in the Australian Act of the provisions required by AUSFTA to harmonise Australia's copyright law with that of the United States led to calls for the introduction of a fair use exception to balance the new, stronger levels of protection provided for copyright owners in Australia (including longer terms of protection, stronger remedies and penalties and new provisions around TPMs). However, despite the Australian Government releasing an Issues Paper to examine 'fair use, fair dealing and other exceptions in

---

58   Copyright (New Technologies and Performers' Rights) Amendment Bill (102-2) (select committee report) at 1.
59   Office of the Minister of Commerce to the Cabinet Economic Growth and Infrastructure Committee *Delayed Review of the Copyright Act 1994* (Cabinet Paper) at [4].
60   The TPP Agreement Amendment Act 2016 (not yet in force).
61   Ministry of Business, Innovation and Employment [MBIE] 'Review of the Copyright Act 1994: Terms of Reference' (29 June 2017) www.mbie.govt.nz.
62   MBIE *Copyright and the Creative Sector* (2016).
63   'Evidence will play an important role in our analysis of issues and any options for reform'; MBIE, above n 61.

the Digital Age',[64] the exceptions introduced into the Australian Act in 2006 included a range of private and domestic use exceptions, but did not include an exception for fair use. Australia's fair dealing provisions were extended to include fair dealing for parody and satire,[65] but the private use exceptions were media-specific and intended primarily to address technological illogicality and consumer practice, such as that sound recordings were not permitted to be reproduced for use on different devices, and that time shifting of television broadcasts was technically illegal.[66]

In 2017, an amending Act[67] removed and/or simplified a number of exceptions, including introducing a new fair dealing exception for the purposes of access by persons with a disability.[68] The amending Act simplified the existing remunerated statutory licences for the educational use of copyright material, by removing '30–40 pages of outdated, technology-specific rules that are no longer relevant in the internet age'.[69] The new simplified provision[70] will allow greater flexibility for schools and universities to negotiate with collecting societies to determine appropriate and effective terms for the educational use of copyright material and payment to rights holders in the digital environment.

None of these amendments, however, delivers the level of flexibility and adaptability for copyright users that is available under the United States doctrine of 'fair use'.[71]

3.3 Proposals for Fair Use in Australia

It has been nearly 20 years since a review of the Australian Act first recommended introducing a fair use–type exception. In 1996, the Copyright Law Reform Committee (CLRC) was asked by the Australian

---

64   Commonwealth of Australia Attorney-General's Department *Fair Use and Other Copyright Exceptions: An examination of Fair Use, Fair Dealing and Other Exceptions in the Digital Age* (Issues Paper, May 2005) apo.org.au.
65   Copyright Act 1968 (Cth), s 41A.
66   Copyright Act 1968 (Cth), ss 109A, 111.
67   Copyright Amendment (Disability Access and Other Measures) Act 2017 (Cth).
68   Copyright Amendment (Disability Access and Other Measures) Act 2017 (Cth), s 113E.
69   Universities Australia 'Universities Welcome Important Copyright Reforms' (press release, 15 June 2017).
70   Copyright Amendment (Disability Access and Other Measures) Act 2017 (Cth), s 113P.
71   See Patricia Aufderheide and Peter Jaszi *Reclaiming Fair Use: How to Put Balance Back in Copyright* (University of Chicago Press, 2011) at 148.

Government to consider how the Copyright Act could be simplified 'to make it able to be understood by people needing to understand their rights and obligations'.[72] In its report, the CLRC recommended the consolidation of the fair dealing provisions into a single section and the expansion of fair dealing to an 'open-ended model' that would not be confined to the 'closed list' of fair dealing purposes. The CLRC recommended that the non-exhaustive list of five fairness factors in s 40(2) of the Australian Act should specifically apply to all categories of fair dealing.[73]

The recommendation was not accepted by the Intellectual Property and Competition Review Committee, which saw no reason to change the current fair dealing provisions and argued that, at that time, the transaction costs of introducing fair use would outweigh the benefits.[74]

There was a further recommendation to introduce fair use made by the Joint Standing Committee on Treaties (JSCOT) in 2004. JSCOT recommended replacing fair dealing with something closer to the United States fair use doctrine 'to counter the effects of the extension of copyright protection and to correct the legal anomaly of time shifting and space shifting' as a result of entering into the AUSFTA.[75] The Australian Government did not, however, enact a fair use exception, stating that, in the public consultation phase, 'no significant interest supported fully adopting the US approach'.[76]

Two more recent reviews have also addressed the effectiveness of Australia's exceptions. The terms of reference for the Australian Law Reform Commission (ALRC) Report into Copyright and the Digital Economy in 2013 included consideration of 'whether the exceptions and statutory licences in the Copyright Act 1968, are adequate and appropriate in the digital environment'.[77] One of the main recommendations in the ALRC's report was that the Australian Act should provide an exception for fair use and it should include both a non-exhaustive list of 'fairness factors' to be considered when determining if a use is fair use, and a non-exhaustive list of illustrative uses or purposes that may qualify as fair

---

72 CLRC, above n 4, at [1.03].
73 CLRC, above n 4, at [2.04] and [6.36]–[6.44].
74 Intellectual Property and Competition Review Committee *Review of Intellectual Property Legislation under the Competition Principles Agreement* (final report, September 2000) at 129.
75 JSCOT—Parliament of Australia, above n 4.
76 ALRC, above n 4, at [4.30].
77 ALRC, above n 4, at 7.

use.[78] In addition, the ALRC report recommended repealing the existing fair dealing provisions and replacing them with a fair use exception.[79] In 2016, the Productivity Commission Report into Intellectual Property Arrangements concluded that Australia's copyright 'exceptions are too narrow and prescriptive, do not reflect the way people actually consume and use content, and do not readily accommodate new legitimate uses of copyright material. Legislative change is required to expand the categories of use deemed to be fair'.[80]

Although both the ALRC and the Productivity Commission have recommended the introduction of a fair use exception, the Australian Government has not yet provided a response. In March 2018, the Australian Department of Communications and the Arts released a consultation paper asking for views on three areas of the Copyright Act 1968 that may benefit from modernisation: flexible exceptions, contracting out of exceptions and access to orphan works.[81]

3.4 Responses to Proposals for Fair Use in Australia

The recommendations of the ALRC and the Productivity Commission, described above, have elicited strong ongoing opposition from Australian copyright owners. The Australian Publishers Association and the Copyright Agency, both of which represent copyright owners, have claimed that to introduce a fair use exception into the Australian Act would stifle local creativity, citing expert evidence to support their claims.[82] The Copyright Council had commissioned a report by accountants PricewaterhouseCoopers, which estimated that introducing fair use in Australia could result in a loss of GDP of more than A$1 billion.[83] Copyright owners referred to this report when objecting to the potential introduction of fair use, arguing that the existence of a fair use exception in the copyright law of the United States, and a fair dealing for education

78   ALRC, above n 4, Recommendation 5-1.
79   ALRC, above n 4, Recommendation 5-4.
80   Australian Productivity Commission, above n 4, at 9.
81   Department of Communications and the Arts *Copyright modernisation consultation paper* (March 2018) www.communications.gov.au.
82   Copyright Agency 'Fair Use' copyright.com.au.
83   Copyright Council of Australia copyright.org.au; PricewaterhouseCoopers *Understanding the Costs and Benefits of Introducing a 'Fair Use' Exception* (February 2016) www.copyright.com.au.

exception in Canada's copyright law, had resulted in the loss of many millions in royalty payments to content producers, plus job losses and the closure or winding back of multiple publishers in those jurisdictions.[84]

The Australian Productivity Commission gave little weight to the report, which did not provide evidence of how this figure was arrived at. The Australian Productivity Commission report noted that '… these concerns are ill-founded and premised on flawed (and self-interested) assumptions'.[85] Rights owners claimed the downturn in the publishing industry in Canada was the direct result of changes to Canadian copyright law, but as the Productivity Commission observed, 'Canada's publishing industry had little to do with copyright exceptions (where fair dealing still prevails) and more to do with other market factors'.[86] A recent (controversial and likely to be appealed) decision from the Federal Court of Canada highlights the difficulty of relying upon fair dealing provisions in the educational context.[87] York University had withdrawn from its licensing arrangement with the Canadian Copyright Licensing Agency, Access Copyright, claiming that the Interim Tariff (the licensing fees) set by Access were not mandatory but voluntary, and that the University would instead follow its own fair dealing guidelines (developed from a generic set of fair dealing guidelines for tertiary institutions prepared by the Association of Universities and Colleges Canada). The Court ruled that York's fair dealing guidelines were not 'fair' and therefore York was bound to pay the Interim Tariff set by Access Copyright.[88]

Although fair use does not protect all educational uses in the United States, there is much more leeway in regard to its scope. Opposition to the introduction of fair use by United States rights holders could reflect concern about the benefit to potential competitors from Australia and New Zealand, rather than the likelihood for harm to creators from the United States. Ben Sheffner, counsel for the Motion Picture Association

---

84   PricewaterhouseCoopers *Economic Impacts of the Canadian Education Sector's Fair Dealing Guidelines* (June 2015) www.accesscopyright.ca. A recent (controversial) decision handed down by a Judge in the Federal Court of Canada has supported the arguments of the Canadian Copyright Licensing Agency, Access Copyright, against a 'fair dealing approach' taken by York University in refusing to pay licensing fees: see *Canadian Copyright Licensing Agency ('Access Copyright') v York University* (2017) FC 669.

85   Australian Productivity Commission, above n 4, at 10.

86   Ibid.

87   *Canadian Copyright Licensing Agency ('Access Copyright') v York University*, above n 84.

88   At [356].

of America (MPAA) is openly supportive of fair use and the reliance of his members on the defence. In a blog post on the MPAA's website, he stated:[89]

> Our members rely on the fair use doctrine every day when producing their movies and television shows – especially those that involve parody and news and documentary programs. And it's routine for our members to raise fair use – successfully – in court. … No thinking person is 'for' or 'against' fair use in all circumstances. … As the Supreme Court and countless others have said, fair use is a flexible doctrine, one that requires a case-by-case examination of the facts, and a careful weighing of all of the statutory factors. Some uses are fair; some aren't.

3.5 Fair Use in New Zealand

While there have been no formal recommendations to introduce a fair use–type defence in New Zealand, there have been a number of submissions made to parliamentary select committees recommending its adoption. Several submissions were made to the committee considering the TPP Agreement Amendment Bill, which was intended to incorporate the requirements of the TPP into domestic legislation. It is noteworthy that the copyright provisions in the CPTPP mainly mirror those in the TPP, with the exception of certain provisions including the proposed TPM and rights management provisions,[90] which have been suspended (although not removed).[91] In regard to the TPP Agreement Amendment Bill, the Libraries and Information Association of New Zealand (LIANZA) and the Auckland Museum[92] both submitted that if the copyright term were to be extended to match United States law, New Zealand should also adopt the United States' 'fair use' exemptions, in order to 'somewhat mitigate the effect of a longer copyright term, rather than the more narrow "fair dealing" exemptions we currently operate within'.[93] In a similar vein, InternetNZ submitted that a review of copyright 'should have the scope to consider a range of options such as a flexible "fair use" right as exists in the USA'.[94] Trade Me Limited, New Zealand's equivalent of eBay, also asked for consideration to be given to rebalancing the Copyright Act by

89   Ben Sheffner 'MPAA and Fair Use: A Quick History' (22 October 2013) MPAA www.mpaa.org.
90   TPP, above n 13, arts 18.68 and 18.69.
91   The other two suspended provisions are the Protection of Encrypted Program-Carrying Satellite and Cable Signals (art 18.79) and Legal Remedies and Safe Harbours, (art 18.2).
92   Auckland Museum 'Submission on the TPP Agreement Amendment Bill 2016' (2016).
93   LIANZA 'Submission on the TPP Agreement Amendment Bill 2016' (22 July 2016).
94   InternetNZ 'Submission on the TPP Agreement Amendment Bill' (22 July 2016).

implementing a United States–style fair use exception, arguing that the flexible approach of a fair use exception would 'cover perceived gaps in the specified exceptions to copyright found in Part 3 of the Copyright Act'.[95] Finally, the Electronic Frontier Foundation TPP Agreement Submission urged Parliament to:[96]

[F]uture proof copyright law to ensure that New Zealand is well placed to take advantage of the next wave of innovation, and the next. Flexible copyright exceptions provide a framework for considering new and innovative uses, as and when they emerge, without the need to go back to the legislative drawing board. A flexible and dynamic exception that is fit for purpose in a digital environment is one that will provide the breathing room for innovation and new uses while ensuring that rights holder's legitimate interests are protected.

Nevertheless, despite calls for the introduction of a fair use–type exception in New Zealand, the New Zealand Government appears more likely to continue to follow the lead of the United Kingdom in matters of copyright. The justification for this approach by the New Zealand Government is that the '[New Zealand Copyright] Act may suffer from similar issues [to the UK CDPA], as it is largely modelled on the UK legislation'.[97]

Rather than suggesting fair use, the Hargreaves review in the United Kingdom had recommended a licensing model, whereby rights could be speedily licensed and effectively protected.[98] The danger of instigating a licensing model to require payment for every use of third-party content, however, is that it could well result in a chilling effect on the cultural growth of society.[99] Indeed, Professor Hargreaves himself has since stated that his preferred option would have been to recommend fair use for the United Kingdom.[100] On another occasion, he described fair use as

---

95   Trade Me Ltd 'Submission on the TPP Agreement Amendment Bill' (July 2016).
96   Electronic Frontier Foundation 'Submission on the TPP Agreement Amendment Bill' (11 August 2016).
97   Office of the Minister of Commerce, above n 59, at [4].
98   Ian Hargreaves *Digital Opportunity – A Review of Intellectual Property and Growth* (May 2011) UK Intellectual Property Office at 4.
99   Yashomati Ghosh 'Jurisprudential Analysis of the Rights of the Users in Copyrighted Works' in Manoj Kumar Sinha and Vandana Mahalwar (eds) *Copyright Law in the Digital World* (Springer, Singapore, 2017) 61. 'The attempts by the copyright holders to limit and regulate the access to copyrighted works through technological and other means will impose huge financial burdens on the consumers of copyrighted works thereby reducing the number of creative works produced in the society.'
100 Ian Hargreaves, 'Digital Opportunity: Powering Innovation through Copyright' (presentation to the Australian Digital Alliance Forum, Canberra, 18 March 2016).

'the backbone of a healthy Internet-economy ecosystem in the US'.[101] As the Australian Productivity Commission noted, Hargreaves 'found it "politically impossible" to recommend fair use for the UK'.[102] To date, similar political resistance has been experienced in Australia where, as discussed earlier in this chapter, various inquiries and reviews of copyright have recommended the adoption of a fair use–type defence but these recommendations have not been acted upon.

There is nothing in the 2017 terms of reference for the upcoming review of the New Zealand Act[103] that suggests the Government has changed its mind. The objectives provided in the terms of reference include to:[104]

- permit reasonable access to works for use, adaption and consumption, where exceptions to exclusive rights are likely to have net benefits for New Zealand
- ensure that the copyright system is effective and efficient, including providing clarity and certainty, facilitating competitive markets, minimising transaction costs, and maintaining integrity and respect for the law …

The terms of reference confirm that 'these objectives are not set in stone, and will be tested through consultation on an issues paper'.[105] Certainly, the desired 'clarity and certainty' described in the above excerpt of objectives will be difficult to achieve if the New Zealand Act is to become flexible enough to ensure that, as stated earlier in the terms of reference, 'our regime is fit for purpose in New Zealand in a changing technological environment'.[106]

It is understandable that the New Zealand Government would wish to avoid the polarised views and the depth of feeling invoked in Australia by the suggestion of the implementation of a fair use–type defence. It is possibly for this reason that the terms of reference conclude with the

---

101 Ian Hargreaves and Bernt Hugenholtz 'Copyright Reform for Growth and Jobs: Modernising the European Copyright Framework' (2013) 13 Lisbon Council Policy Brief 1.
102 ALRC, above n 4, at 6.39.
103 MBIE, above n 61.
104 MBIE, above n 61, at 2.
105 MBIE, above n 61, at 2.
106 MBIE, above n 61.

assertion that 'Evidence will play an important role in our analysis of issues and any options for reform' – that is, the Government proposes an evidence-based review.[107]

Focusing on evidence of current uses of copyright works, however, carries the risk that the review could support narrowly drafted user exceptions. Indeed, this may be why the Australian copyright industry and various representative groups of rights owners opposed to fair use called for such a review of the Australian Act. For example, the Australasian Performing Right Association/Australasian Mechanical Copyright Owners Society (APRA/AMCOS) submitted to the ALRC that 'many of the criticisms of the existing fair dealing exceptions are made in an academic context, and are not evidence based'.[108] Others called for any reform to the exceptions in the Australian Act to be evidence-based.[109] Thus, while superficially an evidence-based review could be seen as an opportunity for New Zealand to craft something better suited to New Zealand conditions, if focused solely on creators' and users' current experiences, the proposed review risks ignoring the potential advantages of fair use in an evolving technological environment and thereby continuing to deny New Zealand's copyright users the flexibility that is found in fair use.

The New Zealand Productivity Commission's inquiry into tertiary education found (albeit rather obviously) that it is difficult to predict with any certainty how technology will develop.[110] With that truism in mind, crafting appropriate permitted exceptions that have the flexibility demanded by the potentially disruptive impact of new technologies on how copyright material is utilised, distributed and monitored will be difficult in the face of objections by well-resourced and determined rights owners who see their traditional sources of income diminishing. It is important that this pressure does not distort the traditional balance necessary to a functioning copyright regime, which both supports the creation of new works and also acknowledges the rights of users of those works during the term of copyright protection.

---

107 MBIE, above n 61, at 3.
108 APRA/AMCOS (Submission 247, ALRC) www.alrc.gov.au.
109 APRA/AMCOS, above n 108; Foxtel (Submission 245, ALRC); AAP (Submission 206, ALRC); AMPAL (Submission 189, ALRC) all at www.alrc.gov.au.
110 New Zealand Productivity Commission *New Models of Tertiary Education: Final Report* (March 2017) www.productivity.govt.nz.

Crafting appropriate permitted exceptions could be done either by the courts interpreting the fair dealing exceptions broadly and adding new purposes, as has happened in Canada,[111] or by Parliament drafting flexible exceptions within the legislation itself. It is unlikely that the New Zealand courts would interpret parliamentary intent broadly as they are traditionally conservative and generally eschew judicial activism.[112] While there has been a trend towards judicial activism, particularly in public law in New Zealand, it is generally in response to:[113]

> Acts which include sections that invite, even instruct, the judges to give priority to vague, amorphous notions like 'the principles of the Treaty of Waitangi' or 'proper respect for cultural, ethnic and ethical beliefs' or 'the intrinsic value of ecosystems' or even 'the maintenance and enhancement of amenity values'.

In two cases,[114] one brought under the former Copyright Act 1962, the other under the present New Zealand Copyright Act, the New Zealand courts had the opportunity to provide a more expansive interpretation of the scope of the permitted exceptions for educational copying. However, in both rulings, the courts have taken a conservative position. Both cases concerned multiple copying by educational institutions for classroom use and in both cases the courts found in favour of rights owners. In the 1991 case *Longman Group Ltd* v *Carrington Technical Institute Board of Governors*,[115] the Court found that copying significant parts of copyright works and using the copies for the same purpose as the original works (education) was not fair dealing and that classroom use by a teacher is not included in private study.[116]

---

111 *CCH Canadian Ltd v Law Society of Upper Canada*, above n 42.

112 Bruce Harris 'Judicial Activism in New Zealand's Appellate Courts' in Brice Dickson (ed) *Judicial Activism in Common Law Supreme Courts* (Oxford University Press, 2007) 273: 'The system of government in New Zealand has long been characterised by a relatively quiet stability, there being a general ethos against the different branches stepping too much out of line. The judiciary on the whole has been a particularly conscientious observer of this ethos. The judiciary is well aware of its obligation to function in such a way as to respect and support the appropriate roles of the other branches of government. One commentator has characterized the current relationship between the courts and the legislature as one of collaboration.'

113 James Allan 'The rise of judicial activism' (1997) 4(4) Agenda 465 at 474.

114 See *Longman Group Ltd v Carrington Technical Institute Board of Governors* [1991] 2 NZLR 574 (brought under the Copyright Act 1962) and *Copyright Licensing Ltd v University of Auckland* [2002] 3 NZLR 76 (brought under the Copyright Act 1994).

115 *Longman Group Ltd v Carrington Technical Institute Board of* Governors, above n 114.

116 At 588.

In 2002, the parties in *Copyright Licensing Ltd v University of Auckland* and others[117] sought clarification as to the meaning of the permitted exceptions for education in the Copyright Act 1994. The universities argued that copying copyright course materials for inclusion in student course packs constituted fair dealing for the purposes of research or private study. The High Court, however, held that the 'purpose' must be that of the person 'doing the copying'.[118] Since the copiers, the universities, were not themselves dealing with the work for the purposes of research or private study, the copying did not amount to fair dealing. In a similar Canadian case, *Alberta (Education) v Canadian Copyright Licensing Agency (Access Copyright)*, the Canadian Supreme Court considered the New Zealand *Copyright Licensing* decision, but took a more expansive view of 'research and private study'. The Supreme Court in Alberta found that there is no such separate purpose on the part of the teacher.[119] Teachers are there to facilitate the students' research and private study and students rely on the guidance of their teachers.[120] The teacher's purpose in providing copies is to enable the students to have the material they need for the purpose of studying.[121] Instruction and research/private study are, in the school context, tautological.[122] (The Supreme Court's ruling must be treated with caution at present, pending a likely appeal from the Federal Court's converse ruling in *Canadian Copyright Licensing Agency ('Access Copyright') v York University*,[123] discussed earlier in this chapter.)

In an equivalent Australian case, *Haines v Copyright Agency Ltd*,[124] the Full Federal Court drew the distinction between an institution making copies for teaching purposes and the activities of individuals concerned with research or study. This finding was confirmed in *DeGaris v Neville Jeffress Pidler Pty Ltd*,[125] which held that the exception only applied if the person who does the copying is the person who does the research or study.

---

117 *Copyright Licensing Ltd v University of Auckland*, above n 114.
118 At [43] and [52].
119 *Alberta (Education) v Canadian Copyright Licensing Agency ('Access Copyright')* (2012) SCC 37, [2012] 2 SCR 345 at [23].
120 At [23].
121 At [23].
122 At [18] and [23].
123 *Canadian Copyright Licensing Agency ('Access Copyright') v York University*, above n 84.
124 *Haines v Copyright Agency Ltd* (1982) 64 FLR 185, 191.
125 *DeGaris v Neville Jeffress Pidler Pty Ltd* (1990) 37 FCR 99 at 105–106.

One possible explanation for the conservative approach by the New Zealand and Australian courts in the above cases and the reluctance of the respective governments to consider fair use might be the perception that fair use is uncertain and ill-defined in law. In the following part this perception is refuted.

4 Arguments For and Against Fair Use

Under United States copyright law, any kind of use can be potentially fair (provided it meets certain criteria). Clearly, fair use offers greater flexibility than a closed list of specific 'fair dealings'. In particular, fair use's flexibility encourages new uses and can be applied to new and developing technologies in a way that fair dealing cannot. It is flexible enough to support future unanticipated uses of copyright works. Conversely, the specificity of each fair dealing provision in the New Zealand and Australian copyright legislation means in practice that users' rights to make fair dealing uses of copyright works are likely to lag behind new technological developments. There is no doubt that both the New Zealand and Australian governments are focused on encouraging the growth of digital technology industries. For example, the New Zealand Government has described digital technology as potentially driving innovation, improving productivity and enhancing the quality of life for all New Zealanders.[126]

Some of the countries in the Asia Pacific region that have already entered into free trade agreements with the United States have amended their copyright laws to create fair use–type exceptions or extended their fair dealing to make it more flexible and open-ended. If New Zealand and Australia intend to compete on a more even playing field in developing technology based industries, they may need to implement similar provisions. This would also be a step towards harmonising the laws in this region.

Although flexibility in law is often desirable, for some aspects of copyright certainty may be more appropriate. For example, in the context of educational users, prescribing the number of pages or percentage that can be copied from a book or journal for distribution to students by teachers provides clear guidance. However, where prescriptive exceptions cover

126 MBIE *The Business Growth Agenda: Building a Digital Nation* (March 2017).

some uses and not others, they become confusing and teachers are likely to either ignore copyright or avoid using third-party content – to the detriment of their students' learning.[127]

In other situations, where new and transformative uses are being made of copyright content, then the strength of fair use is in its flexibility. It is this very flexibility that creates uncertainty about what the law is, and gives rise to a number of criticisms.[128] Some argue that it is likely that adoption of a fair use doctrine would result in more time and money expended on litigation.[129] Although, Barton Beebe's research refutes this argument, as he indicates the cost of litigation may have deterred many parties. In addition, some users may choose not to rely upon fair use due to the very perception of its uncertainty.[130] Beebe systematically reviewed and analysed all 306 reported opinions from 215 cases in the Federal United States courts between 1978 and 2005 that made substantial use of the s 107 four-factor test. He found that this was 'a surprising low number of opinions for such an important area of copyright law, particularly one that has received so much academic attention'.[131] He continues:[132]

> It is all the more surprising in light of Federal Judicial Center data that suggests that a steady average of approximately 2000 copyright infringement complaints were filed per year in federal district courts during the same period. A number of factors may account for the paucity of reported fair use opinions, the most obvious being that many fair use disputes may never reach the courts.

Matthew Sag has also published research in this area.[133] Sag claimed that his work:[134]

---

127 Tomasz Kasprzak, Olga Jurkowska and Alek Tarkowksi *Creator, Rebel, Guardian, Unsuspecting User: Teachers and Modern Educational Practices* (Communia, Warsaw, 2017).
128 June M Besek and others *Copyright Exceptions in the United States for Educational Uses of Copyrighted Works* (The Kernochan Center for Law, Media and the Arts, Columbia University School of Law, 2013).
129 Besek, above n 128 at 64.
130 Barton Beebe 'An Empirical study of US Copyright Fair Use Opinions, 1978-2005' (2008) 156(3) U Penn L Rev 549.
131 At 565.
132 Ibid.
133 Matthew Sag 'Predicting Fair Use' (2012) 73 Ohio St LJ 47 at 51.
134 ALRC, above n 4, at 4.126.

> [D]emonstrates that the uncertainty critique is somewhat overblown: an empirical analysis of the case law shows that, while there are many shades of grey in fair use litigation, there are also consistent patterns that can assist individuals, businesses, and lawyers in assessing the merits of particular claims to fair use protection.[135]

Despite the lack of empirical research to back up claims of uncertainty and likely litigation, the New Zealand Government continues to voice concerns. In 2012, the Hon Craig Foss wrote:[136]

> In the US, both right holders and users have the benefit of the US courts developing and applying the fair use defence over many years across a wide range of alleged infringing actions. If a fair use defence was introduced in New Zealand, it would most likely take a number of years for the New Zealand courts to develop a comparable body of case law. Until that body of case law was developed, I am concerned by the possibility that users would be deterred from undertaking legitimate activity due to fear of litigation on the breadth and purpose of a fair use defence. On the other hand, specific exceptions may be able to allow an appropriate range of uses of copyright works without the need for litigation to show that those uses are appropriate.

The argument that New Zealand does not have a comparable body of case law and that therefore the introduction of fair use would be inappropriate is unsound. A dearth of case law in a particular area is generally not an impediment to the legislature or the courts. For example, when New Zealand implemented the Consumer Guarantees Act 1993, based on Saskatchewan consumer protection law, the courts relied on Saskatchewan precedents as well as pre-1993 New Zealand case law. If New Zealand were to introduce fair use, the relevant body of United States decisions on aspects of fair use would be available for guidance. Nevertheless, it is possible that the fear of uncertainty may have prompted the terms of reference for the review of the New Zealand Act to identify 'clarity and certainty' as an objective of the New Zealand copyright regime.[137]

---

135 See also Aufderheide and Jaszi, above n 71. The authors have created 'codes of best practice in fair use' for various user groups in the United States, allowing users to reclaim 'their rights under the law'.
136 Letter from the Hon Craig Foss to Professor Stuart McCutcheon (Vice-Chancellor University of Auckland) regarding fair use (21 May 2012).
137 MBIE, above n 61.

4.1 Criticisms of Fair Use

Although, as has been shown, there is much support for introducing fair use into New Zealand copyright law, this is by no means a universal view. For example, Graeme Austin notes that the New Zealand Copyright Act already has a number of exceptions that do not require an assessment to be undertaken as to whether or not a use is fair. [138] Such exceptions, for example, permit the decompilation of copyright software in order to create an interoperable program.[139] In the United States, this activity remains subject to the requirements of the fair use defence. Austin warns that:[140]

> a government supported by properly resourced and sufficiently expert policy analysts should be well-equipped to craft specifically tailored defences and exceptions as new problems present themselves – without importing the many intractable problems associated with the US-styled fair use defence.

Given the more than 10-year delay in reviewing the New Zealand Act, however, it seems fanciful to think that Government officials will be able to keep pace with fast-paced changes in technology as they present themselves. The Minister identified problems with the Act in 2013, but a decision to review the Act was not made for another four years, with the implementation likely to be another one or two years away.

The debates around the introduction of fair use into the copyright laws of New Zealand and Australia, although following similar lines, have thus far tended to be confined within each separate jurisdiction. Any changes to the copyright legislation of both countries need to take into account the terms of CER.[141] The objective of CER is to harmonise the laws of New Zealand and Australia in order to 'create a seamless trans-Tasman business environment'.[142]

---

138 Graeme W Austin 'The Two Faces of Fair Use' (2012) 25(2) NZULR 285 at 315.
139 Copyright Act 1994 (NZ), ss 80A–80C.
140 Austin, above n 138, at 317.
141 Australia – New Zealand Closer Economic Relations Trade Agreement (signed 28 March 1983, entered into force 1 January 1983) [CER].
142 New Zealand Ministry of Foreign Affairs and Trade [MFAT] 'Single Economic Market' mfat. govt.nz.

5 Harmonisation of the Copyright Law between Australia and New Zealand: CER

New Zealand and Australia have had close ties since they were both colonised in the late 18th and early 19th centuries. The Australian states were originally independent and self-governing, with New Zealand a dependency of New South Wales until 1840. Following the signing of the Treaty of Waitangi, New Zealand became a separate colony of Great Britain. With a common language, heritage, religion and way of life, there was a proposal to unify the Australian states and New Zealand into a single Australasian state.[143] A New Zealand Royal Commission, established in 1899 to consider whether or not New Zealand should become part of Australia, reported against federation after strong opposition from trade unions who were against Australia's 'coloured labour' and defensive of New Zealand's working conditions and social legislation.[144] While New Zealand decided against becoming part of Australia, New Zealand remains in the Australian Constitution as one of the British colonies that might be admitted into the Commonwealth of Australia.[145] Despite many differences, the relationship between New Zealand and Australia has always been relatively close, with New Zealand Māori trading flax, wheat and potatoes to Australia from as early as the 1820s[146].

There have been various trade agreements between Australia and New Zealand, the most recent being CER in 1983,[147] entered into in recognition of one of the broadest and most mutually compatible economic and trading relationships in the world.[148] The commitment was to create a seamless trans-Tasman business environment, making it as easy for New Zealanders to do business in Australia as it was to do business in and around New Zealand, and included measures to unify policy, laws and regulatory regimes in both countries. In 2009, New Zealand and Australia

---

143 John Farrar 'Closer Economic Relations and Harmonisation of Law Between Australia and New Zealand' in PA Joseph (ed) *Essays on the Constitution* (1995) 158.

144 Honourable Justice Michael Kirby 'The Unfinished Trans-Tasman Business' (2002) 28(2) Commonwealth Law Bulletin 1083 at 1085.

145 Commonwealth of Australia Constitution Act 1900 (Cth), s 6.

146 Claudia Orange *The Story of a Treaty* (2nd ed, Bridget Williams Books, Wellington, 2013) at 7 (doi.org/10.7810/9781927131442).

147 Belton, above n 23.

148 MFAT 'NZ-Australia Closer Economic Relations' (30 September 2016) www.mfat.govt.nz.

reaffirmed their commitment towards harmonisation by an agenda aiming to create a Single Economic Market (SEM), 'designed to create a seamless trans-Tasman business environment'.[149]

To date the harmonisation process has not included any attempt to harmonise copyright legislation, despite there being major differences between the two copyright regimes. As Susy Frankel has observed:[150]

> Australia and New Zealand currently have different terms of copyright, different standards of originality, different ownership rules in copyright, different defences to infringement of copyright, different ways of treating parallel imports of copyright material and trade marked goods and different approaches to functional designs. Additionally, when cases get to court further inconsistencies may develop. This happens even where the laws seem on their face to be alike so that in formal terms there is apparent harmonisation, but in substantive terms there is not.

The problem of having differing laws between such close trading partners is highlighted by a recent case where differences between the two regimes resulted in an Australian company trading in New Zealand having damages awarded against it for copyright infringement. The case, *Jeans West v G-Star Raw*, involved clothing that, despite being mass-produced and therefore an industrial design, in New Zealand is protected by copyright in the two-dimensional drawings or patterns for the clothing.[151] In Australia, however, industrially applied design drawings are not eligible for copyright protection but must be registered under the Designs Act 2003 to obtain protection.[152] JeansWest Australia had assumed New Zealand copyright law was the same as Australian law when it imported into New Zealand jeans that it had copied from G-Star Raw. It did not obtain advice or make the inquiries necessary to inform itself as to the different copyright position in New Zealand.

---

149 MFAT, above n 142; and MFAT 'Joint Statement by Prime Ministers Rudd and Key' (21 August 2009) www.beehive.govt.nz.
150 Susy Frankel and Megan Richardson 'Trans-Tasman Intellectual Property Coordination' *Regulatory Reform Toolkit* ch 18 www.regulatorytoolkit.ac.nz (footnotes omitted).
151 Copyright Act 1994 (NZ), s 75.
152 *JeansWest Corporation (NZ) Limited v G-Star Raw CV and G-Star Australia Pty Limited* [2015] NZCA 14.

Attempts to harmonise the laws of Australia and New Zealand have to date been largely unsuccessful. As noted by Cheryl Saunders:[153]

> … sensitivity about national sovereignty and the political reality of different constituencies with different attitudes and needs have put some brake on the breadth and depth of integration. There is no single tariff, in deference to the different competitive strengths of the two countries; no signs of a single currency, despite occasional murmurings; and no agreement to include telecommunications within the single market.

Given the differences between the two countries' copyright legislation it would take a major overhaul of both Acts to harmonise the law in this area. However, if Australia implements a fair use exception, under CER New Zealand lawmakers will be obliged to consider harmonising the New Zealand Act with the Australian Act before any changes can be made to it.

Following the withdrawal of the United States from the TPP, and the replacement of the TPP by the CPTPP, focus will likely turn to Asia as a market for both Australian and New Zealand goods and services. Noting that several of the potential new trading partners for New Zealand and Australia – Singapore, Taiwan, South Korea and the Philippines – have all implemented fair use–type exceptions and, coupled with the increasing importance of technology-based industries, New Zealand and Australia will face increasing pressure to have a more flexible principle-based exception in their copyright laws if they wish to remain competitive in this area.

6 RCEP: Harmonisation with the Wider Asian Pacific Region

As discussed above, following the demise of the TPP, both the Australian and New Zealand governments have entered into the CPTPP with the other parties to the TPP. In addition, both countries are party to negotiations for the Regional Comprehensive Economic Partnership (RCEP), which currently involves the 10 Member States of the Association of Southeast Asian Nations (ASEAN) – Brunei Darussalam, Burma (Myanmar), Cambodia, Indonesia, Laos, Malaysia, the Philippines, Singapore, Thailand, Vietnam – plus China, India, Japan and South Korea.[154]

---

153 Cheryl Saunders 'To Be or Not to Be: the Constitutional Relationship between New Zealand and Australia' in David Dyzenhaus, Murray Hunt and Grant Huscroft (ed) *A Simple Common Lawyer: Essays in Honour of Michael Taggart* (Hart, Oxford, Portland, Or, 2009) 255.
154 See Yu, above n 16.

There have been two leaked texts of the intellectual property chapters of the trade agreement. Although the latest leak reveals there is no requirement for the members to increase the term of copyright, the availability of copyright limitations and exceptions is limited by the same narrow language as is found in the TPP.[155] Commenting on the released text, Jeremy Malcolm observed that:[156]

[a]lthough the same narrow three-step test is also found in the Berne and TRIPS conventions, the overall impact of this is that the treatment of limitations and exceptions in RCEP begins from a very negative starting point.

The leaked text reveals that Australia has proposed an amendment, based on art 18.66 of the TPP:[157]

Each Party shall endeavour to provide an appropriate balance in its copyright and related rights system by providing limitations and exceptions … for legitimate purposes including education, research, criticism, comment, news reporting, libraries and archives and facilitating access for persons with disability.

Australia has also proposed that parties:[158]

may adopt or maintain limitations or exceptions to the rights described in paragraph 1 for fair use, as long as any such limitation or exception is confined as stated in paragraph 3.

Currently, of those countries negotiating the RCEP, South Korea, the Philippines and Singapore already have a fair use exception and, without the United States as part of the equation, the ability to enact a fair use exception becomes more feasible and possibly necessary if New Zealand and Australia are to remain competitive.

---

155 '2015 Oct 15 version: RCEP IP Chapter' (19 April 2016) Knowledge Ecology International keionline.org [RCEP]. RCEP art 2.5 and TPP art 18.65 each requires that exceptions and limitations in domestic laws must comply with the three-step test.
156 Peter K Yu 'The RCEP and Trans-Pacific Intellectual Property Norms' (2017) 50 Vanderbilt Journal of Transnational Law 673; and Jeremy Malcolm 'RCEP: The Other Closed-Door Agreement to Compromise Users' Rights' (2016) Electronic Frontier Foundation www.eff.org/deeplinks/2016/04/rcep-other-closed-door-agreement-compromise-users-rights.
157 RCEP, above n 155, art 2.5.
158 RCEP, above n 155, art 2.5.

The following section describes the different approaches by some Asian Pacific countries to introducing a more flexible fair use exception into their domestic copyright laws; generally in response to increased protections for rights owners, following entering into FTAs with the United States.[159]

7 Approaches to Fair Use in the Asian Pacific Region

7.1 The Philippines

The Philippines introduced a copyright code in 1998, which provided limitations on the copyright owner's exclusive rights[160] in addition to a fair use clause closely modelled on that of the United States.[161] Rather than a response to an FTA with the United States, the Philippines is a developing country with 'acute social and economic inequalities' that needed flexibilities within copyright legislation to ensure imported copyright works such as books and films are accessible to students. The 11 enumerated limitations include unlimited use of broadcast works and brief excerpts from the 'general cinema repertoire of feature films' provided they are deleted within a reasonable period;[162] inclusion of 'a work in a publication, broadcast or other communication to the public, sound recording or film, if such inclusion is made by way of illustration for teaching purposes and is compatible with fair use'.[163] These limitations are all subject to an interpretation which would not conflict with the normal exploitation of the work and would not unreasonably prejudice the right holder's legitimate interest.[164]

---

159 Korea – United States FTA 2012 [KORUS] (signed 30 June 2007, entered into 15 March 2012), United States – Singapore FTA (signed 3 September 2003, entered into force 1 January 2004). See Corbett, above n 6.

160 The Intellectual Property Code of the Philippines, Republic Act 8293, Republic of the Philippines, 1998, Part IV, Chapter VIII, art 184.

161 Sec. 185.

162 Sec. 184(f).

163 Sec. 184(e).

164 Sec. 184.2.

7.2 South Korea

Unlike New Zealand and Australia, South Korea is a civil-law country; however, the Korea – United States FTA (KORUS) enabled Korea to introduce a flexible fair use provision into the Korean Copyright Act in 2012.[165] As Professor Song So Jong observed:[166]

> Since Korea is a risk taking country rather than a risk averse country, Korea decided to introduce the fair use doctrine six years ago: the fair use doctrine for the benefit of innovations not only for the industry and users but also for creators as well in a fast changing internet environment.

While KORUS did not mandate the introduction of exceptions, it opened the possibility with two restrictions: in connection with the reproduction right expanded to cover 'temporary storage in electronic form'; and qualifying the fair use exception by referring to the three-step test.[167] The result was a combination of the United States–style fair use and the three-step test. The fair use clause is codified in art 35*ter* of the Korean Copyright Act, which consists of two paragraphs. The first paragraph states that it is permissible to use works when such use does not conflict with the normal exploitation of works and does not unreasonably prejudice the legitimate interests of rights holders. The purposes of 'news reporting, criticism, education, research, etc.' were removed in a 2016 amendment for fear of a restrictive misinterpretation that fair use is allowed only for the listed purposes.[168]

The second paragraph has a list of factors, similar to the United States fair use provision, to be considered in determining if a use is fair:[169]

1. The purposes and characters of the use, including whether or not such use is for profit;
2. The category and nature of the works;
3. The amount and substantiality of the portion used in relation to the whole work; and
4. The effect of the use on the existing or potential market or value of the work.

---

165 Sang Jo Jong 'Fair Use in Korea' (paper presented at Australian Digital Alliance Copyright Forum 2017, Canberra, 24 February 2017).
166 Jong, above n 165, 1.
167 KORUS, above n 159, art 18.4 footnote 11.
168 Article amended on 22 March 2016.
169 Open Net Korea 'Changes Induced by Open-Ended Fair Use Clause: Korean Experiences' (24 October 2016) opennetkorea.org.

Before the enactment of the fair use clause, the most commonly relied-upon defences to a claim of copyright infringement were the specific limitations for quotation and private use. However, both were codified in restrictive terms and courts interpreted them narrowly. The Korean courts continue to interpret the law narrowly, however the open-ended fair use clause has 'induced, albeit slowly, changes the judicial practices'.[170]

7.3 Singapore

Similar to Australia and New Zealand, Singapore's copyright law has its origins in United Kingdom copyright law. The United Kingdom Imperial Copyright Act of 1911 was enacted simultaneously in Singapore and the United Kingdom. Under the 1911 Imperial Copyright Act, limitations and exceptions to copyright law were narrowly defined, essentially protecting fair dealings only for private study or research. In 1987, the Singapore Copyright Act received major revisions to make it more able to adapt to emerging technologies that did not exist in the early 20th century. Fair dealing was limited to very specific purposes: private study or research;[171] criticism or review;[172] reporting current events or news;[173] and copying for the purpose of judicial proceeding or professional advice.[174]

In 2005, the Copyright Amendment Act came into force and adopted an open-ended approach to exceptions and limitations to copyright.[175] The modifications of the Singapore Copyright Act in 2005 were in response to an FTA with the United States,[176] which required Singapore to extend the term of copyright from life plus 50 to life plus 70 years[177] and copyright infringement became a criminal offence, sanctioned with imprisonment and hefty monetary fines.[178] The introduction of more flexible copyright exceptions sought to rebalance the needs of users and copyright holders.

---

170 Open Net Korea, above n 169.
171 Copyright Act 1987 (Sing), s 35.
172 Section 36.
173 Section 37.
174 Sections 38 and 106.
175 Roya Ghafele and Benjamin Gibert 'A Counterfactual Impact Analysis of Fair Use Policy on Copyright Related Industries in Singapore Laws' (2014) 3(2) Laws 327.
176 United States – Singapore Free Trade Agreement, above n 159, art 16.4.10: 'Each Party shall confine limitations or exceptions to exclusive rights in Articles 16.4 and 16.5 to certain special cases which do not conflict with a normal exploitation of the work, performance, or phonogram, and do not unreasonably prejudice the legitimate interests of the right holder.'
177 Copyright Act 1987 (Sing), s 28.
178 Section 136.

Clearly, as trading opportunities in the Asian Pacific region escalate, and as the subject matter of that trade moves to copyright-protected goods, New Zealand and Australian entrepreneurs will be disadvantaged without equivalent exceptions in their respective copyright laws to their Asian trading partners. This issue is one that their governments should take very seriously.

8 Conclusion

Despite the compelling arguments in favour of fair use, neither New Zealand nor Australia appears likely to implement fair use in the short term. The Australian Attorney-General George Brandis said in 2013 that the proposed test lacked certainty, and risked artists and creators 'being cheated of the fair compensation for their creativity'.[179] New Zealand has a new Labour-led coalition Government that includes the Green Party, which previously introduced a bill to implement fair use. However, without a strong lead from Australia, it would take a brave New Zealand Government to ignore the demands of well-funded overseas rights owners, making it unlikely we will see a fair use–style defence to copyright infringement introduced in New Zealand.[180]

Entry into the CPTPP provides less incentive for New Zealand to amend its Copyright Act to counterbalance the increased protections for rights owners that would have been introduced had the TPP been ratified. In any event, similarly to the Australian Government, the New Zealand Government may be wary of introducing fair use because they believe it could create uncertainty for the business community. Australia may be concerned about introducing such a change because of the strong reaction from rights owners. However, both countries risk missing opportunities that an open-ended exception such as fair use offers. In Australia, there is likely to be continuing pressure to implement the recommendations of the two reviews that explored the introduction of fair use and concluded that a fair use–type exception was in the best interests of Australia. To ignore these reviews, and the move to fair use in other jurisdictions

179 George Brandis, Attorney-General of Australia 'Statement to the Senate Tabling of ALRC Report on Copyright and the Digital Economy' (speech to Australian Senate, 13 February 2014) www.alrc.gov.au/sites/default/files/pdfs/140213_-_statement_-_alrc_report_copyright_2.pdf.
180 Gareth Hughes, a list member of Parliament representing the Green Party, proposed a new s 40A as an amendment to the TPP Agreement Amendment Bill on 8 November 2016; www.legislation. govt.nz.

that have their basis in English fair dealing law, risks consigning Australia and New Zealand to a digital backwater reliant on trading in minerals, dairy products and meat. The presence of a conservative judiciary in New Zealand suggests there is little hope of a broad interpretation of the closed list of exceptions in New Zealand. Even if Australia were to implement fair use, the agreements in place since 1985 to create closer economic ties between Australia and New Zealand appear to have made little progress in relation to copyright exceptions. The potential benefits to both countries of introducing a fair use exception may be difficult to quantify in economic terms. However, should fair use not be introduced, the social legitimacy of copyright law in both countries could be irretrievably damaged.

7

Open Government Data Licences in the Greater China Region

Jyh-An Lee[1]

1 Introduction

Governments around the world create and collect an enormous amount of data that covers important environmental, educational, geographical, meteorological, scientific, demographic, transport, tourism, health insurance, crime, occupational safety, product safety and many other types of information.[2] This data is generated as part of a government's daily functions.[3] Given the exceptional social and economic value of some government data, former United States President Barack Obama

---

1   Copyright © 2018 Jyh-An Lee. Associate Professor at the Faculty of Law in the Chinese University of Hong Kong. The author is grateful to Susan Corbett and Jessica Lai for their helpful comments. This study was supported by a grant from the Research Grants Council in Hong Kong (Project No. CUHK 14612417).
2   Keiran Hardy and Alana Maurushat 'Opening Up Government Data for Big Data Analysis and Public Benefit' (2017) 33 CLSR 30 at 31; National Archives *UK Government Licensing Framework for public sector information* (5th ed, January 2016) [UK Licensing Framework]; Joshua Tauberer *The Principles and Practices of Open Government Data* (2nd ed, self-published, 2014); Katleen Janssen 'The Influence of the PSI Directive on Open Government Data: An Overview of Recent Developments' (2011) 28 Government Information Quarterly 446 at 446; Barbara Ubaldi *Open Government Data: Towards Empirical Analysis of Open Data Initiatives* (Organisation for Economic Cooperation and Development, Working Papers on Public Governance 22, 2013) at 4.
3   Miriam Marcowitz-Bitton 'Commercializing Public Sector Information' (2015) 97 JPTOS 412 at 413.

described it as a 'national asset'.[4] For various policy reasons, in recent years, open government data (OGD) has become a popular governmental practice and an international movement associated with free access to government data by everyone.[5] 'Open government' has therefore acquired a new meaning empowered by digital technologies and data science.[6] It is estimated that more than 250 national or local governments from around 50 developed and developing countries have launched OGD initiatives.[7] Data.gov, established by the United States Federal Government, and Data. gov.uk, launched by the British Government, are both notable examples of data portals through which governments make their data available to the public.[8] In the Greater China region, Taiwan led the wave by promoting OGD as a national policy in 2012. China's Premier Le Keqiang made a public statement in 2015 supporting OGD, whereas Hong Kong built its first OGD portal in 2016. These developments are discussed in more detail later in the chapter.

In July 2013, G8 leaders signed the G8 Open Data Charter, which outlined five fundamental open data principles.[9] Two years earlier, the international OGD movement led to the establishment of the Open

---

4   The White House Office of the Press Secretary 'Obama Administration Releases Historic Open Data Rules to Enhance Government Efficiency and Fuel Economic Growth' (press release, 9 May 2013).

5   See Joel Gurin *Open Data Now: The Secret to Hot Startups, Smart Investing, Savvy Marketing, and Fast Innovation* (McGraw-Hill, New York, 2014) at 216–218; Anneke Zuiderwijk and Marijn Janssen 'Open Data Policies, Their Implementation and Impact: A Framework for Comparison' (2014) 31 Government International Quarterly 17 at 17; Teresa Scassa 'Public Transit Data Through an Intellectual Property Lens: Lessons About Open Data' (2014) 41 Fordham Urb LJ 1759 at 1760; Deirdre Lee, Richard Cyganiak and Stefan Decker *Open Data Ireland: Best Practice Handbook* (Department of Public Expenditure and Reform, Government of Ireland, May 2014) at 26.

6   See Jillian Raines 'The Digital Accountability and the Transparency Act of 2011 (DATA): Using Open Data Principles to Revamp Spending Transparency Legislation' (2013) NYL Sch L Rev 313 at 321–324; Nataša Veljković, Sanja Bogdanović-Dinić and Leonid Stoimenov 'Benchmarking Open Government: An Open Data Perspective' (2014) 31 Government Information Quarterly 278 at 278–279; Jeremy Weinstein and Joshua Goldstein 'The Benefits of A Big Tent: Opening Up Government in Developing Countries: A Response to Yu & Robinson's The New Ambiguity of "Open Government"' (2012) 60 UCLA Law Rev Disc 38 at 40–41 (noting the distinction between and the convergence of the 'technologies for open data' and 'politics of open government') citing Harlan Yu and David G Robinson 'The New Ambiguity of Open Government' (2012) 59 UCLA Law Rev Disc 178 at 205.

7   'Open Data in 60 Seconds' The World Bank opendatatoolkit.worldbank.org.

8   Data.gov www.data.gov; Data.gov.uk data.gov.uk; see Gurin, above n 5, at 10–11 and 218; Yu and Robinson, above n 6, at 198 and 200; Jean-Louis Monino and Soraya Sedkaoui *Big Data, Open Data and Data Development* (Wiley-ISTE, New Jersey, 2016) vol 3 at xxxv (noting that these are the two leading nations globally in promoting open data policies); Esteve Sanz 'Open Governments and Their Cultural Transitions' in Mila Gascó-Hernández (ed) *Open Government: Opportunities and Challenges for Public Governance* (Springer, New York, 2014) 1 at 11 (describing the role of Data.gov).

9   *Open Data Charter* (Cabinet Office (UK), Policy Paper, 18 June 2013) at 8.

Government Partnership (OGP), 'a multilateral initiative that aims to secure concrete commitments from governments to promote transparency, empower citizens, fight corruption, and harness new technologies to strengthen governance'.[10] The OGP was initiated by eight national governments (Brazil, Indonesia, Mexico, Norway, the Philippines, South Africa, the United Kingdom and the United States)[11] with the proclamation of the Open Government Declaration on 20 September 2011.[12] Sixty-seven additional national governments have joined the OGP since its incorporation.[13] In total, 75 governments altogether have made more than 2,500 commitments to implement open data policies.[14] International organisations, such as the World Bank, have also actively advocated for and implemented open data policies.[15]

Businesses are also embracing the OGD trend as reflected in new strategies, applications, products and services. For example, Microsoft introduced the 'Open Government Data Initiative' to promote the company's Window Azure online platform as a tool for OGD.[16] Government data has become an increasingly important strategic source for entrepreneurship, innovation and economic growth.[17] Businesses may aggregate, repack and redistribute the data, develop new applications and platforms, combine the data with other information or explore novel ways to add value to government data. Enterprises can make use of such data to provide services relating to travel, business planning, medical decisions and so on.[18] The commercial value of this volume of government data is increasingly apparent in the 'Big Data' technology environment, where enormous amounts of datasets are analysed digitally to discover patterns

---

10   'About OGP: What is the Open Government Partnership?' Open Government Partnership [OGP] www.opengovpartnership.org.
11   'Open Government Declaration' OGP, above n 10.
12   OGP, above n 10.
13   OGP, above n 10.
14   OGP, above n 10.
15   See 'World Bank Open Data' World Bank data.worldbank.org.
16   See Steve Clayton 'Microsoft's Open Government Data Initiative with Windows Azure' (11 May 2009) Microsoft Developer blogs.msdn.microsoft.com; Marius Oiaga 'Windows Azure Powers Microsoft Open Government Data Initiative' (7 May 2009) Softpedia news.softpedia.com.
17   See the discussion below, Section 3.2.
18   See Frederik Zuiderveen Borgesius, Jonathan Gray and Mireille van Eechoud 'Open Data, Privacy, and Fair Information Principles: Towards a Balancing Framework' (2015) 30 Berkley Tech LJ 2073 at 2081.

of natural or social phenomena or human behaviours.[19] A number of non-profit organisations, such as the Open Data Institute, Open Knowledge Foundation and the Sunlight Foundation, have also actively taken part in the OGD movement in different ways.[20]

OGD policy involves various legal issues, ranging from personal data protection,[21] citizens' right of access to government information or freedom of information,[22] the attribution of legal liability[23] and appropriate parties to release and receive government data.[24] Intellectual property (IP) and licensing thereof has both been viewed as a cornerstone for OGD, in terms of structuring the government–user relationship[25] and, from a cynical perspective, as one of the main obstacles to the release of governments' data in accordance with the OGD ideology.[26] Government agencies may delay the release of the data because they are uncertain about the best licensing arrangement of the data they hold. Entrepreneurs may hesitate to use or reuse government data if there is no reliable licensing or clear legal arrangement governing it.[27] Tim Berners-Lee, inventor of the World

---

19   See Monino and Sedkaoui, above n 8, at 30–33 and 38; Michael Chui, Diana Farrell and Steve Van Kuiken 'Generating Economic Value Through Open Data' in Brett Goldstein and Lauren Dyson (eds) *Beyond Transparency: Open Data and the Future of Civic Innovation* (Code for America, San Francisco, 2013) 163 at 163; Joel Gurin 'Big Data and Open Data: How Open Will the Future Be?' (2015) 10 IS JL Poly for Info Socy 691 at 699–700 (2015); Hardy and Maurushat, above n 2, at 30–31; Ubaldi, above n 2, at 5–7; see also Maureen K Ohlhausen *The Social Impact of Open Data* (Federal Trade Commission, 23 July 2014) (addressing the relationship between Big Data and OGD from the perspective of the United States Federal Trade Commission).

20   See Lee, Cyganiak and Decker, above n 5, at 28–31.

21   See Gurin, above n 5, at 183–195, 232; Micah Altman and others 'Towards a Modern Approach to Privacy-Aware Government Data Releases' (2015) 30 Berkley Tech LJ 1976 at 2006–2010, 2048–2059; Hardy and Maurushat, above n 2, at 34; Jeff Jonas and Jim Harper 'Open Government: The Privacy Imperative' in Daniel Lathrop and Laurel Ruma (eds) *Open Government: Collaboration, Transparency, and Participation in Practice* (O'Reilly Media, 2010); Borgesius, Gray and van Eechoud, above n 18, at 2086–2093, 2107–2114, 2125–2129; Mashael Khayyat and Frank Bannister 'Open Data Licensing: More Than Meets the Eye' (2015) 20 Info Poly 231 and 244–245; Zuiderwijk and Janssen n 5, at 22, 26; Lee, Cyganiak and Decker, above n 5, at 63–65; Ubaldi, above n 2, at 43.

22   See Tauberer, above n 2, at 87–89, 125; Jeffrey D Rubenstein 'Hacking FOIA: Requests to Drive Government Innovation' in Brett Goldstein and Lauren Dyson (eds) *Beyond Transparency: Open Data and the Future of Civic Innovation* (Code for America, San Francisco, 2013) 81; Gurin, above n 19, at 700–701; Marcowitz-Bitton, above n 3, at 419–423; Lee, Cyganiak and Decker, above n 5, at 21; Ubaldi, above n 2, at 4–5, 37.

23   Zuiderwijk and Janssen, above n 4, at 22.

24   See David Robinson and others 'Government Data and the Invisible Hand' (2009) 11 Yale JL & Tech 160 (arguing that private sector, commercial or non-profit organisations, rather than the government, are better suited to deliver OGD).

25   See Ubaldi, above n 2, at 37.

26   See Khayyat and Bannister, above n 21, at 232; Janssen, above n 2, at 452 (noting that quite a few French Governments had been struggling with licensing policies toward OGD).

27   Ubaldi, above n 2, at 11.

Wide Web, provided a 5-Star Scheme to evaluate the degree of dataset reusability.[28] The scheme's initial 1-Star level sets the most fundamental requirement for OGD, which is that data should be accessible online under an open licence.[29] However, this scheme neither illustrates what is an appropriate open licence for OGD, nor explains why an open licence matters for OGD. In other words, this scheme advocates for the implementation of open licensing for OGD without further definition of this type of licence and its association with OGD.

This chapter focuses on legal issues associated with OGD licences in the Greater China region – namely, Hong Kong, Mainland China and Taiwan. Different government agencies with different policy goals have set different legal terms under which they will release their data. These terms reflect policy considerations that differ from those contemplated in business transactions or shared in typical commons scenarios, such as free or open source software communities.[30] They also concern some fundamental IP issues that are not covered by, or analysed in depth in, the current literature.

The aim of this chapter is to provide a comprehensive legal analysis of open data licences or terms in Hong Kong, mainland China and Taiwan. This study argues that the choice and design of an open data licence forms an important element of a government's information policy. Part 2 introduces the concept and characteristics of OGD, which emphasises citizens' easy and timely access to government data. The features associated with OGD have begun to form an increasingly universal principle adhered to around the world. Part 3 identifies the primary policy goals of OGD, which include the enhancement of governmental transparency, accountability, public participation, the improvement of democracy and public service quality and the advancement of innovation and economic development. These policy goals should be the deciding factors in the design and choice of licence. Part 4 explores the licences and terms design for OGD in Hong Kong, mainland China and Taiwan. Part 5 examines the major legal issues pertaining to the licensing of OGD in the three jurisdictions mentioned above. Part 6 concludes the findings of this chapter.

---

28   James G Kim and Michael Hausenblas 'By Example …' 5 Star Open Data 5stardata.info.

29   Ibid.

30   See Jyh-An Lee 'New Perspectives on Public Goods Production: Policy Implications of Open Source Software' (2008) 9 Vand J Ent & Tech L 45 at 50–53; Molly Shaffer Van Houweling 'The New Servitudes' (2008) 96 Geo LJ 885 at 925–926.

2 The Concept of Open Data

OGD, sometimes referred to as open Public Sector Information (PSI),[31] represents policies or practices that make data held by the public sector digitally available and accessible for reuse or redistribution for free or at a nominal cost. According to the European Union (EU) Directive on the Re-Use of Public Sector Information, '[o]pen data policies … encourage the wide availability and re-use of public sector information for private or commercial purposes, with minimal or no legal, technical, or financial constraints'.[32] Commentators may link the open data movement to other similar movements, in which information is released and widely disseminated by digital technologies and through the internet.[33] Those movements include open access, open educational resources, open standard and free or open source software initiatives.[34]

A number of organisations and individuals have provided their own definitions of, or criteria for, open data. For example, a working group led by Carl Malamud, a renowned advocate for open internet and OGD, first suggested eight principles for open data in December 2007.[35] These principles include complete, primary, timely, accessible, machine processable, non-discriminatory, non-proprietary, and licence-free.[36]

---

31 Zuiderwijk and Janssen, above n 5, at 17.

32   Amending Directive 2003/98/EC on the Re-Use of Public Sector Information [2013] OJ L175/1 [EU Amending Directive]; see Hardy and Maurushat, above n 2, at 30; Tauberer, above n 2, at 95; Lee, Cyganiak and Decker, above n 4, at 4; Ubaldi, above n 2, at 6; Gurin, above n 5, at 9 ('Open Data can best be described as accessible public data that people, companies, and organizations can use to launch new ventures, analyze patterns and trends, make data-driven decisions, and solve complex problems'); Borgesius, Gray and van Eechoud, above n 18, at 2075 ('[o]pen government data refers to data released by public sector bodies, in a manner that is legally and technically re-usable'); but see Luca Leone 'Open Data and Food Law in the Digital Era: Empowering Citizens Through ICT Technology' (2015) 10 Eur Food & Feed L Rev 356 at 358 (claiming that there is no generally accepted definition of open data or OGD).

33   See Yu and Robinson, above n 6, at 187–188; Sanz, above n 8, at 3–5 and 8–11 (describing a series of openness movements enabled by the internet, including the free/open source software movement, and their relations to OGD).

34   See Tauberer, above n 2, at 12–13, 93; Scassa, above n 5, at 1779–1780; Yu and Robinson, above n 6, at 187–188; Weinstein and Goldstein, above n 6, at 40 (noting that OGD represents 'a new alignment of open source and transparency').

35   Open Gov Data 'The Annotated 8 Principles of Open Government Data' (8 December 2007) Open Gov Data opengovdata.org.

36   Open Gov Data, above n 35; Tauberer, above n 2, at 187–188; Khayyat and Bannister, above n 21, at 242; Ubaldi, above n 2, at 8.

Open Knowledge International (OKI), a British non-profit network advocating for free access to, and the sharing of, information globally, defines open data as 'data that can be freely used, re-used and redistributed by anyone – subject only, at most, to the requirement to attribute and [*sic*] sharealike'.[37] According to OKI's definition, there should be no discrimination in regard to different uses of government data.[38] Therefore, '"non-commercial" restrictions that would prevent "commercial" use, or restrictions of use for certain purposes (e.g., only in education), are not allowed'.[39]

Finally, the Sunlight Foundation has published its *Open Data Policy Guidelines* to illustrate OGD best practices.[40] The International Open Data Charter, a collaboration between governments based on the G8 Open Data Charter, identifies six principles of open data: open by default; timely and comprehensive; accessible and usable; comparable and interoperable; for improved governance and citizen engagement; and for inclusive development and innovation.[41]

In sum, most open data advocates concur on the principles of timeliness, comprehensiveness and that the data must be openly accessible.[42] In addition, two other noteworthy principles, 'open by default' and 'open format', are supported by most open data advocates. These are discussed below.

2.1 Open by Default

Many believe that it is a general principle that government data should be openly and freely available online, whereas the non-disclosure of government data should be an exception. A government's proactive disclosure of data is essential to its transparency and democratic governance.[43] In other words, governments should open their data by default unless there is a compelling reason, such as national security or privacy protection, to keep the data confidential.[44] This principle is

---

37   'What is Open Data' Open Data Handbook opendatahandbook.org.
38   Open Data Handbook, above n 42.
39   Open Data Handbook, above n 42.
40   'Open Data Policy Guidelines' Sunlight Foundation sunlightfoundation.com.
41   'Principles' Open Data Charter opendatacharter.net.
42   See Tauberer, above n 2, at 98–99 and 115; Ubaldi, above n 2, at 24.
43   Borgesius, Gray and van Eechoud, above n 18, at 2084.
44   See Gurin, above n 5, at 219.

recognised in the G8 Open Data Charter[45] and in the open data policies of the EU and the United Kingdom.[46] It can also be found in New York City's *Technical Standards Manual*, which states that:[47]

> [a]ll public data sets must be considered open unless they contain information designated as sensitive, private, or confidential as defined by the Citywide Data Classification Policy or information that is exempt pursuant to the Public Officers' Law, or any other provision of a federal or state law, rule or regulation or local law.

2.2 Open Format

Government data should be made available in formats that are suitable for all types of use.[48] The data should be in formats that are machine-readable, downloadable, usable and distributable.[49] Such formats are typically open or non-proprietary industrial protocols and formats.[50] Put differently, '[a]n open format is one that is platform independent, machine readable, and made available to the public without restrictions that would impede the re-use of that information'.[51] Extensible Markup Language (XML) is an example of open format, enabling interoperability of data from diverse sources.[52]

In Tim Berners-Lee's Five-Star Open Data Scheme, 'using non-proprietary formats' is at the Three-Star level.[53] An open format can effectively promote the analysis and reuse of data.[54] The Obama Administration endorsed releasing government data in 'computer-readable' forms.[55] Similarly, in the Open Government Declaration created in

---

45   Open Data Charter, above n 41.
46   See Gurin, above n 5, at 219.
47   New York City Department of Information Technology and Telecommunications *NYC Open Data: Open Data Policy and Technical Standards Manual* (November 2016) at 3.4.1.
48   Tauberer, above n 2, at 99.
49   See Raines, above n 6, at 324; Ubaldi, above n 2, at 24.
50   Tauberer, above n 2, at 99; see also Teresa Scassa and Robert J Currie 'New First Principles? Assessing the Internet's Challenges to Jurisdiction' (2011) 42 Geo J Intl L 1017 at 1067 (noting that efforts to control format in the OGD settings are fading).
51   Peter R Orszag *Memorandum for the Heads of Executive Departments and Agencies* (Executive Office of the President Office of Management and Budget, Memorandum 10–16, 8 December 2009).
52   See Leone, above n 32, at 358.
53   Kim and Hausenblas, above n 28. The scheme measures open data in terms of how well data is integrated into the web: Five Star is the highest level and One Star is the minimal level. See Tim Berners-Lee 'Linked Data'(18 June 2009) www.w3.org.
54   Tauberer, above n 2, at 100–101.
55   'Technology' Obama White House Archive obamawhitehouse.archives.gov.

September 2011, the United States and seven other signatory countries agreed to 'provide high-value information, including raw data, in a timely manner, in formats that the public can easily locate, understand and use, and in formats that facilitate reuse'.[56]

3 Policy Goals Underlying Open Data

OGD brings important social, economic and democratic value to society.[57] Likewise, it can promote both public and private interests.[58] An EU Directive on the Re-Use of Public Sector Information further highlights the value of open data policies:[59]

> Open data policies ... which promote the circulation of information not only for economic operators but also for the public, can play an important role in kick-starting the development of new services based on novel ways to combine and make use of such information, stimulate economic growth and promote social engagement.

OGD policies are tasked with changing the way people run governments and do business via freely available government data.[60] Therefore, the aim of some OGD policies is to build an ecosystem with multiple functions. Identifying policy goals for OGD and setting priorities are also critically important for the design of data governance and relevant legal structures, including licences. In Part 3, I briefly analyse the policy goals underlying OGD.

---

56   OGP, above n 10.
57   See Peter Conradie and Sunil Choenni 'On the Barriers for Local Government Releasing Open Data' (2015) 31 Government Information Quarterly 10 at 10.
58   See Gurin, above n 5, at 218.
59   EU Amending Directive, above n 32.
60   Gurin, above n 5, at 9.

3.1 Transparency and Accountability

OGD promotes the transparency of government and the policymaking process, which underpins accountability and democracy.[61] Transparency involves the disclosure of actions taken by the public sector.[62] Government data can definitely shed light on government activities. Some government data, such as that pertaining to public spending, distribution of revenue and subsidy, is critically important for government accountability.[63] Therefore, by enabling the monitoring of government activities, open data can help reduce corruption.[64]

The former Obama Administration identified its open data policy goal as increasing transparency, participation and collaboration,[65] which will eventually advance the quality and efficiency of the services provided by the government.[66] Likewise, the French Government's OGD policy aims to promote government accountability and make good use of the 'collective intelligence of its citizens'.[67] The Australian Government similarly acknowledged how public access and the reuse of government information could enhance public participation and democracy.[68] The World Bank stated that open data 'encourages greater citizen participation in government affairs' and 'supports democratic societies'.[69] Therefore, OGD has been viewed as a tool to advance public scrutiny, political

---

61   See Lee, Cyganiak and Decker, above n 5, at 4; Hardy and Maurushat, above n 2, at 33; Tauberer, above n 2, at 132; Chui, Farrell and Van Kuiken, above n 19, at 163–164; Janssen, above n 2, at 446; Leone, above n 32 at 356 and 358; Marcowitz-Bitton, above n 3, at 413; Scassa, above n 5, at 1760; Veljković, Bogdanović-Dinić and Stoimenov, above n 6, at 280; Yu and Robinson, above n 6, at 196–197; Zuiderwijk and Janssen, above n 5, at 17; Ubaldi, above n 2, at 4 and 11–12; Weinstein and Goldstein, above n 6, at 46; Judith Bannister 'Open Government: From Crown Copyright to the Creative Commons and Culture Change' (2011) 34(3) UNSW LJ 1080 at 1089 (stating that open access to government information improves transparent decision-making and the quality of democracy); Tiago Peixoto 'The Uncertain Relationship Between Open Data and Accountability: A Response to Yu and Robinson's the New Ambiguity of "Open Government"' (2013) 60 UCLA L Rev Discourse 200 at 202 and 207 (arguing that open date enables transparency, which may lead to accountability).

62   Peixoto, above n 61, at 203.

63   Borgesius, Gray and van Eechoud, above n 18, at 2083.

64   See Marcowitz-Bitton, above n 3, at 416; 'Starting an Open Data Initiative' World Bank opendatatoolkit.worldbank.org.

65   Borgesius, Gray and van Eechoud, above n 18, at 2083–2084; Sanz, above n 8, at 10.

66   Hardy and Maurushat, above n 2, at 32; Orszag, above n 51, at 1; Scassa, above n 5, at 1760; Yu and Robinson, above n 6, at 196 and 201; Zuiderwijk and Janssen, above n 5, at 17; Borgesius, Gray and van Eechoud, above n 18, at 2085–2086 (illustrating how open data promotes public sector efficiency and improves the quality of public service); Peixoto, above n 61, at 202 (arguing that OGD enables participation, which fosters better services and policies).

67   Borgesius, Gray and van Eechoud, above n 18, at 2083.

68   Bannister, above n 61, 1091–1092.

69   World Bank, above n 64.

accountability,[70] participation and the quality of government services. Ideally, these features will combine to improve the governance of, and trust in, the public sector.[71]

3.2 Economic Development

OGD has been described as constituting a crucial strategy to build a 'data-driven economy'.[72] The immense volume and diversity of government data may bring great commercial value to enterprises.[73] Put more clearly, OGD is an abundant free resource that fuels a wide range of new innovative products, apps, services and business models associated with data reuse and analysis.[74] Additional value is then created 'by means of crowdsourcing, user tracking, and data analytics'.[75] Various commercial uses of government data may further encourage economic development.[76] In other words, a properly designed OGD policy can unlock the value of PSI to the public sector.[77]

On 9 May 2013, when the United States Office of Management and Budget and the Office of Science and Technology Policy announced its Open Data Policy, President Obama signed an Executive Order to promote OGD and stated that: [78]

> [Open data can] fuel more private sector innovation … And talented entrepreneurs are doing some pretty amazing things with it … Starting today, we're making even more government data available online, which

---

70   Yu and Robinson, above n 6, at 182.

71   Open Data Charter, above n 41.

72   Leone, above n 32, at 358.

73   See Leone, above n 32, at 356; Marcowitz-Bitton, above n 3, at 413; Scassa, above n 5, at 1773–1774 (describing the commercial value of transit data); Gurin, above n 5, at 693–696.

74   See Gurin, above n 5, at 23–35 and 218–219; Chui, Farrell and Van Kuiken, above n 19, at 163 and 168; Janssen, above n 2, at 446; Marcowitz-Bitton, above n 3, at 416; Conradie and Choenni, above n 57, at 10 (stating that 'the release of [government] data for a broader use may give a boost to the creative industry, which in return leads to innovative applications and techniques').

75   Michael Halberstam 'Beyond Transparency: Rethinking Election Reform from an Open Government Perspective' (2015) 38 Seattle UL Rev 1007 at 1028.

76   See Lee, Cyganiak and Decker, above n 5, at 4; Scassa, above n 5, at 1760–1761; Zuiderwijk and Janssen, above n 5, at 17; Gurin, above n 5, at 217 (stating that open government datasets 'can have a powerful impact for the public good and economic growth'); Gianluca Misuraca, Fransesco Mureddu and David Osimo 'Policy-Making 2.0: Unleashing the Power of Big Data for Public Governance' in Milo Gascó-Hernández (ed) *Open Government: Opportunities and Challenges for Public Governance* (2014) 171 in Christopher G Reddick (series ed) *Public Administration and Information Technology* (Springer, 2014) vol 4 at 171 (describing the benefit brought by OGD in the commercial field).

77   See Borgesius, Gray and van Eechoud, above n 18, at 2080.

78   The White House Office of the Press Secretary, above n 4.

will help launch even more new startups. And we're making it easier for people to find the data and use it, so that entrepreneurs can build products and services we haven't even imagined yet.

The European Commission has also highlighted the potential for significant economic gains to come from OGD.[79] Similarly, both the United Kingdom[80] and Australian[81] governments have stated that OGD could greatly benefit the economy. A number of studies have estimated that the economic value brought by OGD in some countries will exceed hundreds of millions, or even trillions, of dollars.[82] For example, the McKinsey Global Institute estimated that open data could unlock an economic value of US$3–5 trillion a year across seven sectors in the United States.[83] In summary, OGD can form an important part of a government's economic policy when it comes to fostering innovation and economic development.

4 Standardised OGD Licences in the Greater China Region

Some OGD advocates believe that true open data should be free from licence restrictions;[84] others claim that without specific open licences, it is too costly for users to search and negotiate with data publishers.[85] For those who believe licences are necessary for OGD, the consensus is that the licences, or terms and conditions, should facilitate optimal access to the underlying data.[86] Government agencies may choose click-

---

79   Zuiderwijk and Janssen, above n 5, at 17.

80   See Gurin, above n 5, at 9; National Archives, above n 2, at 6; Janssen, above n 2, at 451.

81   Bannister, above n 61, at 1091.

82   See Borgesius, Gray and van Eechoud, above n 18, at 2082; Lee, Cyganiak and Decker, above n 5, at 18–19; Chui, Farrell and Van Kuiken, above n 19, at 166; Marcowitz-Bitton, above n 3, at 424; Ubaldi, above n 2, at 15.

83   James Manyika and others 'Open Data: Unlocking Innovation and Performance with Liquid Information' (October 2013) McKinsey & Company www.mckinsey.com.

84   See Tauberer, above n 2, at 106 and 144–145; Yu and Robinson, above n 6, at 196; Yochai Benkler 'Commons and Growth: The Essential Role of Open Commons in Market Economies (Book Review)' (2013) 80 U Chi L Rev 1499 at 1551 (claiming that OGD is subject to no constraint).

85   See, for example, Lee, Cyganiak and Decker, above n 5 at 6; Federico Morando 'Legal Interoperability: Making Open Government Data Compatible with Businesses and Communities' (2013) 4 Italian J Libr Archives & Info Sci 441 at 442 (introducing the viewpoint that 'the distribution of data also requires … licensing').

86   Ruth Okediji 'Government as Owners of Intellectual Property? Considerations for Public Welfare in the Era of Big Data' (2016) 18 Vand J Ent & Tech L 331 at 336.

use or standardised licences, such as a Creative Commons licence,[87] or they may choose to develop their own licensing terms.[88] The primary advantages of using standardised licences are saving costs associated with creating a bespoke licence, achieving order and efficiency, and achieving interoperability between licences.[89] The use of standardised licences does not necessarily equate to harmonised copyright laws. Standardised licences aim to help copyright owners, including governments, license their content easily and efficiently, whereas international harmonisation proposals, such as the Asian Pacific Copyright Code proposed by Adrian Sterling and the Asian Pacific Copyright Association, aim to implement copyright systems in different jurisdictions and, eventually, create a mutually applicable dispute resolution system.[90] In this section, I introduce the licences or terms of use adopted in Hong Kong, Mainland China and Taiwan and analyse their similarities and dissimilarities.

4.1 Hong Kong

In 2014, the former Financial Secretary of Hong Kong, John Chun-wah Tsang, announced the Government's plan to make Hong Kong a smart city.[91] Among others, an important initiative was to make all government information available online.[92] Consequently, the Office of the Government Chief Information Officer (OGCIO) has overhauled its open data portal to facilitate a wide range of value-added data reuse.[93] The revamped portal, data.gov.hk, came into existence in March 2015 and covers 18 dataset categories.[94] It is estimated that there are more than

---

87 See Marcowitz-Bitton, above n 3, at 439; Lee, Cyganiak and Decker, above n 5, at 67.

88 See Food and Drug Administration (FDA) 'Terms of Services' (22 March 2014) Open FDA open.fda.gov.

89 See Khayyat and Bannister, above n 21, at 238; Marcowitz-Bitton, above n 3, at 434; Naomi Korn and Charles Oppenheim 'Licensing Open Data: A Practical Guide' (June 2011) Discovery discovery.ac.uk at version 2.0; Kent Mewhort 'Creative Commons Licenses: options for Canadian Open Data Providers' (1 June 2012) CIPPIC: Canadian Internet Policy and Public Interest Clinic cippic.ca (noting the benefit of interoperability brought by CC licences).

90 Adrian Sterling 'Asian Pacific Copyright Code' this volume.

91 John Chun-wah Tsang, Hong Kong Financial Secretary '2014–15 Budget Speech' (Legislative Council of the Hong Kong Special Administrative Region of the People's Republic of China, 26 February 2014).

92 Chun-wah Tsang, above n 91.

93 'Open Data' Legislative Council of the Hong Kong Special Administrative Region of the People's Republic of China www.legco.gov.hk.

94 Data.gov.hk data.gov.hk.

6,000 datasets on this portal. In the same year, Hong Kong was ranked 34th among 122 countries and areas in the 2015 Global Open Data Index released by OKI.[95]

Under the 'Terms and Conditions of Use' found on the portal, the OGCIO outlines two provisions to regulate the licensing of government data.[96] Article 8 stipulates: (1) what a user can and cannot do and (2) the government's disclaimer regarding any liability arising from the use of the subject data.[97] Users 'are allowed to browse, download, distribute, reproduce, hyperlink to, and print in their original format the Data for both commercial and non-commercial purposes on a free-of-charge basis'.[98] Users should 'reproduce and distribute the Data accurately, fairly and sufficiently'.[99] Moreover, users should not only attribute the source from the government, but also acknowledge the government's IP ownership over the data.[100] Article 9 defines the 'commercial purpose' of art 8.[101] These two provisions, especially art 8, play a crucial role in regulating the legal relations between the Hong Kong Government and data users.

4.2 Mainland China

China's Premier Li Keqiang stated in March 2015 that government data should be public wherever possible 'unless it is relevant to national security and privacy'.[102] Shanghai and Beijing were the first cities to begin OGD policies in mainland China.[103] The National Bureau of Statistics was the first central government agency that released OGD,[104] followed

---

95 'Place overview' Global Open Data Index index.okfn.org.
96 'Terms and Conditions of Use' Data.gov.hk data.gov.hk.
97 At 8.
98 At 8.
99 At 8.
100 At 8: 'you shall identify clearly the source of the Data and acknowledge the Government ownership of the intellectual property rights in the Data and in all copies thereof including but not limited to paper copies, digital copies and copies placed on other websites.'
101 At 8–9.
102 Eleanor Ross 'Why Open Data Doesn't Mean Open Government' *The Guardian* (online ed, United Kingdom, 2 December 2015).
103 Joel Gurin 'The People's Republic of Open Data?' (11 December 2014) Open Data Now www.opendatanow.com.
104 National Bureau of Statistics of China data.stats.gov.cn.

by the State Intellectual Property Office (SIPO)'s open patent database.[105] A number of local governments, such as Zhejiang Province,[106] Qingdao City[107] and Zhanjiang City,[108] have also established OGD portals.

Most Chinese government agencies building OGD portals do not provide terms of use or licensing agreements for users. As of March 2017, only the City of Beijing,[109] Zhejiang Province[110] and Qingdao City[111] have statements on legal rights and obligations regarding the use of their OGD. Beijing uses the term 'Disclaimer', whereas Zhejiang uses the term 'Statement of the Website'.[112] Beijing's Disclaimer covers not only a disclaimer made by the government, but also the users' obligations with regard to the use of government data.[113] Qingdao provides two documents to regulate users' use of the data, namely a 'disclaimer'[114] and the 'Licence Agreement of Qingdao City's Open Data Portal'.[115]

In the City of Beijing's and Qingdao's Disclaimers, users are granted the right to use the OGD for free,[116] but Beijing does not allow users to transfer the data to any third party.[117] Qingdao's Disclaimer similarly provides for free use of the data but reserves the right to charge users in the future.[118] Qingdao's 'License Agreement of Qingdao City's Open Data Portal' provides that users are licensed to 'download, reproduce, and distribute' the data and initiate commercial or non-commercial development, based on the data released by the portal.[119] However, Qingdao's License Agreement prohibits users from charging any third party for the data obtained from the portal.[120]

---

105 State Intellectual Property Office of the PRC patdata.sipo.gov.cn.
106 Zhejiang Provincial Government Portal data.zjzwfw.gov.cn.
107 Open Data of Qingdao Government qingdao.gov.cn/data.
108 Zhanjiang Data Service Network data.zhanjiang.gov.cn.
109 'Disclaimer' BJ Data www.bjdata.gov.cn.
110 'Statement of the Website' Zhejiang Provincial Government Portal www.zjzwfw.gov.cn.
111 Open Data of Qindao Government, above n 107.
112 'Disclaimer' BJ Data, above n 109; 'Statement of the Website' Zhejiang Provincial Government Portal, above n 110.
113 'Disclaimer' BJ Data, above n 109.
114 'Disclaimer' Open Data of Qingdao Government, above n 107.
115 'Licence Agreement of Qingdao City's Open Data Portal' Open Data of Qingdao Government, above n 107.
116 'Disclaimer' BJ Data, above n 109; Open Data of Qingdao Government, above n 107.
117 'Disclaimer' BJ Data, above n 109.
118 'License Agreement of Qingdao City's Open Data Portal' Open Data of Qingdao Government, above n 107.
119 'License Agreement of Qingdao City's Open Data Portal'.
120 'License Agreement of Qingdao City's Open Data Portal'.

Like many other OGD licences, Beijing's Disclaimer requires users to attribute the portal as the source.[121] It also includes a disclaimer indicating that the government is not responsible for the integrity, accuracy or whether the underlying data is up to date.[122] Similar disclaimers can also be found in Qingdao's Disclaimer[123] and Zhejiang's 'Statement of the Website'.[124] Beijing's Disclaimer further stipulates that the application developed by users should be approved by the government and that the government has the power to delete or block the application afterwards if the application is found to violate the law.[125] Zhejiang has made it clear in its 'Statement of the Website' that the government owns copyright in the text, picture, audio, software and other forms of data from its portal.[126] The Statement provides that users are required to obtain a licence from the government for the use of data.[127] However, there is no standardised licence agreement on the website.

4.3 Taiwan

The Taiwan Government released a Cabinet's executive resolution in November 2012 regarding OGD policy, followed by the other detailed rules, such as 'Open Government Data Operating Principle for Agencies of the Executive Yuan', the 'Essential Requirements for Government Open Data Datasets' and the 'Regulations for the Use of the Government Open Data Platform'.[128] In 2013, the National Development Council established the Government Open Data Platform, which collects various open government datasets from both central and local government agencies.[129] In November 2013, the Industrial Development Bureau, under the Taiwan Ministry of Economic Affairs, released and started to implement the 'Open Data Application Promotion Plan'.[130] Taiwan ranked number one among 122 jurisdictions in the 2015 Open Data Index, released by the Open Knowledge Foundation (OKFN).[131]

---

121 'Disclaimer' BJ Data, above n 109.

122 'Disclaimer' Open Data of Qingdao Government, above n 107.

123 'Disclaimer'.

124 'Statement of the Website' Zhejiang Provincial Government Portal, above n 110.

125 BJ Data above n 109.

126 'Statement of the Website' Zhejiang Provincial Government Portal, above n 110.

127 'Statement of the Website'.

128 'e-Government position: An Outline of the Government Open Data Promotion Situation in Taiwan' National Development Council (NDC) www.ndc.gov.tw.

129 See Data.gov.tw data.gov.tw.

130 Industrial Development Bureau *Overview of Open Data Development in Taiwan* (Ministry of Economic Affairs, Taiwan, November 2013).

131 Global Open Data Index, above n 95.

The Taiwan Government published the 'Open Government Data License, version 1.0' on 27 July 2015, for the release of OGD.[132] The licence includes seven articles, which provide the definitions of 'data providing organization', 'user' and 'open data'.[133] The licence grants users with a 'perpetual, worldwide, non-exclusive, irrevocable, royalty-free copyright licence to reproduce, distribute, publicly transmit, publicly broadcast, publicly recite, publicly present, publicly perform, compile, adapt to the Open Data provided for any purpose'.[134] Like many OGD licences, the licence requires users to attribute the data source[135] and provides a disclaimer for government agencies that release data.[136] In May 2016, the licence was approved by the Open Definition Advisory Council in the OKI as conforming to its open definition and was included in its conformant licence list.[137]

5 Legal Analysis of the OGD Licences

The enforceability of a public (open source) licence was recognised by the United States courts in *Jacobsen v Katzer*, in which the United States Federal Circuit acknowledged the value that open source projects bring to society and reaffirmed the copyright holders' freedom to license their copyright on their own terms.[138] The open licences or terms of use associated with OGD, introduced in the previous section, share a number of similarities, though differ in many ways. An attribution requirement and a governmental disclaimer are quite common. In this section, a number of important issues arising from the design of a licence, or its terms and conditions, will be analysed.

5.1 Charges

'Free of charge' is a principle that is normally found in OGD policies. For example, the Taiwan Government has made it clear in its 'Open Government Data License, version 1.0' that the '[t]he Data Providing

---

132 'Open Government Data License: version 1.0' (27 July 2015) NDC data.gov.tw.
133 At 1.
134 At 2.
135 At 3.
136 At 6.
137 Herb Lainchbury 'Announcement: 'Open Government Data License Taiwan 1.0' Approved' (2 May 2016) Open Knowledge International discuss.okfn.org.
138 *Jacobsen v Katzer* 535 F 3d 1373 (Fed Cir 2008) at 1381–1382.

Organization grants User a perpetual, worldwide, non-exclusive, irrevocable, *royalty-free* copyright license'.[139] All the licences or terms associated with OGD in the Greater China regions, introduced in the previous section, likewise state that the data is provided free from any royalty. Therefore, users or licensees do not need to pay for the licensed materials.

Nonetheless, as mentioned previously, in its Disclaimer, the City of Qingdao reserves the right to charge users in the future.[140] From a comparative perspective, the United Kingdom's Charged Licence charges users to use government data. A reasonable explanation for such a difference is that the United Kingdom Government designed the Charged Licence and the government has certain practical considerations to reflect on, including the cost of implementing open data policies. It should also be noted that the United Kingdom Government has deliberately placed two restrictions on the adoption of the Charged Licence: (1) this licence is an exception; and (2) charges should be limited to the costs arising from 'the re-use of information'.[141] This exception, though not yet implemented, is probably designed to retain more financial flexibilities for public agencies with regard to some unique types of data.

Charging a reasonable fee for the use of government data is also permitted in the EU PSI Directive.[142] According to the Directive, the fee must be limited to 'the marginal costs incurred for their reproduction, provision and dissemination' and the charges 'shall not exceed the cost of collection, production, reproduction and dissemination, together with a reasonable return on investment'.[143] Although both the Charged Licence and the EU PSI Directive allow charging for the use of government data, the EU PSI Directive conflicts with the public interest concerns of OGD policy. The Directive permits using open data as a tool to collect 'a reasonable return on investment' in addition to 'the cost of collection, production, reproduction and dissemination'.[144] However, since the generally accepted OGD policy's goal is to promote transparency, accountability, participation and economic development,[145] open data should not be used as a finance

---

139 'Open Government Data Licence: version 1.0' Data.gov.tw data.gov.tw at 2.1 (emphasis added).
140 Open Data of Qingdao Government, above n 107.
141 National Archives, above n 2, at 4.
142 EU Amending Directive, above n 32.
143 Article 6(3).
144 Article 6(3).
145 See above, Part 3.

tool to benefit the government.[146] Therefore, the charges provision in the PSI Directive is obviously not the best practice for OGD policy. For the same token, the reservation provision, with regard to charges in Qingdao's Disclaimer, may create unnecessary uncertainties for OGD users.

5.2 Restriction of Data Use

In order to maximise the use of government data, a substantial segment of the open data community suggests that licensing terms should be the least restrictive or subject to minimal constraints.[147] Nevertheless, 'minimal constraint' does not mean no constraints at all.[148] Accordingly, what constitutes 'minimal constraint' becomes an issue when the policy goal is to maximise the use of government data. Attribution is the most common restriction in public licences, and is discussed in section 5.5 below. Since fostering innovation, new business models and economic development are some of the primary policy goals of OGD, restrictions other than attribution also need to be scrutinised.

Based on the study of licences and other terms applying to users of OGD in the Greater China region, those in Mainland China tend to be more restrictive than those in Hong Kong and Taiwan. For example, Beijing's Disclaimer prohibits users from transferring the data to third parties.[149] However, many new applications associated with OGD involve the transfer of government data. Qingdao's License agreement prohibits users from charging any third party for the data obtained from the portal.[150] It is unclear from Qingdao's License agreement if users can charge for providing third parties with the raw subject data, which has been extended or improved with other value-added services or information.

Beijing's Disclaimer goes further: providing that the applications developed by users are subject to government approval, following that the government has the power to delete or block the applications.[151] This restriction, which is seldom seen in other jurisdictions, reflects the

---

146 See Chris Corbin 'PSI Policy Principles: European Best Practice' in Brian Fitzgerald (ed) *Access to public sector information: Law, technology & policy* (Sydney University Press, Sydney, 2010) vol 2 161 at 167.
147 EU Amending Directive, above n 32, at 3.
148 But see Chui, Farrell and Van Kuiken, above n 19, at 164 (claiming unrestrictive rights to use government data).
149 BJ Data, above n 109.
150 Open Data of Qingdao Government, above n 107.
151 BJ Data, above n 109.

political reality of the region, which tends towards government control of information and market activities. All these restrictions may discourage new business models and value-added service built upon OGD.

In summary, a government's choice of open licensing terms is quite different from that of the private sector. Businesses or communities usually link the choice over terms to contributors' incentives to contribute, costs to provide this incentive and the sustainability of the commons' projects.[152] However, such considerations may not exist in the context of government data that is continuously generated as an outcome of governmental functions. In other words, a government's selection of open data licences tends to reflect its policy goals, which are typically not the same as those addressed in private business or commons settings.

5.3 Licence Compatibility

Compared to the OGD terms released in other jurisdictions in the Greater China Region, Taiwan's Open Government Data License is uniquely devised with a compatibility provision. This provision serves to facilitate the compatibility between different versions of the licence and between the licence and Creative Commons Attribution License 4.0 International.[153] From a comparative perspective, such compatibility provisions are quite common in OGD licences outside of the Greater China Region.[154] Compatibility, or interoperability, between licences means users can legally combine works that are subject to different public licences.[155] Licence compatibility is especially important in scientific fields, such as environmental protection and climate change, where users have an urgent need to use data from sources with different licences.[156] Because

---

152 See Clark D Asay 'A Case for the Public Domain' (2013) 74 Ohio St LJ 753 at 773–780; Jyh-An Lee 'Organizing the Unorganized: The Role of Nonprofit Organizations in the Commons Communities' (2010) 50 Jurimetrics J 275 at 313 (noting that commons communities can sustain by using licensing terms to coordinate individual contributors).

153 NDC, above n 132.

154 See, for example, 'Open Database License (ODbL) v1.0' Open Data Commons opendatacommons.org at 4.4(e); Mewhort, above n 89, at 3 and 20–21 (noting that the British Open Government Licence was intentionally crafted to be compatible with CC licenses).

155 See Christopher S Brown 'Copyleft, The Disguised Copyright: Why Legislative Copyright Reform Is Superior to Copyleft Licenses' (2010) 78 UMKC L Rev 748 at 772–774; Jyh-An Lee 'The Greenpeace of Cultural Environmentalism' (2010) 16 Widener L Rev 1 at 32–33; Martynas Mockus and Monica Palmirani 'Open Government Data Licensing Framework' in Andrea Kő and Enrico Francesconi (eds) *Electronic Government and the Information Systems Perspective* (Springer, 2015) 287 at 290–292; Morando, above n 85, at 445–448.

156 See Estelle Derclaye 'The Role of Copyright in the Protection of Environment and the Fight Against Climate Change: Is the Current Copyright System Adequate?' (2014) 5(2) WIPO J 152 at 158.

public licences and declarations aim to facilitate greater distribution and reuse of the subject materials, such public licences inevitably include a compatibility provision so that users can legally combine content licensed under different licences.[157]

5.4 Government Data in the Public Domain

Some scholars and policymakers assert that, from a policy perspective, the works created by state employees should be in the public domain and not protected by IP at all.[158] For example, the Dutch Council of State opined in 2009 that the City of Amsterdam could not legally impose any restriction on a company's use of the City's database because it was built with tax money.[159] In other words, the City's government did not own the database. In countries like the United States, there are statutory public domain rules that prohibit the federal government from copyrighting works it produces; however, governments may still own copyrights assigned by others.[160]

Even if a government can own copyright, the originality standard may prevent it from claiming copyright over a government database.[161] Originality is the standard for copyright protection internationally,[162] and in the Greater China region as well.[163] Courts in Mainland China

---

157 See 'Open Government Licence for Public Sector Information' National Archives www.national archives.gov.uk.

158 Okediji, above n 86, at 338–339; Gurin, above n 5, at 9 ('governments should make the data they collect available to taxpayers who've paid to collect it'); Marcowitz-Bitton, above n 3, at 415 (introducing the argument that government works 'should be accessible to all, uninhibited' by the argument that taxpayers shall have free access to government-generated data).

159 Janssen, above n 2, at 451.

160 17 USC § 105 ('[c]opyright … is not available for any work of the United States Government'); see also Marcowitz-Bitton, above n 3, at 420 (explaining that '[t]he reason behind 17 U.S.C. § 105 is to ensure that government information remains in the public domain in order to best serve the public interest'); Okediji, above n 86, 343–345 (explaining the evolution of public domain rule on government works in the United States).

161 See Beth Ford 'Open Wide the Gates of Legal Access' (2014) 93 Or L Rev 539 at 546.

162 See Sterling, above n 90.

163 In Mainland China, art 14 of Copyright Law of the PRC 1990 (China) states that: 'A collection of preexisting works or passages therefrom, or of data or other material which does not constitute a work, if manifesting the originality of a work by reason of the selection or arrangement of its contents, is a compilation. The copyright in such compilation shall be enjoyed by the compiler, provided that the exercise of such copyright does not prejudice the copyright in the preexisting works'. Article 2 of Implementing Rules for Copyright Law 1991 (China) stipulates: 'The term "works" as referred to in the Copyright Law means intellectual creations with originality in the literary, artistic or scientific domain, insofar as they can be reproduced in a tangible form.' Originality requirement can be found in Copyright Ordinance 1997 (Hong Kong), s 2(1)(a): 'original literary, dramatic, musical or artistic work.' Article 7.1 of Copyright Act 2016 (Taiwan) states that: 'A compilation work is a work formed by the creative selection and arrangement of materials, and shall be protected as an independent work.'

and Taiwan have ruled that originality requires independent creation and a minimum degree of creativity.[164] In Hong Kong, originality requires authors to show the exercise of skill and judgment.[165] Consequently, facts, or information automatically generated by a machine or algorithm, cannot be protected by copyright because they lack originality.[166] Database creators gain copyright protection of compilations and databases only if the selection, coordination or arrangement of the contents is sufficiently original.[167] However, this is not the case for some government databases, which include statistics, census data, fiscal data, budget information, parliamentary records, election records, property registration, facts about school locations and performance, other factual information, or that are created automatically and mechanically by machine.[168] In other words, government databases often lack originality and therefore cannot be protected by copyright.[169] This may explain why government agencies in Mainland China do not typically provide a licence agreement or terms for the use of copyright works. If the database is not copyrightable, from a copyright perspective there is no need to design such a licence or appropriate terms. Instead, the courts will likely treat any terms of use relating to access and use of such a database as contractual.[170]

---

164 See Jyh-An Lee 'Copyright Protection of Database in Taiwan' (2011) 188 Taiwan L Rev 36 at 39; Taiwan Intellectual Property Office (TIPO), Interpretation No. 980427a, April 27, 2009; *Changchun Publishing Group v Ji Lin University Publishing & United Book City* Jilin HC Ji Min San Zhi ZhongZi 68(2015).

165 Kenneth Wong and Alice Lee *Intellectual Property Law and Practice in Hong Kong* (Sweet & Maxwell, Hong Kong, 2014).

166 See Frederick Abbott, Thomas Cottier and Francis Gurry *International Intellectual Property in an Integrated World Economy* (3rd ed, Wolters Kluwer, 2015) at 535; Scassa, above n 5, at 1782–1783 and 1787–1788.

167 See *Feist Publications Inc v Rural Telephone Services Company* 499 US 340 (1991) at 345.

168 See Marcowitz-Bitton, above n 3, at 413 (stating that government data includes 'national statistics, budget information, parliamentary records, data about the location of schools and their performance, information about crimes, election records, financial data, and more') and 415; Okediji, above n 86, at 334; Tauberer, above n 2, at 115 ('government data normally represents facts about the real world (who voted on what, environmental conditions, financial holdings)'); Borgesius, Gray and van Eechoud, above n 18, at 2094 (noting that government data includes statistics, land registries, business registers, or earth observation data); Lee, above n 5, at 54–56 (noting that common high-value datasets are those of company register, insolvency and bankruptcy record, government contract, various statistics, and so on); Ubaldi, above n 2, at 6 and 23 (noting that government data consists of business information, registers, geographic information, meteorological information, social data on statistics and transport information).

169 See Marcowitz-Bitton, above n 3, at 415; Scassa, above n 5, at 1785; Paul Miller, Rob Styles and Tom Heath 'Open Data Commons, A License for Open Data' (22 April 2008) CEUR Workshop Proceedings ceur-ws.org (similarly holding that data, datasets and databases are mostly not copyrightable creative works); Scassa, above n 5, at 1776 (stating that it is difficult to identify authorship in government data).

170 *Jacobsen v Katzer*, above n 138. Note: this was a decision of the United States Supreme Court.

In sum, government databases are not protected by copyright unless they meet the originality standard in copyright law. Although some government databases may attain the relevant threshold of original expression in their jurisdiction and, thus, qualify for copyright protection, most government databases do not, such as mundane collections of statistics, factual information or information automatically produced by machine or algorithm. Governments in EU countries can obtain sui generis protection for their databases if they made a substantial investment into the creation of the databases.[171] However, this sui generis right is not available in the Greater China jurisdictions.

Typically, copyright or neighbouring rights protect works subject to open licences, such as Creative Commons licences. Similarly, most open data licences are designed based on the presumption that the subject government's data or database is protected by copyright.[172] For example, Hong Kong's Terms and Conditions require users to recognise the government's ownership of IP in the data.[173] Taiwan's Open Government Data License identifies itself as a copyright licence.[174] Beijing's Disclaimer provides that the government owns property rights over the content.[175] Article 1 of Zhejiang's Statement of the Website is the 'declaration of copyright' of all content on the website.[176]

The use of copyright-dependent terms and statements logically imply that the relevant terms of use do not apply to databases that are not protected by copyright. Nonetheless, a significant number of databases in those OGD portals are automatically and mechanically created, and, therefore, not copyrightable. Consequently, the legal (or, more specifically, copyright-dependent) arrangements around the access and use of databases may not be consistent with the legal status of the databases.

---

171 Directive 96/9/EC on the Legal Protection of Databases [1996] OJ L77/20 at 20.
172 Scassa, above n 5, at 1804; Tauberer, above n 2, at 107 ('[w]hen a work is copyrighted, a license is required to undo or partially undo the all-rights-reserved default rule') and at 144 ('[o]pen licensing … is subject to copyright protections'); Bannister, above n 61, at 1099 ('Creative Commons licensing movement aims to provide a standardised infrastructure for the open licensing of copyright protected material').
173 See Terms and Conditions of Use, above n 96.
174 NDC, above n 132.
175 BJ Data, above n 109.
176 Zhejiang Provincial Government Portal, above n 110, at 1.

I now consider the situation in regard to governments that apply public licences to databases that are not protected by copyright or database rights. What is the legal effect of such licences? It is possible that governments do not conduct due diligence regarding the legal status of the subject data and databases. Based on the author's personal experiences of providing OGD consultation to the public sectors in the Greater China region, this is most likely because of government mentality regarding control over data and databases. Government officials may hesitate to recognise the public domain nature of the sorts of databases over which they are accustomed to exerting their full control. They may not understand that although the government is in charge of database governance, the government cannot legally claim database ownership (in terms of copyright). Nevertheless, they may claim ownership of the physical copy of the database or control access and use through their possession of the database.

From a legal perspective, it is worth exploring the effects of these licences and terms of use if the underlying database is in the public domain. There are two possible approaches to this question, both of which are based on an implication of the *Jacobsen v Katzer* ruling suggesting that contract law applies to public licences.[177] The first interpretation is that the contract may be void, or partly void, as an illegal contract, given that the subject matter database in the contract is not owned by the licensor and is in the public domain. The database should thus be free to everyone.[178] If the underlying database is not protected under applicable law, a licence is unnecessary.[179] Indeed, asserting copyright over public domain materials may at worst be defined as 'copyfraud': an activity that may stifle creativity and free speech.[180]

The second possible solution is to recognise the validity of the agreement and treat it as a binding contract between the database holder and the user. Expressed differently, even if there are no underlying IP rights to support a copyright licence,[181] the agreement itself is still a contract that can legally

---

177 *Jacobsen v Katzer*, above n 138.
178 See Marcowitz-Bitton, above n 3, at 438.
179 'Comments on the Open Database License Proposed by Open Data Commons' Creative Commons sciencecommons.org.
180 Jason Mazzone 'Copyfraud' (2006) 81 NYU L Rev 1026 (2006) at 1028–1030.
181 But see Christopher M Newman 'A License Is Not a "Contract Not to Sue": Disentangling Property and Contract in the Law of Copyright Licenses' (2013) Iowa L Rev 1101 at 1114 (noting that a licence needs to be granted by the titleholder of the property).

oblige database users to fulfil attribution or other duties.[182] This contract theory has, however, been criticised as imposing unnecessary restrictions on public domain resources.[183]

Even if the open licence agreement is valid and enforceable between the licensor and licensee, whether the database is protected by copyright makes an important difference when the licensor attempts to enforce their legal right against a third party. Given the transparent nature of OGD policy, it is quite possible that third parties have not obtained the database directly from the government, but from elsewhere. These third parties may argue that they are not parties to public licences or term of use and thus are not bound by the licence agreement. While contractual or licensing rights and obligations are in personam and, thus, restricted to the specific parties to the contract or licence, property rights are in rem and good against third parties. The risk of third party use of government data in the public licence sphere is higher than that of third party use in a proprietary licensing scenario, as, with the latter, the number of licensees is limited and the licensor may adopt various contractual or technical measures to control the flow of licensed materials. By contrast, those adopting public licences usually have much less understanding and control regarding the flow of licensed materials. Traditionally, even though copyright owners cannot sue the third parties for breach of the licence agreement, they can still claim copyright infringement against them.[184] Nevertheless, if the subject database is in the public domain, the database originators will not have any grounds to sue the third party who does not comply with the licence agreement. Instead, the originator might be able to sue the licensee.

5.5 Attribution

Almost all OGD licences or terms in the Greater China region contain an attribution requirement. This practice would involve a fundamental inquiry into the relationship between copyright and attribution. Normally, a right of attribution is a moral right.[185] Authors may not retain ownership of their copyright but they can require users or licensees to attribute credit to them. By claiming the original copyright ownership over databases,

---

182 Creative Commons, above n 179.

183 Jyh-An Lee 'Licensing Open Government Data' (2017) 13 Hastings Bus LJ 207 at 234.

184 See also Brown, above n 155, at 767 ('if the user [of a CC license] cannot rely on the license then they will have no way to know whether their use constitutes copyright infringement').

185 Berne Convention for the Protection of Literary and Artistic Works 1161 UNTS 31 (opened for signature 9 September 1886, entered into force 5 December 1887), art 6*bis*.

governments justify using public licences to entail users giving credit on the basis of moral rights, although, technically, a government cannot be an author and, thus, cannot have moral rights. Governments may be owners of copyright, but only individuals can be authors with moral rights. Therefore, in this context, attribution is a contractual requirement.

Since OGD policies normally promote access to, and reuse of, data for free or at nominal costs,[186] every restriction in the licensing terms that increases users' costs needs to be justified. Therefore, it is worth exploring why attribution is necessary in open data licences. Some researchers argue that the attribution requirement is a government's instrument to control speech because every restriction on the use of data is a form of censorship.[187] This argument is flawed in at least three ways: first, free speech as a constitutional right is still subject to some limitations;[188] second, there is no empirical evidence or theoretical support indicating that the attribution requirement in OGD licences generates a chilling effect or any barriers to freedom of speech; and third, it is not articulated why governments would intend to restrict speech via the attribution requirement. We can hardly imagine how a government would be able to use the attribution requirement to silence others from voicing opinions with which it disagrees.

Some other scholars have suggested that attribution can guarantee the accuracy and reliability of the data provided by governments.[189] However, such an argument may not be validated if we read through government data licences. It is quite costly to maintain the accuracy and precision of data.[190] Poor quality has been a problem for government data;[191] consequently, making it openly available highlights its incompleteness and inaccuracy. Most open data licences include a liability disclaimer refusing to take responsibility for the data's accuracy, correctness or completeness. The data or database is licensed by the licensor 'as is' and without any warranty of data quality. The disclaimer provision in traditional public

---

186 See above n 32.
187 Tauberer, above n 2, at 109.
188 See David S Bogen 'The Origins of Freedom of Speech and Press' (1983) 42 Md L Rev 429 at 431 and 436–437; Irene M Ten Cate 'Speech, Truth, and Freedom: An Examination of John Stuart Mill's and Justice Oliver Wendell Holmes's Free Speech Defenses' (2010) 22 Yale JL & Human 35 at 69; Ronald J Krotoszynski 'A Comparative Perspective on the First Amendment: Free Speech, Militant Democracy, and the Primacy of Dignity as a Preferred Constitutional Value in Germany' (2004) 78 Tul L Rev 1549 at 1551 and 1554–1559.
189 See Marcowitz-Bitton, above n 3, at 414–415.
190 Tauberer, above n 2, at 118.
191 See Gurin, above n 5, at 233; Tauberer, above n 2, at 149.

licence agreements is typically subject to IP infringement claimed by third parties,[192] but, in open data agreements, the disclaimer provision also excludes any legal liability associated with data error.[193] If the attribution terms in open data licences are intended to ensure data quality, then the disclaimer provisions become unnecessary in the licence agreement.

The right to be identified, or right of attribution or paternity, is the most important category of moral rights.[194] Leaving aside the fact that governments cannot have moral rights, it is worth examining a government's attitude toward appropriate attribution from the perspective of moral rights theory. It should be noted that a government's generation of data differs from that of individuals or enterprises making creative works. Most government data and databases are produced as a by-product of a government's daily functions.[195] Therefore, although correct attribution can provide non-pecuniary rewards or incentives to authors of creative works,[196] the same cannot be justified in the context of government data. In addition, attribution rights have traditionally represented an artist's personal connection to his or her creative works.[197] This personal link hardly exists in the generation of government database. More importantly, as noted above, moral rights are personal rights, which pertain only to authors. Businesses, governments and other organisations, therefore, cannot claim moral rights.

---

192 See Stephen McJohn 'The GPL Meets the UCC: Does Free Software Come with a Warranty of No Infringement?' (2014) 15 J High Tech L 1 at 19.

193 For example, all CC licences come with this disclaimer: 'Unless otherwise separately undertaken by the Licensor, to the extent possible, the Licensor offers the Licensed Material as-is and as-available, and makes no representations or warranties of any kind concerning the Licensed Material, whether express, implied, statutory, or other. This includes, without limitation, warranties of title, merchantability, fitness for a particular purpose, non-infringement, absence of latent or other defects, accuracy, or the presence or absence of errors, whether or not known or discoverable.'

194 See Paul Goldstein and Bernt Hugenholtz *International Copyright: Principles, Law and Practice* (3rd ed, Oxford University Press, 2013) at 361; Mira T Sundara Rajan 'Creative Commons: America's Moral Rights?' (2011) 21 Fordham Intell Prop Media & Ent LJ 905 at 926.

195 See above n 3.

196 See Jane C Ginsburg 'Moral Rights in a Common Law System' (1990) 1(4) Ent L Rev 121 at 122; Catherine L Fisk 'Credit Where It's Due: The Law and Norms of Attribution' (2006) 95 Geo LJ 49 at 56–60; Asay, above n 152, at 792 (noting that attribution is a significant drive for contributions in free or open source software or open content communities).

197 See Elizabeth M Bock 'Note: Using Public Disclosure as the Vesting Point for Moral Rights under the Visual Artists Rights Act' (2011) 110 Mich L Rev 153 at 161–162; Robert C Bird 'Moral Rights: Diagnosis and Rehabilitation' (2009) 46 AM Bus LJ 407 at 426 ('*Le droit moral* [moral right] … addresses legal rights that acknowledge a personal legal connection between an author and her creations'); Adolf Dietz 'Moral Rights and the Civil Law Countries' (1995) 19 Colum VLA JL & Arts 199 at 207 (noting that moral rights in the Germany Copyright Act focus on the authors' personal relationship with his or her creative works).

Nonetheless, governments occasionally gain political advantages from the attribution requirement because it helps to craft a public impression that they have released some valuable data to society. In this sense, governments, just like authors of creative works, benefit from situations where the relationship between the makers and their works is visible.[198] Greg Lastowka correctly indicated that attribution helps creators gain advantages in the reputation market.[199] The same reasoning can be applied to governments' open data licences in which the attribution requirement may help them earn a positive public reputation.

Another argument in favour of attribution is the 'public interest theory', which states that the public can benefit from the disclosure of attribution.[200] This theory is more suited to OGD policy. As the primary goal of OGD is to promote transparency, accountability and economic development, the public has a stake in knowing whether the data is provided by the government and which government agency provided which data, dataset or database. The disclosure of this information can better enable citizens to assess the performance of government agencies and whether, and to what extent, the data release can help economic development.

6 Conclusion

Open data may contribute to the achievement of a wide range of social, economic and political goals. Nevertheless, it also involves a variety of legal issues. The choice (or design) of a licence, or the terms of use for OGD is not only a legal issue but also a policy issue. Based on an analysis of the legal environment for OGD in the Greater China region, this study argues that a government's decisions regarding open data licences reveal the priorities of its policy goals, which may be associated with transparency,

---

198 See Silke Von Lewinski *International Copyright Law and Policy* (Oxford University Press, Oxford, 2008) at 51.
199 Greg Lastowka 'Digital Attribution: Copyright and the Right to Credit' (2007) 87 BU L Rev 41 at 60–61; Bock, above n 197, at 168 ('integrity and attribution are concerned with the reputation of the artist').
200 See Ginsburg, above n 196, at 122; Fisk, above n 196, at 54 ('[a]ttribution is a type of signal, and it operates in labor and other markets plagued by information asymmetries in which reliable signals are important'); Henry Hansmann and Marina Santilli 'Authors' and Artists' Moral Rights: A Comparative Legal and Economic Analysis' (1997) 26 J Legal Stud 95 at 107 (noting that public interests are enhanced by attribution rights, which prevent the public from being misled about the work); Margaret Ann Wilkinson 'The Public Interest in Moral Rights Protection' (2006) Mich St L Rev 193 at 212–216 (analysing moral rights' public-interests function in information provision).

accountability, collaboration, economic growth or political control. If the primary policy goal is to promote innovation and economic development, the terms or licences of OGD should be the least restrictive. Based on this line of reasoning, the provision in Beijing's Disclaimer regarding government's control of applications developed by users implies that control of information is a higher priority than innovation and economic development on the government's agenda.

As a significant number of government databases in the Greater China region do not meet the originality requirement and thus are not copyrightable, these licences may not prove effective in many OGD scenarios. In Greater China jurisdictions, where there is no sui generis database right, these licences may not be legally effective for non-copyrightable data and databases.

Moreover, attribution is the most common, and occasionally the only, requirement in OGD licences. The existence of this design in open data licences cannot be explained by traditional copyright theories because the data can hardly present a government's personality and governments do not need user attribution as an incentive to generate data. Nonetheless, these provisions can be understood by applying the public interest theory of moral right, suggesting that the public can benefit from the disclosure of attribution. As the primary goal of OGD is to promote transparency, accountability and economic development, the public has a vested interest in knowing whether the government provides the data and which government agency has produced it.

Through a study of OGD licences in the Greater China region, this chapter not only illustrates different phases of OGD development but also analyses potential and unsettled copyright issues therein, such as moral rights and the legality of licences associated with uncopyrightable materials. The dynamic OGD experiences from three main jurisdictions in the Greater China region, namely mainland China, Hong Kong and Taiwan, are, therefore, valuable for others that aim to implement OGD policies for various policy goals.

Part 4: Non-authors?

8

Putting Artists and Guardians of Indigenous Works First: Towards a Restricted Scope of Freedom of Panorama in the Asian Pacific Region

Jonathan Barrett[1]

1 Introduction

'Freedom of panorama'[2] permits use of certain copyright-protected works on public display; for example, anyone may publish and sell postcards of a public sculpture.[3] The British heritage version of freedom of panorama, which is followed by many jurisdictions in the Asian Pacific region,[4] applies

---

1   Copyright © 2018 Jonathan Barrett. Senior Lecturer, School of Accounting and Commercial Law, Victoria University of Wellington.

2   The term 'freedom of panorama' recently came into common usage in English. It appears to be derived from the Swiss German 'Panoramafreiheit', which itself has only been used since the 1990s, despite the exemption existing in German law for 170 years. See Mélanie Dulong de Rosnay and Pierre-Carl Langlais 'Public artworks and the freedom of panorama controversy: a case of Wikimedia influence' (2017) 6(1) Internet Policy Review.

3   Incidental copying of copyright works is not considered to be a feature of freedom of panorama. See Copyright Act 1994 (NZ), s 41.

4   Asian Pacific countries are those west of the International Date Line (IDL), as defined for the purposes of the Asian Pacific Copyright Association (APCA) in Brian Fitzgerald and Benedict Atkinson (eds) *Copyright Future Copyright Freedom: Marking the 40 Year Anniversary of the Commencement of Australia's Copyright Act 1968* (Sydney University Press, Sydney, 2011) at 236.

to buildings, sculptures and works of artistic craftsmanship on permanent display in a public place or premises open to the public.[5] These objects may be copied in two dimensions, such as photographs. (Traditionally, this is known as reproducing 'the round' in 'the flat'.[6]) Owners of affected works may find themselves in competition in the market with others who are permitted to exploit those works, albeit in the flat.[7] Furthermore, works on public display are commonly exposed to derogatory treatment.[8]

The impact of freedom of panorama on Indigenous[9] artists is arguably most acute because their works may not be intended for commercial exploitation.[10] Indeed, some works are sacred and should not be revealed to outsiders.[11] An Indigenous artist whose work is exploited by outsiders may face serious community sanctions for failing in their guardianship

---

This definition mostly excludes British, European and United States copyright interests. However, any division of jurisdictions based on a construct such as the IDL will inevitably lead to arbitrary results. And so, while most of the United States' territories will be excluded, Guam lies west of the IDL. Likewise, French Polynesia will be mostly excluded but Wallis and Futuna lie west of the IDL, as does Francophone New Caledonia. Conversely, the Cook Islands and Niue, which are territories within the Realm of New Zealand, lie east of the IDL.

5   See Copyright, Patents and Designs Act 1988 (UK), s 62.

6   See JM Easton and WA Copinger *The Law of Copyright in Works of Literature, Art, Architecture, Photography, Music and the Drama* (5th ed, Stevens and Haynes, London, 1915) at 192.

7   In *Radford v Hallensteins Bros Ltd*, New Zealand's leading case on freedom of panorama, the artist argued that a chain store's use of an image of his sculpture, by trivialising it, would deter serious collectors from buying miniature reproductions of the sculpture: see *Radford v Hallensteins Bros Ltd* DC Auckland CIV-2005-004-3008, 6 June 2006; *Radford v Hallensteins Bros Ltd* HC Auckland CIV-2006-404-4881, 22 February 2007; *Radford v Hallensteins Bros Ltd* [2009] DCR 907.

8   For example, Antony Gormley, *STAY* (2015/2016), a sculpture installed in Christchurch's Avon river, 'has been dressed in a high-viz vest and even an All Black jersey'. See Charlie Gates '$800k Antony Gormley statue acting as a weed catcher' *The Press* (online ed, Christchurch, 7 June 2006). Moral rights, which protect authors' non-economic interests in their works, are generally unaffected by freedom of panorama. See Berne Convention for the Protection of Literary and Artistic Works 1161 UNTS 31 (opened for signature 9 September 1886, entered into force 5 December 1887), arts 6*bis* and 9 [Berne Convention]. However, in practice, artists are unlikely to assert their moral rights, even when the person in breach can be identified, because of the high costs of litigation in New Zealand.

9   The term 'Indigenous' is sufficiently problematic for the United Nations to avoid formulating a definition. Nevertheless, Indigeneity is reliably indicated by a group's continued expression of a distinct culture, despite colonisation or other domination. Minority groups within postcolonial societies, such as Māori within New Zealand, are likely to self-identify as Indigenous, but it is reasonable to assume that on the international stage, non-Europeans in ex-colonial countries, such as Samoans, have similar interests to minority groups in preserving their traditional expressions of culture. Consequently, this chapter adopts a broader than normal conception of Indigeneity.

10   See *Bulun Bulun v R & T Textiles* [1998] ALR 157.

11   See *Re Terry Yumbulul v Reserve Bank of Australia; Aboriginal Artists Agency Limited and Anthony Wallis* [1991] FCA 448; 21 IPR 481.

obligations.[12] Indigenous peoples inhabit many countries in the Asian Pacific region, either in a minority or a majority; their artistic works may be adversely affected by excessively liberal freedom of panorama provisions.

The issues are exemplified by Ra Vincent's *Wai-titi Landing* (2005),[13] which is a sculpture consisting of two pouwhenua (land-marking posts) and is situated near Parliament on Molesworth Street in Wellington, New Zealand. The Wellington Tenths Trust donated the sculpture to the city in the belief that it 'symbolises partnership between the city and local Te Atiawa/Taranaki people'.[14] Māori sculptures in the public space are typically gifted for particular purposes; they are treasures that Māori, through their carvers,[15] have chosen to share with others. They are not commodities launched onto the market. Such artefacts may be open to public view but should not be game for commercial exploitation by anyone. Yet, several images of the sculpture are available for purchase on Alamy, an online stock photograph collection affiliated with Getty Images.[16] Vincent is not identified as the sculptor. Conversely, Alamy ensures that its images cannot be downloaded without payment.[17]

This chapter argues that the Asian Pacific Copyright Code should adopt a restricted scope of freedom of panorama for the benefit of artists in general, but specifically for Indigenous artists and the guardians of their works.[18] The chapter is structured as follows: first, relevant international treaty considerations are identified, in particular, art 9 of the Berne

---

12   See Miranda Forsyth 'Intellectual Property Laws in the South Pacific: Friend of Foe?' (2003) 7(1) J South Pac L www.paclii.org.

13   This example has been taken from Jonathan Barrett 'Time to Look Again? Copyright and Freedom of Panorama' (2017) 48(2) VUWLR 261 at 280.

14   See '11. Two pouwhenua, Wai-titi Landing', Wellington Sculptures www.sculptures.org.nz.

15   According to Māori tradition, pūmanawa (creative talent) 'comes to the individual through the parents and down through one's ancestry … Whakapapa [genealogy] determines the distributions of talents': see Hirini Moko Mead *Tikanga Māori: Living by Māori Values* (Huia, Wellington, 2003) at 254–255.

16   Alamy www.alamy.com.

17   Alamy and Getty Images have been accused of wrongly offering copyright images for sale, and other sharp practices: see Ben Challis 'High Noon for Getty Images as a Photographer Bites Back' (2 August 2016) The 1709 Blog www.the1709blog.blogspot.co.nz.

18   In this chapter, 'guardian' refers to those people or groups who may or must protect particular works. In Te Reo Māori (the Māori language), they are denoted 'kaitiaki'. The trustee of a deceased artist's estate might play a comparable role in western culture. The types of artworks considered in this chapter are limited to things that currently attract copyright protection. Ancient cultural treasures in the public view are, for example, excluded. The Waitangi Tribunal comprehensively analysed Māori expectations about kaitiakitanga (guardianship) of their taonga (cultural treasures) and intellectual property rights. See Waitangi Tribunal *Ko Aotearoa Tēnei: A Report into Claims Concerning New Zealand Law and Policy Affecting Māori Culture and Identity* (Wai 262, 2011).

Convention for the Protection of Literary and Artistic Works (Berne Convention);[19] second, in order to more effectively engage with the 30 or so Asian Pacific jurisdictions, a taxonomy of freedom of panorama provisions is constructed;[20] third, freedom of panorama provisions across the region are surveyed; fourth, focusing on the proportionality requirement of art 9(2) of the Berne Convention,[21] a proposal for harmonised freedom of panorama across the Asian Pacific region is put forward.

2 International Considerations

This part of the chapter sketches the international agreements relevant to freedom of panorama.

2.1 Berne Convention

The Berne Convention, which is administered by the World Intellectual Property Organization (WIPO),[22] establishes minimum copyright standards for its signatories,[23] including an author's 'exclusive right of authorizing the reproduction of [qualifying] works, in any manner or form'.[24] Furthermore, non-signatory counties which are members of the World Trade Organization (WTO) must also comply with the key Berne provisions.[25] Consequently, the only Asian Pacific countries which are not obliged to the follow art 9 of the Berne Convention are Marshall Islands, Nauru, Palau and Timor-Lesté. The Berne Convention implicitly permits, but does not mandate, freedom of panorama. Article 9(2) provides:[26]

---

19 Berne Convention, above n 8, art 9.
20 At the time of writing, I had not accessed the copyright legislation, if any existed, of the Marshall Islands or Timor Lesté.
21 Berne Convention, above n 8, art 9(2).
22 Berne Convention, above n 8; Asian Pacific countries that are not members of the World International Property Organization (WIPO) are: Marshall Islands, Federated States of Micronesia, Nauru, Palau, Solomon Islands and Timor-Lesté. See WIPO 'Member States' www.wipo.int.
23 Agreement on Trade-Related Aspects of Intellectual Property Rights 1869 UNTS 299 (adopted 15 April 1994, entered into force 1 January 1995) [TRIPS Agreement], art 9, provides: 'Members shall comply with Articles 1 through 21 of the Berne Convention (1971) and the Appendix thereto.'
24 Berne Convention, above n 8, art 9(1).
25 Asian Pacific countries that are neither members nor observers (future members) of the WTO are: Cook Islands, Kiribati, Marshall Islands, Federated States of Micronesia, Nauru, Niue, Palau, Timor-Lesté, and Tuvalu. See WTO 'Groups in the WTO: updated 7 April 2017' www.wto.org. TRIPS, above n 23, art 9(1), only incorporates arts 1–21 (excluding art 6*bis*) of the Berne Convention, above n 8.
26 See also TRIPS, above n 23, art 13.

It shall be a matter for legislation in the countries of the Union to permit the reproduction of such works in certain special cases, provided that such reproduction does not conflict with a normal exploitation of the work and does not unreasonably prejudice the legitimate interests of the author.

Article 9(2) establishes a three-step test to gauge the acceptability of an exception to the fundamental rights of copyright owners.[27] Broadly, this requires a balancing of the interests of copyright owners and users, and is essentially a question of proportionality.[28] In the Asian Pacific region, any consideration of the proportionality of freedom of panorama must take particular account of the interests of Indigenous artists.

2.2 United Nations

Various United Nations instruments are relevant to the protection of traditional knowledge, including the United Nations Educational, Scientific and Cultural Organization (UNESCO) Convention for the Protection of the World Cultural and Natural Heritage;[29] UNESCO Convention for the Safeguarding of the Intangible Cultural Heritage;[30] and the United Nations Declaration of the Rights of Indigenous Peoples 2007.[31] These instruments are noted but will not be considered further in this chapter.

2.3 Model Laws

The imperative for Indigenous peoples' interests in their traditional knowledge to be balanced against western conceptions of individual copyright has been recognised in certain 'model laws', which are templates for domestic laws.[32]

---

27   Berne Convention, above n 8, art 9(2); For an analysis of the three-step test, see Sam Ricketson and Jane C Ginsburg *International Copyright and Neighbouring Rights: the Berne Convention and Beyond* Volume 1 (2nd ed, Centre for Commercial Law Studies, Queen Mary College, London, 2006) at [13.10]–[13.27].

28   See Christophe Geiger, Daniel Gervais and Martin Senftleben 'The Three-Step Test Revisited: How to Use the Test's Flexibility in National Copyright Law' (2014) 29(3) Am U Int L Rev 581 at 583.

29   Convention for the Protection of the World Cultural and Natural Heritage 1037 UNTS 151 (opened for signature 16 November 1972, entered into force 17 December 1975).

30   Convention for the Safeguarding of the Intangible Cultural Heritage 2368 UNTS 3 (opened for signature 17 October 2003, entered into force 20 April 2006).

31   *United Nations Declaration on the Rights of Indigenous Peoples* GA Res 61/295, A/Res/61/295 (2007).

32   WIPO *Tunis Model Law on Copyright for Developing Countries* (UNESCO, 1976); see Lida Ayoubi 'Copyright Harmonisation in the Asian Pacific Region: Weaving the Peoples Together?' in this volume.

2.3.1 Tunis Model Copyright Law

The Tunis Model Copyright Law for Developing Countries (Tunis Model Law) recognises the economic importance of national folklore for less and least developed countries.[33] (Indigenous people within more developed countries may be considered to be in a position analogous to citizens of developing countries.) The Commentary on the Tunis Model Law provides that 'in developing countries national folklore constitutes an appreciable part of the cultural heritage and is susceptible [to] economic exploitation, the fruits of which should not be denied to those countries'.[34] The Commentary further notes:[35]

> The object of [section 6 Works of national folklore] is to prevent any improper exploitation and to permit adequate protection of the cultural heritage known as folklore, which constitutes not only a potential for economic expansion, but also a cultural legacy intimately bound up with the individual character of each people. On these twofold grounds, works of folklore deserve protection, and the economic and moral rights in such works will be exercised, without limitation in time, by the competent national authority empowered to represent the people that originated them.

Section 7 of the Tunis Model Law permits:[36]

> the reproduction of works of art and of architecture, in a film or in a television broadcast, and the communication to the public of the works so reproduced, if the said works are permanently located in a place where they can be viewed by the public.

2.3.2 Pacific Model Law 2002

In 2002, the Secretariat of the Pacific Community agreed on a Pacific Regional Framework for the Protection of Traditional Knowledge and Expressions of Culture, including the Pacific Model Law (Pacific Model Law).[37] 'The Pacific Model Law is an IP-based sui generis

---

33   WIPO, above n 32, at 17.
34   At 17.
35   At 39.
36   Section 7.
37   Secretariat of the Pacific Community *Regional Framework for the Protection of Traditional Knowledge and Expressions of Culture* (Secretariat of the Pacific Community, 2002) www.forumsec.org [Pacific Model Law].

system … It creates new IP, or IP-like, rights.'[38] Part 4 of the model law 'sets out the procedure for obtaining the prior and informed consent of the traditional owners to use their traditional knowledge or expressions of culture for a non-customary use (whether or not of a commercial nature)'.[39] Specifically, s 15(1) provides:[40]

> A prospective user of traditional knowledge or expression of culture for a non-customary use (whether or not of a commercial nature) may apply to the Cultural Authority to obtain the prior and informed consent of the traditional owners to use the traditional knowledge or expressions of culture.

Indigenous peoples' control over their expressions of culture is acutely relevant to freedom of panorama.

3 Survey of Asian Pacific Provisions

This part of the chapter establishes a taxonomy of regional freedom of panorama provisions. The purpose here is to aid effective engagement with the different provisions of the more than 30 Asian Pacific jurisdictions. Classification is for convenience purposes only and provides no more than a rough guide.

3.1 British Heritage

British heritage copyright law is prominent in the Asian Pacific region. Many Asian Pacific jurisdictions were once British colonies or protectorates of Australia or New Zealand, such as the Cook Islands, whose own copyright legislation has traditionally followed United Kingdom law.[41] To reiterate, the basic British heritage copyright exemption for freedom of panorama applies to buildings, sculptures and works of artistic craftsmanship, which are on permanent display in a public place or premises open to the public. These objects may be copied in two-dimensional forms, such as

---

38   Secretariat of the Pacific Community *Guidelines for Developing National Legislation for the Protection of Traditional Knowledge and Expressions of Culture Based on the Pacific Model Law 2002* (Secretariat of the Pacific Community, 2006) at 7.
39   Pacific Model Law, above n 37, at 7.
40   At 7.
41   On New Zealand's following of United Kingdom copyright legislation, see Geoff McLay 'New Zealand and the Imperial copyright tradition' in Uma Suthersanen and Ysolde Gendreau (eds) *A Shifting Empire: 100 Years of the Copyright Act 1911* (Edward Elgar, Cheltenham, 2013) at 30.

photographs or television broadcasts. Australia,[42] Nauru,[43] Singapore[44] and the Solomon Islands[45] follow this model precisely. Variations are mostly determined by the vintage of the United Kingdom legislation followed – whether it is the 1911,[46] 1956[47] or 1988 Act.[48] Fiji,[49] Hong Kong,[50] New Zealand,[51] Niue[52] and Tokelau[53] all follow the 1988 legislation. Occasionally, British heritage copyright provisions appear to have been filtered through a locally dominant jurisdiction. For example, while

---

42   See Copyright Act 1968 (Cth), s 65.

43   English laws of general application in force on 31 January 1968 were adopted by Nauru, see Custom and Adopted Laws Act 1971 (Nauru), s 4.

44   See Copyright Act 1987 (Singapore), s 63.

45   See Copyright Act 1987 (Solomon Islands), s 7.

46   Copyright Act 1911 (UK), s 2(1) provided:

> … the following acts shall not constitute the infringement of a copyright:—

> (iii) The making or publishing of paintings, drawings, engravings, or photographs of a work of sculpture or artistic craftsmanship, if permanently situated in a public place, or building, or the making or publishing of paintings, drawings, engravings, or photographs (which are not in the nature of architectural drawings or plans) of any architectural work of art:

47   Copyright Act 1956 (UK), s 9 provided:

> (3) The copyright in a work to which this subsection applies which is permanently situated in a public place, or in premises open to the public, is not infringed by the making of a painting, drawing, engraving or photograph of the work, or the inclusion of the work in a cinematograph film or in a television broadcast. This subsection applies to sculptures, and to such works of artistic craftsmanship as are mentioned in paragraph (c) of subsection (1) of section three of this Act.

> (4) The copyright in a work of architecture is not infringed by the making of a painting, drawing, engraving or photograph of the work, or the inclusion of the work in a cinematograph film or in a television broadcast.

48   Copyright, Patents and Designs Act 1988 (UK), s 62 (as amended) provides:

> (1) This section applies to—

> > (a) buildings, and

> > (b) sculptures, models for buildings and works of artistic craftsmanship, if permanently situated in a public place or in premises open to the public.

> (2) The copyright in such a work is not infringed by—

> > (a) making a graphic work representing it,

> > (b) making a photograph or film of it, or

> > (c) making a broadcast of a visual image of it.

> (3) Nor is the copyright infringed by the issue to the public of copies, or the communication to the public, of anything whose making was, by virtue of this section, not an infringement of the copyright.

49   See Copyright Act 1999 (Fiji), s 67(1).

50   Copyright Ordinance 2007 (Hong Kong), s 71.

51   See Copyright Act 1994 (NZ), s 73.

52   In terms of Niue Act 1966 (Niue), s 686, New Zealand copyright law generally applies in Niue. However, Niue may pass laws which amend the Niue version of the Act but not the New Zealand version.

53   New Zealand law applies in Tokelau: see New Zealand Law Rules 2004 (Tokelau), s 3.

the New Zealand Copyright Act 1962 broadly followed the Copyright Act 1956 (UK), the former included murals in freedom of panorama,[54] whereas the latter did not.[55] New Zealand exempted murals until its 1994 Copyright Act commenced, whereas the Cook Islands continued to include murals in its freedom of panorama exemption until 2013.[56]

Tonga has never been a colony of a western power,[57] but has close ties to the United Kingdom and has adopted the English Common Law. Nevertheless, Tongan copyright law does not follow United Kingdom law, and permits 'the private reproduction of a published work in a single copy … where the reproduction is made by a person exclusively for his own personal purposes'.[58] However, this permitted use does not extend to reproducing, inter alia, 'a work of architecture in the form of building or other construction' or 'any work in cases where reproduction would conflict with a normal exploitation of the work or would otherwise unreasonably prejudice the legitimate interests of the author or other owner of the copyright'.[59]

3.2 United States Heritage

The United States, whose law applies in the Commonwealth of the Northern Mariana Islands and Guam, limits freedom of panorama to architectural works in the public space.[60] However, in line with United States copyright law,[61] Micronesian (FSM) legislation includes a fair use provision.[62] The Philippines also has a general fair use provision.[63] (The interaction between fair use and freedom of panorama lies beyond the scope of this chapter.)

---

54 See Copyright Act 1962 (NZ), s 20(5).
55 See Copyright Act 1956 (UK), s 9(3).
56 See Copyright Act 1962 (NZ), s 20(5), which applied in the Cook Islands in terms of the Cook Islands Act 1915 (NZ), s 627(1)). Section 627 remains on the New Zealand statute books despite the enactment of the Copyright Act 2013 (Cook Islands), which repeals the application of New Zealand copyright legislation in the Cook Islands.
57 See Sophie Foster and Sione Latukefu 'Tonga' (2016) *Encyclopaedia Britannica* www.britannica.com.
58 See Copyright Act 2002 (Tonga), s 8.
59 Section 8(2).
60 The United States provision only includes buildings in the freedom of panorama exemption: see 17 USC § 120(a). For a discussion, see Bryce Clayton Newell 'Freedom of Panorama: A Comparative Look at International Restrictions on Public Photography' (2011) 44 Creighton L Rev 405.
61 On the United Sates influence over Micronesian (FSM) law, see 'Australia-Oceania: Micronesia, Federate States of' (15 June 2017) Central Intelligence Agency www.cia.gov.
62 See Annotated Code 2014 Title 35 35 USC § 107.
63 See Intellectual Property Code, Republic Act No. 8293 (Philippines), s 185.

3.3 French Heritage

France's ratification of the Stockholm Act 1967 of the Berne Convention included the following declaration:[64]

> The Government of the French Republic ... declares that the said Convention shall be applicable to the territory of the French Republic in Europe, to the overseas territories of New Caledonia, French Polynesia, St. Pierre and Miquelon, Wallis and Futuna Islands and the French Southern and Antarctic Territories.

French law applies in its Polynesian territories, such as Wallis and Futuna.[65] France has transferred certain legislative competence to New Caledonia with a view to future independence.[66] Protection of Indigenous Kanak interests will be a principal motivation for developing laws differently from municipal French codes.[67] Currently, New Caledonia's intellectual property code is a clone of the Code de la propriété intellectuelle 1992.[68] Whether changes to the mother code will be adopted in New Caledonia is a matter of speculation.

Distinguished by its championing of authorial interests, French law has not traditionally recognised freedom of panorama.[69] However, with effect from 7 October 2016, a limited freedom of panorama has been introduced by Loi pour une République Numérique, art 39,[70] which amends art L.122-5 of Code de la Propriété Intellectuelle, which limits an author's rights after divulgation, and is akin to fair dealing in British heritage copyright systems. And so, it is not breach of an author's rights for a natural person to reproduce or represent an architectural work or sculpture, which is permanently situated on a public road, provided this

---

64   WIPO 'Paris Notification No. 70 Paris Convention for the Protection of Industrial Property Ratification of the Stockholm Act by the French Republic' (notification, 12 May 1975) www.wipo.int.
65   Save for Wallis and Futuna, the territories which comprise French Polynesia lie east of the international date line. The laws of France generally apply in French Polynesia: see 'Australia-Oceania: French Polynesia' (26 June 2017) Central Intelligence Agency www.cia.gov.
66   See Loi du pays n° 2012-2 du 20 janvier 2012 relative au transfert à la Nouvelle-Calédonie des compétences de l'Etat en matière de droit civil, de règles concernant l'état civil et de droit commercial (New Caledonia).
67   See Régis Lafargue 'The Unity of the Republic vs. Living together on the Same Land: New Caledonia from Colonization to Indigenousness: Law at the Center of a Major Culture Issue' (2014) 46(2) J Legal Pluralism 172.
68   Code de la Propriété Intellectuelle (France); see Loi n° 92-597 du 1er juillet 1992 relative au code de la propriété intellectuelle (partie législative) (New Caledonia).
69   See *Ashby Donald v France* [2013] ECHR 287.
70   Loi pour une République Numérique (France), art 39; Code de la Propriété Intellectuelle (France), arts L.122–125.

is not done commercially.[71] The new rule will no doubt remove certain anomalies,[72] but, as Marie-Andrée Weiss notes, the lack of a definition of commercial use (*usage à caractère commercial*) is likely to raise new problems.[73] Would, for example, free blogs, which enjoy some support by advertising, be able to claim the exemption?

Despite its faults, the new French law represents an attempt to balance the interests of authors and others, as required by art 9(2) of the Berne Convention.[74] There is nothing to suggest that British heritage systems have revisited the balance of their liberal freedom of panorama exemptions since the exemption was introduced in 1911.[75] The French law usefully indicates that a balanced freedom of panorama rule can give members of the public reproduction permission but also protect authors' interests from commercial exploitation.

3.4 Other Civil Law Heritage

Four civil-law jurisdictions – Japan, Korea, Taiwan and the Russian Federation – have broadly similar freedom of panorama exemptions, which are distinguished by their restrictions on non-authorial, commercial exploitation of public works.

---

71   In French: Les reproductions et représentations d'oeuvre architecturale et de sculptures, placée en permanence sur la voie publique, realisées par des personnes physiques, à l'exclusion de tout usage à caractère commercial.

72   For example, while the Eiffel Tower (which was built in 1889) is in the public domain, the tower's lighting was installed in 2003 and is copyright protected. This meant that, prior to 2016, a tourist could freely photograph the tower by day but not by night under the copyright-protected lighting: see 'IP and Business: Using Photographs of Copyrighted Works and Trademarks' *WIPO Magazine* (online ed, 2 April 2006) www.wipo.int.

73   Marie-Andrée Weiss 'The new, but narrow, French freedom of panorama exception' The 1709 Blog (18 October 2016) www.the1709blog.blogspot.co.nz.

74   Berne Convention, above n 8, art 9(2); Directive 2001/29/EC on the Harmonisation of Certain Aspects of Copyright and Related Rights in the Information Society [2001] OJ L 167/10 [InfoSoc] permits but does not mandate freedom of panorama. The Swedish Supreme Court's response to freedom of panorama and InfoSoc has been to prevent the not-for-profit WikiMedia from reproducing images of publicly displayed works. See *Bildupphovsrätt i Sverige (BUS) ek för v Wikimedia Sverige*, Ö 849-15, 4 April 2016. The case does not appear to be available in English. For a discussion of the case, see Nedim Malovic 'Swedish Supreme Court defines scope of freedom of panorama' (2016) 11(1) JIPLP 736.

75   See Copyright Act 1911 (UK), s 2(1)(iii).

3.4.1 Japan, Korea and Taiwan

The Japanese exemption applies to all works of art, permanently located 'in open places accessible to the public, such as streets and parks, or at places easily seen by the public, such as the outer walls of buildings'.[76] However, sculptures may only be reproduced in three-dimensional form for personal use, and, generally, 'reproduction of an artistic work exclusively for the purpose of selling its copies and sale of such copies' is prohibited.[77] This aversion to commercial exploitation of works in the public space is akin to the French approach, but direct French influence on Japanese copyright law in this area is not obvious.[78] Korea's freedom of panorama provision is substantially similar to that of Japan.[79] Taiwan's provision is also similar to that of Japan,[80] with the key distinguishing feature being a prohibition on commercial exploitation.

3.4.2 Russian Federation

Due to the unavailability of a reliable translation of the Civil Code, including all amendments, the scope of freedom of panorama in the Russian Federation is unclear. The text of the Code available through WIPO permits reproduction of works permanently located in a public place 'except for cases when the imaging of the work in this way is the main object of the reproduction, broadcast or cable transmission or when an image of the work is used for commercial purposes'.[81] WikiMedia indicates that freedom of panorama does not apply to public artworks but states 'exceptions for works of architecture, urban development, and garden and landscape design, which were added under consultation with Wikimedia Russia, have taken effect with the Civil Code amendments as of October 1, 2014'.[82] It seems certain, however, that commercial exploitation of publicly displayed works is not permitted without the copyright owner's permission.

76   Copyright Law of Japan (Japan), art 45.
77   Article 46.
78   On the broad influence of French and German civil law on Japanese copyright law see Dennis S Karjala and Keiji Sugiyama 'Fundamental Concepts in Japanese and American Copyright Law' (1988) 36(4) Am J Comp L 613 at 613.
79   See Copyright Act 2009 (Korea), s 35.
80   Copyright Act 2014 (Taiwan), art 58.
81   See Civil Code of the Russian Federation 1994 (as amended 2011) art 1276.
82   See 'Commons: Freedom of panorama' WikiMedia Commons (2017) commons.wikimedia.org.

3.5 China and Malaysia

The freedom of panorama provisions of China and Malaysia defy easy categorisation or identification of provenance but may offer the broadest scope of freedom of panorama.

3.5.1 China

China's freedom of panorama provision reflects the language used in art 9(2) of the Berne Convention inasmuch as it implies a consideration of proportionality. Covering 'a work of art of art put up or displayed in outdoor public place',[83] the provision is wider than the British heritage version since all artistic works are covered, and there is no explicit permanence of display requirement. Conversely, indoor works are not exempted. No restrictions appear to apply to the means of copying, such as recreating a sculpture in a three-dimensional reproduction. Furthermore, a commercial motive is expressly permitted. Despite the broad licence of the Chinese approach, in which regard we might speculate about the tradition of social 'ownership' of artworks in the public space,[84] the moral right to be identified as the author is explicitly mentioned and other authorial rights must not be prejudiced. This latter requirement reflects the proportionality element of art 9(2) of the Berne Convention.[85]

3.5.2 Malaysia

Despite the common-law basis of its legal system, Malaysia does not follow British heritage copyright law with regard to freedom of panorama. Its broad exception provides that authorial rights do not extend to controlling 'the reproduction and distribution of copies of any artistic work permanently situated in a place where it can be viewed by the public'.[86] This provision is notable because freedom of panorama is not restricted to three-dimensional artistic works in the public space.

---

83   See Copyright Law of the People's Republic of China 1999, art 22.
84   See, generally, William P Alfred *To Steal a Book is an Elegant Offense: Intellectual Property Law in Chinese Civilization* (Stanford University Press, Redwood City (Cal), 1995).
85   Berne Convention, above n 8, art 9(2).
86   Copyright Act 1987(2) (MY), s 13.

3.6 Miscellaneous

Any impact the Netherlands (in Indonesia), Portugal or Indonesia (in Timor-Lesté), the other ex-colonial powers in the region,[87] may have had on their previous colonies' copyright law does not appear to have any lingering influence over freedom of panorama.[88] The relevant provisions of other Asian Pacific jurisdictions defy neat classification, and, indeed, vary considerably. The possibility of unreliable translation must also be taken into account.

The Cambodian exception is prima facie wide in its scope, provided moral rights are respected. Article 25 of the Law on Copyrights and Related Rights 2003 provides:[89]

> If there is a clear indication of the author's name and the source of work, the following acts are not subjected to any prohibitions by the author ... The reproduction of graphic or plastic work which is situated in the public place ...

However, this broad exception applies 'when this reproduction doesn't constitute the principle [*sic*] subject for subsequent reproduction'.[90] Concerns for inaccurate translation noted, this qualifier may restrict the scope of the exception to incidental reproduction. If so, freedom of panorama, as contemplated in this chapter, is not a permitted use.

3.7 Public Display Right–Only

The Cook Islands,[91] Indonesia,[92] Palau,[93] Papua New Guinea,[94] Samoa[95] and Vanuatu[96] do not provide for freedom of panorama but establish a public display right. The Attorney-General of the Federated States of Micronesia has the power to regulate similarly.[97] The typical provision allows public display of originals or copies of works, other than via films,

---

87 German colonisation of several Pacific islands, including Samoa, appears to have been too brief to have had any lasting influence on copyright law.
88 But see above n 63, on the Philippines fair use provision.
89 Law on Copyright and Related Rights 2003 (Cambodia), art 25.
90 Article 25.
91 Copyright Act 2013 (Cook Islands), s 23.
92 Law of the Republic of Indonesia 2014 about Copyright (Indonesia), art 15.
93 Consolidated Legislation Real and Personal Property Title 39 (Palau) 39 PNC § 821.
94 Copyright and Neighbouring Rights Act 2000 (Papua New Guinea), s 16.
95 See Copyright Act 1998 (Samoa), s 15.
96 See Copyright and Related Rights Act 2000 (Vanuatu), s 18.
97 See Annotated Code 2014 Title 35 Copyrights, Patents and Trademarks (Federated States of Micronesia), § 107.

slides, television images or similar forms of communication, without the artist's permission. However, the work must have been divulged. The right to display works publicly is relevant to freedom of panorama because original copies of works entering the public space become susceptible to unauthorised reproduction or derogatory treatment. From a guardianship perspective, works may enter the public space which were never intended to leave the aegis of a particular community.

3.8 No Explicit Exemption

The copyright laws of Kiribati[98] and Tuvalu[99] are minimalist and do not mention either freedom of panorama or a public display right.

3.9 Summary of Survey

While noting the risk of oversimplifying disparate laws in the search for convenient commonalities, freedom of panorama provisions in the Asian Pacific region can be sorted into five loose categories – these may be termed: British heritage; United States heritage; French heritage; other civil law; and Chinese and Malaysian. The key features of these categories are summarised in tabular form below. For more detail, see the Appendix to this chapter.

Table 1: A comparison of the key features of freedom of panorama in the Asian Pacific region.

	British heritage	US heritage	French heritage	Other civil law	Chinese (Malaysian)
Works covered	Three-dimensional	Architectural works only (and fair use)	Three-dimensional	All	All
Period of display	Permanent	All times	Permanent	Permanent	All times
Scope of public visibility	Outdoor and indoor	Outdoor	Outdoor (public way)	Outdoor	Outdoor (anywhere)
Permitted form of copying	Two-dimensional	Two-dimensional	Any (unclear)	Two-dimensional	Any
Restrictions on commercial exploitation	None	None	Permission required	Permission required	None

Source: Author's summary.

---

98   See Laws of the Republic of Kiribati Revised Edition 1980 (Kiribati), Chapter 16 Copyright.
99   See Copyright Act 1916 (Tuvalu).

4 Evaluation and Recommendation

The underpinning premise of this chapter is that the principle of proportionality established by art 9(2) of the Berne Convention ought to inform a freedom of panorama exemption.[100] The Berne Convention does not prescribe precise provisions for Member States' copyright legislation but does establish minimum standards. A general exemption from the fundamental principle of authors' exclusive exploitation rights – indeed, the fundamental principle itself – was only included in the text of the Convention in 1967.[101] This late inclusion partly accounts for the heterogeneity of freedom of panorama exemptions seen across the Asian Pacific region. But, analogous to European Union directives, which harmonise laws across diverse legal cultures but do not require uniformity in actual legislation, it is not far-fetched to propose restrictions on freedom of panorama in the Asian Pacific region. Harmonisation would not mean that countries which do not already recognise freedom of panorama would be required to do so, but countries which have unusually broad exemptions would be required to enact restrictions.

The principal interest-holders and the interests which should be appropriately balanced are:

1. Authors should be able to exploit their works in accordance with art 9(1) of the Berne Convention and to enforce their moral rights in terms of art 6bis.[102]

2. Cultural guardians should be able to protect their communal interests in cultural expressions in terms of UNESCO principles, the Pacific Model Law and so forth.

3. Not-for-profits, such as WikiMedia, should be able to disseminate images of copyright works in the public space to entertain and educate in terms of proportionate fair dealing rules or fair use principles, as contemplated in Berne Convention, art 9(2).

4. The general public should not be subjected to arbitrary rules about reproducing works in the public space and should normally be able to publish (for example, Facebook, Snapchat and so forth) images of public display works. For example, the two-dimensional and

---

100 Berne Convention, above n 8, art 9(2).
101 See Ricketson and Ginsburg, above n 27, at [11.06].
102 Berne Convention, above n 8, arts 9(1) and 6*bis*.

three-dimensional distinction is arbitrary. Why should an amateur artist be able to sketch a public statue but not attempt to make a three-dimensional model?

5. Entrepreneurs may have an expectation of commercially exploiting works created by others but the justification for this is far from obvious.[103]

It is submitted that a fairer and more coherent balance may be struck between these competing interests than we currently find in freedom of panorama provisions in the Asian Pacific region. But, by drawing on the different provisions, we may craft a generic freedom of panorama provision suitable for regional harmonisation. The table below sets out the key features of the proposed provision, which aims to be better than current arrangements, if not perfect.[104]

Table 2: Proposal for freedom of panorama.

Criterion	Scope	Justification
Works covered	All works in public places	Avoids arbitrary distinction between two- and three-dimensional works
Period of display	Displayed at any time	Avoids arbitrary distinction between permanent and public displays
Scope of visibility	Outdoor and indoor	Avoids arbitrary distinction between permanent and public displays (museums and galleries may restrict copying as a condition of entry)
Permitted form of copying	Any	Avoids arbitrary distinctions between two-dimensional and three-dimensional copies
Not-for-profit reproduction	Permitted unless owner objects	Establishes a proportionate default rule which favours not-for-profits and general public
Commercial reproduction	Prohibited unless owner agrees	Establishes a proportionate default rule which favours artists and guardians

Source: Author's proposal.

In accordance with art 9(2) of the Berne Convention and art 13 of the Agreement on Trade-Related Intellectual Property Rights (TRIPS), the Asian Pacific Copyright Code para D proposes limitations and exceptions to copyright be confined to 'certain special cases' and should 'not conflict with a normal exploitation of the work and do not unreasonably

---

103 I have in mind here direct commercial exploitation, as seen in the examples discussed in the Introduction, rather than indirect commercial benefit; for example, when a blogger on public artworks attracts advertising revenue.

104 Practical issues of permission could, in particular, prove problematic.

prejudice the legitimate interests of the rights owners'.[105] This approach would accommodate freedom of panorama arrangements, as varied as British and French heritage protections of the rights of the author, or new particular Asian versions. The legal heterogeneity of the Asian Pacific region prevents harmonisation based on common historical experience; rather, we need to look for commonalities across disparate cultures.

Everywhere, the majority of artists struggle to make a living. But, in the Asian Pacific region, consideration for the interests of Indigenous people must play a prominent role. In this context, empowering all artists (and guardians of their works) to prevent non-consensual exploitation of artworks in the public view is imperative. Conversely, users should not be subject to distinctions that appear irrational, such as between permanently and temporarily displayed artworks and permitted reproduction in 'the flat' but not in 'the round'.

5 Conclusion

Berne Union members negotiated the text of art 9(2) long after a variety of freedom of panorama exemptions had been enacted across different jurisdictions. Nevertheless, every WIPO and WTO member is obliged to ensure that its exemptions from copyright are restricted to 'certain special cases', do 'not conflict with a normal exploitation of the work', and do 'not unreasonably prejudice the legitimate interests of the author'. Broadly, this last requirement calls for a proportionate balancing of the interests of artists, including guardians of their works, and users. It seems unlikely that the broad, century-old British heritage exemption, which is followed in many Asian Pacific jurisdictions, has ever been subjected to a rigorous proportionality assessment. In contrast, French law has until recently refrained from recognising freedom of panorama. (That refusal is not, of course, subject to proportionality testing since Berne Union members are not required to provide exemptions to the fundamental author's reproduction right enshrined in art 9(1).)

In the Asian Pacific region, every country has either been the subject of colonialism or includes Indigenous communities who are dominated by an alien culture. It is trite that western conceptions of individualised intellectual property rights do not fit well with Indigenous conceptions

---

105 See Adrian Sterling 'Asian Pacific Copyright Code' in this volume.

of traditional knowledge and cultural production and protection. In this context, the idea that an artwork, which an Indigenous community gifts to another community, might become fair game for commercial exploitation by anyone must be considered unacceptable. Freedom of panorama should not extend that far. Conversely, in a dominant legal-economic system, which is fundamentally informed by individual property rights, it is implausible to think that traditional arrangements might escape unscathed from collision with that hegemony. A compromise must be sought which does least harm.

A balanced freedom of panorama exemption should not only adequately protect artists' and guardians' interests, it should also remove the arbitrary binary oppositions for users between: 'in the flat' or 'in the round'; graphic works or sculptures; temporary or permanent displays; and two-dimensional or three-dimensional reproduction. It is absurd to think that, say, a tourist taking a photograph of a mural that will be displayed in a public place for a finite period of time ought to be concerned about copyright infringement. (Galleries have the prerogative to decide whether artworks may or may not be photographed,[106] and increasingly in public galleries, prohibition is the exception.) It seems perfectly reasonable that a tourist in Wellington, who sees *Wai-titi Landing*, should think they are entitled to take a 'selfie' in front of it and post that image on Facebook,[107] just as much as they might include an image of the sculpture incidentally in a panning shot of the Parliamentary precinct. But a director of a fashion shoot who wishes to use the sculpture as a principal feature should reasonably expect the need to obtain permission, as should anyone who seeks a direct financial benefit from reproducing images of the sculpture.

Drawing on the best elements of freedom of panorama exemptions across the region, but excluding the least desirable features, this chapter proposes the following for the Asian Pacific Copyright Code: no distinction should be drawn between two-dimensional and three-dimensional works or between permanently and temporarily displayed works or whether they are displayed out of doors or indoors; no distinction should be drawn between two-dimensional and three-dimensional reproduction; however, non-commercial and commercial exploitation should be distinguished.

---

106 See Simon Stokes *Art and Copyright* (2nd ed, Hart Publishing, Oxford, 2012) at 67, n 160.

107 On possible Indigenous objections to this approach, see S Corbett and M Boddington 'Copyright Law and the Digitisation of Cultural Heritage' (Centre for Accounting, Governance & Taxation Research, Working Paper Series, WP No. 77, September 2011).

As a compromise, it is proposed that non-commercial reproduction should be permitted as a default; whereas commercial reproduction should only be allowed with permission. In either case, artists, owners or guardians would be able to prevent offensive reproduction.

Appendix: Summary of Asian Pacific Freedom of Panorama Provisions

Country Statute	Summary of freedom of panorama provision
British heritage copyright schemes	
Australia	
Copyright Act 1968, s 65 Compare: Copyright Act 1956 (UK)	(1) This section applies to sculptures and to works of artistic craftsmanship of the kind referred to in paragraph (c) of the definition of artistic work in section 10. (2) The copyright in a work to which this section applies that is situated, otherwise than temporarily, in a public place, or in premises open to the public, is not infringed by the making of a painting, drawing, engraving or photograph of the work or by the inclusion of the work in a cinematograph film or in a television broadcast.
Fiji	
Copyright Act 1999, s 67(1) Compare: Copyright Act 1956 (UK); and Copyright Act 1962 (NZ)	This section applies to— (a) buildings; and (b) works (being sculptures, models for buildings, or works of artistic craftsmanship) that are permanently situated in a public place or in premises open to the public. (2) Copyright in a work to which this section applies is not infringed by— (a) copying the work by making a graphic work representing it; (b) copying the work by making a photograph or audiovisual work of it; or (c) broadcasting, or including in a cable programme, a visual image of the work. (3) Copyright is not infringed by the issue to the public of copies, or the broadcasting or communication to the public or inclusion in a cable programme, of anything the making of which was, under this section, not an infringement of copyright.
Hong Kong	
Copyright Ordinance 2007, s 71 Compare Copyright, Patents and Designs Act 1988 (UK)	(1) This section applies to— (a) buildings; and (b) sculptures, models for buildings and works of artistic craftsmanship, if permanently situated in a public place or in premises open to the public. (2) The copyright in such a work is not infringed by— (a) making a graphic work representing it; (b) making a photograph or film of it; or (c) broadcasting or including in a cable programme service a visual image of it …

Country Statute	Summary of freedom of panorama provision
Nauru	
Custom and Adopted Laws Act 1971, s 4 Compare: Copyright Act 1956 (UK)	The Copyright Law of England applies in Nauru because, according to the Custom and Adopted Laws Act 1971 of Nauru, the common law and statutes of general application, which were in force in England on 31 January 1968, are adopted as laws of Nauru.
New Zealand	
Copyright Act 1994, s 73 Compare: Copyright Act 1988 (UK)	This section applies to the following works— (a) buildings: (b) works (being sculptures, models for buildings, or works of artistic craftsmanship) that are permanently situated in a public place or in premises open to the public. (2) Copyright in a work to which this section applies is not infringed by— (a) copying the work by making a graphic work representing it; or (b) copying the work by making a photograph or film of it; or (c) communicating to the public a visual image of the work. (3) Copyright is not infringed by the issue to the public of copies, or the communication to the public, of anything the making of which was, under this section, not an infringement of copyright.
Niue	
Niue Act 1966, s 686	The Copyright Act 1994 shall be in force in Niue in the same manner in all respects as if Niue were for all purposes part of New Zealand, and the term 'New Zealand' as used in that Act shall, both in New Zealand and in Niue, be read as including Niue accordingly. See also Tāoga Niue Act 2012.
Singapore	
Copyright Act 1987, s 63 Compare: Copyright Act 1968 (Cth); and Copyright Act 1956 (UK)	(1) This section shall apply to sculptures and to works of artistic craftsmanship of the kind referred to in paragraph (c) of the definition of 'artistic work' in section 7. (2) The copyright in a work to which this section applies that is situated, otherwise than temporarily, in a public place, or in premises open to the public, is not infringed by the making of a painting, drawing, engraving or photograph of the work or by the inclusion of the work in a cinematograph film or in a television broadcast.
Solomon Islands	
Copyright Act 1987, s 7 Compare: Copyright Act 1968 (Cth)	(7) The copyright in— (a) any sculpture; or (b) any work of artistic craftsmanship of the kind described in the definition of 'artistic work' in subsection (1) of section 2, which is permanently situated in a public place, or in premises open to the public, is not infringed by the making of a painting, drawing, engraving or photograph of the work, or the inclusion of the work in a cinematograph film or in a television broadcast. (8) The copyright in a work of architecture is not infringed by the making of a painting, drawing, engraving or photograph of the work, or the inclusion of the work in a cinematograph film or in a television broadcast.

Country Statute	Summary of freedom of panorama provision
Tokelau	
Application of New Zealand Law Rules 2004, s 3	New Zealand law applies to intellectual property.
Tonga	

Copyright Act 2002, s 11	(1) … the private reproduction of a published work in a single copy shall be permitted without the authorisation of the author or owner of copyright, where the reproduction is made by a person exclusively for his own personal purposes.
	(2) The permission under subsection (1) shall not extend to reproduction—
	    (a) of a work of architecture in the form of building or other construction …
	    (e) of any work in cases where reproduction would conflict with a normal exploitation of the work or would otherwise unreasonably prejudice the legitimate interests of the author or other owner of the copyright.

Specific national provisions	
Cambodia	
Law on Copyrights and Related Rights 2003, art 25	If there is a clear indication of the author's name and the source of work, the following acts are not subjected to any prohibitions by the author … The reproduction of graphic or plastic work which is situated in the public place, when this reproduction doesn't constitute the principle [sic] subject for subsequent reproduction.
China	
Copyright Law of the People's Republic of China 1990, art 22	In the following cases, a work may be used without permission from, and without payment of remuneration to, the copyright owner, provided that the name of the author and the title of the work are mentioned and the other rights enjoyed by the copyright owner in accordance with this Law are not prejudiced … (10) copying, drawing, photographing or video-recording of a work of art put up or displayed in an outdoor public place.

Country Statute	Summary of freedom of panorama provision
Japan	
Copyright Law of Japan, arts 45 and 46	Art 45. (1) The original of an artistic work or a photographic work may be publicly exhibited by its owner or with his authorization. (2) The provision of the preceding paragraph shall not apply with respect to the permanent location of the original of an artistic work in open places accessible to the public, such as streets and parks, or at places easily seen by the public, such as the outer walls of buildings. Art 46. It shall be permissible to exploit artistic works permanently located in such open places as mentioned in paragraph (2) of the preceding Article and architectural works by any means not falling within any of the following items: (i) multiplication of a sculpture and offering it to the public by transfer of ownership of its copies; (ii) imitative reproduction of an architectural work and offering it to the public by transfer of ownership of its copies; (iii) reproduction of a work for the purpose of locating it permanently in such open places as mentioned in paragraph (2) of the preceding Article; (iv) reproduction of an artistic work exclusively for the purpose of selling its copies and sale of such copies.
Korea	
Copyright Act 2009, s 35	(1) The owner of the original of a work of art, etc. or a person who has obtained the owner's authorization, may exhibit the work in its original form: provided that this provision shall not apply if the work of art is to be permanently exhibited in a street or park, on the exterior of a building, or other places open to the public. (2) Works of art, etc. exhibited at all times at an open place as referred to in the proviso of Paragraph (1) may be reproduced and used by any means, except those falling under any of the following cases: 1. Where a building is reproduced in another building; 2. Where a sculpture or a painting is reproduced in another sculpture or a painting; 3. Where the reproduction is made in order to exhibit permanently at an open place, as prescribed under the proviso of Paragraph (1); and 4. Where the reproduction is made for the purpose of selling its copies.
Russian Federation	
Civil Code of the Russian Federation 1994 (as amended 2011) art 1276	A photographic work, an architectural work or an artistic work that is permanently located in a place open to the public may be reproduced, broadcast or transmitted by cable without the consent of the author or other right holder and without paying out a fee, except for cases when the imaging of the work in this way is the main object of the reproduction, broadcast or cable transmission or when an image of the work is used for commercial purposes.

Country Statute	Summary of freedom of panorama provision
Taiwan	
Copyright Act 2014, art 58	Artistic works or architectural works displayed on a long-term basis on streets, in parks, on outside walls of buildings, or other outdoor locales open to the public, may be exploited by any means except under the following circumstances: 1. Reproduction of a building by construction of another building. 2. Reproduction of a work of sculpture by production of another sculpture. 3. Reproduction for the purpose of long-term public display in locales specified in this article. 4. Reproduction of artistic works solely for the purpose of selling copies.
Thailand	
Copyright Act 1994, s 37	A drawing, painting, construction, engraving, molding, carving, lithography, photograph, film, video broadcast or any similar use of an artistic work, except for an architectural work, which is openly located in a public place shall not be deemed an infringement of copyright in the artistic work. 38. A drawing, painting, engraving, molding, carving, lithography, photograph, film or video broadcast of an architectural work shall not be deemed an infringement of copyright in the architectural work.
Malaysia	
Copyright Act 1987(2), s 13	… the right of control … does not include the right to control … (d) the reproduction and distribution of copies of any artistic work permanently situated in a place where it can be viewed by the public.
Vietnam	
Law on Intellectual Property (No. 50/2005/ QH11), art 25	Cases of use of published works where permission or payment of royalties and/or remunerations is not required include … h/ Photographing or televising of plastic art, architectural, photographic, applied-art works displayed at public places for purpose of presenting images of such works.
Public display provisions only	
Cook Islands	
Copyright Act 2013, s 23	(1) A person does not infringe copyright in a work if the person publicly displays a work or copies of the work— (a) for the purposes of promoting the work, testing the work, or training users of the work; and (b) without the authorisation of the owner of the copyright in the work.

Country Statute	Summary of freedom of panorama provision
Federated States of Micronesia	
Annotated Code 2014 Title 35 Copyrights, Patents and Trademarks, § 107	§ 107. Limitation on exclusive rights—Fair use. Notwithstanding the provisions of section 106 of this chapter, the fair use of a copyrighted work, including such use by reproduction in copies or phonorecords or by any other means specified by that section, for purposes such as criticism, comment, news reporting, teaching (including multiple copies for classroom use), scholarship, or research, is not an infringement of copyright. In determining whether the use made of a work in any particular case is a fair use the factors to be considered shall include: (1) the purpose and character of the use, including whether such use is of a commercial nature or is for nonprofit educational purposes; (2) the nature of the copyrighted work; (3) the amount and substantiality of the portion used in relation to the copyrighted work as a whole; and (4) the effect of the use upon the potential market for or value of the copyrighted work. § 109. Other limitations on exclusive rights of specific works. Other limitations on exclusive rights of specific works or exemptions of certain performances and displays may be prescribed by the Attorney General in rules and regulations consistent with sections 107 and 108 of this chapter.
Indonesia	
Law of the Republic of Indonesia 2014 about Copyright, art 15	(1) Unless otherwise agreed, the owners and/or holders of Creation photography, paintings, drawings, works of architecture, sculpture, or other artistic works the right to make announcement of a work in a public exhibition or multiplication in a catalog produced for exhibition purposes without the consent of the Creator.
Palau	
Consolidated Legislation Real and Personal Property Title 39 (Palau) 39 PNC § 821.	Notwithstanding the provisions of section 814, the public display of originals or copies of works shall be permitted without the authorization of the author or copyright owner, provided that the display is made other than by means of a film, slide, television image or otherwise on screen and provided further that the work has been published or the original or the copy displayed has been sold, given away, or otherwise transferred to another person by the author, copyright owner, or their successors in title.

Country Statute	Summary of freedom of panorama provision
Philippines	
Intellectual Property Code, Republic Act No. 8293, s 184.1	Notwithstanding the provisions of Chapter V, the following acts shall not constitute infringement of copyright … j. Public display of the original or a copy of the work not made by means of a film, slide, television image or otherwise on screen or by means of any other device or process: Provided, that either the work has been published, or, that the original or the copy displayed has been sold, given away or otherwise transferred to another person by the author or his successor in title; 184.2. The provisions of this section shall be interpreted in such a way as to allow the work to be used in a manner which does not conflict with the normal exploitation of the work and does not unreasonably prejudice the right holder's legitimate interests.
Papua New Guinea	
Copyright and Neighbouring Rights Act 2000, s 16	Notwithstanding the provisions of Section 6(1)(g), the public display of originals or copies of works may be made without the authorisation of the author, provided— (a) that the display is made other than by means of a film, slide, television image or otherwise on screen or by means of any other device or process; and (b) that the work has been published or the original or the copy displayed has been sold, given away or otherwise transferred to another person by the author or his successor in title.
Samoa	
Copyright Act 1998, s 15	Despite section 6(1)(f), the public display of originals or copies of works shall be permitted without the authorisation of the author: PROVIDED THAT— (a) the display is made other than by means of a film, slide, television image or otherwise on screen or by means of any other device or process; and (b) the work has been published or the original or the copy displayed has been sold, given away or otherwise transferred to another person by the author or his or her successor in title. Section 30 A person who, without the consent of the competent authority referred to in section 29(4), uses a traditional cultural expression in a manner not permitted by section 29 commits an offence in breach of a duty under law, and is liable to the competent authority referred to in section 29(4) for damages, injunctions and any other remedies as the Court may deem fit.

Country Statute	Summary of freedom of panorama provision
Vanuatu	

Copyright and Related Rights Act 2000, s 18	(1) A person may display in public the original or copies of a work if:
	  (a) the display is made other than by means of an audiovisual work, slide, television image or otherwise on screen; and
	  (b) either:
	    (i) the work has been published; or
	    (ii) the original or the copy of the work displayed has been sold, given away or otherwise transferred to another person by the author or his or her successor in title.
	(2) The display of the work in accordance with subsection (1) is not an infringement of the copyright in the work.
	(3) The display in public of the original or copies of a work by means of an audiovisual work, slide, television image or otherwise on screen is not an infringement of copyright in the work if its inclusion in such is only incidental to the principal matters being represented.

Commonwealth of the Northern Mariana Islands	
US legislation applies, i.e. 17 USC § 120(a)	The copyright in an architectural work that has been constructed does not include the right to prevent the making, distributing, or public display of pictures, paintings, photographs, or other pictorial representations of the work, if the building in which the work is embodied is located in or ordinarily visible from a public place.
Guam	
US legislation applies, i.e. 17 USC § 120(a)	The copyright in an architectural work that has been constructed does not include the right to prevent the making, distributing, or public display of pictures, paintings, photographs, or other pictorial representations of the work, if the building in which the work is embodied is located in or ordinarily visible from a public place.
Kiribati	
Laws of the Republic of Kiribati Revised Edition 1980, Chapter 16 Copyright	Minimalist legislation, no mention of public display etc.
Tuvalu	
Copyright Act, 1916	Minimalist legislation, no mention of public display etc.

Source: Author's summary of legislation, as listed in table.

9

The Development of Performers' Rights in New Zealand: Lessons for the Asian Pacific Region?

Jessica C Lai[1]

1 Introduction

Performers' rights have never been in the limelight in New Zealand. In fact, it is probably safe to say that performers' rights have generally taken a backseat to authors' rights in the Asian Pacific region. This is illustrated by the fact that the Asian Pacific Copyright Code makes very little reference to performers and, even then, only in a perfunctory manner.[2] As discussed in this chapter, the historical notion of the 'lowly performer' next to the idea of the 'romantic author' contributed towards this. At the same time, New Zealand and several Asian Pacific nations are under pressure to increase protections for performers as a result of international trade agreements. However, little scholarship in New Zealand or the Asian Pacific has addressed the nature or impact of performers' rights vis-à-vis authors' rights, whether from a theoretical, practical or empirical perspective. This chapter analyses the potential expansion of performer's

---

2   Adrian Sterling 'Asian Pacific Copyright Code' in this volume at C.2, D.1 and E.2.

rights, arguing that the expansion is either unnecessary because of the growing reach of copyright, or can have little practical effect (or perhaps the wrong effect, depending on one's policy aims) if done incorrectly.

Being a common-law country, New Zealand intellectual property law is predominantly grounded in utilitarian and law and economics philosophies, which do not lend themselves to cultivating performers' rights.[3] In comparison, natural rights theory still holds powerful sway over France, for example,[4] which has a strong and history-laden *droits des artistes-interprètes*.[5] In New Zealand, there has never been a case on performers' rights and very little has been written about them.[6] At the time of writing, New Zealand was neither a member of the Rome Convention (for the Protection of Performers, Producers of Phonograms and Broadcasting Organizations)[7] nor the World Intellectual Property

---

3   During the Industrial Revolution (1760–1840), Lockean labour theory (a natural rights theory) was used in England to justify property rights in literary works. However, by the mid-19th century, Lockean theory had given way to utilitarianism and consequentialist thinking, bringing patent law into the Modern Era. Though natural rights theory is still used today to justify the protection of intellectual property rights, we tend to focus less on the mental labour or creativity of works/inventions in order to justify property rights and instead look at the value of the immaterial thing itself with respect to economic or quasi-economic perspectives. See Brad Sherman and Lionel Bently *The Making of Modern Intellectual Property Law: The British Experience, 1760–1911* (Cambridge University Press, Cambridge, 1999) at 23–24 and 173–176. Note: certain interpretations of Lockean labour theory hold it as an instrumentalist or consequentialist theory; Justin Hughes 'The Philosophy of Intellectual Property' (1988) 77 Geo LJ 287 at 305–306.

4   In Continental Europe, copyright protection was and continues to be grounded in Kantian and Hegelian natural rights theories related to personality and individuality. See Immanuel Kant 'On the Injustice of Counterfeiting Books' in JAL Sterling *World Copyright Law* (2nd ed, Sweet & Maxwell, London, 2003); Georg Wilhelm Friedrich Hegel *Grundlinien der Philosophie des Rechts* (F. Meiner, Leipzig, 1911) (translated ed: Thomas M Knox (translator) *Philosophy of Right* (Oxford University Press, Oxford, 1967)).

5   Translation: *Performers' rights* – see Code de la Propriété Intellectuelle 1992 (France) (as at 10 April 2017), arts L212-1–L212-15.

6   One finds only two pages on performers' rights in Susy Frankel *Intellectual Property in New Zealand* (2nd ed, LexisNexis, Wellington, 2011) at 313–314. See *Intellectual Property Law* (online loose-leaf ed, LexisNexis) at [COP169]–[COP170], for a discussion on Part IX of the Copyright Act 1994, which deals with performers' rights; Owen Morgan 'Appendix C Performers' Rights' in *Intellectual Property Law* (online loose-leaf ed, LexisNexis) at [2120]–[2124] also deals specifically with performers' rights and offers a short overview of the development of performers' rights in New Zealand up to and including the Copyright Act 1994. However, both rely almost exclusively on case law from the United Kingdom, or case law from New Zealand dealing with similar terms used in copyright. The reliance on United Kingdom case law arises because Part IX of the Copyright Act 1994 is based significantly on Part II of the Copyright, Designs and Patents Act 1988 (UK) [CDPA 1988] (as originally enacted), though there are differences.

7   International Convention for the Protection of Performers, Producers of Phonograms and Broadcasting Organizations 496 UNTS 43 (adopted 26 October 1961, entered into force 18 May 1964) [Rome Convention].

Organization (WIPO) Performances and Phonograms Treaty (WPPT).[8] Indeed, New Zealand did not have any protection of performers' rights until the Copyright Act 1994,[9] when it implemented a weak form of performers' rights as neighbouring rights.[10] In other words, a 'performance' is not a copyright work, but performances are attributed a kind of protection, different from that conferred upon authors. It is clear that the implementation of performers' rights in 1994 only came about as a consequence of New Zealand's ratification of the World Trade Organization (WTO) Agreement on Trade-Related Aspects of Intellectual Property Rights (TRIPS).[11] Like the Rome Convention and WPPT, TRIPS predominantly deals with phonograms or sound recordings,[12] and not audiovisual works or films.[13] While attempts to create an agreement on audiovisual works eventually led to the signing of the WIPO Beijing Treaty on Audiovisual Works in 2012,[14] very few countries have ratified this Treaty and New Zealand is not a signatory.[15] That is to say, New Zealand has no international obligations relating to visual performances. Nevertheless, when New Zealand implemented the

---

8   WIPO Performances and Phonograms Treaty 2186 UNTS 203 (adopted 20 December 1996, entered into force 20 May 2002) [WPPT]. For a treatise on the development of international performers' rights generally, see Owen Morgan *International Protection of Performers' Rights* (Hart Publishing, Portland, 2002).

9   Performers' rights had been discussed in New Zealand before this, but there was never any particular drive or persuasive arguments for New Zealand to adopt performers' rights. See Dalglish Committee *Report of the Copyright Committee* (1959) at 125–127; Department of Justice *Reform of the Copyright Act 1962 – A Discussion Paper* (1985) at 22; and Department of Justice *The Copyright Act 1962 – Options for Reform* (1989) at 33–36.

10   With respect to performers' rights, the Copyright Act 1994 significantly mirrored the CDPA 1988 (UK), which was shortly modified by the Copyright and Related Rights Regulations 1996, s 20, to introduce a right to equitable remuneration (discussed below).

11   Agreement on Trade-Related Aspects of Intellectual Property Rights 1869 UNTS 299 (adopted 15 April 1994, entered into force 1 January 1995) [TRIPS]. See Ministry of Economic Development (MED) *Performers' Rights: A Discussion Paper* (July 2001) at [30]. The MED is now part of the Ministry of Business, Innovation and Employment (MBIE).

12   The terms phonograms and sound recordings traditionally have different meanings, with phonograms tending to relate to the civil-law neighbouring rights system, whereas 'sound recordings' usually refers to the common-law copyright-integrated protection. See Daniel J Gervais *The TRIPS Agreement: Drafting History and Analysis* (4th ed, Sweet & Maxwell, Croydon, 2012) at [2.201]. The terms are used interchangeably in this article.

13   As the name suggests, audiovisual works can comprise both the visual and aural components of a recording, though they may only contain the former; see Beijing Treaty on Audiovisual Works (adopted 24 June 2012), art 2(b) [Beijing Treaty]. In comparison, a film only refers to the visual component; see Copyright Act 1994 (NZ), s 2(1), which defines 'film' as 'a recording on any medium from which a moving image may by any means be produced'.

14   Beijing Treaty, above n 13.

15   Of the Asian Pacific, only China and South Korea signed and ratified the Beijing Treaty, while Japan and Russia did not sign the treaty but acceded to it.

TRIPS Agreement,[16] it did not discriminate between performers of sound recordings and performers in films,[17] instead extending the rights to both types of performers.

The Ministry of Economic Development (MED) reviewed performers' rights in 2001 and confirmed that there 'has been little discussion of the rights of performers in New Zealand, and these rights are not well understood'.[18] The MED released a Discussion Paper on performers' rights, raising a myriad of questions to consider. However, it received few submissions (21), and this outcome was interpreted as suggesting 'New Zealand's performers' rights regime [was] neither well understood nor utilised in performance-based industries'.[19] The outcome was essentially a recommendation that nothing be changed.[20] The MED did, however, advise that performers' rights be re-reviewed in the future.[21] At the time of writing, this review has not taken place. However, when the Comprehensive and Progressive Agreement for Trans-Pacific Partnership (CPTPP)[22] comes into force,[23] New Zealand will have to modify its performers' rights, including the implementation of the WPPT (but not the Rome Convention or Beijing Treaty).[24] With respect to performers' rights, the CPTPP is more or less identical to its predecessor, the Trans-Pacific Partnership (TPP), except that New Zealand will not have to extend the protection period from 50 to 70 years.[25]

---

16   Via the enactment of the Copyright Act 1994.

17   The Copyright Act 1994, s 2 defines a film as 'a recording on any medium from which a moving image may by any means be produced', and a sound recording as '(a) a recording of sounds, from which the sounds may be reproduced; or (b) a recording of the whole or any part of a literary, dramatic, or musical work, from which sounds reproducing the work or part may be produced,— regardless of the medium on which the recording is made or the method by which the sounds are reproduced or produced'.

18   MED, above n 11, at [2].

19   Office of the Associate Minister of Commerce *Performers' Rights Review* (2001) at [12].

20   At [1].

21   At [6].

22   Comprehensive and Progressive Agreement for Trans-Pacific Partnership (signed 8 March 2018, not yet in force) [CPTPP]. The official signed version is not yet public. The CPTPP developed from the Trans-Pacific Partnership Agreement (signed 4 February 2016) [TPP]. All the provisions relating to the substantive performers' rights remain in place, except term of protection (art 18.63 was suspended).

23   CPTPP, above n 22, art 30.5.

24   CPTPP, above n 22, art 18.8.2(f); Rome Convention, above n 7; Beijing Treaty, above n 13.

25   See above n 22. New Zealand will have to amend its ratifying legislation accordingly; Trans-Pacific Partnership Agreement Amendment Act 2016, s 28 (replacing s 193) [TPP Agreement Amendment Act]. The WPPT, above n 8, art 17, only requires 50 years of protection for performers' rights.

On 8 April 2016, the Ministry of Business, Innovation and Employment's (MBIE; successor to the MED) released a Regulatory Impact Statement (RIS) regarding the implementation of the intellectual property chapter of the TPP Agreement.[26] While the RIS did not discuss all aspects of the TPP intellectual property chapter, it included a section on performers' rights. Following this, the TPP Agreement Amendment Bill was introduced on 9 May 2016.[27] Rather conspicuously, no mention was made of performers' rights during the Bill's first reading.[28] The Foreign Affairs, Defence and Trade Committee examined the Bill and reported back on it on 27 October 2016 (TPP Agreement Amendment Bill 133-2).[29] The Committee did not comment on performers' rights and the substantive clauses remain unchanged, despite the fact that 11 of the 85 submissions made on the Bill provided comments on the performers' rights.[30] Within the first half of November 2016, the Bill swiftly passed its second reading, went through the Committee of the Whole House and had its third and final reading,[31] with virtually no mention of performers' rights.

Generally, the Copyright Act 1994 does not distinguish between sound recordings and films.[32] The TPP Agreement Amendment Act 2016, however, does, introducing 'stronger' rights for sound recordings but not for films.[33] The legislature only applied the new rights to sound recording to minimise the effect of implementing the TPP and WPPT.[34] The TPP Agreement Amendment Act 2016 also introduces moral rights for sound recordings and films, but more extensively for the former.[35] The Act will

---

26   MBIE *Regulatory Impact Statement: Analysis of Options Relating to Implementation of Certain Intellectual Property Obligations under the Trans-Pacific Partnership Agreement* (8 April 2016) [MBIE RIS].

27   Trans-Pacific Partnership Agreement Amendment Bill 2016 (133-3).

28   (12 May 2016) 713 NZPD 11059.

29   See Ministry of Foreign Affairs and Trade (MFAT) *Trans-Pacific Partnership Agreement Amendment Bill: Departmental Report for the Foreign Affairs, Defence and Trade Committee* (MFAT, September 2016) [MFAT Departmental Report].

30   MFAT Departmental Report, above n 29, Annex A at 67–78. The 11 submissions were from: The Electronic Frontier Foundation; The International Association of Music Libraries (NZ); Mr Jobson; Legislation Design and Advisory Committee; Library and Information Association of New Zealand Aotearoa; MBIE; New Zealand Institute of Patent Attorneys; New Zealand Law Society; Recorded Music, APRA AMCOS, Independent Music New Zealand, The New Zealand Music Commission, and The Music Managers Forum; Te Whakakitenga o Waikato Inc; and Universities New Zealand.

31   On: (3 November 2016) 718 NZPD 14756; (8 November 2016) 718 NZPD 14839; and (10 November 2016) 718 NZPD 14978 and (15 November 2016) 15044, respectively. The Bill received its Royal Assent on 21 November 2016.

32   Copyright Act 1994.

33   TPP Agreement Amendment Act 2016, s 18.

34   MBIE RIS, above n 26, at [262].

35   TPP Agreement Amendment Act 2016.

have to be amended in light of differences between the TPP and CPTPP, however the Act's provisions on performers' rights should not change. In all likelihood, any legislative amendments will only come into force if the CPTPP comes into force.[36]

The TPP/CPTPP aside, the proposed changes and issues discussed here are pertinent. First, if New Zealand were ever to achieve an elusive European Union – New Zealand free trade agreement (FTA),[37] it would in all likelihood require that New Zealand ratify the WPPT. Indeed, the leaked 15 October 2015 version of the Regional Comprehensive Economic Partnership (RCEP)[38] intellectual property chapter indicates that it would also require New Zealand to ratify the WPPT, as well as the Rome Convention and Beijing Treaty.[39] A majority of the RCEP nations have already ratified the WPPT.[40] It thus seems that the WPPT performers' rights will be semi-harmonised across much of the Asian Pacific region, whether as a result of some regional attempt to codify copyright and neighbouring rights, or the CPTPP, RCEP or another FTA. This makes the analysis of the impact of ways in which New Zealand would or could implement the WPPT important. Second, even if it were not the case that New Zealand will eventually have to ratify the WPPT,[41] the broader discussion on the relevance of performers rights in New Zealand (and, indeed, the Asian Pacific region), as they exist or in a 'stronger' form, is important.

As seems the tradition in New Zealand, little has been said about the proposed changes to performers' rights. This chapter does so. The purpose is not to critically analyse current law and the potential changes in detail, but to ask the broader question of the relevance of performers' rights in New Zealand and what it would mean to have 'stronger' rights. Part 2 'sets the scene' by briefly outlining performers' rights under the Copyright

36   As is the case under the TPP Agreement Amendment Act 2016, s 2(2).
37   New Zealand has long sought such an FTA; see MFAT 'New Zealand-European Union FTA' New Zealand Foreign Affairs and Trade www.mfat.govt.nz. The beginning of negotiations for such an agreement was announced on 30 October 2015; John Key 'NZ takes significant step towards an EU FTA' (press release, 30 October 2015).
38   Between Brunei Darussalam, Cambodia, Indonesia, Laos, Malaysia, Myanmar, the Philippines, Singapore, Thailand, Vietnam, Australia, China, India, Japan, South Korea and New Zealand.
39   '2015 Oct 15 version: RCEP IP Chapter' (19 April 2016) Knowledge Ecology International www.keionline.org at arts 1.7.6(f) and (h)–(i); WPPT, above n 8; Rome Convention, above n 7; Beijing Treaty, above n 13.
40   For example, of the RCEP countries: Brunei Darussalam, Indonesia, Malaysia, Philippines, Singapore, Australia, China, Japan and South Korea.
41   WPPT, above n 8.

Act 1994 and what changes could be introduced if New Zealand has to implement the WPPT.[42] Part 3 assesses performers and performances in contradistinction to authors and works from a theoretical perspective, examining whether it makes sense that copyright law holds the 'romantic author' in higher esteem than the 'lowly performer'. The chapter then looks at the actual situation in New Zealand from different perspectives, to address the significance of performers' rights and the need for, and potential effects of, introducing 'stronger' rights (as would be required by the implementation of WPPT). It asks whether introducing 'stronger' rights would improve the position of performers in reality.

2 Performers' Rights in New Zealand

Presently, New Zealand has only minimal protection of performers' rights.[43] Performers only have personal rights for economic rights (rather than property rights)[44] and have no moral rights. New Zealand law does go beyond its TRIPS obligations by protecting performers of sound recordings and films, where TRIPS only requires the former. There are two kinds of economic performers' rights: primary and secondary.

2.1 Primary Economic Rights

Primary rights relate to a live performance itself, namely its recording, broadcast or communication to the public, rather than to a recording of a performance or a copy thereof. The Copyright Act 1994 states that any performers' rights are infringed if someone records (meaning in a sound recording or film)[45] the whole or a substantial part of a performance,[46] without consent.[47]

---

42   Copyright Act 1994; WPPT, above n 8.
43   The Copyright Act 1994 does not define 'performer', but 'performance'; Copyright Act 1994, s 169(a).
44   Performers also cannot assign away their rights, though they can be passed by testamentary disposition; Copyright Act 1994, s 194.
45   Section 169.
46   Section 169.
47   Section 171(1)(a). Compare CDPA 1988 (UK), s 182(1)(a).

The Copyright Act 1994 additionally makes it an infringement of a performer's rights to communicate *live* to the public the whole or any substantial part of a performance, without consent.[48] The right to 'communicate to the public' is defined broadly under the Copyright Act 1994, as 'communicate means to transmit or make available by means of a communication technology, including by means of a telecommunications system'.[49] It thus includes what international law calls broadcasting, communication to the public and also making available to the public.

The TPP Agreement Amendment Act 2016 would not make any changes to the primary economic rights.[50]

2.2 Secondary Economic Rights

Secondary rights pertain to the exploitation of a recording or copy thereof. Sections 172–174 of the Copyright Act 1994 state that it is an infringement of performers' rights to use a (sound or film) recording of a performance without consent in the following ways:[51]

- To show in public, play in public, communicate to the public the whole or a substantial part of a performance, if the recording was made without the performer's consent, and the user knew or had reason to believe that there was no consent.[52]

- To copy a recording, if the user knew or had reason to believe that the recording was made without consent.[53]

- To copy a recording for a purpose other than that for which the performer gave consent to the recording.[54]

- To copy a recording that was made in accordance with an exemption under ss 175–179 or 181–191 for a different purpose.[55]

- To import a recording that the importer knows or has reason to believe is an illicit recording.[56]

---

48 Copyright Act 1994, s 171(1)(b). Compare CDPA 1988 (UK), s 182(1)(b).
49 Copyright Act 1994, s 2.
50 TPP Agreement Amendment Act 2016.
51 Copyright Act 1994, ss 172–174; Note: Morgan has stated that there is problem with the secondary rights in the Copyright Act 1994 because performance is defined as 'live performance' and it is not possible to do the infringing acts with a live performance; Morgan, above n 6, at Appendix C [2133]. However, he is clearly mistaken, as ss 172–174 pertain to recordings of performances.
52 Copyright Act 1994, s 172. Compare CDPA 1988 (UK), s 183.
53 Copyright Act 1994, s 173(1).
54 Section 173(3)(a).
55 Section 173(3)(B).
56 Section 174(1)(a). Compare CDPA 1988 (UK), s 184(1)(a).

- In the course of business, to possess, sell, let for hire, offer or expose for sale or hire, or distribute, a recording that the importer knows or has reason to believe is an illicit recording.[57]

It is these rights that will be affected if New Zealand has to implement the WPPT.[58] The WPPT specifically requires that performers of phonograms have the exclusive right to authorise:

- the direct or indirect reproduction;[59]
- the distribution (making available of the 'original and copies') 'through sale or other transfer of ownership';[60]
- the commercial rental of the 'original and copies';[61]
- the making available, by wire or wireless means, 'in such a way that members of the public may access them from a place and at a time individually chosen by them'.[62]

These are positively phrased and transferable,[63] and are, thus, property rights.

The TPP Agreement Amendment Act 2016 retains the status quo for films. It introduces a new set of property rights for the secondary economic rights for sound recordings, as displayed in Table 1.

---

57 Copyright Act 1994, s 174(1)(b). Compare CDPA 1988 (UK), s 184(1)(b).

58 WPPT, above n 8; If the TPP comes into force, New Zealand will have to amend the Copyright Act 1994 to meet WPPT standards. See CPTPP, above n 22, arts 18.58, 18.60 and 18.62.3(a). See also the art 18.57 definitions of 'broadcasting' and 'communication to the public'.

59 WPPT, above n 8, art 7.

60 Article 8. An open (and highly controversial) question remains whether distribution is only for tangible copies of performances, or includes digital distribution.

61 WPPT, above n 8, art 9.

62 WPPT, above n 8, art 10. Article 15 also includes a right to a single equitable remuneration 'the direct or indirect use of phonograms published for commercial purposes for broadcasting or for any communication to the public'. However, subarticle 3 allows countries to opt out of the right. The right is not specifically required by the CPTPP, above n 22. New Zealand has not implemented art 15 of the WPPT, above n 8, in the TPP Agreement Amendment Act 2016. This is consistent with the MED's statement that 'a right of remuneration would represent an additional cost that is likely to be passed on to the consumer. A remuneration right also leads to an outflow of moneys in a country like New Zealand, which is a net importer of performances. The outflow will occur because overseas performers will be entitled to be remunerated in New Zealand alongside domestic performers. Although there will be some money flowing into New Zealand from New Zealand performances exploited in other countries, it is unlikely to be enough to balance the outflow'. See MED, above n 12, at [109].

63 The WPPT does not explicitly state that these rights are transferable, above n 8. However, art 5(1) states that moral rights stay with performers even upon the transfer of their economic rights, implying that economic rights are transferable.

Table 1. Possible Implementation of the WPPT.

WPPT Right	TPP Agreement Amendment Act 2016[1]	Amendment to the Copyright Act 1994[2]
Reproduction	Copying	s 174C
Distribution	Issuing copies to the public	s 174D
Rental right	Issuing copies to the public	s 174D
Making available	Communicate to the public	s 174B

[1] TPP Agreement Amendment Act 2016, s 24.
[2] Copyright Act 1994.
Source: Author's summary.

As noted above, 'communicate to the public' includes making available to the public in New Zealand.[64] As defined in the Copyright Act 1994, 'issuing copies to the public' includes distribution and rental.[65] The TPP Agreement Amendment Act 2016 states that the economic rights of performers of sound recordings (but not films) are 'personal or moveable property' rights and states that performers can assign their rights, or dispose of them by testament, and exclusively licence them.[66] The 2016 Act specifically stipulates performers' secondary rights in films would remain personal rights.[67]

New Zealand chose to differentiate between films and sound recordings with respect to the new introduced property rights in order to minimise the impact of its TPP obligations.[68] However, the differentiation demonstrates a hierarchy of value of performers, with performers of sound recordings sitting higher than performers of films, which one also observes at the international level where the WPPT enjoys more status and acceptance compared to the Beijing Treaty.[69]

---

64   Copyright Act 1994, s 2.
65   Section 9.
66   TPP Agreement Amendment Act 2016, s 29, implementing ss 194E–194K.
67   TPP Agreement Amendment Act 2016, s 29, implementing ss 194C and 194D.
68   CPTPP, above n 22.
69   WPPT, above n 8; Beijing Treaty, above n 13.

2.3 Performers' Moral Rights

Rather unsurprisingly, TRIPS does not require the protection of moral rights of performers; this mirrors the explicit exclusion of authors' moral rights in TRIPS.[70] New Zealand also does not protect the moral rights of performers, because moral rights are linked to particular categories of copyright works and a performance is not a work.[71]

The WPPT requires that states protect moral rights of performers, again with respect to performances fixed in phonograms and also 'live aural performances', namely:[72]

- the right to claim to be identified as the performer; and
- the right to object to any 'distortion, mutilation or other modification of his performance that would be prejudicial to his reputation'.

The TPP Agreement Amendment Act 2016 contains these two rights.[73] It grants the right to be identified to both performers in sound recordings and films, but more broadly for the former.[74] Performers of sound recordings (not films) would also be protected from 'distortion, mutilation, or other modification', in relation to the whole or any part of a performance,[75] that is 'prejudicial to the honour or reputation of the performer'.[76]

Per the 2016 Act, moral rights would not be assignable, but could be disposed by testament.[77] The 2016 Act would allow performers to waive their moral rights.[78] This is not possible in all countries, particularly not in civil-law countries, like France and Germany, which justify their laws on natural rights theory. However, the instrument provided in the 2016 Act to performers to waive their moral rights is analogous to that which allows authors to waive their moral rights,[79] and is in accordance with an economics theory approach.

---

70 TRIPS, above n 11, art 9(1).
71 See Copyright Act 1994, s 14(1).
72 WPPT, above n 8, art 5(1).
73 Compare CDPA 1988 (UK), ss 2015C–205H, as amended 1 February 2006 by The Performances (Moral Rights, etc.) Regulations 2006 (SI 2006/18) and 31 October 2003 by The Copyright and Related Rights Regulations 2003 (SI 2003/2498).
74 TPP Agreement Amendment Act 2016, s 18, implementing s 170A.
75 TPP Agreement Amendment Act 2016, s 18, implementing s 170I(2).
76 TPP Agreement Amendment Act 2016, s 18, implementing s 170F.
77 TPP Agreement Amendment Act 2016, s 29, implementing ss 194A and 194B.
78 TPP Agreement Amendment Act 2016, s 18, implementing s 170H.
79 See Copyright Act 1994, s 107(2).

3 The Historical 'Lowly Performer'

Performers' rights exist as neighbouring rights to copyright. In New Zealand, and most (if not all) western countries, performances are not copyright works.[80] As mere 'conduits' or 'interpreters' of existing literary and musical works,[81] singers, dancers and actors are not considered to have added any creativity over and above the existing works and, thus, have no separate copyright for their performance. This conceptualisation of the author/composer as having primacy over the performer stems in part from the contraposition of the romantic author and the lowly performer in the 18th and 19th centuries.[82] Ruth Towse has also suggested that the hierarchy was influenced by the introduction of copyright for composers as authors in the late 19th century, which raised the relative status of composers.[83] That authors/composers rank higher than performers is also a consequence of the fact (or belief) that copyright works come first; there must be something for a performer to perform.[84] Andreas Rahmatian discussed this, stating that, while a performance animates a work, it does not create an object of copyright protection because:[85]

> the object of protection is already the written piece recorded in a score or recorded on a sound recording as a past musical event: time and the necessary volatility and imprecision which time entails have been removed.

---

80   See Copyright Act 1994, s 14(1). There is, after all, no property in a spectacle; *Victoria Park Racing & Recreation Grounds Co Ltd v Taylor* [1937] HCA 45. Some discussion has been made about whether performers should have copyright; see Department of Justice, *The Copyright Act 1962 – Options for Reform*, above n 9, at [10.2]–[10.11]; and, in the United Kingdom, Gerald Dworkin 'The Whitford Committee Report on Copyright and Designs Law' (1977) 40(6) MLR 685 at 690–691.

81   The words of songs and the music to those songs are usually separate works. An exception may be rap, where the words cannot be separated from the music. See *Brown v Mcasso Music Production Ltd* [2005] EWCC 1 (Cpwt) at [6]–[7] and [45]–[46], which held that Mr Brown's changes to lyrics made him a co-author of the literary work of the song 'Mr High Roller'. While Judge Fysh did not go so far as to say that Mr Brown also had copyright in the music, the importance of the lyrics of rap for the overall song contributed to the finding that Mr Brown was a co-author.

82   Ruth Towse 'The Singer or the Song? Developments in Performers' Rights from the Perspective of a Cultural Economist' (2007) 3 Rev L & Econ 745 at 746–747.

83   At 748.

84   Notably, it does not seem to be an issue for co-authorship whether contributions occur in series or parallel; see Alison Firth 'Music and Co-Authorship/Co-Ownership' in Andreas Rahmatian (ed) *Concepts of Music and Copyright: How Music Perceives Itself and How Copyright Perceives Music* (Edward Elgar, Cheltenham, 2015) 143 at 257.

85   Andreas Rahmatian 'The Elements of Music Relevant for Copyright Protection' in Andreas Rahmatian (ed) *Concepts of Music and Copyright: How Music Perceives Itself and How Copyright Perceives Music* (Edward Elgar, Cheltenham, 2015) 78 at 89.

Rahmatian, however, noted that this is not always the case and 'in reality one precipitates the other and they are often inseparable in the creative process, for example in improvisation'.[86] Thus, while Rahmatian indicated the importance of chronology for copyright law, he also highlighted that copyright cannot take into account the temporal aspect of music and music-making. In the quote above, he also implied that copyright's need for static and definable property prevents us from recognising performances as works, because performances have an inherent temporal character. The allusion to the ephemeral nature of performances leads us to the next point.

It is not always easy to see the contribution made by a performer,[87] nor can one simply separate a performance from the work that is being performed.[88] The boundaries of the performance are difficult to define, in contrast to the boundaries of a literary work or musical work.[89] In explaining why performances are not recognised as works in contrast to the work they are performing, Mathilde Pavis stated that 'the work of the author has clear boundaries'.[90] While lyrics and compositions may have clearer boundaries than performances, it is arguably incorrect to say that they have clear boundaries. Many questions remain open regarding the delineations of copyright works, for example: when there are several versions (or drafts),[91] when a work changes depending on the user,[92] when a work contains something biological or when the work is incomplete,[93] the line between a musical work and an adaptation, derivative work or substantial rearrangement,[94] what is functional/utilitarian as opposed to

---

86 At 117.

87 Mathilde Pavis 'Is There *Any*-Body on Stage? A Legal (Mis)understanding of Performances' (2016) 19 JWIP 99 at 106.

88 Towse, above n 84, at 752.

89 Pavis, above n 89, at 106.

90 Pavis, above n 89, at 106.

91 *Sweeney v Macmillan Publishers Ltd* [2002] RPC 651.

92 For example, video games and *Komesaroff v Mickle* [1988] RPC 204 (VSC). In *Komesaroff v Mickle*, the court held that sand and air between two glass planes was not a work of artistic craftsmanship, because the sand landscape resulted from the user not the maker.

93 *Kelley v Chicago Park District* 635 F 3d 290 (7th Cir 2011); and *Massachusetts Museum of Contemporary Art Foundation, Inc v Büchel* 593 F 3d 38 (1st Cir 2010). As discussed by Michael J Madison 'Understanding Access to Things: a Knowledge Commons Perspective' in Jessica C Lai and Antoinette Maget Dominicé (eds) *Intellectual Property and Access to Im/material Goods* (Edward Elgar, Cheltenham, 2016) 17 at 31–38.

94 Rahmatian, above n 86, at 115–116; and Shane O'Connor 'A Critical Evaluation of the Law of Copyright Authorship in Relation to Derivative Musical Works' (2014) 3(2) Westminster L Rev.

expression,[95] or where the line is between the idea and the expression (including within music).[96] Indeed, there is a significant discourse regarding the concept and bounds of the musical work.[97] In any case, given that the existing categories of copyright works are by no means clear-cut, that performances have nebulous boundaries is not a strong reason to find against copyright.[98]

Towse criticised the fact that authors/composers are given primacy over performers, noting that there are far more songs and musical works in existence than will ever be performed, and authors/composers need their works to be performed, otherwise they have little value.[99] Noting that the chronological chain of events is irrelevant because authors/composers and performers have mutual need for each other,[100] Towse stated:[101]

> incentives to perform must be taken into account if copyright is to achieve its goal of not only stimulating the creation of works but also their publication. The unperformed song has little value either to the composer or to society at large.

Singers and musicians are, after all, the ones that make lyrics and compositions famous. Additionally, Alison Firth has discussed that musical and dramatic works are designed to be performed and that a performance can end up defining the work, particularly when fixation is achieved by recording a performance.[102]

95　For example, *Star Athletica, LLC v University Brands, Inc* (USSC, Docket No.15-866) regarding whether certain aspects of designs (stripes, chevrons, zigzags and colour blocks) for cheerleading outfits are copyrightable or a functional/utilitarian. In the lower court, the majority of the 6th Circuit held Varsity's designs were distinctive graphic works, separate from the function of the outfits (6th Cir, Docket No. 14-5237, 19 August 2015).

96　Rahmatian, above n 86, at 111–116.

97　See John Butt 'What is a "Musical Work"? Reflections on the Origins of the "Work Concept" in Western Art Music' in Andreas Rahmatian (ed) *Concepts of Music and Copyright: How Music Perceives Itself and How Copyright Perceives Music* (Edward Elgar, Cheltenham, 2015) 1.

98　Patents are arguably also granted for objects that are poorly delineated. See e.g. James Bessen and Michael J Meurer *Patent Failure: How Judges, Bureaucrats, and Lawyers Put Innovators at Risk* (Princeton University Press, New Jersey, 2008).

99　Towse, above n 84, at 752.

100　At 764.

101　At 752. Note the analogies between this argument and arguments that patent law needs to take into account post-grant incentives to ensure the commercialisation of patented inventions; see Edmund Kitch 'The Nature and Function of the Patent System' (1977) 20(2) JL & Econ 265; and Ted Sichelman 'Commercializing Patents' (2010) 62 Stan L Rev 341.

102　Firth, above n 86, at 152. See also Dalglish Committee, above n 9, at 125. The definitions of literary, dramatic and musical works in s 2 of the Copyright Act 1994, also make it clear that many works are meant to be performed.

That copyright law does not recognise the performer as bringing any extra creativity has been challenged as reflecting an outdated philosophy of performance.[103] Pavis argued that performers can undertake creative choices when interpreting a work and usually enough to satisfy the level of creativity (or originality) required to have copyright, namely 'time, skill and effort' (or skill, judgment and/or labour), a very low standard in New Zealand.[104] Furthermore, Towse has argued that, purely from a Lockean perspective, a performer should be entitled to a share in the revenue for any value that he/she adds.[105]

To be clear, this is not to say that performers should, thus, have copyright or 'stronger' neighbouring rights (as would be introduced by the TPP Agreement Amendment Act 2016),[106] but to refute the notion that the 'romantic author' necessarily sits higher on the creative scale (and consequently also the value scale) than the 'lowly performer'. Nevertheless, while lyrics are literary works, screenplays are dramatic works, compositions are musical works, and sound recordings and films are works in themselves, each with authors (including producers and directors for sound recordings and films, respectively), performances are not works and performers do not have copyright for their performances. As discussed further below, performers might nevertheless be authors (Part 4.3). This is not just because they are often also composers, lyricists, screenplay writers or choreographers, but because their performances may have certain aspects that qualify as part of copyright works.

---

103 See Pavis, above n 89; and Aurore Vinant, 'Le danseur, interprète et/ou auteur?' (2014) 2 Recherches en danse 1. Compare Phillip Johnson and Sheldon W Halpern 'When is a Performance not a Performance (but a Copyright Work)?' (2014) 4(3) QMJIP 236, which discusses *Garcia v Google* 743 F 3d 1258 (9th Cir 2014) – a case where the majority found that a performance was a separate copyright right. But see *Conrad v AM Community Credit Union*, case no 13-2896 (7th Cir 2014), which held that an actress' performance was not a copyright work. Notably, the disconnect between copyright law and philosophy on the role of the author is also dated and we are stuck on the notion of the romantic author; see Lionel Bently 'Copyright and the Death of the Author in Literature and the Law' (1994) 57 MLR 973. Compare Martin Parker Dixon 'Creativity and Possessive Interests' in Andreas Rahmatian (ed) *Concepts of Music and Copyright: How Music Perceives Itself and How Copyright Perceives Music* (Edward Elgar, Cheltenham, 2015) 50 at 66 who states that it is 'sheer hubris' to remove authors and artists from the equation.

104 The latter is the test in New Zealand, per *Ladbroke v William* [1964] 1 All ER 465 (HL). See also *Henkel v Holdfast NZ Ltd* [2007] 1 NZLR 577 at [38] per Tipping J, confirming that the threshold for originality is low in New Zealand and looks at 'how much skill and labour has gone into its creation'. See also *University of London Press Ltd v University Tutorial Press Ltd* [1916] Ch at 608–609 per Peterson J, stating that originality 'does not require that the expression be in an original or novel form, but that the work must not be copied from another work – that it should originate from the author'.

105 Towse, above n 84, at 754.

106 TPP Agreement Amendment Act 2016.

Performers' rights differ from classical copyright because they are not for a work, but for a particular performance. As alluded to above, performances have been argued to be ephemeral, lacking in tangibility or materiality,[107] and this is confirmed by the fact that a performance of a work is not a fixation of it; the performance would have to be recorded and then there would be fixation of the underlying works. However, in a way, performers' rights relate to something far less abstract than classical copyright works. This is because performers' rights relate to a specific embodiment of a work. Another person can re-enact the performance, copy the intonation, pitch, syncopation and pausing,[108] for example, but will not be infringing performers' rights (though perhaps copyright in any underlying works) unless they use or copy the actual embodiment or performance. This is analogous with films and sound recordings (modern categories of copyright works),[109] which are also less abstract as they protect a particular embodiment of underlying works.[110]

4 Do Performers' Rights Matter?

While performers might be just as deserving of rights as authors, being equally as creative and playing a pivotal role on the dissemination of authors works, this is not to say that existing performers' rights in the Copyright Act 1994, or the 'stronger' rights proposed in the TPP Agreement Amendment Act 2016, necessarily create the best environment for performative creativity.[111] Indeed, performers' rights are perhaps, by and large, of little practical importance in New Zealand because:

- Performers' rights have been largely ignored by government, practitioners, academics and performers themselves.
- Common-law countries have been relatively apathetic to performers' rights and moral rights generally.
- Performers potentially have copyright as authors if they modify the underlying works enough to qualify for a new work.
- Contract law dominates any intellectual property.

107 As discussed by Pavis, above n 89, at 107.
108 See *Elizabeth Coffey v Warner/Chappell Music Ltd* [2006] EWHC 449 (Ch) at [5]–[6].
109 In New Zealand, the Copyright Act 1962, s 7, only covered literary, dramatic, musical, and artistic works. The Copyright Act 1994, s 14(1), introduced both 'films' and 'sound recordings' as categories of works.
110 Indeed, one could view a sound recording or film as an embodiment of an embodiment of a work.
111 Copyright Act 1994; TPP Agreement Amendment Act 2016.

The questionable importance of performers' rights in New Zealand will be expanded upon here.

4.1 Perceived Relevance for New Zealand

Arguments for 'stronger' performers' rights are analogous to those for authors' rights; namely, that exclusive rights are required to offer extrinsic incentives for creativity.[112] Similarly, reasons against performers' rights are also the same as those against authors' rights; in particular, that performers – like authors and artists – have other intrinsic incentives to create. Additionally, just as authors' (and publishers') rights emerged after the invention of the printing press and separation of an author from his or her work,[113] performers' rights arose in Europe with the development of recording technologies, and then broadcasting technologies, and the separation of performers from – and replacement of performers with – their performances.[114] In either case, the creative parties were concerned with the unauthorised fixation of their works and the use of those fixations.

A noted above, New Zealand only introduced performers' rights because it had to under its TRIPS obligations.[115] If one looks at the historical discussion on performers' rights in New Zealand, there has never been a local push for the introduction or expansion of performers' rights. In 1959, the Report of the Copyright Committee stated:[116]

> There is reason to believe that these problems [as in Europe], such as the threat to the livelihood of musicians, do not exist to anything like the same extent in New Zealand. There are few full-time professional musicians in this country and it is probable that the growth of radio, in particular, far from harming musicians, has given them an audience which they would not otherwise have had.

In 1989, the Law Reform Division of the Department of Justice noted that there did not appear to be any need to protect performers' rights, as there was 'no evidence that unauthorised fixation of performances

---

112 For example, Office of the Associate Minister of Commerce, above n 19, at [7].

113 See William Cornish 'Conserving Culture and Copyright: A Partial History' (2009) 13(1) Edin L Rev 8.

114 Morgan, above n 8, at 54–59; and Towse, above n 84, at 748; and John Williamson 'For the Benefit of All Musicians? The Musicians' Union and Performers' Rights in the UK' in Andreas Rahmatian (ed) *Concepts of Music and Copyright: How Music Perceives Itself and How Copyright Perceives Music* (Edward Elgar, Cheltenham, 2015) 167 at 181–182.

115 TRIPS, above n 11.

116 Dalglish Committee, above n 9, at 126.

constitute[d] a problem in New Zealand'.[117] In its 2001 Discussion Paper, the MED acknowledged that New Zealand only had performers' rights because of its international obligations and not due to any theoretical (whether economic- or natural rights–based) justifications.[118] Indeed it noted that, with respect to performers' rights, the economic incentive argument was weak because performers in New Zealand had very little knowledge about their rights, such that the rights could not constitute any kind of incentive to perform.[119] New Zealand nevertheless has burgeoning music and film industries. Arguably, other legal regimes hold far greater sway over the film industry, such as tax and employment law. Moreover, in light of the fact that featured singers and musicians may in fact have copyright if they modify any underlying work to a sufficient extent to be original (as discussed below, part 4.3), certain performers arguably already have enough of an incentive.

Indeed, creative industries have strong non-economic incentives, such as the drive for self-expression, communication, respect from one's peers and 'fame', or the pursuit of 'art for art's sake'.[120] There is a compelling argument to be made that inappropriately offering extrinsic rewards for activities that are primarily motivated by intrinsic grounds can have a 'crowding out effect' and either fail as an incentive or even act as a disincentive.[121] That is, offering extrinsic rewards where intrinsic motivations pre-exist can crowd out or remove those intrinsic motivations, potentially forever, and can even discourage the behaviour it is meant to incentivise.[122]

---

117 Department of Justice, *The Copyright Act 1962 – Options for Reform*, above n 9, at [10.11].

118 MED, above n 11, at [16]–[17].

119 MED, above n 11, at [16]. See also Dalglish Committee, above n 9, at 126, which noted that 'there appears to be no demand for it in New Zealand by performers themselves'.

120 See Jiarui Liu 'Copyright for Blockheads: An Empirical Study of Market Incentive and Intrinsic Motivation' (2010) 38(4) Colum JL & Arts 467; and Jessica Silbey *The Eureka Myth: Creators, Innovators, and Everyday Intellectual Property* (Stanford University Press, Stanford, 2014). Note that similar arguments are made regarding non-economic reasons to invent in the patent law discourse, such as the prestige associated with invention (possibly the opportunity for co-authorship), altruistic desires (to 'save the world') and the chance to participate in the advancement of science. See Yochai Benkler 'Commons-Based Strategies and the Problems of Patents' (2004) 305 Science 1110 at 1111; and Robin Feldman 'The Open Source Biotechnology Movement: Is it Patent Misuse?' (2004) 6(1) Minn JL Sci & Tech 117 at 161.

121 Bruno S Frey and Reto Jegen, 'Motivation Crowding Out' (2001) 15(5) J Econ Surv 589 at 589–591.

122 See also Bruno S Frey 'Crowding Out and Crowding In of Intrinsic Preferences' in Eric Brousseau, Tom Dedeurwaerdere and Bernd Siebenhüner (eds) *Reflexive Governance for Global Public Goods* (Massachusetts Institute of Technology, Massachusetts, 2012) 75; Bruno S Frey and Felix Oberholzer-Gee 'The Cost of Price Incentives: An Empirical Analysis of Motivation Crowding-Out' (1997) 87(4) Am Econ Rev 746; and more broadly Bruno S Frey *Arts and Economics* (Springer, Heidelberg, 2000).

Moreover, other initiatives supporting the arts may prove to be better promoters of creativity than property or property-like rights.[123] There is no concrete evidence that copyright and neighbouring rights are the ideal means to offer extrinsic rewards and not, for example, prizes, direct state subsidies,[124] or public/private patronage. This is not to say that extrinsic rewards have no role in the creative sector, but rather that the picture is complex and we have to be careful about the type and extent of extrinsic rewards we put forward.

As with patents and copyright, it is arguable that financial or economic incentives are only required for employers, investors or right holders, rather than inventors, authors or performers. Much invention occurs in the absence of patents, for example, by researchers in universities and publicly funded organisations, but pharmaceutical companies are heavily reliant on patents. At the same time, while songwriters and authors might be incentivised by intrinsic motivations, music producers and book publishers are less likely to invest in commercialisation in the absence of intellectual property protection. Analogously, it is music producers that are more susceptible to incentives created by copyright and related rights, as opposed to performers. This is, of course, a simplistic view, based on generalisations. The role of patents varies across differing industries. For example, motivations in the software industry are not the same as those in the pharmaceutical industry. Equally, there are authors and artists who are motivated by economic incentives, and there are music producers and book publishers that do not seek to profit. However, the general point is that incentive arguments for 'stronger' performers' rights are arguably weak.

In 2001, the MED stated that, as a net importer of performances, an extension of performers' rights would predominantly benefit foreign – and not local – performers, and would lead to a net outflow of royalties from New Zealand.[125] It is difficult to see how this is the case when there is no right to remuneration. How much foreign performers get depends on their contracts with their producers. Normally, they would contract to allow their producers to reproduce their performances and distribute copies, internationally. Even if their contracts stipulate that they receive

---

123 Office of the Associate Minister of Commerce, above n 19, at [42]–[43].
124 Copyright and neighbouring rights are a form of indirect subsidies, as are state-funded music or drama schools or faculties at universities and colleges.
125 MED, above n 11, at [26].

a certain royalty for each public performance or communication, or each copy made or sold, this has (almost) nothing to do with New Zealand's law on performers' rights. It is a matter of contract law and, as noted, the terms of contract are usually stipulated to be international to simplify matters.

This position is supported by the statement made by the Ministry of Foreign Affairs and Trade (MFAT) in January 2016 that:[126]

> Giving performers new rights is unlikely to incentivise an increase in the number of performances, an increase in the number of sound recordings created from performances, or in the distribution and sale of sound recordings in the New Zealand market. The New Zealand market is a small market by world standards. Most performers are therefore likely to base their production and distribution decisions on the conditions in large overseas markets like the US and Europe rather than on the regulatory conditions in the New Zealand market.

As noted above, other areas of law appear to be more important for incentivising foreign investment in the film and music industries. New Zealand's 'untouched' landscape is another relevant factor for the film industry. Indeed, if anything, strong performers' rights are likely to be a disincentive to invest in New Zealand, as investors (that is, producers) will want to negotiate away any rights that performers hold.[127]

The MED further noted that there did not seem to be any evidence that performers' rights or infringement thereof was an issue in New Zealand.[128] As stated at the beginning of this chapter, there has never been a performers' rights case in New Zealand and, indicative of the general indifference to performers' rights, the MED only received 21 submissions in response to its Discussion Paper. None identified any substantial problem with the existing regime and very few supported any move for New Zealand to extend protection for performers, or to accede to the WPPT or an international agreement on audiovisual works.[129] However, it is important to note that most of the submissions were from producers or users of performances. The few submissions from performers supported the extension of performers' rights.[130]

---

126 MFAT *Trans-Pacific Partnership: National Interest Analysis* (25 January 2016) at 90 [MFAT NIS].
127 Morgan, above n 8, at 49. See also Department of Justice *Reform of the Copyright Act 1962 – A Discussion Paper*, above n 9, at 22.
128 MED, above n 11, at [26].
129 Office of the Associate Minister of Commerce, above n 19, at [12].
130 At [36].

Overall, reporting on the review, the Cabinet paper prepared by the Office of the Associate Minister of Commerce stated:[131]

> There would appear to be no substantive benefit to New Zealand from making changes to the performers' rights regime at present. An extension of performers' rights would not necessarily result in increased or better performances, as performers appear to have a range of other incentives that encourage performance. These include incentives that are not primarily economic. Further, as New Zealand is a net importer of performances, any extensions to rights could simply flow overseas rather than to New Zealand.

As is common in the realm of intellectual property in New Zealand, the MED Discussion Paper and the report on the review often mention the need to be mindful of 'international developments' and changes made by other like jurisdictions. However, the conclusion wrought represents one of a few examples of New Zealand deciding not to follow these 'international developments', instead opting to retain the status quo.

In 2016, having signed the TPP, New Zealand had no choice but to start implementing 'stronger' performers' rights. Nevertheless, MBIE's RIS was consistent with the MED's reservations and stated that its objectives were: to keep amendments to the minimum required to meet TPP and WPPT requirements; to ensure that the correct balance is met between performers and producers, and performers and users; and to minimise any regulatory and business compliance costs introduced.[132] It is correct to be wary of extending performers' rights more than is necessary. As noted by the MED in 2001:[133]

> There have been *no studies conducted in New Zealand on the economic consequences of extended performers' rights*. Studies in Australia and Canada however, suggest that extended performers' rights may act as disincentives to the production of performances.

---

131 At [4].

132 MBIE RIS, above n 26, at [262].

133 MED, above n 11, at [119] (emphasis added), citing Steven Globerman and Mitchell P Rothman *Copyright Revision Studies: An Economic Analysis of a Performers' Rights* (Canadian Bureau of Consumer and Corporate Affairs, Ottawa, 1981); and Australian Federal Bureau of Transport and Communications *Economic Effects of Extended Performers' Rights – Paper prepared for the Department of Communications and the Arts* (Department of Communications and the Arts, Canberra, 1996).

Fifteen years later, MFAT made a similar statement. In explaining why the new provisions only apply to aural and not visual aspects of performances, MFAT noted: 'It has not been established that going beyond TPP and WPPT obligations would result in a net benefit to New Zealand.'[134] The reservations indicated by the MED, MBIE and MFAT should be commended, as recent years have seen New Zealand roll full steam ahead with broadening and strengthening certain areas of intellectual property, despite the similar lack of economic studies on the particular situation in New Zealand.[135] This is not to say that broadening performers' rights could not be an overall boon for New Zealand, but rather that we cannot presume this until there has been a full economic investigation into the matter.

4.2 Performers Rights and Moral Rights in Common-Law Countries

A note should be made regarding the general apathy towards performers' rights and moral rights in common-law countries. New Zealand did not have either until it enacted the Copyright Act 1994.[136] This is, of course, connected to the history of copyright law in England, which was about protecting publishers and copying. It was not really about authors and it most certainly was not about performers. Copyright has always been based more in utilitarian or law and economics theory. In comparison, performers' rights and moral rights have a strong history in Central Europe, where natural rights philosophies dominate.[137] France's *droit d'auteur* (or author's right) has, thus, always been author-centric, as its name suggests, and civil-law jurisdictions tend to have robust moral rights. Similarly, France has a separate *droit des artistes-interprètes* (performers' right).

The historical and philosophical differences continue to create divergences today. Even though many common-law countries now have moral rights, they are seldom used or held out as an integral part of copyright law. Similarly, there are few cases on performers' rights in the United Kingdom,

---

134 MFAT Departmental Report, above n 29, Annex A at 70.

135 For example, regulatory data exclusivity and patent term extension. See Susy Frankel and Jessica C Lai, *Patent Law and Policy* (LexisNexis, Wellington, 2016) at ch 10.

136 This is despite the fact that New Zealand has been a Party to the WIPO Berne Convention for the Protection of Literary and Artistic Works, 828 UNTS 222 (adopted on 9 September 1886), since 1928.

137 See above n 4.

none in New Zealand, and – as the discussion above indicates – little interest in further developing performers' rights. This reflects a continued understanding of a hierarchy of creative beings, with the romantic author on top and the lowly performer clearly below. Indeed, the differentiation between performers on sound recordings in comparison to performers of film or audiovisual works reflects a further demarcation in hierarchy, with the musician or composer sitting higher than the actor or dancer.

The differences between the two legal systems plays out in a subtler way, which impacts performers' rights. This relates to the standard of originality. The standard is very low in common-law jurisdictions, New Zealand included. In contrast, it is famously higher in civil-law jurisdictions, where it typically requires that there be an imprint of the author's personality.[138] Because common-law jurisdictions have such a low standard of originality, performers can sometimes be authors or co-authors and, to a degree, a performance can constitute a work. This being the case, performers' rights are arguably of less relevance in common-law countries than in civil-law jurisdictions.[139]

4.3 Performers as Authors/Performances as Works?

Copyright envisages the traditional composer, playwright or choreographer as a lone creature, who is singularly the creative genius behind any given work. Copyright has a clear delineation between the author and the performer. However, in reality, there is no fine line between the two. It is hard to imagine that there ever was. Instead, performers often bring something more than just performance skills. They often rearrange music, adapt music, or change lyrics; actors often ad lib or improvise many of their lines. This can make them authors of rearrangements, co-authors of musical, literary or dramatic works, if the additions or rearrangements reach the required level of originality. Keeping in mind that the level of

---

138 Note, however, that there is 'an unstoppable trend towards a more objective criterion of originality'; Ramón Casas Vallés 'The Requirement of Originality' in Estelle Derclaye (ed) *Research Handbook on the Future of EU Copyright* (Edward Elgar, Cheltenham, 2009) 102–132 at 112. Moreover, although differences between copyright and *droit d'auteur* may not have entirely disappeared, interpretations of originality are converging (at 113). See also Sam Ricketson and Jane C Ginsburg *International Copyright and Neighbouring Rights: The Berne Convention and Beyond* (2nd ed, Oxford University Press, Oxford 2006) at para 8.05. For a comparison of the two traditions see the seminal study by Alain Strowel *Droit d'auteur et copyright: Divergences et convergences. Etude de droit compare* (Bruxelles, Bruylant, 1993).

139 One could speculate that performers' rights are more important in jurisdictions with higher standards of originality because it is very difficult for performers to be authors.

originality required in common-law countries is low, it might commonly be the case that performers have copyright, but as authors rather than as performers.[140]

As far as the author is aware, New Zealand does not have any case law on the matter. However, United Kingdom case law is highly illustrative of the general trend of copyright expanding its understanding of the author. In *Brooker v Fisher*,[141] the England and Wales Court of Appeal held that Mr Fisher, an organist who improvised changes to Mr Brooker's composition during rehearsal, which were later recorded, was a co-author of the rearrangement. Mr Brooker was the author of the original musical work. What was eventually recorded was a rearrangement made by Mr Fisher, who was deemed to be a co-author of the rearrangement. Two things should be noted. First, Mr Brooker was the 'traditional' composer. He composed the music and lyrics, before putting a band together to perform his works. In contrast, Mr Fisher composed via performance. The corollary to a performer being an author through performance is that performance can define the work. Second, the fixation of Mr Fisher's work was via sound recording, not writing. Fixation via non-written means is specifically allowed in New Zealand, for works and rearrangements, and can be 'in writing or otherwise'.[142] When fixation is via sound or film, the question arises of what exactly the work encompasses.

The bounds of the 'musical work' or 'dramatic work' are by no means clearly defined. In *Coffey v Warner/Chappell Music Ltd*,[143] the England and Wales High Court was quick to hold that the following were 'interpretation or performance characteristics by the performer, which is not the legitimate subject of copyright protection in the case of a musical work':[144]

> The claim, as now formulated, is that the recording of Forever After '*includes* an original musical work *comprising* the combination of vocal expression, pitch contour and syncopation of or around the words "does it really matter"' [emphasis added]. She refers to this as 'the Work'.

---

140 This has been the case in the United Kingdom, see *Bamgboye v Reed* (2002) EWHC 2922; and *Brooker v Fisher* [2008] EWCA Civ 287. See Luke McDonagh 'Rearranging the Roles of the Performer and the Composer in the Music Industry – the Potential Significance of Fisher v Brooker' (2012) 1 IPQ 64 at 68–70 and 75–76; and O'Connor, above n 96.
141 *Brooker v Fisher* [2008] EWCA Civ 287.
142 Copyright Act 1994, ss 15 and 34(2).
143 *Coffey v Warner/Chappell Music Ltd* [2005] EWHC 449 (Ch).
144 At [4]–[5] and [11].

By 'voice expression' is meant, in effect, 'timbre' (illustrated by a comparison between the 'gravelly' vocal expression of one well known performer and the 'twangy' vocal expression of another). By 'pitch contour' is meant 'the general shape of the pitches to which the words "does it really matter" [in Forever After] are sung' rather than, as I understood it, the notes themselves. By 'syncopation of or around the words "does it really matter"' is meant the 'unnatural metrical stress' given to the syllables of those four words 'in terms of their placement within the two bars [in which they are sung] and the unusual rhythmic and durational stress in terms of their elongated durations'.

The Court was clear that aspects of performance are not the subject of copyright protection. However, the problem was possibly more that the plaintiff used language that was simply too clear about performance. Perhaps, had the plaintiff used copyright-acceptable language, her case might have been stronger. To illustrate the point, in *Hyperion v Sawkins*,[145] what the England and Wales Court of Appeal accepted as forming part of the musical work included aspects that were very performance-based. Regarding 'performing editions' that Dr Sawkins had recreated from out-of-copyright music by Michel-Richard de Lalande, Mummery LJ stated:[146]

> Hyperion's arguments ignore the fact that the totality of the sounds produced by the musicians are affected, or potentially affected, by the information inserted in the performing editions produced by Dr Sawkins. The sound on the CD is not just that of the musicians playing music composed by Lalande. In order to produce the sounds the musicians played from Dr Sawkins' scores of his edition.

His Honour continued:[147]

> It is wrong in principle to single out the notes as uniquely significant for copyright purposes and to proceed to deny copyright to the other elements that make some contribution to the sound of the music when performed, such as performing indications, tempo and performance practice indicators, if they are the product of a person's effort, skill and time ...

In essence, the Court held that all the instructions for performance written down by Dr Sawkins in his performing editions (piano/forte/fortissimo, adagio/allegro/allegrissimo, gentile/furioso, for example) were part of the musical works. But what if a work is fixed by sound recording? What is

---

145 *Hyperion v Sawkins* [2005] EWCA Civ 565.
146 At [49].
147 At [56].

then recorded as being part of the work? If a work is more than just the musical notes and their lengths, how do we know from a sound recording what the instructions for performance are that form part of the work?

In fact, Mummery LJ noted that:[148]

> Music must be distinguished from the fact and form of its fixation as a record of a musical composition. The score is the traditional and convenient form of fixation of the music and conforms to the requirement that a copyright work must be recorded in some material form. But the fixation in the written score or on a record is not in itself the music in which copyright subsists. There is no reason why, for example, a recording of a person's spontaneous singing, whistling or humming or of improvisations of sounds by a group of people with or without musical instruments should not be regarded as 'music' for copyright purposes.

Of course, though fixation can be by writing or otherwise, this is not to say that a work fixed by sound recording must, thus, include more than just notes and words. Mummery LJ conflated substance with form.

All the same, the result is that some aspects of performance when recorded can constitute part of a copyright work. The question is which aspects of performance? For example, if performance instructions are part of a musical work, then a performer choosing to not follow those instructions might create a rearrangement. If recorded, the performer could then be the author of the rearrangement.[149] No one else would be able to imitate the way that the rearranger played the piece, not even the author/owner or licensee of the original piece. The rearranger would essentially have copyright for the performance as a work.

The same issues arise with visual performances. Mummery LJ also noted:[150]

> In principle, there is no reason for regarding the actual notes of music as the only matter covered by musical copyright, any more than, in the case of a dramatic work, only the words to be spoken by the actors are covered by dramatic copyright. Added stage directions may affect the performance of the play on the stage or on the screen and have an impact on the performance seen by the audience. Stage directions are as much part of a dramatic work as plot, character and dialogue.

---

148 At [53].
149 See *Redwood Music v Chappell* [1982] RPC 109 (QB), which held that even an unauthorised rearrangement can have copyright and the rearranger is the owner. However, there is infringement.
150 At [55].

But, if stage directions also constitute part of the dramatic work, what is the dramatic work when fixation is via film? Is not then every pause, stress on certain words, eyebrow raise or dramatic turn of the head, for example, a stage direction? And if one had a licence to perform the dramatic work, could one be liable for breach of the moral right to integrity of the work if one performed the words differently?

It is one thing to say that a musical work is more than the notes and their length, or that dramatic work is more that the words, but it is something else entirely to deal with the consequences of such a statement. One of the reasons why Dr Sawkin's performing instructions were considered part of the musical works is undoubtedly that they were in the correct form. That is, in a form that copyright accepts, written down on the score. In contrast, Ms Coffey used descriptive performance language. This is not to say the Ms Coffey had a valid case, but that she could have made a stronger case. Despite Mummery LJ's statement regarding non-written forms of fixation, it is hard to imagine that a court would be open to accepting aspects of performance as part of a copyright work when presented in a sound recording or film.[151] This is, however, the logical next step from *Hyperion v Sawkins*.[152]

If the trend is that performers can be authors and it seems that performances might become works, the question then arises of what we need performers' rights for. Copyright, after all, offers a broader system of protection, protecting something abstract and not individual embodiments. The answer to the question requires the recognition that very few performers reach the level of skill or success where they can create an original rearrangement or adaptation and be authors or co-authors. It is only lead actors, band members and named artists who have this potential. Such performers often have copyright anyway, because they are singer-songwriters or dabble as screenwriters, producers or film directors. The majority of performers are background actors, singers or dancers, sessional musicians or members of an orchestra, who would not have the opportunity to be authors via performance. It is perhaps these performers who require performers' rights.

---

151 The history of copyright stemming from the introduction of the print press, with sound recordings and films being relatively new categories of works, means that there is an inherent snobbery regarding the medium of fixation.

152 *Hyperion v Sawkins*, above n 147.

It is worth noting that performers who do not bring 'something more' to become authors of rearrangements or derivative works, or co-authors of copyright, are not less deserving of performers' rights. First, unlike copyright, performers' rights are devoid of any assessment based on quality. The action of performance alone equates to subsistence. Second, even if a performer does not do anything that qualifies as 'original' in the copyright sense, this is not to say that they do not bring something worthy of protection. Members of symphony orchestras are illustrative; they follow the score before them and the instructions of the maestro, but it would be ungenerous and untrue to say that they are not highly skilled and do not bring something to the table, possibly even something indescribable.

4.4 Commercial Reality

Economic situations change. Fifteen years passed between the MED review and MBIE's RIS.[153] It is possible that much had altered in this period and perhaps New Zealand had since become ripe for 'stronger' performers' rights, particularly with respect to the majority of performers – that is, those who do not have 'star power' or who do not have the opportunity to create original works. The film industry in 2017 is not the same as the film industry of 2001. This is not only because of international blockbusters like the 'Lord of the Rings' and 'The Hobbit' movies,[154] but also the impact of local films and television, such as 'Boy' and 'Hunt for the Wilderpeople'.[155] Similarly, the music industry has developed significantly, with many artists having international repute, such as Lorde and Brooke Fraser.

Furthermore, technology changes. As information and communication technologies have affected the realm of copyright, these technologies arguably also affect performers' rights. For example, one could argue that the increased ease with which one can record and distribute

---

153 MED, above n 11; MBIE RIS, above n 26.
154 Peter Jackson (dir) 'The Lord of the Rings: The Fellowship of the Ring' (2001); Peter Jackson (dir) 'The Lord of the Rings: The Two Towers' (2002); Peter Jackson (dir) 'The Lord of the Rings: The Return of the King' (2003); Peter Jackson (dir) 'The Hobbit: An Unexpected Journey' (2012); Peter Jackson (dir) 'The Hobbit: The Desolation of Smaug' (2013); Peter Jackson (dir) 'The Hobbit: The Battle of the Five Armies' (2014).
155 Taika Waititi (dir) 'Boy' (2010); Taika Waititi (dir) 'Hunt for the Wilderpeople' (2016).

performances might justify stronger performers' rights and also some level of harmonisation of such to allow for international protection and enforcement.[156]

Still, given the contractual nature of the relationship between performers and producers, it is questionable whether modifications to performers' rights will result in any concrete changes to these contracts and the reality of New Zealand performers (or performers anywhere). The Copyright Act 1994 states that a person who has recording rights may bring an action of infringement on behalf of the performer, without their consent (unless the performer expressly requires that consent be obtained).[157] A person having recording rights includes a person (or his/her assignee) with an exclusive recording contract, or someone authorised by that person (or his/her assignee) to make recordings or copies of recordings for the purpose of commercial exploitation.[158] One can infer from this that performers can contract around their rights, even though they are personal rights and not property rights in the Copyright Act 1994.[159] As a result, performers can, in effect, assign away their rights by exclusively contracting broad consent; for example, an exclusive recording contract, including the exclusive right to communicate and copy the recording for any purpose.

If the relationship between performers and producers is dominated by contract law, giving performers property rights will not change their situation, as it does not affect their bargaining power. At the end of the day, the bargaining power of any artist will depend on his or her reputation and the market demand for that artist, and also the relative bargaining power of the producer. That is, while performers with star power, who tend to be copyright authors/owners anyway (because they are authors or co-authors, whether in a classical sense or via performance), can essentially demand the contracts that they want; performers with less star power achieve less favourable contractual terms. This is not affected by performers' rights, regardless of whether they are personal rights or property rights.

---

156 There is very little research on the impact of digital technologies on the performing arts. For a survey of the existing literature, see Ruth Towse 'Performing Arts' in Ruth Towse and Christian Handke (eds) *Handbook on the Digital Creative Economy* (Edward Elgar, Cheltenham, 2014) 311.

157 Copyright Act 1994, s 196(2). Compare CDPA 1988 (UK), ss 185–188, which is much more explicit about exclusive recording rights than the Copyright Act 1994.

158 Copyright Act 1994, s 169.

159 Copyright Act 1994.

As the Department of Justice noted in 1989, before New Zealand had any performers' rights, 'it is open to a performer to obtain such rights by contract with a record or film maker'.[160] The Department of Justice was, thereby, acknowledging that performers with enough bargaining power would be able to demand performers' rights in their contracts. Of course, one requires something to bargain around, which may be some kind of performers' rights, but might also be the simple ability to decide whether or not one is willing to perform. The primacy of contract law over any performers' rights is also reflected by the fact that featured artists usually have individual contracts, stipulating any fixed payment plus royalty rates for box office or CD sales, for example, whereas backing singers and musicians (non-featured or session musicians) and extras tend to be paid a flat rate, one-off payment.

As an illustration, New Zealand has no right to equitable remuneration for performers, nor will it if it implements the CPTPP.[161] Nevertheless, Recorded Music NZ exists, which collects certain licensing revenues for performers of sound recordings.[162] It is obvious from the discussion above that producers are under no statutory obligation to share their licensing revenues with performers. Recording Music NZ collects revenues from producers who opt to share their licensing revenues, from public performance and communication of the sound recording, with performers, splitting the revenues 50:50.[163] This requires that both the producer and the performer register with Recorded Music NZ. This relationship may arise through contract. In other words, a performer with a strong balance of power might insist that his/her contract include a provision requiring that both producer and performer be registered with Recorded

160 Department of Justice *Reform of the Copyright Act 1962 – A Discussion Paper*, above n 9, at 22. See also Department of Justice *The Copyright Act 1962 – Options for Reform*, above n 9, at [10.8]–[10.9].
161 See above n 62.
162 This paragraph is based on an email from Dean Cameron (Distribution & Member Services Manager) to the author regarding 'RMNZ / Performer Rights' (10 October 2016). Recorded Music NZ manages the rights of sound recording right holders, namely recording artists and recording labels. It was previously known as PPNZ Music Licensing. PPNZ was established in 1957 under the name Phonographic Performances (NZ) Limited.
163 Recorded Music NZ does not itself collect revenues, but works together with the Australasian Performing Right Association Limited, Australasian Mechanical Copyright Owners Society Limited (APRA AMCOS), Australia and New Zealand's main (but not only) collecting society for performing and mechanical rights. APRA AMCOS manages the rights of songwriters, composers and music publishers. Recorded Music NZ has a joint licensing initiative with APRA AMCOS, offering a 'OneMusic licence' for all public performance licensing, offering a single music licence covering performing rights (but not mechanical rights) and sound recording rights. On APRA AMCOS, see Susy Frankel *Intellectual Property in New Zealand* (LexisNexis, Wellington, 2011) at 182–184.

Music NZ and that the licensing revenues be shared accordingly. As at 10 October 2016, around 2,500 artists were registered with Recorded Music NZ. At the same time, if New Zealand were to implement 'stronger' performers' rights, artists with less bargaining power will nevertheless end up contracting away their rights. It will still be performers with enough bargaining power and producers who are more open to sharing their royalties that register with Recording Music NZ.

A way to overcome imbalances in bargaining strength is via the introduction of non-waivable, non-alienable rights to equitable remuneration, which tend to be collectively managed.[164] This is an entitlement protected by a liability rule rather than a property rule.[165] Rights to equitable remuneration are often considered to be 'lesser' rights, compared to rights to exclude. However, in cases where the right holder is in a weak bargaining position, such rights are arguably 'greater' as they cannot be negotiated away as a consequence of an imbalance of bargaining power. Put another way, rights to exclude are not stronger rights in practice if they can be easily bargained away. Indeed, as noted by Towse, regarding performers in the United Kingdom and a right to equitable remuneration for sound recordings compared to assignable individual exclusive rights,[166] the latter might not change anything for performers, or might in fact decrease the bargaining power and income of performers. This is because contracts will either continue to be standardised or individual negotiation will result in performers being undercut because the market is overcrowded with performers.[167] This perspective is supported by the fact that the Musicians Union (MU) in the United Kingdom achieved a great deal for its members, including royalties for mechanical reproduction of records,

---

164 See above n 62.

165 See Guido Calabresi and A Douglas Melamed 'Property Rules, Liability Rules, and Inalienability: One View of the Cathedral' (1972) 85(6) Harv L Rev 1089. As a response to Calabresi and Melamed's article, Epstein has argued that property rights should dominate because most things do not have a cash-value equivalent and liability rules create instability or a destabilising of possession, expectations and transactions; Richard A Epstein 'A Clear View of the Cathedral: The Dominance of Property Rules' (1997) 106 Yale LJ 2091.

166 In 1996, performers of sound recordings were given the right to 'equitable remuneration' if the performance was played in public, communicated to the public or made available to the public; CDPA 1988 (UK), s 182D, as amended 1 December 1996 by The Copyright and Related Rights Regulations 1996 (SI 1996/2967). The same Regulations introduced the individual property rights for performers (ss 183A–182CA). The United Kingdom now has the Performing Artists Media Rights Association (PAMRA), which is the largest collecting society for performers of music in the United Kingdom.

167 Towse, above n 84, at 758 (emphasis added).

despite the lack of performers' rights throughout the 20th century.[168] Private agreements between record companies and the MU additionally gave the latter some control over third party use of records, as the MU required that the record companies restricted certain uses in public places by licence.[169] Thus, the role of contracts remains crucial and arguably central.

Furthermore, introducing individual assignable property rights could make non-star performers vulnerable, as the removal of collective bargaining could lead to producers taking a 'divide and rule' approach.[170] Given that most performers are not superstars, it is likely that 'stronger' individualised performers' rights are unlikely to benefit most (if any) performers. It would likely be more advantageous for the majority to work as a collective, whereas it likely makes no difference for the minority superstars, who benefit from strong bargaining power in any case.

Common-law countries are generally wary of liability rules, including non-waivable rights to adequate remuneration. The concept is, however, widespread and accepted in Central Europe, which often connects the liability rule with compulsory collective management.[171] Large collecting societies have significant bargaining power, which is important for the artists that they represent. New Zealand has essentially introduced a very Central European subject matter (performers' rights), but has attempted to do it in a common-law manner (with no liability rules). The result is less than convincing.

The introduction of moral rights for performers is arguably of equally little practical consequence. This is because moral rights can be waived and this is standard in industry contracts between performers and producers of sound recordings and films. However, the waivers are only valid between the performers and copyright owners, meaning that performers would still

---

168 Williamson, above n 116, at 177–178.
169 Williamson, above n 116, at 178–179. This was in an agreement between the Musicians Union and Phonographic Performance LTD (PLL), which consisted of EMI and Decca.
170 Towse, above n 84, at 758–759.
171 The author-centric system in Central Europe has many more rights that cannot be waived or transferred. The end effect of this can be that collective management is the only viable means to enforce copyright or for authors to be remunerated for the use of their works with respect to certain rights. Consequently, Continental Europe has also developed many copyright rights that are remuneration-based, many of which are subject to compulsory collective management. On collective management, see Mihály Ficsor *Collective Rights Management of Copyright and Related Rights* (WIPO, Geneva, 2002); and Daniel Gervais (ed) *Collective Management of Copyright and Related Rights* (Kluwer Law, Alphen aan den Rijn, 2010).

have moral rights against third parties. Furthermore, as with economic rights, performers with more bargaining power will be able to retain any introduced moral rights.

The relative subordinate nature of performers' economic and moral rights next to contract law was acknowledged by MFAT in its National Interest Analysis, which stated:[172]

> While performers would be given new rights over the copying and distribution of recordings of their performances, the potential impact of these new rights may be limited in practice. This is because performers would be able to assign their rights to third parties. ...
>
> In practice New Zealand performers already receive royalties for rights connected to their performance through contractual arrangements and it is not clear that the flow of royalties would be likely to increase to any significant degree.
>
> The new rights for performers may benefit some New Zealand performers. It could give some better bargaining power when entering into recording contracts. However, this is unlikely to significantly change the bargaining dynamics or substantive outcomes of contracts between performers and the producers of sound recordings in most cases.

In other words, the impact of the new rights would be minimal, because the resultant position of performers would continue to be ruled by contracts between performers and producers. Giving performers 'stronger' rights in the form of property rights would not affect their bargaining power.

In essence, one can view the introduction of property rights that can be assigned away from two perspectives: (1) a genuine but ineffectual attempt to give performers greater protection; or (2) an intentionally ineffectual implementation of international law, to keep down costs for users, knowing that contract law and bargaining power will dominate. New Zealand has clearly opted for the latter.

---

172 MFAT NIS, above n 128, at 89.

5 Final Thoughts

Regardless of whether the CPTPP comes into force, New Zealand will likely have to introduce 'stronger' performers' rights for sound recordings at some point, making them definitively property and not personal rights, and giving performers moral rights over their performances. It is not in question whether performers deserve rights in comparison to authors. It is quite clear that the conceptualisation of the 'romantic author' next to the 'lowly performer' is dated and simply incorrect. It is, however, debatable how any given jurisdiction can best protect performers, in the sense of creating a conducive atmosphere for creativity via performance. Whether neighbouring rights are the correct method is dubious.

Case law from the United Kingdom indicates that performers can have copyright when they rearrange or modify a musical work enough that they overcome the standard of originality. Given the similarities between the categories of works in the United Kingdom and New Zealand, and the low standard of originality in New Zealand, it is likely also the case in New Zealand that performers can be authors. If performers can be authors, they do not need performers' rights.

Not all performers are, however, in the position to be authors. One could, thus, conclude that performers' rights are important for less creative performers – those who do not bring anything original in the copyright sense. However, the most important factor for such performers will not be the strength of performers' rights, but the reputation and demand for a performer and, thereby, that performer's bargaining power and ability to negotiate a favourable contract, whether in relation to a music producer, venue owner or broadcaster. The introduction of assignable and waivable rights (as per the TPP Agreement Amendment Act 2016) does not change this. One has to have some rights as a performer, but the stronger one's bargaining power, the fewer rights are required. For example, Beyoncé probably does not require any more than primary rights. If one is not allowed to record her without her consent or to transmit her live performances, she already has a lot to bargain with vis-à-vis record companies and venues, and to control the use of her performances. With her bargaining power, Beyoncé could negotiate terms of contract regarding reproduction, distribution and royalties, regardless of whether she has those rights under law.

Performers' rights should, hence, be geared towards performers who do not have the opportunity to create original works and who do not have 'star power'. What one must acknowledge is that the idea that 'stronger' rights – that is, property rights – equate to improving a performer's position is mistaken. Introducing 'stronger' rights that can easily be signed away does not change the imbalance of bargaining power that most performers face. The question then arises of whether a liability rule would, in effect, be more conducive towards supporting performative creativity.

While this chapter has predominantly dealt with the New Zealand situation, several of its conclusions apply equally to the Asian Pacific region. Namely, the conclusions about the comparative creativity of authors compared to performers, and the importance of contract law and relative bargaining power. Moreover, most Asian Pacific nations do not have a history steeped in Central European natural rights theory, including those that have civil-law systems. Instead, copyright and neighbouring rights are, typically, either artefacts of colonialism or a result of international trade agreements. If the Asian Pacific region is to take a particular perspective on performers' rights, different from that embodied in the WPPT, and codify this, it should allow for a system that fits its various cultures and commercial realities.

Taking a step back, there is a key question that has yet to be answered: why should the Asian Pacific region harmonise (to any degree) performers' rights beyond its WPPT obligations? So long as nations are aware of the relationship between performers' rights and contractual bargaining power, and act accordingly to meet their policy aims, it might be in the region's interest to stick with the WPPT and its flexibility.

Conclusion

Shubha Ghosh[1]

These papers from the 2016 proceedings of the Asian Pacific Copyright Association (APCA) demonstrate the vitality of copyright scholars focusing on the Asian Pacific region. Several of the papers show a depth of understanding on a range of issues, such as traditional knowledge, performance rights, free trade agreements, fair use and open government data. Some of the papers provide a theoretical framework as a window into regional debates. The theory suggests that regional studies can be generalised into broader principles that shape international intellectual property law. There is more than a promise in this volume for a vital scholarship on Asian Pacific copyright law. What have we learned and where should we be headed?

An initial question is why an Asian Pacific–centred copyright law? In the United States, copyright is rife with moral panic; a confused field in the shadow of patent law and digital rights. Why would the field be vital anywhere else? Furthermore, the Asian Pacific region is a diverse one with multiple religions, languages, economies and histories that potentially undermine any coherent perspective. Can there be a coherent copyright law that meets the needs of the various industries, consumers and cultural groups? At the threshold, the prospect for an Asian Pacific Copyright is not promising.

But what seems to be a vice can prove to be a virtue. As copyright in the United States falls into a moral panic, lessons can be gleaned from such failures, both actual and perceived. An Asian Pacific Copyright Code can revitalise the field, reinvigorating debates through a reconsideration of foundational principles. The diversity of the Asian Pacific region provides

---

1   Copyright © 2018 Shubha Ghosh.

the ingredients for a healthy re-examination and reformulation of copyright law. Expressive activity, the domain of copyright, takes many forms in the Asian Pacific region through the complexity of trading patterns and the rich cultural mix of traditional expression and modern artistic forms. This mix is made more complex by the multiplicity of languages, religions and interactions with other regions, whether Europe, the Americas or South Asia. Identifying and developing an Asian Pacific copyright holds much promise for revitalising copyright. A deep scholarly dive into the issues facing the region invites new lessons that can be exported to the rest of the world through better informed baselines for a global system of copyright.

The chapters in this volume each contribute to this enterprise. Readers have engaged already with the high-quality work presented here. For those readers who have chosen to consult the Conclusion first before perusing the rest, be advised that there is much valuable thought here. Return immediately to page one and read this Conclusion afterwards. What I have gleaned from my reading are three sets of lessons that can guide future research in Asian Pacific copyright scholarship and global copyright law and policy more broadly. The editors have divided this volume into the themes of 'Norm-making', 'Norm-taking', 'Users and Access' and 'Non-authors'. While these are instructive markers, I propose dividing the lessons from these articles into three more basic categories: the economics, the culture and the politics of copyright.

Since copyright has traditionally found justification in economics, I turn to that category first. The traditional story is the familiar one about incentives. Copyright provides a set of exclusive rights designed to benefit authors, those who create original works. What counts as a work and what counts as original is a choice about what types of creative works society wants to incentivise through exclusive rights. In some circumstances, the exclusive rights granted to the copyright owner may conflict with the rights of other creators or with beneficial uses, such as for education, research or news. When such conflicts arise, limitations on the exclusive rights are needed, through specific exceptions or general limitations such as fair use or fair dealing.

Economic incentives are complicated. They are implemented in order to create markets for the copyrighted works. These markets can extend across several industries and across borders. Several chapters demonstrate this complexity in the Asian Pacific context. Professor Yu offers a descriptive account of pending multilateral trade regimes that might structure Asian

Pacific markets based on copyright. He warns of the risks inherent in adopting the strong protections and enforcement measures required by such regimes, pointing out the likelihood of countries in the Asia Pacific that are already party to free trade agreements with high standards putting pressure on other jurisdictions to similarly strengthen their copyright laws. While noting that many countries of the region are developing nations, for which strong copyright protections are not necessarily beneficial, Yu also points out that the situation is complex as there is some evidence that stronger rights can result in development. Thus, Yu urges parties to the proposed multilateral trade agreements to understand both sides of the coin. Professor Ayoubi offers a rigorous and valuable analysis of the interests of indigenous people, particularly with respect to Traditional Cultural Expressions, in the emerging economic system. Her chapter points to the problems of legal harmonisation, and implicitly economic integration, in taking account of the interests of all members of society. Human rights considerations, as she advocates, may address the problems of harmonisation and integration. Flexibility for nation states in protecting the rights of indigenous people is necessary in defining the economics of copyright, especially if the incentives created work against the interests of traditionally marginalised groups. Professor Lai's excellent chapter on performers' rights in New Zealand offers a focused discussion of the economics of copyright as applied to performers. Her chapter presents a thoughtful argument for structuring copyright incentives through liability rules to ensure compensation while limiting misappropriation. How contracts are negotiated and enforced with respect to performance rights is an important topic for future research and legal advocacy to ensure that her important ideas are implemented effectively.

What Professors Ayoubi and Lai show is how cultural background can shape economic incentives and markets. Cultural theories of copyright go beyond pecuniary incentives to understand why expressive works are created. Cultural theories, also, highlight how culture is disseminated outside the market system. Oral and written transmission across generations, integration of works into community practices, such as religious rituals, and shared understandings of the sacred are just some examples of how works are transmitted to communities and their members. A central problem in cultural theories of copyright is determining what uses should be permitted and which should be allowed within the legal system. Should groups for whom a work has cultural meaning be allowed legally to prevent exploitation through commercialisation or transformation of the sacred work? Or should creative redefinition and remixing be allowed? Professors Ayoubi and Lai suggest possible ways to answer these questions, whether through human rights limitations on copyright or through legal mechanisms of contract and liability. Their chapters are at the intersection of economic and cultural theories of copyright, serving as both critique and analytical framework for assessment of the law.

The chapter by Professors Johnson, Wright and Corbett examines fair use, as it exists under United States copyright law, as an important copyright doctrine to import into Australian and New Zealand legislation. Their argument is grounded in the need for limitations on copyright, and the flexibility of fair use in facilitating the development of new industries and new uses. Such flexibility is essential, they argue, for integration into the knowledge economy. Their argument is in part on the need for correct economic incentives, but their analysis delves into the cultural challenges of importing foreign law into the Australian and New Zealand contexts. These challenges are further explored by Professors Stoianoff and Wright, who discuss the need for appropriate legislative intervention to protect traditional cultural expressions and knowledge from misuse by third parties under the auspices of broad user rights such as fair use. They draw upon earlier work with Indigenous Australian communities to propose a way forward that could be encapsulated in Professor Sterling's draft Asian Pacific Copyright Code and that would achieve an appropriate balance between the interests of indigenous communities in the Asian Pacific region to custodianship of their traditional knowledge, on the one hand, and the permitted exceptions for users in copyright laws, on the other hand. Professor Barrett offers a detailed analytical framework for how to recast and reform existing rights to address practices in the creation of two-dimensional works, specifically ones that capture three-dimensional works such as buildings and statuary (the so-called right to panorama). His proposal for reform suggests ways in which the law can protect customary practices while also recognising the rights of copyright owners.

What undergirds much of the debate over copyright is a political question of how reform occurs and how various interests, whether economic or cultural, are represented in the law. Professor Long provides a useful summary of arguments for the incorporation of privacy interests in copyright law. She focuses on the copyright–privacy interface promulgated by technological developments in a plethora of areas – from notice and takedown regimes, to drones and other surveillance techniques, to the unauthorised online circulation of personal images. She explains that at least one advantage of introducing personal privacy issues into copyright law might be that it would provide courts with the opportunity to take a more nuanced approach to assessing relief in copyright disputes. Professor Corbett provides a rigorous and concrete discussion of digital rights management as imported into New Zealand. Her chapter shows sensitivity to the administrative context for implementing copyright law and the need for both legal development and flexibility through administrative rule making. She points to an important factor in the success of importing copyright laws: the creation of political institutions for fitting the laws to unique social contexts particular to the nation state. Professor Lee's chapter complements this point about administration through advocacy for open government data. Transparency and accountability guide how law is implemented and develops. Citizens need to know how government reaches its decisions and how it collects information from the public. His call for open government policies with respect to data collection and use emphasises how public-minded political institutions are needed for citizen participation in creating the rules that will structure economic and cultural interactions.

The Asian Pacific region provides a rich environment for academic debate on the economics, cultural context and politics of copyright. As these chapters show, copyright as field is a vital one in the region and touches upon a range of concerns across countries in the region. These nine chapters serve as a bellwether for how copyright debates can be transformed. They also serve as models for future scholarship from the APCA and from scholars committed in creating a copyright law that serves creators, participants in cultural communities and political actors, within and beyond the Asian Pacific region.

Index

Note: locators that contain an 'n' indicate the reference appears in a footnote. For example, 32n77 indicates footnote 77 on page 32.

www.ingramcontent.com/pod-product-compliance
Lightning Source LLC
Chambersburg PA
CBHW040819280326
41926CB00093B/4593